DESERT TRAVELLER

W9-BRJ-914

ALSO BY KATHARINE SIM

Malayan Landscape
Those I Have Loved
Flowers of the Sun: On the Malay Pantun
Costumes of Malaya
A Career with the Malayan Railway
Journey Out of Asia


*Fiction*

Malacca Boy
The Moon At My Feet
Black Rice: A Story of Opium Smuggling
The Jungle Ends Here

# DESERT TRAVELLER

## The Life of Jean Louis Burckhardt

Katharine Sim

PHOENIX
PRESS

PHOENIX PRESS
5 UPPER SAINT MARTIN'S LANE
LONDON WC2H 9EA

A PHOENIX PRESS PAPERBACK

First published in Great Britain
by Victor Gollancz Limited in 1969
This paperback edition published in 2000
by Phoenix Press,
a division of The Orion Publishing Group Ltd,
Orion House, 5 Upper St Martin's Lane,
London WC2H 9EA

© Katharine Sim, 1969

The moral right of Katharine Sim to be identified as the author
of this work has been asserted by her in accordance with
the Copyright, Designs and Patents Act 1988.

All rights reserved. No part of this publication may be
reproduced, stored in a retrieval system, or transmitted,
in any form or by any means, electronic, mechanical,
photocopying, recording or otherwise, without the prior
permission of the copyright owner and the above
publisher of this book.

This book is sold subject to the condition that it may not
be resold or otehwise issued except in its original binding.

A CIP catalogue record for this book is available from the
British Library.

Printed and bound in Great Britain by
Butler & Tanner Ltd, Frome and London

ISBN 1 84212 086 7

To Peter Randolph
with sincere gratitude

# Contents

# Illustrations

### LINE DRAWINGS

*Author's Introduction*

# The Forerunner

# The Forerunner

## JEAN LOUIS BURCKHARDT

"—a haggard land infested with wild beasts and wilder men, a region whose very fountains murmur the warning words 'Drink and away!' What can be more exciting? what more sublime? Man's heart bounds in his breast at the thought of measuring his puny force with Nature's might, and of emerging triumphant from the trial. This explains the Arab's proverb, 'Voyaging is victory'. In the Desert, even more than upon the ocean, there is present death; hardship is there, and piracies, and shipwreck, solitary not in crowds, where, as the Persians say, 'Death is a Festival' and this sense of danger, never absent, invests the scene of travel with an interest not its own."

*Burton*

LOOKED AT EVEN singly the highlights of Jean Louis Burckhardt's career are powerful enough to have given him lasting fame in the popular mind.

To have discovered Petra, the long-lost "rose-red city",[1] as well as the Great Temple of Rameses II at Abu Simbel; to have made the Islamic pilgrimage to Mecca disguised as a Muslim haji —and to have lived to write the most accurate and detailed account of the holy city ever received in Europe[2]—were alone outstandingly important achievements. Important not only to future historians and map-makers, and to the explorers of Nubia and the Middle East, but indeed to all the thinking world.

At the time—the early nineteenth century—these astounding exploits, his courage in carrying them out, the exceptional accuracy and brilliance of his observations won him wide acclaim and high praise.

Both Jordan's Petra and the fabulous Nubian temples of Abu Simbel have long been household words. His discoveries caused "great sensation and interest": he was quite overcome by the compliments which he then received "from all sides". But, always a humble man, he was too modest to repeat any of these praises even in letters to his mother[3]—the person to whom he devoted all the love of a warm, affectionate nature.

Today the names Petra and Abu Simbel ring out among those of the strangest, most beguiling and gorgeous artefacts of this planet. Popularly they stand as symbols evoking two countries, both of which are vast store-houses of historical and archaeological treasures—countries which form the very background and sub-stance of our civilisation—the Holy Land, and Egypt in Nubia. But by some curious twist of fate the man who, among other brilliant exploits, revealed those long lost places to the modern world has received only too little recognition. For perhaps as much as a hundred years now his fame has been considerably less than he deserves, and yet he is unquestionably a giant among the great explorers of the nineteenth century.

On hearing the name Burckhardt some people—those not specifically familiar with things Middle Eastern—think first of the renowned historian, Jakob, who has been described as "the wisest man of the nineteenth century". Although born of different branches, both men were descendants of the same Swiss family, which originated centuries ago in the Black Forest area, and in Christoph Burckhardt, who came to settle in Basle in 1523, they have a common ancestor.[4]

Some people too have asked me why I wanted to write this book. I suppose it is the kind of question that always seems surprising to a writer but, since it has been so often put to me, I will try to answer it here.

I was about four years old when I first heard of Petra as a magical roseate city with a dark and narrow entrance. So the longing to see it for myself was always somewhere in my mind, in the back of it or in the forefront according to the course of events. In 1960, driving home overland with my husband from Calcutta to Calais, the dream at last became reality, nearly 150 years after Burckhardt's discovery of the place. It was then that I first read of Jean Louis, the young "Anglo-Swiss". Perhaps the fact that my father too had come of an old Swiss family did something to whet my appetite still further for knowledge of this so intrepid explorer. In the Lebanon I learned a little more about him: it had been in the face of grave danger that he had penetrated the jealously guarded lost city, and only by the means of an ingenious strategem was he able to outwit its fierce Arab custodians. So it was that after six myth-shrouded centuries he restored to all cognisant peoples Petra—the Biblical *Sela* in the wilderness.

My interest in the indefatigable, unassuming and utterly dedicated man grew inevitably. I decided to write about him: the more I studied his work and personality the less could I understand why his name was not better known today.

I visited Abu Simbel in 1964, the final year of its ancient siting. I went to Basle and was shown his father's fine town mansion— the "Kirschgarten"*—by the kindness of Dr Carl Burckhardt-Sarasin with whom I have often corresponded since. Later I went to Malta, Louis' starting point, and to southern Turkey. I had already travelled in Syria, Lebanon, Jordan and eastern Turkey. In 1967 I planned to revisit Syria and Egypt, especially the southern part of the Sinai peninsula which I had previously seen only tantalisingly from the deck of a ship in the Red Sea, but the outbreak of the Arab-Israeli war put an end to that.

For obvious reasons I could not go to Mecca and Medinah, but I have several good friends in Malaysia who have made the pilgrimage to the holy cities. A long familiarity with the Islamic world, as I have known it over the course of many years in South-East Asia with its ardent Arab links, helped me to have at least some understanding of the Muslim outlook. Largely because of this I felt almost convinced at various stages of my reading that Louis must have been a Muslim, or at least have seen eye to eye with the precepts of pure Islam—which would not be difficult for any thinking man. Later, as I came to know him better, I began to

* Now a museum.

change my mind somewhat. However, I give the facts as I have found them and may the reader decide whether or not he did actually cross that particular Rubicon. If so it was almost certainly spiritually and intellectually only, for it seems clear that he did not undergo any formal initiation ceremony, so there would have been no need for him to renounce his original Christian upbringing—and he certainly believed in God.

Although the roots of "modern civilisation are planted deeply in the highly elaborate life of those nations which rose to power over 6,000 years ago, in the basin of the eastern Mediterranean",[5] the new science of archaeology did not flower until the nineteenth century to give us solid proof of this fact. It is useful to remind oneself from time to time of all that has happened archaeologically in the areas concerned, particularly the Nile region, in the brief period of the last 200 years or less—which is only an ephemeral hour in comparison with the thousands of epochs gone.

A great deal of what was known of the Nile valley remained, as we are all aware, a mystery until some time after Napoleon's invasion of Egypt in 1798 and the subsequent lucky find by the French officer, Bouchard, of the Rosetta Stone. The repetition of such very common knowledge seems necessary here merely in order to place Jean Louis in time. His remarkably fruitful though tragically few years—1809-17—in the Levant, Africa, and Arabia fell within the period when the marvels of Egypt had already been studied although not fully comprehended, for the hieroglyphs of the Rosetta Stone were not deciphered until 1822.

Born in Switzerland in 1784, son of a wealthy patrician soldier and merchant of Basle, Louis grew up in an age that was catastrophic for his freedom-loving country. Feeling against Napoleon and the Republican French naturally ran high: it was an acid that bit cruelly into the lives of all the Burckhardts, as a family and as individuals. For Louis it etched a totally unforeseen career, one which fate, conspiring with the devastating events of the era, caused him to adopt. For he was not, as Burton for instance was later, a born explorer; he became one through determination, vigour, and a rather mysteriously persistent vindication of self.

He might have been a soldier, a naturalist, a diplomat, perhaps a musician, even a statesman. Indeed, he was a most accomplished European, in the true modern sense of the word, and although serious minded, a perfectionist and an idealist, he was an extremely likeable, kindly, genial man, and a very good companion—as many of his friends bore witness. Physically he was strong and handsome, with firm, regular features and tense grey eyes. He was intellectually adaptable, gifted in languages and music, he had a retentive memory, he possessed highly acute powers of observation; and was fascinated by the new sciences.

He was well ahead of his time; in thinking—notably on Africa —he was certainly decades in advance. So he was a forerunner not only in the matter of the new territories he explored but in spirit also—in the method and manner of the approach to his problems, the careful planning, the well-judged risks. Although a product of the eighteenth and early nineteenth century, living still in an age of Goethean greatness—and he was an admirer of Goethe—he was, or rather he made himself, a liberal-humanist— as his actions, his work and his ideas all prove.

He enjoyed the good things of life but he strove constantly against materialism. This, no doubt, is one of the reasons for his passionate love of the desert—its simplicity, beauty, and cleanliness in refreshing contrast with the complexity and unnaturalness of life in towns. He had serious reasons for this battle with himself, this endless striving, for his father, although a courageous, high-spirited patriot and a good citizen, was undeniably hottempered and self-indulgent. Louis was well aware of these failings: while he was only sixteen or seventeen, at Leipzig University he ran up debts out of all proportion to his allowance. It was an occurrence which seems to have preyed on his conscience to such an extent that literally years were to pass before he felt he had lived down his youthful follies.

So altogether life was not easy for him; he had a long battle to fight with himself as well as with innumerable hardships. Sometimes one almost feels that he knew his life was to be brief: though never in his letters or journals did he give any indication of such an attitude, in fact it is rather the reverse—he often spoke hopefully of the future and of his return. But the vital force of his drive was so tremendous that one is compelled to think that it derived partly from a subconscious awareness of the shortness of life. Or else it was that strangely persistent sense of atonement for the traumatic event in Leipzig which goaded him ever harder along each difficult course he undertook.

The Burckhardts' hatred of the new France was balanced by an equally strong admiration for England, for the very same qualities that for a thousand years had been the pride and mainspring of their own country—freedom, love of peace, and independence. And now above all they admired the staunch way the English stood against France, which for many years continued to be the greatest military power yet known on earth.*[6]

Therefore it was to England that Louis turned, determined to serve England and none other since he could not fight for his own country. Wordsworth's "Two Voices" were indeed strong at that time and explain the *rapport* existing then—as it still does, I think, today though differently—between the two countries, and the sonnet helps one to understand something of the Burckhardts' strength of feeling towards England.

So it was that this young Swiss came to fill a place unique in the story of Britain's explorers and, next to Mungo Park, he was undeniably the most notable traveller employed by England in the early days of African exploration.[7] I say unique deliberately for although there had been one or two other foreigners before him working for England in this field, their achievements bear no real comparison with his, and yet England surprisingly enough has neglected to honour him. He should rank very close to Mungo Park, who as it happens was a far less humble man.

A quarter of a century after Burckhardt's death, Dr Andrew Crichton, in a brief memoir, wrote this of him:

the celebrated oriental traveller, although a foreigner by birth, is so intimately associated with the exertions of British enterprise in the cause of physical and geographical discovery that England may justly claim him as her adopted son.[8]

* 1793-1815.

One could wish that she would do so—with honest pride and gratitude.

Since his death many famous names have emerged in the gathering fever of exploration of the "Black Continent", overshadowing as so often happens those of a forerunner forgotten now—except by the archaeologist, or the serious traveller in the Middle East, by whom Burckhardt's name is always honoured. Such travellers, with the exception of a suspect few, have never been unwilling to give him his due; his journals were consulted and many have quoted him. Burton himself wrote of the energetic Burckhardt "whose name has ever been held in the highest repute".9

Louis certainly possessed very much more than common talents. William Leake in his "Memoir"* said that it would be from "the public and posterity" that his memory would:

> receive its due reward of fame, for it cannot be doubted that his name will be held in honourable remembrance as long as any credit is given to those who have fallen in the cause of science . . .

One cannot help thinking that as a man of inimitable resource, verve and imperturbability he would, in modern times, have made a superb "cloak and dagger" agent—quick-thinking and latent histrionic talents came to his aid in many dangerous situations.

His was always a lonely figure; isolated among countless perils he acted as path-finder, laid foundations for those who came after him. Not for military expeditions as such—though those inevitably did come—but for humanity, through his contribution to a wider understanding of the world and its peoples—the Arabs particularly, above all the Bedouin—and also through his deep sympathy for Islam. This at a time when the spirit of the East was unrevealed to the great majority of orientalists, who saw

* The "Memoir" in Burckhardt's *Travels in Nubia*: Leake was himself a well-known writer and traveller; he edited several of Louis' travel journals.

its colour and fascination but from the *outside*, and as superiors. He saw it clearly, and from within. A weaker man, however, might easily have become over-involved, especially in the company of barbaric slave-traders, as Louis was at times when he had to travel as one of them. Another man might, for instance, have succumbed to the voluptuous Abyssinian beauties in the Sudan, who entertained the traders openly and unashamedly each night with their regal charms and their intoxicating liquor. Louis had to keep himself aloof, not only for reasons of natural fastidiousness but for personal safety, and the success of his mission. So, of course, he was held in great contempt by this callous band of licentious brutes—his fellow-travellers.

London society proved unhelpful to him for a long and un-happy time, yet he retained an unfailing admiration for the English, not only through his congenial contacts with the learned and the scientific men of the day but, it seems, for the nation in general. Eventually it was through the brilliant Sir Joseph Banks that Louis undertook the incredibly difficult and dangerous assignment which was to be his aim and career. This mission, on behalf of London's African Association,\* was to have been a search for the Niger's course, a journey to be made from Egypt, travelling westerly with pilgrim caravans returning from Mecca through the Fezzan and then south towards the Niger. It took fifty days to journey from Cairo to the Fezzan, and ninety from the Fezzan to Timbuctu.

The cruel irony of Louis' story is that all his great achievements were as training and background for this immense project: for which end he had made himself supremely fitted when his tragically early death robbed him of ultimate triumph.

During the initial years of preparation his first duty was to perfect himself in his role as an Arab, a task to which he applied himself with all his scholarly devotion for two-and-a-half years —studying in Aleppo, and travelling also into the desert, learning

---

\* Sir Joseph Banks, who had sailed with Captain Cook and done much to help him, already the President of the Royal Society and known as the "Father of Research", had helped to found the African Association in 1788; it was later incorporated in the Royal Geographical Society, in 1831.

to live with danger. He went to Palmyra and beyond, reaching the most easterly forgotten outposts of the Roman Empire on Euphrates, and in the west finding the lost Apamea, the Seleucid city on the Orontes. He was robbed, stripped naked, blistered by the sun, in frequent danger, but learning all the while.

The year of Bonaparte's retreat from Moscow saw the start of Louis' first long journey south to Cairo, through Syria. As he went he explored the unknown Hauran, found the first Hittite inscriptions ever to be seen by a European traveller, and in Jordan, as we know, after discovering Petra he ultimately reached Egypt, having ridden fast with a small group of hard-bitten Bedouin across the dreaded Desert of Tyh.

Louis then felt himself to be almost prepared to undertake the great journey to the interior, but once he was in Egypt he realised that he now needed intimate knowledge of the African world, especially of the pilgrims, and the African Arab who is so vastly different from the Syrian or the Bedouin.

There was not likely to be a pilgrim caravan returning through the Fezzan for some time, and it so happened, for various reasons, that there was none until too late—not until the end of 1817. A remorselessly bitter stroke of fate that was hard to bear.

Rather than wait indefinitely in Egypt he decided to go south beyond the First Cataract, all unknown territory then, and to him must be given the credit of instigating archaeological finds of much of the ancient land of Kush: that part of Nubia destined to vanish this century under the huge lake of Nile waters building up behind the new High Dam—a fantastic tract of sands that have hidden and perhaps still hide "whole pages of man's history".[10] On this journey he followed the colossal bend of the Nile, not then explored: he went further than any European had previously penetrated,[11] and defying the ferocious local Kashifs and Beys he managed to get as far south as was possible without risking death at the hands of rebel Mamluks;* on the way he remarked the Ballana tumuli—those of the "X-group" people. Then, on his return north, he found the Great Temple of Rameses II, the

* The Mamluks, once powerful race of slave-kings, had fled into Dongola after Mohammed Ali's blood-bath of 1811.

heroic "Ozymandias", at Abu Simbel, almost completely buried in the sand drifts of millennia.

During the course of his second Nubian-Sudan journey he also covered vast areas of new territory, with the brutal slave-traders, from the lost Kingdom of Meroë to the Red Sea. Later, in Sinai where he went to avoid the plague months in Cairo, he traced the hitherto unknown shape of the Gulf of Akaba.

For him nearly all the wonders that he saw were tantalising in the extreme, for he was constantly suspect and in danger; he travelled at speed, always unostentatiously, disguised as a poor Syrian sheik; often in great discomfort, thirsty, hungry, literally in rags, but while his strength lasted he was equal to every event, and he delighted in the march, particularly that of the desert.

His was a sincere, an ardent personality; with a touch of the romantic perhaps, not as Lawrence had it, but in that natural histrionic ability which I have already mentioned. The unfortunate early event in Leipzig had formed him into a firmly level-headed man of great good sense, but not altogether a happy one since he craved affection, and he was too often lonely. Whether it was his loneliness, an awareness of life's brevity, or his conscience that drove him to work so hard is difficult to decide. But his written output—seven detailed volumes for the African Association composed not in his mother-tongue but in English, during six years of arduous life, Arabic study, extensive travel and, in addition, severe illness—is alone a *tour de force*. If not always easy reading, he is often vastly entertaining in a dry way, and he certainly takes one along with him on the road.

In the oriental landscape of the period his figure stands between the brave flamboyant Bruce and the brilliant, loving, and much-loved Burton, as something of an enigma, but undoubtedly a keystone in the story of the exploration of the region.

A great man: in Switzerland he is certainly not without honour, and it seems to me that not only his name but his writings and his deeds deserve to be more widely known in English, and in German-speaking countries, and in the Arab world too. Therefore this book is intended as an introduction to Jean Louis Burckhardt, the man and his travels, to this "adopted son" of England who lived and worked dangerously, strenuously in her service, and who died in so doing.

During his lifetime, although he was human and warm in his relationships with people, one is conscious of tragedy, of being in the presence of a man who was ready to lay down his life, if need be, to secure his integrity. He was literally one of those tragic human sacrifices which, it appears, do have to be made in man's history. Atavistically such sacrifices were made deliberately to secure the safety of the masses—to please the gods perhaps. In recent times they have been made, and still are, in the polite name of science. Man's reasons for sacrifice, both modern and ancient, appear to be identical, although to us, naturally, the excuse of science seems the more rational. But whichever way one regards human sacrifice it looks as if the need does derive from some fundamental law.

In Arabia, in 1815, when Louis faced Mohammed Ali, the great Pasha of Egypt, and spoke of his travels, although he was to *some* degree still acting a part the words[12] that he used then—despite their concealment of his ultimate aim and despite their Arabic flavour—do express what had become reality for him. I think that they are a key to much of his character. He said:

Men's lives are predestined; we all obey our fate. For myself, I enjoy great pleasure in exploring new and unknown countries and becoming acquainted with different races of people. I am induced to undertake journeys by the private satisfaction that travelling affords and I care very little about personal fatigue.

# Author's Acknowledgements

I AM INDEBTED TO many people for their help and kindness. Notably Robin Hallett, expert on the history and early exploration of Africa, without whose practical assistance and academic advice in the initial stages of research I sometimes think I might have lost my way in unravelling background fact and detail; the patient encouragement and sympathy of John Smith, my literary agent; and the kind generosity of Peter Randolph who on my behalf had the *Briefe* most excellently translated, without which work I could not have written this book.

Among many others to whom I am indebted are the three scholars who have so kindly read and checked the book in proof: Professor Richard Hill, of Durham University and of the Department of History, Abdullahi Bayero College, Kano, Nigeria; Professor Peter Shinnie of Birmingham University and the Department of Archaeology, University of Khartoum; and Miss Christine Cashin of the Oriental Department of the University Library, Cambridge. The libraries of the Royal Geographical Society and of the University Library Cambridge; the Egyptian Exploration Society; the National Army Museum; the William Salt Library; the National Portrait Gallery; the Records Office; the School of Oriental and African Studies; the Museums and Archives of Basle; the Historical Manuscripts Commission; the British Museum Reading Room and Studio staff; Dr Carl Burckhardt-Sarasin; Professor Max Burckhardt; Mon. C. L. Burckhardt; Frau Myrte Schwabe-Burckhardt; Miss Vivienne Burckhardt; Mr Joseph Frisch; Mr Joseph Fenech; Mr Paul Gardner; Professor T. H. G. James; Haji Ja'amat bin Karamdin; Mr Rex Keating; Mr Stanley Mayes; Mr Louis Naudi; Dr de Pasquale; Mr J. D. Pearson; Mr Michael Prawdin; Dr Fikri

Riad; Mr Moursi Saad el-Din; Sir Hannibal Scicluna; Dame Barbara Salt; Lady Salt; Cdr John Stringer; Mr Jack Waddell.

For descriptive detail in the final passages I drew on Burton, Lane, and the *Westcar Diary*. The ultimate coming of the long-delayed caravan is based on an eye-witness' account, that of Henniker.

Lastly, I owe my gratitude to the enduring sympathy and support of my husband and sons who lived, and sometimes suffered with me, for the best part of five years through much of the various quests and problems arising out of the story of this brilliant and tragic man.

K. S.

## NOTE

I am extremely grateful for all the advice I have received on the modern transliteration of Arabic words: notably Wahhabi, hajji and sheikh.

The reason why I have not followed these most modern ideas on transliteration is largely personal. It was familiarity with the Arabic-derived words in the Malay language that led me to spell haji as such—for so it is in romanised Malay—rather than hajj, or hajji, as in correct modern Arabic and Turkish transliteration.

For the spelling of sheikh, I have followed the 1942 edition of the *O.E.D.* which gives, as first alternative, the spelling, sheik. With the name, Boghoz, I have followed Burckhardt's own spelling, Boghos.

K. S.

*Part I*

# The Early Years

Die Neujahrsgratulation im Kirschgarten

# CHAPTER ONE

## *Swiss Childhood*

Two Voices are there; one is of the Sea,
One of the Mountains; each a mighty Voice:
In both from age to age thou did'st rejoice,
They were thy chosen music, Liberty!
But there came a Tyrant: . . .
*Wordsworth, in 1789*

ANCIENT CITY OF Roman origin, place of great importance in the Middle Ages, capital of a canton which has belonged to the Swiss Federation since 1501, Basle stands poised splendidly at the heart of Europe—where three frontiers meet, and where the mountain-turgid Rhine angles sharply north, dividing Germany and France.

Since quite early in the sixteenth century Basle has been the home of an old respected family—the Burckhardts. Here, in 1768, Rudolf Burckhardt contracted a youthful marriage. It was not a success—his bride was the shallow-minded young daughter of Basle's mayor, and Rudolf was a somewhat pampered young man only eighteen years old.

Rudolf's father, Gedeon Burckhardt, prosperous silk ribbon manufacturer, had died while in his early thirties. Although an elegant, cultured man of intelligent appearance he had so doted on his young son that by the age of ten, when his father died, the boy had already been seriously spoilt.

The ancestral home was spacious; it stood in a large garden with meadows and vineyards behind it, but soon Rudolf wanted something grander for himself and the mayor's daughter. He could well afford to be extravagant since, while he was growing up, both the manufacturing side and the forwarding agency part of the family business had flourished in the capable hands of his energetic mother. So an imposing new mansion, the "Kirschgarten"— named after its mass of flowering cherry trees—was built in the Elizabethan Strasse to his precise and lavish wishes. The young couple moved into this splendid town house in 1777: on the surface all was prosperity and beauty but only a year later divorce proceedings commenced.

Rudolf was an ambitious man, and he was considerably more than the soldier and merchant-councillor that he appeared to be— he was a collector, a music lover, a generous patron of the arts. He was also a great whip; he enjoyed driving his own carriage and spirited four with enviable panache through the charming streets of old Basle. He was well-educated, he had travelled with his tutor, he was a good linguist, and a very efficient business man. He steered clear of politics, which was wise since he was hot-tempered, but soldiering was a passion with him and occupied much of his time—indeed he founded and commanded the first Corps of Riflemen in the Canton of Basle.

He cherished high ambitions for his sons—he had five children in the ten years of his first marriage. He was well aware that his father had spoilt him; in consequence he swung to the other extreme by bringing up his children in spartan severity—no *duvet* even in the bitterest of winters. Indeed it was said that one child died in infancy from the ill effects of cold. For Rudolf had a dogged belief in his own infallibility. This failing, allied with a fiery temperament—he was inclined to use violent language should his own opinions be crossed—brought him near to death during the devastating upheavals caused throughout Europe by the French Revolution. The Revolution, and of course the subsequent Napoleonic era, had disastrous repercussions in Switzerland, politically, militarily and economically.

With what seems remarkable ease the divorce went through, mainly on the grounds of Rudolf's complaints that his wife brought up the children to shallow and arrogant ways.*

* To people of a later age, and in countries where divorce is still something of a calamity if not as in Victorian days a social disgrace, this may seem rather strange, but no doubt even then for members of the Lutheran Reformed

Three years later—while he was still quite young, only thirty-one—Rudolf married again, this time a very different girl. She was Sara Rohner, the twenty-year-old daughter of the first secretary to Basle's hospital, a woman of character, charm and sympathy, a devoted and profoundly loved wife and mother. She did not come of a wealthy family but of a more stable one perhaps, imbued with a stronger but a more gentle philosophy than a hollow belief in the power of riches alone.

In this second marriage Rudolf found great happiness and contentment. Sara shared his outlook on life, his interest in the arts, she apparently also understood his tirades and must have been able in her gentleness to calm his passionate temper. Her children adored her, and it was largely through her efforts that the brothers and sisters of both marriages held together during the difficult years that followed the Revolution. Their son, Georg, was born in 1783.

Tiring of the rather philistine company of the prosperous merchants of old Basle, Rudolf and Sara now began to visit Lausanne for a part of each year; soon it became a haven for them in which they could forget the endless mercantile topics of their home town. Not only was it more peaceful on Lac Léman but, since Rudolf had many aspirations, the dull society prevailing then in Basle did not satisfy him and he thirsted for the milieu which he knew—from his student days—existed so pleasantly in Lausanne.

In 1783 Gibbon also escaped to Lausanne, from "noisy and opulent London", to the house of his intimate friend, Deyverdun —"La Grotte" standing in its four-acre garden above the lake. Deyverdun, a charming epicurean, lover of nature, an easy-going, somewhat indolent man, was a personal friend also of Rudolf, and he sometimes travelled to Basle to stay at the "Kirschgarten".[1] Among Rudolf and Sarah's other Lausanne friends was the Charrière de Sévéry family. Madame de Sévéry was an attractive, elegant woman: indeed her whole family was entirely delightful.

Church, to whom marriage was not a sacrament, not only was divorce no scandal but it was easier to obtain in nineteenth-century Switzerland than it is even today in, for instance, twentieth-century England.

Gibbon gradually acquired "solid and tender friendship" with them, every day seeking and finding opportunities of meeting.[2]

So it was that Rudolf came to know Gibbon—the short, fat English genius who so dearly loved the Swiss. In return Rudolf admired him greatly, not only intellectually but as an Englishman, a member of a proud race that stood for freedom: Rudolf was a staunch Anglophile.

The beauty of Lausanne, the conservative, very English views of visiting English aristocracy, and those of their own friends, the intellectual interests of congenial men and women, all were a source of delight and refreshment to Rudolf and Sara in dire times of impending change and terror. For dark wings of danger yet to come already hovered menacingly above the horizon.

Their friends, the de Sévérys, owned the Château of Mex, and a house in Lausanne itself, 33 Rue de Bourg, where the Burckhardts relaxed.

At the same time, likewise facing the unimpeded view, a rich landscape of meadows and vineyards around the lake "and the prospect far beyond the lake crowned by the stupendous mountains of Savoy",[3] Gibbon at "La Grotte" was working on the fifth volume of his momentous *Decline and Fall*.

In Lausanne, towards the end of 1784, on 25 November, the Burckhardts' second son was born. They called him Jean Louis, or Johann Ludwig, but from his letters he was known mostly as Louis.

During that autumn a fifteen-year-old Corsican boy was transferred from the Royal Military School of Brienne le Château to the Military School of Paris—the young Bonaparte, training for war.

At the same time an Albanian boy of identical age, destined to be Pasha of Egypt, was also learning the art of war but in a very different school—the wild mountains of his native country.[4] This was the young Mohammed Ali, preparing himself, though as yet unwittingly, for a great role in the Ottoman Empire.

Oddly enough, the Swiss boy born that autumn day in quiet Lausanne was destined to lead a life deeply affected directly and indirectly by these three famous men: the rotund little English-

man at work among his books above the serene lake; the young
Corsican who was to alter the face of Europe and singe far wider
shores with his paranoic torch of war; and the fiery Albanian
boy who was to become the founder of modern Egypt.

Louis came to love Lausanne, but Basle was home: the "Kirschgarten", the town, the *munster*'s warm red sandstone pile, the
swift-flowing curve of the Rhine, the mountains and the mellow
countryside beyond. He knew Basle's fountains and narrow lanes,
its tall gabled *Rathaus* where his father presided at meetings, its
Rheinsprung—where some of his friends lived—its mediaeval
houses where vivid geranium flowers glowed against dark carved
shutters and where, below each window, fallen petals lay like
small drops of blood bright on grey flagstones. Here the only
sounds would be a burble of pigeon voices, the gentle splash of
water, a distant jingle of carriages and horses' hooves from wider
streets below.

The *munster* rears twin Gothic towers high above the Rhine:
from its quiet paved terraces set in a green foam of trees, sheer
rocky cliffs descend to the turbulent river below. In the shadow of
the building, in a chestnut-shaded *platz* there stands a fountain
where the horned head of a satyr spouts the sweet water of Basle
into a wide stone trough. It was made in 1784, the year of Louis'
birth, the date is engraved upon it. Any boy would have looked
at this fountain and its date and felt privately that the satyr and the
water had some special significance for him—being as it was
exactly the same age as he. Sara too, no doubt, in later lonely
years could hardly have passed it by without a thought for her
most adventurous of sons, he who knew the desert's thirst.

The "Kirschgarten" was a busy house in those still prosperous
years of Louis' childhood. The ground floor served as offices for
the silk business and the forwarding agency, on either side of the
stone-flagged entrance hall clerks bent over their desks, or went
scurrying to and fro with papers, messages, bills and orders.
Above the offices sunlight shone in through high windows to
flood the wide well of Rudolf's ornate staircase, where Corinthian
columns and golden balustrades rose like gilded lilies from the

plain working floor below to a marbled hall above, to the balconies, and painted and panelled upper rooms of style and grandeur where the family lived. There was the "garden room" with Watteauesque murals, the tapestry drawing-room; fans left by visitors—refugees from the French court—decorated the walls of the main salon, from which pleasant room a small chapel opened out.

There was much to delight an eager child: beautiful porcelain stoves, a rare Chinese wallpaper, and the "rose-closet" mentioned in family correspondence. This is a little boudoir where, since he idolised his mother, Louis must often have sat to talk with her; obviously it had memories for him. Its walls were painted with innumerable red roses by a Viennese artist; originally created for the mayor's daughter this costly piece of rococo had been romantically commissioned by Rudolf to represent the roses he had laid before her at the time of his proposal. If the painted blooms reminded Sara of the earlier marriage she was too sensible a woman to be bothered by such things, too successful with the step-children and with her own three—Rosine was born two years after Jean Louis—and too happy with her devoted husband to begrudge the youthful romanticism of this little "closet".

So Louis grew up at the "Kirschgarten" with his brother Georg and his sister Rosine, whom he loved dearly. They were taught at home by a tutor; they all adored their gentle, intelligent mother and, despite their father's strictness, they were happy. It was a full and satisfying life. Each year at the pre-Lent carnival season they thrilled to the drums of Basle's *Fasnacht*. At the stroke of four in the morning, when every light was extinguished, the whole town would wait in darkness until, simultaneously from many different points, the drums began to rattle and throb out a loud tattoo: a vibrant tumultuous background of sound swelling to the skirl of accompanying fifes. At this signal the streets quickly filled with people and with bands of macabre masked figures. In his early teens[5] Louis took part masked in the revels; it is a time when sober Basle goes mad, and all normal reserve is thrown aside.

The New Year had much meaning for the Burckhardts, as Louis

was never to forget, and there was another annual event in their lives, a private one—the family gathering of 14 October, called "Burckhardt Day". This tradition, dating from the Middle Ages, is still retained by the present Burckhardts of Bastle, who celebrate it generally with a dinner-party, often followed by music.

Throughout the year musical evenings were frequent events at the "Kirschgarten", the big house sparkling with lighted chandeliers resounded then to the melodies of Bach, Scarlatti, Handel, Clementi, and other contemporary composers.

Music was an important part of Louis' development. His talent for it showed early: he was considered a good enough player at the age of seven to deserve one of the new pianofortes for his own use—this Rudolf ordered especially for him from London.* By that time Louis' French too was already excellent. But life was not all work and chamber music for this clever child: he learnt to ride early, and, when he was old enough, to handle a gun. He was a fast runner, and a strong swimmer, as his later adventures prove, but his eyesight was not keen for distance, and on several occasions in manhood he was to lament that he was not as fine a shot as he would have liked—in the manner of the alpine chamois hunters of his country.

There was plenty for his imagination to feed upon. Great names, such as Goethe, Gibbon, Lavater, were familiar household ones. Rudolf had entertained Goethe at the "Kirschgarten" when the poet arrived from Weimar on his visit to Switzerland. Having already met Rudolf in Germany he came to call at the new mansion, then one of the "beautiful stone palaces of Basle",[6] and was charmed by the brilliant show of its wrought-iron window guards which, in that era, were remarkable for being painted in "lively colours reminiscent of parrots' cages".[7] Although Louis was not yet born at the time of this visit, he must frequently have heard of it from his father, who was proud of his acquaintanceship with the great poet.

There were also the musicians, and the young painters and

* It was probably a Broadwood "square", since at this period the London masters were undoubtedly the finest in Europe, the Seven Years War having driven many German workmen to England.

architects whom Rudolf assisted by his patronage. All this must have been a stimulating background for the children.

But there were increasing economic difficulties brought about by the situation in France that now disastrously affected Swiss trade in general and particularly that of the silk merchants of Basle, whose main export markets had been Germany, France, and Italy, now totally lost to Switzerland through the economic and the military consequences of the Revolution. Despite this Rudolf was able to plan the building of a country house, a decision made all the more necessary because, through the contrivances of the French minister there, Geneva was already coming under French dominance even in 1793, a fact which would soon have put an end to the Burckhardts' annual Lausanne visits.

The country house, called "Erndthalden",* was designed in deliberate contrast with the "Kirschgarten". Following the still novel Rousseau trend for the natural life, the architect created not a castle-like country seat as was customary among the landed gentry of the age but an Emmenthal-style farmhouse built entirely of wood. It was an innovation, the only house of its kind in the entire canton,[8] and to the children it became a paradise.

"Erndthalden" was near the village of Gelterkinden on the edge of the wooded Jura, at a distance of only five miles from Basle along the carriage road to Luzern. Louis was ten years old when he first began to taste the joys of living in the countryside. The place had a fresh, sweet-scented tranquillity most individually its own: Louis' thoughts constantly returned to it in later years of hardship and he refers often to the house and the surprises of the flowery meadows with obvious nostalgia. "Erndthalden" stood on a hill overlooking the richly fertile valley of the meandering Ergolz. To the south—hills and mountains, lonely chalets, tiered vineyards, and high pastures; to the north the slopes of the Jura, dark but not unfriendly. The pleasing early morning clonk of cowbells would mingle softly in cool water rhythm with a distant ringing of church bells and the soughing of the wind in the firs. Each year with mounting impatience the children welcomed the summer months that would see their release from the hot con-

* Meaning "Harvest Slopes".

fines of town. From "Erndthalden" tracks and footpaths led into the woods where Louis, Georg and Rosine loved to play; there is a charming picture of the three of them painted in 1795, all with flowing locks. Georg, very handsome, in tall top hat, is apparently searching, with the dark-haired Rosine, for Louis who is hiding behind a tree—there is something oddly symbolic as well as touching about this painting.

There was a look-out tower, a hut on a rock, a trout stream, orchards, numerous sunlit slopes, and the sweet flower-filled meadows. Near the house an old barn had been converted into a chapel. The peace and beauty of the place inspired Lavater, the Zurich poet, philosopher and physiognomist, to write a song in praise of the quietness of "Erndthalden" and the noble spirit of his hosts. The learned Lavater, of penetrating eye and remarkable mien, was a close friend of Rudolf, and sometimes preached in the "Erndthalden" chapel.*

For a year or two more this pleasant routine of town and country life endured. But all too soon the even tenor of family affairs was to be totally disrupted by an event infinitely more far-reaching for the Burckhardts in its effects than the growing economic crisis. It was a dangerous incident that occurred while France was fighting the Austrian dominions, and while the ravages of war were spreading along the Rhine, and beyond the Alps now as far as the Po Valley. The occurrence all but cost Rudolf his life, and was to alter the entire fortunes of his family. When this storm broke Louis was just twelve, an impressionable age, and the events of this time form one of the major keys to the understanding of his character.

Even then, with war raging all around, Rudolf felt that given the aid of Germany, still England's ally, French influence might yet be excluded from Switzerland. The deep sympathy and warmth which he had long felt towards England—France's hereditary enemy—did much to give him hope. Ever warm in approval, Rudolf was also too open about his dislikes. He loathed

* The song which Lavater wrote, known as the "Erndthalden Song", is in the family archives. Unfortunately, this charming house was destroyed by fire under a later owner.

the Revolutionary principles, French new thought was utterly unacceptable and he did not hesitate to voice his opinions, and— as so lively and successful a man—he had probably long since evoked the jealousy of some of the more stolid citizens of Basle, some of whom favoured France. Now he was to find himself disappointed and betrayed.[9]

Before this personal catastrophe fell, Swiss officers, and officers of the besieging army alike, had found a warm welcome at the "Kirschgarten". Unfortunately, as Rudolf could not refrain from comments of disgust whenever the French were mentioned in his house—inevitable among soldiers—spies reported him, and very soon his name was heading the list of the enemies of France in Basle.

A few days after Louis' twelfth birthday, on the night of 30 November 1796, the Austrians attacked the bridgehead on Cobbler's Island, before Hünigen. In the darkness a detachment of Austrians broke on to Basle territory before the Swiss could prevent them. The French concluded that this transgression over the neutral border was part of a conspiracy between Austrian and Swiss officers, and with some of his fellow officers Rudolf was involved—very nearly fatally.

A few weeks later, the Council of Basle demanded a detailed inquiry and arrested the officers concerned. Rudolf was imprisoned on the charge of high treason. This dangerous accusation was eventually dismissed, but a long trial ensued, and the leader of the Basle democrats' party, favouring France, demanded severe punishment. Rudolf was deprived of his captaincy of the Riflemen, and forbidden to attend meetings of the Great Council. Deeply hurt and offended, he left Basle for good and withdrew to "Erndthalden"—he had already handed over the management of his flagging business to his elder sons, Johann and Gedeon. He was forty-six years old.

The great armies of France, having burst like a tidal wave from her own frontiers to spread across Europe, flooding forth misery and devastation all in the so plausible name of "freedom", soon set Switzerland in flames. The subjugation of the Cantons brought tragedy and personal ruin to many. But first, in 1797, came the Treaty of Campo Formio and the end of Austrian power. Then England alone remained to resist the gigantic forces of the Republican machine. Bonaparte, now abandoning the idea of invading the British Isles, was planning to strike at the English through Egypt.

1798: Basle at Carnival time—no drums or dancers that year— then early in the same spring news reached "Erndthalden" that the French Republican army was advancing against Berne. The moment he heard this, Rudolf rode away over the mountains, and at Berne he fought as a private with the troops gathered there to defend the town. He had at least the satisfaction of taking part in one victory, but when Berne fell to the invader during a second onslaught, Rudolf rode sadly home to "Erndthalden". The French ransacked the city and used the treasures they took in fitting out their expedition against Egypt the following year.

For centuries the Swiss cantons had been allies of France, bound to her by treaties faithfully kept, often shedding blood in her service: now the treatment they received was so devilishly treacherous and so unprovoked that it excited the indignation of all Europe. In their heroic struggle the Swiss were regarded as martyrs in the cause of freedom:[10] of Wordsworth's two mighty Voices one was now stilled—the Tyrant had come.

Until the subjugation of the Cantons there had been:

no country in Europe in which happiness and contentment more generally prevailed among the inhabitants for not withstanding the variety of governments and independent commonwealths within that small territory, a mild spirit of liberty pervaded their several constitutions, and the property of the subject was secured against every kind of violation.[11]

Although good soldiers, the Swiss had never been fired with the spirit of conquest and, since the establishment of the Everlasting League of the "forest cantons" in 1291, they had scarcely ever had occasion to oppose a foreign power, and there had been no troubles among themselves that had not been easily settled.

Now the French forced these free-spirited, long independent states into one republic under the Helvetic Directory which, formed after the French model and established at bayonet point, promptly reduced that once happy little country to abject humility and ruin—all in the name of "liberty, equality and justice".[12]

For the Burckhardt family a new threat arose: a re-trial of the offending officers of the Hünigen bridgehead affair was publicly demanded by the French *chargé d'affaires* of the Directorium. However, after a month of suspense the case fortunately was dismissed. But now Rudolf and many of his friends decided that the time had come to emigrate, not only to save their lives but in the hope of liberating Switzerland from the outside with Allied aid. So it came about that the Swiss patriot *émigrés* joined the Allied Armies.*

These self-exiled men travelled to Vienna and on to Munich. Rovéréa's Battalion Company was one of several Swiss levies to fight in British service. It was in this company that Rudolf now served, with the rank of colonel, on a military council to Rovéréa, and Rovéréa's "Swiss Legion", as the English called it, saw much hard fighting.

When Rudolf went into exile, Louis and his brother Georg were sent away for further education, to Neuchâtel, which was not yet under the French Directorate.

All these distressing scenes, the danger, strain and suffering, were to have a permanent effect on the boys, inspiring them both with a loathing of French Republican ways and principles so vehement that it was to shape Louis' destiny in a totally un-expected way: and to Georg it brought the tragic fate of a pro-longed imprisonment eventually causing mental disorder. It was not until many years later that relatives discovered him languish-ing in a French lunatic asylum: he was brought back to Basle where Rosine nursed him devotedly until he died in old age.

* The reputation of the Swiss as soldiers was still very high. A few years earlier, Wickham, the British minister at Berne, had hoped to gain the service of some Swiss regiments, but the cantons had not been willing at the time to accept recruitment.

Thus, through the hated French oppression the family was split and divided: the mother and Rosine at "Erndthalden", the father in Germany, the elder brothers struggling to keep the business alive in Basle, the two youngest boys at school in Neuchâtel.

Louis could not forget that it was France which had brought this upon his family and his country. It was this detestation of the Republic which made him resolve with bitter determination not only never to live under the yoke of France, but also never to serve any country not actively opposed to her.

This then was the turbulent background of his adolescence; indeed at fourteen his childhood was already virtually over.

# CHAPTER TWO

## *In Malta—the Start of the Adventure*

A man truly becomes Man when in quest of what is most
exalted in him. Each hero, saint or sage stands for a victory
over the human situation.

*André Malraux*

MALTA, 1809: a great wind sweeping across the two sister
islands had moaned all night through rock and crevice. Now the
Grand Harbour glittered in morning sunshine. Senglea's golden
fortifications reflected a dancing sea-borne light: voices rang out
along the Barriera quay from the semi-circular Fish Market,
a graceful little building blessed by Neptune; the shouts of sailors
aboard ships below arose echoing off the honey-coloured heights
of old Valletta's stalwart walls. There was a pleasant tang of
brine, ozone, fresh fish and a hint too of spices on the morning
air.

The clean fierce wind, warm sunshine, the lively aspect of
a busy harbour taut with trade, bustling with the multifarious
confusion of this interim period in Malta's long history were
enough to quicken any pulse. To an energetic, vigorous, ambitious
young man the whole scene was as refreshing as a draught of
potent wine. It aroused Louis' curiosity, stimulated his imagination, blew away the accumulation of the doubting years, the
anxiety and the disillusionment painfully experienced in Germany
and in London.

He had not been long at school: in 1800 when he was just
sixteen he had been sent to Leipzig University. Above all else, he
craved serious learning; he had tried to work hard, had striven to
avoid disrupting influences, gay companions. But cheerful, full of
a natural *joie de vivre* he became involved—got badly into debt

through gambling and other extravagances—and during almost all the Leipzig years he longed for the more inspiring environment of Göttingen University.

Still at Leipzig in the summer of 1804 he had to write a desperate plea to his half-brother, Johann: fresh debts accrued during a "far from frugal" winter were crippling him. He owed everyone—for books, clothes, rent, even lecture fees. Altogether his debts amounted to something over 640 *thalers*: a sum worth about £100 sterling at that time, now in actual purchasing power the equivalent of £250, but—and this is the point—today's accepted "psychological value"[13] of such a sum represents something near the £1,500 mark. One *has* to grasp this in order to understand the gravity of Louis' predicament, and the intense shame that he felt. It seems to have helped to shape his character and to carve out his extraordinary determination, it partly explains the utter dedication of the man he became.

Johann's reply was a stiff rebuke and a direct question: why had he not appealed to their father? But Louis had thought should Rudolf know the state of his affairs he would certainly ask him to return and all chances of a career would be ruined.

> Mother would be utterly cast down with grief. She would consider me lost and that, by God, I am not. . . . Please help me while you are able to help . . . [*he wrote*] . . . Do you really think that I should suffer, perhaps all my life, the consequences of a single year? My conscience, my fear and my future oppress me and crush me . . .

Hating to deceive his parents, to lose their trust, he had implored Johann to reconsider his decision, and help him. Perhaps the parents could have been spared their anxiety over this, Louis' second lapse, had Johann thought fit. Louis had written on feverishly:

> . . . My fate is at stake. It will never depend so much on you as it does now . . . show me a middle course, support me with your advice, and if you believe that you do not neglect your

obligations to our parents, help me . . . in any case relieve me of the agonising uncertainty.

As always your faithful and loving
L. Burckhardt.

Even this heart-felt appeal failed dismally. The whole story had come out and, worse still, Johann had shown Louis' letters to Sara, making him appear not only shockingly extravagant but, infinitely more grievous to him who loved her so dearly, insincere also. The hurt caused all round was profoundly wounding —more so to Louis than to the others concerned perhaps as he was its cause. Indeed it left so great a scar on his conscience that it was to be ten years before he felt justified in believing he had fully atoned for failing parental trust—especially at a time of distress and war.

Eventually, at Göttingen he had been much happier, fascinated by the sciences, inspired by the great Blumenbach, the handsome, distinguished, famous scholar whose influence soon extended to almost all branches of science.

Louis' year at Göttingen passed only too quickly, Then, after a farewell visit to his mother in Switzerland when he was twenty-one, he travelled across bleak northern Germany, and sailed to England to seek, on a cousin's advice, an administrative position in London in military, or the civil service. This cousin, Christoph Burckhardt, son of a Basle banker, had over-confidently led Rudolf to believe that he had sufficient influence in England to help Louis secure for himself an excellent position there. Christoph, it seems, was a man of easy promises, and it so happened that Rudolf's and Louis' trust in him was ill-founded.

Louis' first sight of the sea, and of ships from many far away places had enchanted him; he reached London by long and weary stages but in high hopes and a buoyancy of spirit. However, difficulties arising from sudden changes of government, nepotism, and other problems, had been endless; soon they began to seem almost insuperable. He discovered early that important introductions were not given lightly on a mere superficial acquaintance at fashionable routs and supper parties. He was rapidly learning more about the English character. But there were some aspects of it that he did not perhaps quite realise then: one, probably, was how extraordinarily little the hurricane of the revolutionary years had ruffled the brilliant surface of English upper-class life. Indeed there were some, perhaps less perceptive English tourists —such as Lady Hester Stanhope, for instance—who had been dazzled by the First Consul, despite all England's proud notions of maintaining individual rights. Such illogicality, in lesser minds, may well be symptomatic of a country that has not known invasion. Something of the Corsican's glitter and power captivated many of those who saw it; Madame de Staël recognised his fascination but she was repelled by his cold and fearful inhumanity.

London, "this vast city" as he called it, must have seemed more than a little bewildering to Louis who had counted hopefully on an English predilection for the Swiss. It is quite true that the English admired and praised the Swiss, and had even tried to respond to their appeal before the French closed in to put an end to a thousand years of liberty. Addington had been deeply moved, Wordsworth had written his famous sonnet, England was appalled by their martyrdom. But was it rather more a theoretical admiration than a practical one? It may have touched the hearts of a few good men and great thinkers, but how much had it really affected that unruffled surface of English society?

In many ways life in London began to prove a kind of hell for him. When money ran short Christoph disappeared, but Louis clung on stoically, determined to face the challenge, doing the round of social duties, reading, studying his English, economising. Everything seemed to conspire against him, and instead of receiving him with open arms and employing his proffered and undoubted talents in her service, England nearly lost this "adopted son" of hers through all but disregarding his presence.

So the months passed, apparently fruitlessly, in London: in a letter of August 1807—over a year after his arrival and at almost the lowest ebb of Louis' spiritual endurance—while battling with dejection he had written to his parents of England, which he still loved, despite everything.

One can in our time breathe freely only in this country. Those who do not know this country have no idea, not even the faintest of what makes the English proud and will always make them victorious.

He was struggling for everything, he told his parents—for their approval, for his own existence—and indeed things had come to such a pitch that he would now undertake any job honesty allowed in order to achieve success.

That autumn he lived through two months when he was "literally in distress". It was a time, he wrote later, which had induced him to fast and pray. He had hardly any money left and he did not want to borrow, he experimented to see how he could work while living on bread and cheese only. He soon discovered that little was needed "to keep the flame of life alight".

This, my dear parents, is how I have lived since and how I probably shall continue to live for some time: to mingle with the great in the daytime, and buy for the evening, secretly in a back street, provisions for a few days. I shall never forget it —and I hope it will do me good.

Through prayer he had at last found consolation, a quiet courage, a new strength. For him it was a kind of spiritual rebirth, and he thought that he had become a better Christian.

Although the society and government contacts from which he had expected so much failed him, he had already met many scientists, learned men and travellers. There was Joseph Planta, Swiss scientist and principal librarian at the British Museum. There was W. G. Browne—a good friend—a man who had travelled dangerously in Africa when Louis had been no more than eight years old. There was Henry Salt who had journeyed as Secretary to Lord Valentia for four years in India, Egypt and Abyssinia. Above all there was Sir Joseph Banks, and the welcoming house in Soho Square where Louis had first called, bearing an invaluable introduction from Professor Blumenbach of Göttingen.

It was most likely in Banks' house that Louis met George Cecil Renouard, a young member of the African Association, a man with whom he corresponded over the years. Renouard must quickly have seen the passionate fire and promise in Louis, for it appears that he was certainly influential in getting Louis his post.[14] This scholarly priest, who had a wide reputation as linguist, geographer, and botanist, later maintained a wide correspondence with the most distinguished orientalists and geographers of Europe.[15] Louis continued to write to him from London when he had gone, in 1806, to Constantinople as chaplain to the British Embassy there.

Sir Joseph Banks was one of the most forward-looking, energetic, genuine and accomplished men in the London of that day: few sincere people ever turned to him in vain.[16] It is not hard to imagine with what sense of relief Louis resorted to this house,* since it had become a rendezvous for all interested in the sciences; there the latest discoveries were discussed, and the most up-to-date scientific papers were available to all. In fact Louis' meeting with Sir Joseph was the turning point from which was to spring his whole career, and although he did not know it then the end of uncertainty was soon to come.

Sir Joseph had long been an extremely active member of the African Association, a society formed by a group of learned and wealthy gentlemen in 1788 to promote the exploration of Africa, then still largely *terra incognita*.[17] Members of this group had recruited some adventurous and daring young men who had already been sent out to penetrate the "dark continent", to find the as yet secret routes of caravans, to determine the most likely means of exploring the interior, and above all to settle the baffling question of the Niger's course, a problem which had long concerned the African Association. Young Ledyard had been one of the first of these men: manly, original, but too impetuous, he had died from an over-dose of medicine while awaiting a long-delayed caravan to the Fezzan. Hornemann, a young German recommended by Blumenbach, had reached the Fezzan, but was now missing on the same venture. By 1806 the African Association had

* Number 32, Soho Square.

quite despaired of having any further news from him, and at the same time Mungo Park was missing on his second, and disastrous, expedition to the Niger. Then in the following year, 1807, the Association had heard of the death of another of their travellers— Henry Nichols, who had died of a violent fever at Old Calabar on the Gulf of Benin.*

Comparing information obtained by travellers on the western side of Africa with that sent back by Hornemann from the Fezzan and Tripoli, it was now decided that any fresh assaults on the interior towards the Niger should be made from the north, travelling first in a westerly direction from Cairo, with returning Mecca pilgrim caravans.

So it was that, on hearing from Renouard of the Association's need, and after careful consideration, Louis decided to offer himself for this dangerous assignment.

When Sir Joseph first saw Louis he may well have been reminded of young Ledyard, the American, whose manliness, "breadth of chest, open countenance, and inquietitude of eye"[18] had promised so much. Ledyard's very impetuosity was a lesson to Louis.

William Martin Leake,† one of the younger members of the Association, wrote this of Louis:

> To a mind equally characterised by courage, a love of science and a spirit of enterprise such an undertaking afforded peculiar attractions, and accordingly it was not long before Burck- hardt made an offer of his services to Sir Joseph Banks, and the Rev. Dr Hamilton. The latter who was at the time treasurer and acting Secretary of the Association, perceiving him un- dismayed by the strong representations of danger, which it was peculiarly right to make to a person of his birth and education, and having found him admirably adapted to the undertaking

* Their latest and most promising explorer was not destined to reach the great river. It was not until 1830 that the English brothers Lander solved a part of the long-vexed question and later still in the 1850's that the German explorer, Barth, by a series of journeys decided the question.

† Traveller, humanist; in Greece a forerunner of the archaeologists, and champion of Grecian liberty.[19]

by his natural and acquired talents, as well as by the vigour of his constitution, laid his offer before the next general meeting in May 1808. The offer was willingly accepted and Burckhardt received his instructions on the 25 January 1809, having diligently employed the interval in London and Cambridge in the study of the Arabic language, and of those branches of science which were most necessary in the situation in which he was about to be placed.[20]

Louis had paid most careful attention to the accounts and reports of those who had gone before him; he knew well enough the value and wisdom of patience in preparation for so great and lonely a mission. The older traveller, W. G. Browne, also influenced him, and impressed upon him the danger of being caught in the act of note-taking. Invariably it evoked suspicion—it had nearly been Browne's undoing on his lonely Nubian journey, and had led to his being "detained" in Darfur for three years.

To reach the still mysterious, much fabled Timbuctu, or any town on the banks of the Niger, it was agreed that Louis should be disguised as a Moorish trader, travelling with pilgrims. The most important initial step was for him to go to Aleppo to study Arabic so fully that he might pass among the people of the caravans as one of them: since Arabs were to be his constant travelling companions "from the confines of Syria to those of the Negro countries" he would have to be fully initiated into their manners and customs as well as their language. So he was to stay in Syria, for a full two years, and he was appointed for a subsequent period of six years with the promise of further support if he were delayed by adverse conditions beyond that time. If he were not heard of before the year 1819 he would be considered lost, and his pay in the hands of the treasurer would be disposed of as he should have directed. He was to receive 10s. 6d. a day plus expenses and lecture fees until he should start his main travels from Cairo, when his salary would be raised to one guinea a day.[*21] A sum of £150 was to be placed at Cairo for his disposal

---

* But Louis in a letter home wrote that he was to have one guinea as soon as he left England (*Briefe*, p. 108).

there to enable him to buy goods and beasts of burden for his journey. On leaving England he was paid £70 sterling, and £55 for his passage to Malta.

He was just able to manage on the half-guinea a day when at Cambridge, but he thought that while travelling as a Muslim he would be able to save. Also, the travel diaries that he would write should bring in a considerable sum. With any surplus money he proposed to buy old Arabic manuscripts whenever possible; they would prove invaluable in furthering Arabic studies in England.

The Association had asked him to make his own draft of how he intended to manage his journeys, and when he handed in his proposals, the Committee agreed with them so completely that they immediately had them copied word for word, signed and handed back to him as his actual orders. This must have been highly gratifying to him, the best possible encouragement, and he told his parents: "I shall do my uttermost to justify the good opinion they have formed of me."

The Association had left it to his judgement as to whether he should go on, and how it should be done; safety was to be paramount. "Continue to try your luck [*the Committee had said*] in pressing forwards [*Sudan*] or to the right or left. If on the contrary you find travelling in the Sudan subjected to great hazards, or the contents of your journal appear to you too important to be exposed even to the smaller risks trace back your nearest way home."

He was to be neither over-rash nor over-cautious, and as rigidly exact in writing down his observations as was possibly consistent with prudence. The members of the Committee had treated him with "great friendship and *delicatesse*", he had a very high respect for them, and obviously the trust was mutual. The Committee expressed their pleasure at the attention he had paid to the instructions given to earlier travellers, and the way in which he had so promptly made himself master of the most important parts of the information the Society had derived from the habits of his predecessors.[22]

One of the first things he did on being accepted by the African

Association was to renounce, in the politest gentlest way imagin-able, so as not to offend his father, his "marriage portion". This was a sum of £1,000 which Rudolf had presented to all his other children on their reaching maturity. Now Louis was at last in a position that enabled him to say that he would never again have to ask for his father's support financially and he wrote that, as he considered Rudolf had spent more on him than on any of his other children, he wished solemnly to declare his renouncement of the marriage portion. He reckoned that his father had spent at least 1,700 *louis d'or* on him since he had left school at the age of sixteen. Since he felt it would be unfair to the family should he receive even a fraction more he made this renouncement formally, by a special document. It was, of course, in a sense repayment, but it was, oddly enough, also a kind of safeguard against himself, for he says quite frankly that he had no desire to be unfair and that such a word would be more than inadequate if he were to return to his father and ask for money.

It is hard to believe that he did not *yet* trust himself, but it must have been so. He must have felt too that he had been over-long bound by obligations to his father, although he writes:

I do not do it because I am shy of obligations. I owe you my deepest and sincerest sentiments and by them I am for ever closely bound to you.

It was his desire for fair play, an action typical of the meticulous care with which he arranged all his affairs from the instant he had the power to do so.

The London period had been a long-drawn testing time, the difficulties he had experienced in the great city had humbled and hardened, though not embittered him. He was strong now: spiritually and physically purged of inherent luxury-loving tendencies; all that it seemed was under control, burned away in the London kiln. In fact, it was rather as if he had been through fire: cruelly tried, he had emerged a true man; his career decided, his ardent ambition at last resolved, most creditably channelled after eight years of searching—his life's course now fixed and dedicated.

Dedicated is the word for such a man; in Malta now at twenty-four he was old for his years, and perhaps a little withdrawn despite his natural warmth and amiability, but the loneliness was self-imposed, a safeguarding necessity. In it one senses that trace of the actor in his blood—a trait which, although he might not have admitted it, spiced the part he had set himself to play. It is in no way derogatory to think that he derived some vicarious enjoyment from the perfecting of this dramatic role. He did so, almost unconsciously but to such a degree—as we have seen—that it is difficult to decide between histrionics and facts, especially in the matter of his Muslim sympathies. The question naturally arises as to what he really did feel about Islam. The family's descendants today are certain that he remained a Christian, though he was not a conventionally religious man. Indeed the only time he mentions religion at all, as it affected him, is in the letter from London recounting that terrible autumn when he had recourse to his Bible, and prayed. From then onwards he had never looked back. He clearly believed in the power of prayer and in God, but this does not in the least mean that he was anything more than a nominal Christian, though it does seem that he considered himself still as being one.

Islam means submission: Louis certainly felt the need to submit —to some power greater than himself. He *had* to be dedicated. Therefore, Islam in its purest sense might well have suited him; possibly it, in fact, did. Even after prolonged study of him, and of his writing and actions, it still remains hard to tell: perhaps even he was not quite clear about it in his own mind.

But one thing is very clear: once the path of his life had been found he submitted immediately and whole-heartedly. Nothing could now deter him from the course set, although there were to be struggles later with his conscience when, always alone, he had to make difficult decisions, the outcome of which he knew would be a further perfecting of his assigned role, but which involved steps that he feared might possibly be misconstrued by those to whom he owed allegiance, the African Association.

Shortly before he left England for Malta—he sailed from Cowes early in March 1809—he signed a formal contract with the Association, and completed his business arrangements. He had arrived in Valletta about the middle of April on this the first stage of his travels for the Association. In Malta the fresh winds from off the sea blowing from Africa, his ultimate destination, put new heart and hope in him, as it were winnowing through the chaff of doubt and anxiety that had so long beset him.

Mr Peter Lee, Mr Chapman (Public Secretary to the Governor), and the Harbour Master, Lieutenant Corner, R.N., were all helpful to him. While waiting his passage to Syria he had gone to live discreetly "out of the way of intruders" in Lieutenant Corner's lodgings overlooking the Grand Harbour. He was now going by the name of Ibrahim bin Abdullah, and he had already adopted disguise on leaving England. He felt that by assuming very early in the adventure the clothes and character of an oriental merchant he would be more secure in the dangerous countries he intended to explore than if his true identity were to become known through the spreading grapevine of inter-port trade— and at the time there was considerable trade between Malta and the harbours of the Barbary coast.

Only too often in his story, as in that of most men of action, he was to be frustrated by periods of delay, waiting for weather, for ships, for intractable traders, for caravans, for firmans, or finance. He endured such times on the whole patiently, turning his tremendous restless energy to some study or other that would pass tedious hours fruitfully. And in his strong, firm handwriting— it is an interesting hand, neither too small nor too large, lively, active, full of a nervous intensity—he wrote long letters, to his parents, to Sir Joseph, to Renouard, and often to a good friend in Cambridge, Dr Edward Clarke.

He remained in Malta for nearly two months awaiting a ship for Syria. But this particular delay was not as irksome as times of uncertainty in London, nor as others yet to come in Africa, since now the sense of adventure, the joy of coming to grips at last with his career pervades all that he wrote with a controlled but lively new urgency. There was that uplift, too, which he had expressed to his parents when the African Association had first engaged him.

The best thing that could have happened has happened now. During this long period [*in Africa and the East*] I shall be accustomed to living more moderately. I shall learn to make do with less and to strengthen my moral and physical character through self-denial. I have at last achieved what I have been craving for during eight years—a definite sphere of activity. I have at last found a goal. And I shall spare neither industry nor effort. I have some intelligence and I shall use it now. But do not overestimate yourself, you might say. I won't. This journey, and what I shall observe while I travel, requires not a genius but a straightforward, clear mind and some ability . . .

He was always modest about his own abilities.

Louis must often have sat in the kiosk window of his room in Lieutenant Corner's lodgings overlooking the Grand Harbour. He had a well-built, stalwart figure, his broad shoulders showed firm beneath the flowing robe, a full turban framed the strong intent face—straight, clean-cut nose, winged lifting well-marked brows above wide, deep-set clear eyes. The right eye the one of the dreamer, the left a little quizzical, more worldly, the whole expression remarkably resolute, his dark beard full and curling (a beard then of course was totally unfashionable, he had grown it while still in England expressly for this venture)—it was a handsome, passionate face.

At the window where he would sit to write he paused often to look out at the fascinating and still unfamiliar nautical life. From the shadow of the lattice shutter he could see into the decks and cabins of vessels below. For one whole day a ship of the former Pasha of Tripoli was moored close beneath and, as he wrote to Banks, he was delighted with the opportunity afforded of "prying unobserved into the Moors' private manners and behaviour to each other". Even the short history of one such day he found instructive—naturally so for a man who refused to allow himself to be bored. There was no time to waste, and he seized on every chance to increase his knowledge of the peoples among whom he hoped to pass unnoticed; not for the sake merely of his own personal safety but, through it, for the advancement of his mission.

Across the harbour beyond the ships and beyond the Knights' imposing walls, bastions, bartizans and vedettes stood the tall honey-gold houses of the town, their façades enlivened with green-painted kiosks jutting on shapely stone corbels. Above them, higher still, rose the drums and domes of some of the numerous churches that make religion a part of that island landscape—red domes ribbed with golden stone, surmounted by lantern campaniles and bells that are tolled from the top.

As Louis grew more accustomed to his oriental dress and to speaking the day's greetings, he passed frequently through the narrow streets and stairways. Making his way up the steep flights (which had so irked Lord Byron that very same year during a brief and rather grudging stay on the island), Louis would climb away from the harbour to the wide Piazza Tesoreria. And so along the narrow spine of Valletta's main artery, then called the Strada Reale,★ where shore-leave sailors stroll today; here Louis rubbed shoulders with Moors from the Barbary coast, but contrived to pass by with no more than a "*salam aleik*". Here he would have caught glimpses of pretty Maltese profiles half-hidden by the great black sails of their *faldettas*. Here too he saw officers of a Swiss Regiment in English service that chanced then to be garrisoned in Malta, and to many of whom he was personally known. This made him all the more cautious in walking about, and in driving to the Palace of San Anton to call on Sir Alexander Ball, for he was as anxious not to have news of his mission percolate back to French-held Europe as he was to hide his true identity in north Africa. He succeeded in passing quite unknown and unnoticed in the streets. It must have been a strange experience and a gratifying one when he realised that he was unrecognised by his fellow Swiss, many of whom were friends or sons of officer acquaintances of his father, but their presence made it all the more

★ Now Kingsway.

difficult for him to visit Sir Alexander at the charming palace in its invitingly leafy gardens.

Napoleon knew well the vital importance of these islands: he had once said that he would prefer to see the British in the Faubourg St Antoine than in Malta, and in 1803 Nelson had called it "a most important outwork to India". But as yet the islands did not belong to England; it was later that Sir Alexander became officially governor—in which post he endeared himself enormously to the Maltese people. At this particular point in time he was guiding island affairs through the interregnum that had followed upon the surrender of the French garrison.

A most likeable man, Sir Alexander was kind to Louis on every occasion and expressed great interest in the success of his travels. Louis enjoyed his friendly and instructive conversation, and only regretted that he dared not risk calling more often.

While he waited in Valletta, he tried to improve his Arabic, but there was little safe opportunity because of the lively trade connections then existing with north Africa; so there must have been many hours for reflection and planning.

It is unfortunate that the letter which he wrote to his parents from Malta is missing. But those which he wrote just before leaving England all contain that longing to atone for the "old way of life" and, as always, the yearning for parental approval. If, as they evidently had, the parents forgave him his former bouts of extravagance, they did not appear to understand that they called his moodiness, nor perhaps had they quite grasped the extent of his fervent ambition. It had been a long, terrible time in London. When it was over he had written:

I have a feeling, dear parents, that we will meet again; do not believe that during my absence I shall be continually in a state of unhappiness and danger. I have lived long enough to have the firm conviction that happiness and contentment originate solely from the mind. If I do my duty in such a creditable enterprise, my mind will be cheerful even when I sleep on the ground and live on flour and water. These are negligible worries compared with the tormenting reproaches of a disturbed conscience or the grief of a mind neglected or by circumstances depressed.

He did sincerely believe that the discoveries he was about to make would be beneficial not only to the civilised world but also to the peoples of the countries he would explore:

There is some danger involved in it but it could have very profitable results not only for myself but also for England, and for the whole of mankind.

He carefully understates the danger, since his concern was constantly for his parents' peace of mind:

The thought that you might believe that I had been led to make such an important step acting in despair or thoughtless rashness, or that you might torment yourselves thinking that I had found an untimely death without being reconciled with my Creator, would deprive me of all courage. . . . You may say that I am too young, that I have not enough experience, that I am not sufficiently cautious and determined and that this will increase any danger from the half-civilised races of Africa. What answer can I give you? I have got to know myself better and through this others too. Since then I have come into contact with many people, had to give way to them and observe them, because I needed them.—So far I have not had a chance to prove my determination either to others or to myself.

For he believed that the quality of a man's determination was to be proved only by the demands necessity made upon it. Another thing he now knew was that he no longer feared death.

The fear of death has left me since I have been at ease with my conscience and, whatever my beliefs are, I shall not hastily expose myself to death, but shall not be afraid either when I am faced by it;—and am I really safer from it here in my room than I shall be on my journey?

We know his sufferings in London had already taught him that materially very little is required to keep the body sustained, and he was glad to have lost weight. There is of course much good in the idea of living frugally, but it can be dangerously over-worked—even possessing so splendid a constitution as he did.

At that time Africa was still very much the fabled continent, full of mysteries, strange beasts and weird legends. He himself was not prejudiced by the fairy-tales that originated from people who had travelled a little but did not speak as eye-witnesses, and he begged his parents to forget all such hearsay fantasies that had impressed the imagination since childhood. He seemed to worry more about his parents' fears for him than he ever did for himself.

All these things that he had written home were deep in his mind, a part of him; whatever his beliefs indeed were, he never wavered in his actions and his courage was never to fail him—even to the so bitter end.

Here in Malta, Africa was close, the very smell of it was on the sea-borne wind, and his thoughts must have turned more and more to the vast little-known continent.

The sun was setting in gold and flame, gilding churches and bastions with fire, the room glowed blood-red and then grew dark. Suddenly from the Moorish ship below a haunting falsetto cry floated up to arouse him from reverie. It was the *mahgrib* call to prayer. He got to his feet, pushing away the writing table, stretched his strong arms, straightened his robes about him, and went to fling wide the half-closed shutter. Small lamps were lit on the decks below, dark-faced figures robed in white flung them-selves down prostrate, stood, bowed and fell forwards again *kiblah*-wards—in the direction of the holy city—engrossed in their evening oblations. For some time he watched intently; when they had finished their prayers he turned to go out. There might be a chance of news that evening from a Greek sea-captain—the news he awaited of a passage to Syria . . .

But, as usually happens in the East, there was still some time yet to wait. Meanwhile, he met Mr Barker, a merchant in Malta, brother of the British Consul then in Aleppo, and through him came by some interesting information about a German explorer.

This was Dr Seetzen, whom Louis thought, as he wrote to Sir Joseph, might be a rival in the field of exploration in the African interior.[23] Seetzen had been sent out to the Levant five or six years earlier by the Duke of Saxe-Gotha to collect manuscripts and "eastern curiosities"—he too had been a student at Göttingen and likewise inspired by Professor Blumenbach. He had little or no money but soon became famous through his success as a collector, so that not only Saxe-Gotha, but later also the Czar of Russia and other wealthy princes continued to finance his travels.[24] After learning Arabic in Syria, Seetzen had travelled to Egypt, and it was from Cairo that Mr Barker received the news that so much interested Louis. On his way south through *Arabia Petraea* Seetzen had tried to discover the lost city of Petra but without success. He intended next to travel down the coast of the Red Sea, and eventually to enter Africa south of the equator.[25] On the way, having made the pilgrimage but sent back no report, he set out in 1811 to follow in Niebuhr's haunted footsteps across *Arabia Felix*. He started off from the Red Sea coast travelling incredibly ostentatiously with a caravan of seventeen camels, only to die of poison two days later at Taes by the order of the Imam of Yemen.[26]

Seetzen was a considerably older man, already in his forties when at Malta Louis first heard of him; passionately interested in travel as well as natural history, he had originally trained as a doctor. Hearing now of his success to date (news of his subsequent fate two years afterwards did not come through until 1815), Louis must have been more than ever grateful for the few medical lessons he himself had received recently in Cambridge.

Cambridge had been a pleasant interlude in every way, a refreshing oasis after London, one to which his thoughts frequently returned, as his correspondence reveals, especially the letters to the delightful Clarke family in whose house Louis had felt completely at home.

At first, Dr Edward Clarke had thought Louis a retiring young man with a naturally grave character to which the stresses brought to bear on his family by the Revolution had added a great depth of seriousness. It is interesting to read this outside opinion while

knowing that during his time in Cambridge Louis was deliberately living very quietly, allowing himself to visit only one house
at all regularly—that of the Clarkes—despite having been made
welcome everywhere. The effects of his London ordeal and self-
disciplining are clearly stamped on the young, tense, bearded
profile in the portraits of this time. Angelica, Dr Clarke's wife,
made an engraving from the Slater original so that Louis'
mother especially might have a copy. But the other early portrait
is more true of him since it shows the fire and strength.

From his letters to Dr Clarke one can see that Louis felt a
warm affection for this family; he wrote frequently in an easy,
friendly manner. Clarke, penetrating the mask of solemnity, soon
saw Louis' real worth, and those qualities for which he became so
distinguished, and was:

> delighted to bring them forward to the notice of friends, to
> whom he also frequently predicted that high degree of reputa-
> tion which he (Louis) afterward attained.[27]

This kindly, lively professor did everything he could to make
Louis' short stay in Cambridge agreeable; the house was open to
him at all times, and access procured to whatever people or books
were likely to be of help to him.

In Cambridge, Louis also knew Dr Herbert Marsh, a man
greatly respected as a scientist, but unpopular because of his
pedantry and enormous self-assurance. His young wife had been
a friend of the Burckhardts, of both father and son, in Leipzig,
where as Mlle La Carrière she had lived with her father, a
merchant. In Germany, Marsh had been pursued by Napoleon's
men, suspected of spying and of being an opponent of the regime;
he had taken refuge in the merchant's house and later married his
daughter. Louis was delighted to have found her in Cambridge,
and together they often talked of Rudolf.

But it is true that most of Louis' happiest Cambridge hours
had been spent in the Clarke household. Dr Clarke was known all
over England as a traveller; in 1806 he had married Angelica
Rush, beautiful, accomplished, wealthy and half his age. There

were some doubts as to the success of their marriage but he was a warm, very human man—he once said that no biped ever lived more happily than he—and Angelica was, in some ways, homely. At the time of Louis' constant visits they had a house at Trumpington, then a pleasant village two miles from Cambridge. Louis, who loved children, obviously liked particularly one of their small offspring, a tiny boy, rather delightfully named Hotspots. He refers to him several times in his letters—notably in one from Damascus when he later wrote to thank Angelica for having taken the trouble to "etch his bearded head". He had some light-hearted advice for Hotspots to be brought up as great a traveller as his father.

> For the life of a traveller is certainly a happy one, so long as success and home return may be expected; I hope to arrive in England in time to make an Arabic scholar of him; we shall then send him from Eton to the Wahabi court, to wrangle with the students at Derayeh, and leave it to his option afterward, either to become a fellow of Jesus College, or an Olema at Medinah.

Under Clarke at Cambridge Louis had studied mineralogy, he had obtained a little knowledge of medicine, and he had attended lectures on chemistry, anatomy and astronomy. The contacts, and lectures, the long London meetings too with W. G. Browne, when a variety of topics were discussed over friendly breakfasts—all were helpful and stimulating. William Hamilton's well-known book on Egypt was published in 1809, and it is likely that Louis was given the opportunity of reading this at least in proof, and he was of course familiar with Rennel's *Geography*, and the invaluable memoirs of Norden, Pocock, Volney, Sonnin, Denon and Wilson.

How rich, full and intoxicating these exciting months must have been after the deadliness before! But he allowed none of it to go to his head, he wanted no fame until he felt it deserved, and this no doubt is partly why in Cambridge he gave an impression of such restraint and gravity. The fact was that it embarrassed him to be treated with distinction (as he was on various occasions) before he had won it; though he sincerely hoped to bring honour to his country one day.

An odd thing had happened during that summer in Cambridge: an extraordinary heatwave occurred and lasted for three days, the thermometer registering 98–100 degrees Fahrenheit in the shade. He seized the opportunity to walk bare-headed across open fields for some thirteen hours, mostly in full sunshine. It was good training, he thought, and so was living on vegetables and water, and sleeping on the bare ground, habits he also practised with typical zeal.

When the time had come to leave England he could tell his parents that he felt he had left only friends behind, and that he was indeed embarking on this formidable journey with considerably more good courage than he had been able to muster when, still under a cloud of his own unhappiness, he had left Leipzig for Göttingen.

Whatever might happen, whether I succeed or not, I shall know how to bear my fate . . . your good wishes and your love, dear parents, will accompany me everywhere . . . your prayers often unite with mine. May Providence grant me a chance to embrace you again . . . God bless you and keep alive your love for your sincerely loving son

Louis.

*Part II*

# Into Asia

# CHAPTER THREE

## *Eastwards—Beyond Antioch*

"What is Fate?" Nasrudin was asked by a scholar. "An endless succession of intertwined events, each influencing the other."

*The Incomparable Mullah Nasrudin*

MR BARKER, OF MALTA, had some baggage—goods and supplies—to send to his brother John, in Aleppo; these he entrusted to Louis' care.

Louis' departure was delayed until 9 June when he sailed at last with a Greek captain, as he thought for Acre. But no sooner was the ship out of sight of the island than he learned that the Caramanian (Karaman) coast of Turkey was their intended destination.

Realising that he had been duped, Louis knew there was no point in protesting, so he set himself to cultivate the good graces of captain and fellow passengers, and consequently a quite amusing voyage ensued. The other passengers were three men from the north African Tripoli, with their Negro slaves; one, a wealthy merchant, was part-owner of the vessel. Louis introduced himself as an Indian Muslim trader on his way home after many years in England. Passengers and ship's company alike believed this story: many searching questions were put to him regarding India, and China too—on the Grand Mogul, the gruesome custom of *suttee*, porcelain pagodas, even the Great Wall, and besides all this he was often asked to speak a little Hindi. He responded by answering in "the worst dialect of the Swiss-German, almost unintelligible to a German, and which, in its guttural sounds, may fairly rival the harshest utterance of Arabic".[1]

So the evenings passed in story-telling, both truth and hearsay, while passengers and crew sat around on deck enjoying the cool sea breezes and smoking their long pipes. For Louis, conversation with the Tripolitan merchant was easy since the man spoke Italian, as well as Turkish, Greek, and his native Arabic. He had some wonderful tales to tell of Bornu and the Sudan, and it was from him that Louis first heard of the interruption of the Mahgribin pilgrim caravans (coming from the far west through the Fezzan, to Cairo and Mecca), caused by the recent Wahabi incursions in Arabia.

This wealthy man, seeing that Louis had brought on board only scanty provisions of rice, dates and so on, soon insisted that he should join his own mess which was "plentifully supplied with all sorts of Barbary dainties". Louis returned this hospitality with manual labour. He helped to clear one of the merchant's coffee bags of rotten beans, preparing it to make a good show for potential Turkish buyers as a sample of the whole stock—an age-old trick. One day a sheep was killed and he learned how to make Barbary sausages and *kus-kus*, and among other jobs he helped to refit the foremast which had been carried away in rough weather off Candia.

Eight days out they sighted Rhodes at a great distance, and two days later they dropped anchor in the little old port of Antalya, which he calls by its ancient name—*Satalia*. It is set on a splendid wide, curving bay at the foot of a fertile plateau that, watered by an out-spreading of countless streams, ends abruptly in sheer cliffs from which the water spouts in foaming white torrents. To the west rise the immense Bey Mountains—a wild off-shoot of the Taurus Range soaring up in magnificent tier upon tier to the Pamphyllian defiles—through which Alexander sent his men 2,300 years ago, while he himself plunged boldly around the seaward end of this stupendous barrier. Snow was lying on these wildly extravagant summits when Louis saw them that June; looming threateningly at dusk, their sheer flanks at dawn take on the innocent colour of nectarines.

Above the low cliffs of the harbour and nestling down into the shelter of the port, white and tawny minarets, red roofs of little Turkish houses were bright in the sunshine; all around grew poplar trees and orchards. Louis saw the remains of Seljuk forti-

fications guarding the harbour entrance, and he remarked on two
fine cascades that descended then on either side of the landing
place, striplings of the river that further back hurtles from the
mountains to water the so fertile plain. It was all very sunny and
beautiful but—there was plague in the town.

This was his first encounter with that scourge of the Near East,
and Antalya was the setting for an incident arising from it which
he tells with evident amusement. The captain tried to forbid
anyone to go ashore, but the merchant, who had already recovered once from the plague, thought himself inoculated and, disregarding the captain's orders, spent four days ashore trading on
his own behalf. The Turks laughed at the captain's precautions;
he would allow no contact, and shoremen were kept at arm's
length, though Louis and some others did go ashore once to fetch
some meat and provisions for the ship's company.

When the wealthy Tripolene had completed his trading he
reappeared alongside accompanied by several cheerful Turks, and
demanded to be taken back on board. But the captain refused to
comply until the Moor had undressed completely and washed
himself and his clothes in the sea. The sun set, but the evening was
still light and so the argument continued between the adamant
Greek and the angry Moor, with Louis looking on, careful no
doubt to conceal the smiles that the comedy evoked, the crew
laughing, the boatload of Turks sympathising with the plump
merchant—since as a Muslim it would have been shameful to
expose his nakedness except in the bath. At last when darkness
fell he was prevailed upon to strip and jump into the sea; "but
nothing would persuade him to allow his clothes to be washed for
fear of having them spoiled; they were afterwards suspended at the
rigging of the foremast that the night air might purify them".

And so the ship sailed again, with the merchant's fine clothing
flapping from the rigging for three full days of quarantine. The
captain considered he had done his duty, and later he told Louis
that on his return to Malta he would feel quite justified in taking
the usual oath that he had had no communication with any infected place.

For these three days they sailed along the southern Anatolian coast within ten leagues of the shore: the great chain of snowy Taurus were always in sight, and each evening the foothills were angry with thunder clouds in which a dazzle of lightning flashed and played.

On 26 June they anchored late at night in the roads of Mersin and the next morning Louis went ashore with some of the other passengers. On myrtle-covered dunes they found a party of grain-selling Turks encamped around a single tent. These lively, hospitable people took them to their village, to the mulberry-shaded terrace of their Aga's house. Servants spread carpets for them, and here they spent the daylight hours of the next four days, very comfortably relaxed. While they talked and smoked the narghile, Louis was undoubtedly learning to imitate what Burton descriptively calls "the usual conglomerate posture" of the Turk.

Louis mentions here that it was impossible, but for the red cap—the fez, which the Greeks of course did not wear—for a stranger to distinguish a Greek from a Turk or, as it then was, man from master.

While the ship was loading Louis persuaded the Moorish merchant to ride with him to Tarsus since he hoped to find a way thence by sea or land to Syria, so a small caravan was formed. In ancient Tarsus they led their horses to the Khan of the Muleteer and themselves went on to the Khan of the Merchants.

These khans, then so important a feature of travel in the Near East, were all much alike: through a narrow entrance one came to a great pile of enclosed buildings set about a quadrangular court-yard, the pattern varying little from Constantinople to Sidon, from Smyrna to Cairo. Some of these buildings or the remains of them can still be seen today, though not in use, and it must have been in part of a similar caravanserai that Christ was born. Rambling, dirty, noisy hostelries, full of smoke and strange, acrid smells, the stench of dung, of varied merchandise—and appetitising aromas too, rice and peppers cooking, *kebabs* savoury on the charcoal. Dim, evil stairways shot with shafts of sunlight were stained, insanitary, festooned with cobwebs. There was a central well in the courtyard, animals stood tethered near it, stables or storage rooms for merchandise and sometimes small cavernous shops of various kinds faced the quadrangle below. Above, giving on to covered verandas or galleries, was the accommodation for travellers; it consisted generally of one or two, or more rooms, with rough and ready cooking and bathing facilities.

It was in Tarsus that Louis had his first experience of the ubiquitous khan. Since the merchant's brother was known here they found "tolerable accommodation", and soon their room was filled with all the foreign merchants staying there, as well as the principal merchants of the town. They sold them a few silk handkerchiefs and coarse cambric, and were "plagued with their company" for the remainder of the day.

In the evening the alley at the gate of the khan was transformed into a dark coffee room, where everybody went to smoke a pipe. As we were strangers we were greeted at our entrance with the usual politeness of Orientals towards travellers: "Peace be with you, you are welcome among us, how are you? God send you a happy evening . . ."

Several merchants treated them to pipes, coffee, ice-water, and *bour*, a drink mixed with liquorice juice: the ice had been brought from the distant mountains. A man with a pleasing voice sang lilting Turkish airs, accompanying himself upon the *saz*.

Louis much enjoyed this party: the great number of queries made about him and his affairs were conveniently answered by his Moorish friend to everyone's satisfaction, and they retired late to bed, sleeping before the open door of their room on the wooden veranda.

The caravan journey from Tarsus to Aleppo took ten days, but at the time there was no overland communication at all since a savage rebel had set himself up in the mountains and taken control of the passes north of Alexandretta. However, the Moor arranged for a passage for Louis on another Greek boat sailing to the Syrian coast.

On departure Louis presented the friendly Tripolene with a

red cambric Glasgow shawl as a keepsake—the merchant had long admired it, thinking it to be Indian stuff—and with many mutual protestations of friendship they said farewell, Louis sincerely hoping to meet the man again in Barbary on his way to the interior.

The boat was a small open three-masted vessel, immensely over-crowded with fifty-six passengers, six crew, and in the hold six horses. Each person had just as much space as his or her body covered, and in this typical deck-passenger discomfort they arrived eventually at Suedieh.

Without the help and support of his friend, the Tripolene, life for Louis became considerably more difficult almost at once: no one spoke Italian, the Latin tongue as they called it, the crew suspected him of being a Frank★ and scoffed at his Arabic. While he was bargaining for a horse and mules to take him and his baggage to Antakia (Antioch) a caravan luckily came down to the coast from Aleppo with Indian goods. He soon arranged with the muleteers for the journey back to Aleppo and then, as he was helping the servants to distribute his baggage into mule loads, he was sent for by the Aga. On entering this local chief's house he remembered to pull off his slippers, and sat down to drink a dish of coffee. By unmistakable gestures of thumb and forefinger the Aga indicated what was needed—cash on the nail, duty that is on the goods which Louis carried.

Louis had marked all the baggage, both his own and the chests for Mr John Barker of Aleppo, with the consul's name, so that he was able to say that he did not know their contents. A bottle of Mr Barker's beer had been broken in the loading, and the Aga's men reported its vile taste. Then, as a sample of the vegetables sent by his brother in Malta to the consul, a potato was produced and tried raw. Louis said "that noble root" excited general laughter and sardonic comments on the great wisdom of sending such revolting stuff so far. Frankish stomachs also came in for some revilement for even enduring such food and drink.

Louis paid the duty but less than was first demanded, while the Aga lolled around boasting of his grandeur and independence,

★ European.

and laughing a great deal at Louis' Cambridge Arabic—which Louis admits "certainly was hardly intelligible".

The route to Antioch is famous for its beauty; they rode through lanes overhung with flowering shrubs, bright and scented too with myrtle and wild oleanders. So on and up over the mountains to the beautiful city itself set in gardens of rose and honeysuckle and surrounded with cultivated fields which, since it was then July, would have been harvested, pecked over by the tall cranes of the White Lake, burnt-off, re-ploughed and probably already re-sown.

The first hint of trouble occurred in Antioch when, being alone, and also because he wished to study their way of living, he followed the muleteers to their khan instead of going to that of the merchants.

His appearance at the khan—his height perhaps, his features, his full curling beard, his colouring—excited considerable curiosity. His small, cell-like, vermin-ridden room was soon besieged by troublesome inquirers who unanimously declared he was a Frank come to Syria for evil purposes.[2] His own protests and those of his muleteer, who did strive to remonstrate, were drowned in the yells of "Infidel!" hurled at him by the mob of muleteers, and also by the townspeople who crowded his doorway to join in the fracas.

When he could make himself heard he managed to appease them, but he soon realised that the intention was to make religion a pretext for practising an *avania* upon him, that is to levy an extortionate tax. And sure enough before long the Aga of Antioch sent his dragoman to get something out of him.

This was a wretched Frank, who pretended to be a Frenchman, but whom I would rather suppose to be a Piedmontese. I pretended complete ignorance of the French language, he therefore asked me in Italian minutely about my affairs, and how I could attempt to travel home without any money or goods to defray the expenses of the journey. I answered that I hoped the Consul, in remuneration of my having carefully watched his effects, would pay the expenses of a camel from Aleppo to

Bagdad, and at that place I was sure of friends to facilitate my farther journey. When the man saw that nothing in my manners betrayed my Frank origin, he made a last trial, and pulling my beard a little with his hand, asked me familiarly "why had I let such a thing grow?" I answered him with a blow upon his face, to convince the bystanding Turks how deeply I resented the received insult; the laugh now turned against the poor drago-man, who did not trouble me any further. I am at a loss to state how I succeeded in sustaining my assumed character; I thought that the major part of the caravan people were gained over to my side, but the townspeople were constant in their imprecations against me. I had been flattered with an immediate departure for Aleppo, but the caravan was detained four days in the Khan. During the whole time of our stay, I spent the day time in the cell of the goods, amusing myself with cooking our victuals; the townspeople, though often assembled before the door of the room, never entered it; in the evening the gates of the Khan were shut, and then I went to sleep with the mule-teers upon the terrace.

This unpleasant situation ended on 10 July. It was still dark when the muleteers prepared to leave: a wonderfully businesslike orderliness prevailed, contrasting with the hurly-burly of visitors and insults during that delay. At once the whole courtyard was divided into squares of different sizes by means of ropes fixed to iron staples driven right into the earth, and although the ropes were little more than an inch above the ground not an animal moved out of its allotted square. Louis looked upon this crowded marshalling with wonder; the walled space teemed with beasts, bales and men, and yet nothing was out of place since all worked or co-operated with the systematic urgency of the custom-hardened caravaneer.

In this first account of the Levant sent home to Sir Joseph, Louis purposely described all these things in full so that they might easily be visualised in his later accounts, and his difficulties understood.

On the second evening out towards Aleppo the caravan was

joined by some other travellers whose curiosity led to fresh inquiries as to Louis and his affairs. Unlike Sir Richard Burton, Louis did not possess a naturally oriental look, but on the other hand some northern Indians, Kurds and many Turks do have light-coloured eyes, and Indo-Aryan features are very similar to European ones. But the curiosity he aroused in these new travellers led to fresh inquiries about his affairs.

Despite a strict watch no one had noticed anything that could directly condemn him as a Frank, but that night, being obliged to leave the encampment at a call of nature, he was followed unseen by two of the new travellers, who afterwards said that they had

"observed some irregularities in the ablutions necessary to be performed on such occasions." (It is an offence to use the right hand for this office since it is the social and the eating hand.)

In consequence of what they pretended to have seen he was pronounced "*Haram*", that is in a forbidden or unclean state. Now he had lost the trust of his companions, and the day's ride was made wretched with taunts and abuse. But he was learning very quickly:

Having been much plagued during the whole day by my fellow travellers, and in the evening also by peasants who had collected round the caravan; I swore that I would not eat any more with any of them. This declaration being somewhat in the Arab style, they were startled at it; and my muleteer especially much pressed me to rejoin their mess; I assured him that I would rather eat nothing and starve, than have any further friendly dealings with men who professed themselves my friends one day, and proved my enemies the next.

Characteristically honest and always anxious not to appear in heroic light, he points out in parenthesis that as this was the last stage of the journey he did not run serious risk of making good his words!

After another day's march, of eight hours across the wide plain, Aleppo's citadel came in sight high on its famous tell, defended in turn by Hittite and Assyrian, and where Abraham is said to have milked his flocks. The caravan's armed horsemen immediately set off at a gallop, wildly and repeatedly firing their guns, while the merchants bustled their jingling mounts to the head of the caravan. One hour later they clattered noisily into the town.

Aleppo's story goes back to the fourteenth century B.C. As Damascus seems an Eden, a heady paradise of an oasis miraculously set on the desert's brink for man's refreshment and delight, so in contrast Aleppo, grey, staid and businesslike, is the dourer of the two, from time immemorial the town of the merchant. For centuries caravans making their way north and west, up the Euphrates from Bagdad and beyond, have turned away from the river to cut across the desert en route for Antioch and the Mediterranean coast with their cargoes of silks, and spices. To the north lie the mountainous fastnesses of Kurdistan; all around Aleppo are the plains, not really desert here, and lying as the place does half-way between the great river and the sea, it became a natural staging post for caravans on the oriental trade route.

Another interesting point about Aleppo—which perhaps made it the safest and most ideal place in which to study Arabic in those dangerous times—it is on the very northernmost latitude of the language. It is here that Arabic ends, and Turkish and the rough dialects of the Asia minor hinterland are first heard.[3] All merchandise coming into Aleppo had to be taken direct to the Customs House Khan, where the baggage was weighed to ascertain the muleteers' freight dues, and for a duty to be paid to the Grand Signior of the Porte. This duty, also the taxation money taken from Christians and Jews, and the *miri*, or general land tax, were the only branches of revenue that the Janissaries, then masters of the town, still allowed the Sublime Porte to retain. Louis already had a clear grasp of the rapacious character of Pashas and Janissaries who, often quite independently of the Porte, levied decimating taxes and *avania* on the local peasantry and farmers.

It was in the Customs House Khan, that he first met Mr Barker, who was soon to become a warm friend; the English consular house stood within these walls.

Having arrived in disguise but under some suspicion it was quite optional as to whether he should continue in his oriental role, or appear among the Europeans as one of them. After a long discussion with Mr Barker, Louis felt convinced that it would be best to live as a European (and he chose to pass as English rather than Swiss lest he should be taken for a Frenchman), until he had so perfected his Arabic that disguise could not be suspect—as indeed it would have been had he set himself up in the bazaar as one of the many merchants there, when no doubt the French consul of Aleppo would have been only too glad to put his activities into any possible dubious light.

On leaving Malta he had imagined that free intercourse existed between Cairo and Aleppo, and therefore that anything he did here in Syria would reflect on his actions when he appeared later in Egypt. But since the great Syrian pilgrim caravan had not departed for Mecca for three years—prevented primarily by the Wahabi incursions in Arabia—practically all commercial contact overland between the two countries had ceased.

So, with Mr Barker's help, his plans were worked out for the best. He continued to use his name of Ibrahim and, in his Turkish dress, passed as he had in Valletta unnoticed in the crowds of street and bazaar. He was received at the consul's house as a travelling English merchant and, as it frequently happened that people coming to the Levant did change their names, nobody wondered in the least at his going by an oriental one. Also, he had no further bother with the muleteers of the caravan who were undoubtedly too wary of the greedy Janissaries, ever prompt to fine trouble-makers, to stir up a row over the matter of statements Louis had made at Antioch regarding his own affairs and origin.

He soon found a good and willing master of Arabic, and began a very serious study of the language, both the literary and the vernacular. He planned to stay in Aleppo until he could express himself with some precision in the common dialect, after which he intended to visit the Bedouin and to live with them in their tents, the best way of learning their manners and of becoming used to the character of the desert Arab. He hoped too to travel to those parts of Syria less known or quite unknown to Europeans to add to existing geography. At the end of a year he would be in a position to know how much further study he would require for real fluency.

He concluded his first Aleppo letter to Sir Joseph by promising never to dwell again at such length on his personal story, and gave his reasons for having written it in full.

> I thought it might be of some interest to the Association, to see how far I was able to succeed in making my way to Aleppo in the disguise in which I left London; unaided as I was by a knowledge of Eastern languages, or a familiarity with Eastern manners. This trial has so far been satisfactory to me, that, in the first place, I am persuaded that nothing of my pursuits transpired at Malta, which will always be of material consequence to me; secondly, in being landed in a remote corner of Syria, I have avoided the general intercourse of a mercantile seaport, such as Acre, Beirout, Tripoli, or Latakia; and finally it has created within me the confidence that whenever I may be able to call in support of a similar disguise, a fluent utterance of Arabic, and a habitude of Oriental manners, I shall easily find means to triumph over such obstacles as those I met with in the Khan at Antakia.

In this he was absolutely right. He was to encounter many such situations, some infinitely worse, some extremely dangerous, and not once did he fail to triumph over them—as he had in that verminous khan at Antioch, alone and unseasoned.

# CHAPTER FOUR

## *The Aleppo Years of Training*

Honourable is her rank, and far-flung in every age her name,
many the Kings who have sought her hand, and privileged
her position in all hearts. How many a hand-to-hand combat
has she excited, how many gleaming blades have been un-
scabbarded for her! . . . She has contended with the days and
the years. . . . This city of Halab, . . . how often has she
superseded the adverb of time by the adverb of place!"

*Abu'l Husain Ibn Jubair*

ALEPPO IS A timeless city. But apparently today we are not
allowed to believe the pleasant mediaeval story, common to both
Arab and Crusader writings, that the name is really derived from
*halab Ibrahim*—the milk of Abraham. Though Abraham kept
large flocks of sheep here and supplied the needy with milk from
them, so says Ibn Battuta, Marco Polo of the Arab world.[4]

Early last century no one knew anything for certain about the
Hittites: and it so happened that it was Louis who made the
initial discovery of Hittite hieroglyphs. He noticed a block of
basalt built in the corner of a house in the bazaar at Hama inscribed in a hitherto unknown form of writing,[5] and reported this
remarkably exciting discovery to London, but not much interest
was taken in it at the time. It was not until nearly sixty years later
that a similar find in an Aleppo mosque eventually led to a chain of
further Hittite discoveries, and the start of decipherment.[6]

Aleppo was to be Louis' base and home for the next two-and-a-
half years: he was happy there; he worked extremely hard, he
made good friends, and he began to travel. They were tentative
excursions at first, then further and further away into the desert,
he lived adventurously, even dangerously, and on several occasions

he explored tracts of land as yet unpenetrated by any European.

In some ways this time of happiness and preparation—he was learning rapidly all the while—was rather as an extension of university, in the fullest and widest sense possible, and it brought him deep satisfaction and peace of mind.

On arrival he took a little house in the town, engaged an Armenian servant and bought, for about 14 *louis d'or* a good horse worth in London more than ten times that amount. He devoted nearly all his time to the study of Arabic, and with his teacher, a venerable Maronite—a bearded charming old Christian Arab— he worked for hours every morning. They would sit side by side on the floor, their elegant Aleppo narghiles standing close, the long tubes mounted with silver and amber mouthpieces coiling to each left hand, Arab manuscript and dictionaries spread on wide Turkish-trousered laps. Sometimes, youthfully, Louis had to suppress an inward laugh when he thought how startled his family would be to see him now outwardly so changed—bearded, voluminously costumed, seated cross-legged on the rug-strewn floor; the glittering hubble-bubbles giving off sharp fragrance of cooled tobacco, blue smoke curving languorous around turbaned heads, while the old Maronite gutturally intoned the swallowed vowels in his deep and throaty Arab voice.

It did not take Louis very long to realise that his German was deteriorating: it was years since he had spoken it, his journals and most of his letters had to be written in English, but—he cheerfully reassured his parents—since Arabic is a language not so much spoken as "gargled" he should be able at least to pick up *Zuridütsch* again on his return.

He was soon practised enough in Arabic to converse with desert sheiks, and with some of the literati among the Turks of Aleppo who visited him occasionally, primarily to consult his much admired Wilkin's *Arabic and Persian Dictionary*, since the local dictionaries were very defective. These learned Turks never failed to exclaim in wonder that a Frank should know more of their language than their own ulemas did. But the standard was not high, the religiosi of Aleppo were not able to cope with passages of difficult grammatic construction, or even to compose

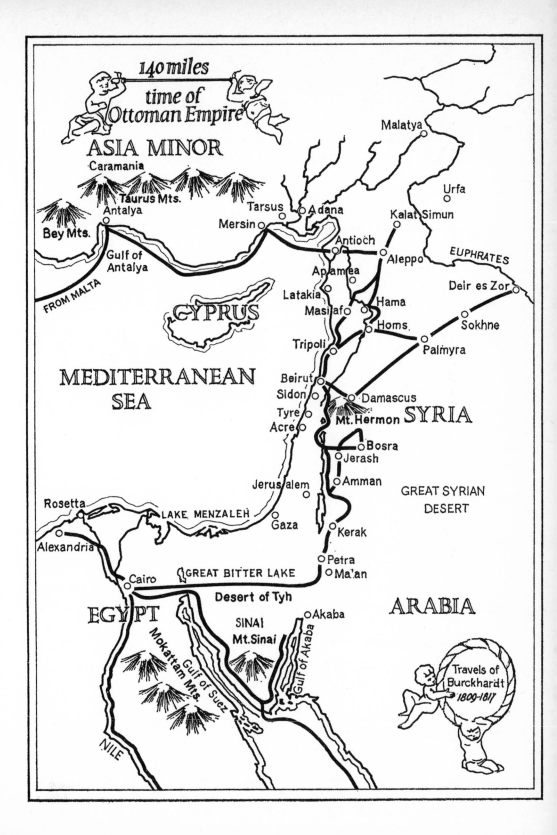

140 miles
time of
Ottoman Empire

ASIA MINOR

Caramania

Taurus Mts.

Antalya

Bey Mts.

Gulf of
Antalya

FROM MALTA

CYPRUS

MEDITERRANEAN
SEA

Rosetta

Alexandria

Cairo

EGYPT

NILE

Mokattam Mts.

Gulf of Suez

LAKE MENZALEH

Desert of Tyh

GREAT BITTER LAKE

SINAI

Mt. Sinai

Gulf of Akaba

Tarsus

Mersin

Adana

Antioch

Kalat Simun

Malatya

Urfa

Aleppo

EUPHRATES

Apamea

Latakia

Masilaf

Hama

Homs

Deir es Zor

Sokhne

Tripoli

Palmyra

Beirut

Sidon

Tyre

Acre

Damascus

Mt. Hermon

SYRIA

Bosra

Jerash

Amman

GREAT SYRIAN
DESERT

Jerusalem

Gaza

Kerak

Petra

Ma'an

Akaba

ARABIA

Travels of
Burckhardt
1809-1817

prose or verse free of errors. In Arabian poetry, Louis discovered, there were some 150 different words for wine alone: shades of the Prophet! Already Louis was learning Arabic proverbs, many of which he was later to compile into a very attractive collection, and he had begun an intensive study of the Koran.

Another task which he set himself during that first winter proved useful: the translation of *Robinson Crusoe* into an Arabian story adapted to oriental taste and custom. In this he was helped by a young locally born European who could neither read nor write Arabic but spoke it fluently, no doubt with the raciest idiom of the bazaar. Louis sent a copy of what he called this "travestied Robinson" to Sir Joseph as some proof of his progress. He called the book *Dur el Bahr*—Pearl of the Seas.

Louis had not been very long in Syria before he saw that the reputation in Europe of the Turks as the terrible ones was a fallacy, although it is a legend that still dies hard. Like most travellers today, he found them to be more full of frankness and good nature than many a people of European stock. He remarked on their mildness and peacefulness of character, and noted their luxuries which he put down as women and horses.[7] But for the Janissaries he had, not surprisingly, nothing good to say. It is almost undoubtedly primarily this hated body of men (and likewise later the Arnauts, the Albanian mercenaries), who have over the centuries vicariously endowed the Turk with his condemning alliterative epithet. The *O.E.D.* gives the figurative meaning of Janissary as "personal instrument of tyranny".

The Janissaries or "new troops" in Turkish, a force originally created by the Ottoman Turks in the fourteenth century, were mainly derived from children of Christians and, as it has often been said, the renegade makes the most bombastic of men. They became the principal infantry force of the Ottomans and made possible the vast conquests of that period.[8]

At the time of Louis' arrival the Janissaries were in complete mastery of the town, having chased out the Pasha. Like all bullies they were cowardly, but when there was skirmishing in the bazaars between them and the religiously fanatical sherifs, firing was abated by common consent if a European went by. Sniping from the minarets also ceased when the Europeans began to pass from one flat roof to another, as was the custom in time of trouble: for it was possible to walk all over the town on the terraces, roof-tops and connecting archways of the streets.

The Janissaries waxed rich by their extortions but they were mainly illiterate and lived poorly, hoarding their gold. They kept the town under despotic rule—indeed murder and theft seldom occurred; any serious quarrels that did arise were generally among "young Janissaries heated with brandy and amorous passion" fighting their rivals after sunset at some prostitute's door.[9]

Mr Barker's *ménage* was a hospitable one, his house was comfortable, even luxurious. An excellent shot himself, he entertained passing travellers and friends with shooting parties. The spread of gardens near Aleppo abounded with woodcock; there was also coursing with salukis of hare or gazelle in the plain, and sometimes hawking. Game of all sorts was abundant: partridge, wild geese, teal, bustard, wild turkey, and even porcupine were often served at Mr Barker's table.[10]

Mr Barker, whose home was Bakewell in Derbyshire, was the "best kind of John Bull": a typical stalwart Englishman, of true English blood—a thing rare enough in the Levant—a man with an admirably strict attention to duty. Louis grew very fond of him, for he was after his own heart—bright, jovial, gay, full of a dry good humour, affectionate and generous to a fault. It was proverbial at Aleppo that "the English consul would give away the whole world if he had it in his hand".[11]

When Louis first met him the consul was nearly forty; he had been married for some years to a bright, attractive woman. A Levantine by birth, Mrs Barker had from childhood spoken Arabic, Greek, French, English and Italian. She had already lost a son, and nearly lost another child at the time of the Russian-provoked threatened break between England and Turkey when she and her husband had fled from Aleppo—a daughter had then been born. Now she was again pregnant; and since Louis soon became a warm friend, Mr Barker asked him to stand as godfather.

Louis spent many happy hours in the Barker household and later, on his return from his tour of the Hauran, his little house having been sold, he went to live with the consul and was made to feel as if in the home of his own family.

> Burckhardt, the great traveller, under the assumed name of "Shaykh Ibraheem", lived several months in Mr Barker's house, and was very much regretted by him on his leaving for Palestine and Egypt, when he had learnt sufficient Arabic to start on his travels. He was much loved at Aleppo, from the amiability of his disposition—sometimes put severely to the test.[12]

At this time the Barker's house was constantly full of young men travelling through Syria not to explore but for pleasure, one of these, a Venetian named Bonaventura Popolani, was notorious for playing practical jokes, often risky ones. While on a partridge shooting expedition at a village some hours distant from Aleppo, he dropped, unseen, a hot coal into Louis' large Turkish riding boots just as they were about to be pulled on, and rushed away before the dénouement. It was far from funny: Louis, writhing from the horrible pain of the burn, fired off his pistol in the direction of Popolani's retreating back "without exactly knowing what he was doing"! The wretched man escaped quite unscathed and was forgiven generously enough by Louis. But on another occasion he very nearly did lose his life through playing a silly trick with a horrific mask on a terrified Turkish nomad.

Besides the Barkers, Louis became friendly also with the Dutch consul, Herr van Masseyk, whose intimate and specialised knowledge of the language and customs of Syria he found of immense interest, and they had another subject in common— horses. For fresh air and exercise Louis rode out every day; he was learning to ride the Turkish way—that is as one with his mount, skilled in sharp swift wheeling turns, and able to throw and fend off the *jerid*, a short javelin, at full gallop.

First firmly assured when the Seleucids made Antioch the third city of the civilised world, the long tradition of the caravan trade lives on in Aleppo still, and the covered *souks*, which are its mart, are a great feature of the town. Here Louis must frequently have wandered in the bustling gloom of the vaults shafted with long dusty beams of light from above, here he must have bargained, fingering wares, practising his Arabic, watching the leather-workers stitching camel-skins dyed with the juice of pomegranate rind. Here, half-deafened by the tin-smiths' clangour, he snuffed the wonderful scents of perfumes and exotic spices—attar, musk, myrrh and patchouli, coriander, cloves, cinnamon and saffron —feasted his eye on the colours of silks, the glitter of gold thread, and puzzled over rare aphrodisiacs, unknown Indian leaves, poisons, powders and strange stones. Here he would have bought his saddles and waterskins, and for himself perhaps a sheepskin coat, a fine woollen aba, a floating *keffieh* of muslin, with black corded silken ropes of the *agal* to bind it to his head.

Above the domed vaults of the *souks*, aloof from the confused din of work and barter, the shrill clatter of the tinsmiths, the braying of donkeys, there is a grass-grown expanse, a strange, lost roof-top place where sheep and goats graze quietly in the sun while life and trade hums below.

Louis' chief pleasure, beside studying and riding, was the ritual of the bath—the almost ceremonial Turkish bath. After a day of the cold, sometimes frost of an Aleppo winter, during the long rains of January or the great heat of summer, it was a delight to be pummelled, soaped and scrubbed, and soused with hot water by aged but dexterous attendants, and then to lie, clean, relaxed and refreshed, for the coffee and smoke that followed. Men and women made separate parties to the baths; evenings were often passed in this way, as had been the custom since the early days of the Levant Company, and it was one of the few regular delights of Aleppo life. It has been said, even today, that there can be no more authentic introduction to the town, since here one may see an unchanging Aleppo. The patrons, as they have been for centuries, range from hard-riding sheiks straight from the desert yearning for cleansing water, to fleshy old habitués, the sybaritic merchants of the town, and in certain establishments "the good-looking boys who still play their ambiguous role".[13]

On his rides and excursions Louis would often have seen the strange white conical beehive houses of northern Syria, like clusters of hard-boiled eggs dumped on the red Syrian soil—the fields of "saffron-tinted rose" of which the poet speaks—and we know that he enjoyed walking by the river in the orchards of quince and walnut, the gardens where "the oft-plucked myrtle grows".

Early in March as that first winter ended, he went to live briefly with a tribe of nomadic Turks or Turkomen of the Reyhanli, at a day's journey from Aleppo. He introduced himself as a physician in search of medicinal herbs and spent a fortnight with these hill men in their winter quarters—about 300 scattered tents of camel hair belonging to thirteen different clans.[14] Here he tasted the *leben* (yoghurt), and lived on honey, rice, eggs and cardamom-flavoured coffee. He admired the beauty and shapely elegance of the nomadic women, who when young were as fair as Europeans, and he learnt that although they were neither harem-bound nor veiled, any moral lapses were always severely punished: even a kiss meant death for the girl offender—and at the hands of her own father or brother. With his nomad host he also visited some Kurds—those magnificent people of fierce and splendid eye—and he rode on to Kalat Simun to see the ruined basilica of Simon Stylites, the pillar-squatting saint, the first to initiate this extraordinary method of self-mortification.

That summer he chanced to meet in town—perhaps in one of those bath houses—a sheik newly arrived from the Great Syrian Desert, a man of the Aneza, then a powerful tribe, or collection of tribes, of Bedouin, a small, strong neatly built people, whose deep-set eyes shine under bushy brows with a fire unknown in northern latitudes. Louis and this sheik ate and drank together, and Louis arranged with him to be taken to Tadmur* in the wilderness, home to his family encampment near by, and back to Damascus. Although this man was indeed a famous robber, Louis felt quite assured about the arrangement since desert sheiks did not normally withdraw their protection once given.

* Palmyra: it was first rediscovered by Englishmen in 1678 but was very little visited until the 1920s.

But he was let down on this excursion: the sheik became frightened for the safety of his own encampment and only two days out Louis was handed over to an underling who had no power to protect him; they were attacked by a party of Mawali Arabs, and Louis was stripped of all but his undershirt. He was in European dress on this occasion, posing as an apothecary's lad from Damascus, he had no money on him to lose, but he did regret his good English watch and compass. However, he managed eventually to reach Palmyra, and was able to "contemplate the wonders" of that perhaps most amazing of all caravan cities, whence the desert drifts away falling in swathes of luminous colour as blue as the sea towards Euphrates.

His friend, William Turner, gives a fuller account of this incident as he had it himself from Louis. Even after rigorous searching Palmyra's sheik could not believe that Louis had no money on him; it must be hidden in an ear, or swallowed. So Louis was confined alone in a room for two days: "but as nothing was forthcoming and the prisoner remained contentedly enjoying his lodging and food" he was set free and allowed to visit the ruins[15]—an incident typical of Louis' coolness.

In the ruins he found a statue, and was removing it when a chief stopped him, swearing it was surely full of gold. Louis bargained that if it were broken and proved to contain gold the man could keep the prize, if there were none he should hand over two piastres (about 2s. 6d.). The Arab shrugged, refusing to take the risk, and Louis was allowed to carry off the statue. History does not relate whether he got it safely back to Aleppo; if so he probably presented it to the Barker household.

Having no money he had to pay for the pleasure of this Palmyra visit with the saddle off his horse's back. But he was not in the least cast-down by his various losses, since, as he reported to Sir Joseph, not only had he seen those so remote, stupendous ruins but there had been excellent opportunities for observing the Bedouin in their own tents—he had stopped each day at a different encampment and had always been received with kindness and hospitality.

This marks the beginning of his growing love for and understanding of the Bedouin, really until his day a much maligned people. The tawny Bedouin he calls them, small, but well-built, and their women he thought beautiful although brown, of slender stature, and there were many who "walked with strikingly elegant gait". He was to write later of this time, when he first encountered these people in the desert, of how whatever preferences he may then have had in general for the European character, he was soon bound to admit that Bedouin with all their faults were "one of the noblest" people he had ever known.

The Bedouin exults in the advantages he enjoys; and it may be said, without any exaggeration that the poorest Bedouin of an independent tribe smiles at the pomp of a Turkish Pasha; and without any philosophical principles, but guided merely by the general feelings of his nation, infinitely prefers his miserable tent to the palace of the despot.

The French call that *le snobisme du desert*. Louis had to admit the Bedouin's rapacity, especially in the vicinity of towns, but he admired

his cheerfulness, wit, softness of temper, good nature and sagacity, which enables him to make shrewd remarks on all subjects rendering him a pleasing and often a valuable companion.

Returning from Palmyra towards Damascus Louis met with some vastly impressive encampments—true nomads, strolling villages as it were on the move, advancing *en masse* over the sandy plain in search of water and pasture. Some outriders led the way, but the main body covered an area at least three miles wide—armed horsemen and camel riders, followed by the she-camels grazing in wide ranks with their young ones; behind them the camels, loaded with tents and provisions and the huge copper pan of each family swaying high, and lastly the women and children riding in their cradle-like saddles. The whole nomadic caravan extended in depth about two-and-a-half miles, that is almost as wide as its gallant frontage. A splendid sight.[16]

Louis was forced on this occasion to remain in Damascus for

seven weeks: various dangers and disorders made it unsafe to travel, and there was news that the Wahabi hordes, the fanatical tribe from Arabia, were approaching the city.

It was then August and very hot. But *el Ghouta*, the green oasis, the girdle of gardens threaded with streams, made Damascus one of the pleasantest places for an enforced stay in the hot season. The famous and oft-sung Barada, the cold or, as the Greeks called it, the golden river provides this oasis. Below bleak hills it divides like a miniature delta into five or more main branches that flow in and around the town spreading freshness and fertility everywhere, creating the green *Ghouta*, filling the *hammams* and the tanks and marble fountains of every house. Below the town the Barada recollects its forces and at little more than a dozen miles beyond it disappears on the verge of the Syrian Desert in the sad swamps of 'Atebeh, the ancient "sea of Damascus". Beyond that, interminable-seeming wastes of fine sand and stone stretch 200 miles or more to Euphrates, and little lies between except to the north-east Zenobia's fabled Palmyra desolate in the wilderness. The ground plan of Damascus has hardly altered since the earliest times despite ravages by sword and fire, and the Street called Straight still cuts through the town—the street where Paul of Tarsus received back his sight at the hands of Ananias.

The poet sang lyrically of Damascus: "encircled by gardens as the moon is encircled by its halo . . . enfolded by them as the calyxes enfold the flower". In season its green orchards hang heavy with fruit, the luscious bursting fig, the apricot, the groaning mulberry tree all swagged with vines, and in autumn red pomegranates, and large brown walnuts that fall thudding to the ground. A place that the desert dweller dreamed of as paradise. Saturdays in Damascus, Ibn Battuta wrote, were for wandering by the river banks, and so it has been through the centuries. People stroll under great spreading branches and between the orchards with their fresh greenery and the gliding waters of the swift Barada, they linger until nightfall, singing their haunting falsetto recitatifs and threnodies, playing the *saz* and *rebaba*, surrendering themselves to that pleasant languor of the senses that the Arab calls *khayf*.

Rumour now formed a labyrinthine web for turbulent Damascene discussion. A few days after Louis' arrival from the desert the Pasha was betrayed and ousted: Soleiman Pasha of Acre then took his place. Most of these affairs were occasioned, or complicated, by a recent Wahabi threat to the town, when Abdulla ibn Saoud, with 6,000 men, mounted on camels, and 400 horsemen, had ransacked some fifty villages of the Hauran, and returned flying into the heart of his dominions.[17]

These flashes of news about the Wahabi are interesting in their effect on Louis' story, and indeed, although he admits to not being able to unravel all the complexities of rumour and events, one important fact emerges clearly: the disruption of the normal course of the pilgrim caravans. As we have seen, it was now six years since the Syrian Haj caravan had been able to reach Mecca. This great caravan included not just the pilgrims of Syria alone, but also those of most of the vast Turkish dominions. The innumerable hosts of Abdullah bin Saoud's army barred the way.[18] This fanatical puritan of Arabia, son of the first heretical reformer, stood firm. He would not allow the ornate retinue—caparisoned *Mahmal* camel, tasselled dromedaries, swaying litters, seraglio tents of linen, all the rich pomp and circumstance of Pasha cavalcade—to approach near the holy cities.

In Damascus, Soleiman of Acre, having ousted the former Pasha, now ruled three Pashaliks—Damascus, Acre and Tripoli —that is to say he was in possession of almost all Syria from Gaza to the neighbourhood of Aleppo and Antioch. Soleiman, a Georgian Christian by birth, had been brought up as a slave—a Mamluk—by the infamous Djezzar, "the Butcher", former Pasha of Acre, whose favourite he became. His own favourite and counsellor now was the rich Jew Haym, whose talents had already been appreciated by "the Butcher", who had also most terribly maimed him—a fact which Lady Hester Stanhope was appalled to discover, and one that Turner, Louis and others have recounted as a story typical of this monster of Acre.

Some years earlier, on returning from a Mecca pilgrimage, Djezzar had found that nearly all the women of his harem were pregnant. He sent for a Jewish doctor and commanded him to feel the pulse of one woman through the arras, as was the custom, and asked if anything strange was the matter with her. When the doctor pronounced nothing wrong, Djezzar called a eunuch and told him to rip open the woman's stomach: the foetus revealed, the doctor was tied up in a sack and flung into the sea. The Mamluks of Acre, having been the violators of the Pasha's harem, saw that their only chance of life was to kill Djezzar; they fired at him but missed. After the fight that ensued the Pasha started a systematic butchery: first he killed all his women; then Haym, the Jewish banker who was presumably considered responsible, had his ears and part of his nose chopped off, and one eye put out. But he was retained for ten years as a prisoner in the seraglio and forced to conduct all Djezzar's most important business affairs.[19] Indeed it was said later that the number of faces in Acre lacking noses and ears was the most striking evidence of the late Djezzar's activities.

Djezzar's favourite, Soleiman, who soon made himself master of Acre after "the Butcher's" death, continued to use the maimed but brilliant Jew in his offices, and in fact it was Haym who now virtually ruled Acre. Three of Haym's close relatives were equally influential in Damascene affairs so that the Christians of the town, writes Louis, were apt to say the Jews of Syria could well flatter themselves that Israel reigned again within her ancient limits.

Louis took a room in Damascus in the house of one of these wealthy Jews, a banker and the factotum of the Pasha—the very man in fact who had betrayed his previous master to Soleiman and forced him to flee to Egypt.

In September, when travel again became safe, Louis made a four-week expedition from Damascus to visit Ba'albek and what is now the Lebanon. Naturally he did not travel by any easy road but, joining a small Tripoli-bound caravan, with them struck up over the steep side of Mount Kassioun. To the north-west stood the red-streaked barrier of the Anti-Lebanon and from the south, stretching out towards it, the great grey, isolated mass of Hermon towered white-turbaned to the clouds.

Just before sunset the caravan paused, and from a saint's tomb high on the mountainside they looked back at all Damascus laid

out below. The oblong of the old inner city framing at its heart
the wide square of the Great Ummayyad Mosque: the pattern of
streets and river-threaded orchards evocative, hallowed by time
and legend from Genesis onwards, through the relatively modern
Graeco-Roman and Byzantine times to the turbulence of Ottoman and Wahabi of that day. Adam was created here, it is said,
here Abraham was born, near here Cain killed Abel, Elisha came
to the city, Mohammed travelled to its gates with his caravans
from Arabia; and here today Aramaic, the language of Christ,
is still spoken, if falteringly, in some outlying hamlets.

After that long sunset look at the beloved city they turned and
rode on into the mountains. Louis noted, as he went, the names of
every village; some days later he reached the river Litanni, and
the high vale of the Beka'a. The time he spent at Ba'albek was
peaceful, and for his own pleasure, since Wood and Dawson's
visit in the 1750s and Volney's lengthy account of it, made in the
year of Louis' birth, had rendered a report unnecessary and he was
free to give himself over to a quiet enjoyment of the place.

Heliopolis, city of the sun: Jupiter's gigantic columns soared,
powerful, slender, golden, masculine, high above the sacrificial
courtyard, where only sun-doped lizards moved along the stones;
racing clouds splashed the rust-red background hills with shadow,
and flights of pigeons, grey and white like the clouds, wheeled
overhead on momentarily flashing wings, splintering the sunlight
above golden Hellenistic splendour. Louis gazed in wonder upon
the famous Cyclopean blocks, lapped from below by a billowing
mass of green walnut foliage as a cliff is by the waves of the sea.
He savoured deeply the monumental richness of the place, its
height and grandeur enhanced as dusk fell over the red vale of the
Beka'a, and darkening clouds came down forbiddingly across
Sannin's snowy crest.

He found the little village of Ras el Ain delightful, small
and homely in contrast with the great temples. Perhaps he stayed
there in a house near the clear spring where, so it is said, Solomon
liked to camp at the time of the full moon as he paused to rest on
the way to Palmyra.

From Ba'albek, Louis went straight up the mountains and over to the high cedars of Lebanon, their gnarled trunks carved with the names of many travellers. He continued along the mountain tops where he was reminded of his own Alpine pasture lands, he looked down on the milk and honey coastline far below, and at the tall horizon of blue sea reaching westward to Cyprus and the far distant isles of Greece. The Maronite convent of Kanobin appeared to him as if suspended in mid-air, supported as it was

υΠΕΡ σΩΤΗΡΙΑC ΤΩΝ ΚΥΡΙΩΝ

ΑΥΤΟΚΡΑΤΟΡΩΝ

. . . . ΑΝΟC ΙΕΡΕΥC ΘΕΟΥ ΠΑΝΟC ΤΗΝ

. . . ΚΥΡΙΛΙ . . . ΕΟΙΝΚΑΙ ΤΟΝ . ΥΝΤΗΥΠΑΥΤΟΥ . . ΙΛΑΝ

. . . ΟΘΙ . ΙΠ . . . . ΡΕΔΘ . ΙΟΥΡΠ . . . ΝΤΑ . . . . ΥΤΗΟ . . .

by a high wall built against the side of the mountain. In its church, which was carved out of the living rock, he noticed with interest many bags of silkworms hung there by peasants for the duration of the winter, before portraits of favourite saints, in the devout hope of thereby securing a good silk harvest in the following season. The owner's names were written in various hands upon each bag. He went on to el Afka to see the source of the Adonis river that each spring "runs purple to the sea", and through Druse territory he came eventually to Banias, the ancient *Caesarea Philippi* and the Dan of the Jews—a place originally devoted to the worship of Pan. Here he was able to make a sketch (reproduced above). As it was then Ramadan, the Fasting Month, he often sat up late at night under the trees, smoking and talking with his guide and any local villagers who came to join them. When he ran out of money he began to return, going south of Mount Hermon across Jebel Heish; beyond lay those ports of the desert, Damascus, Homs and Hama, and the great desert itself unfolding ever eastward in jewel blue veils of shimmering light. As he returned towards Damascus, he was able to learn the names of many villages and hamlets during the lengthy sessions of Ramadan nights, when the men grew merry, animated by the usual tension of the day-long fast, their interest aroused by his lively curiosity.

This time he remained in Damascus for two weeks only, in order to recover from an infected blister (perhaps something resulting from Popolani's stupid trick), and he was busy planning a tour of the Hauran, an area better known today as Jebel Druse. This was a journey which interested him enormously, particularly as it would be his first exploratory one; no European had as yet visited this mountainous country of the Druses except Dr Seetzen, the German traveller who about four years earlier had seen a part of it. Louis thought that he would have already reported on this but in fact his account was lost. So this tour of Louis' proved of exceptional interest to Sir Joseph Banks and his colleagues in London who, as the reports came in, were able to congratulate themselves on fresh geographical information gained as well as on how rapidly their traveller was learning, and actively adapting himself to, the life and conditions in these preparatory years. Their friendly replies added greatly to Louis' happiness and confidence.

Even at the extreme end of the last century Baedeker warned that a journey into the Hauran could only be made when the country was in an unusually quiet state—always rare enough in Syria—and that it was best undertaken with a Druse escort, although one soldier would be sufficient for the plains of the Hauran "unless the tribes were actually fighting".[20]

Eighty-three years before that was written Louis entered the territory unattended, dressed as a peasant in sheepskin and *keffieh*, and riding "a miserable horse", which he brushed and fed himself, and with no more than 80 piastres, that is about £4 sterling, in his girdle. But he did take the precaution of arming himself with several useful letters of recommendation addressed to Turkish officials and to Greek village priests in the area.

He left Damascus by the Gate of God, the Bab Allah, on the Mecca road, which he remarked might more appropriately be called Bab-el-Maut, the Gate of Death, since scarcely a third of the pilgrims ever returned from the holy city. But perhaps to the devout it has the same meaning either way.

Although it was the patrimony of Abraham and also once one of the great granaries of the Roman Empire, the Hauran is now a thirsty, stony, dun-coloured place. Only the sight of Hermon's sacred summit crowning the 9,000 feet of its isolated massif does something to relieve the dreariness of a march into these savage strata of black basalt—the uninviting, forbidding, even sinister country of Jebel Druse.[21]

In Louis' day the Druses were not as firmly established in this wild and tortuous landscape as they became during the second half of the nineteenth century, after the massacre of Lebanese Christians, for which they were held in part responsible. Louis wrote of them to Dr Clarke saying that he felt they were the only people in Syria who had any idea of a commonwealth; with regard to each other they were free but they were despotic in their dealings with the other inhabitants of the mountains. In his view he felt that if Syria "were ever to emerge from its deadly slumber" it might be through the influence of the Druses, who might be strong enough to "throw off their allegiance to the Porte and regenerate the nation's deplorable state".[22]

An enigmatic and fascinating people, a heretical sect who have been a religious minority since the early days of Islam. Seetzen was scared of them for they could be dangerous. They are also brave and beautiful, famed for their blue eyes, for their lovely unveiled women, who wear the wimple—the exalted horned head-dress—and narrow-waisted gowns of deep rich colours. The men, equally magnificent, made splendid marksmen and dashing horsemen. It is perhaps worth recalling that it took the French, in more recent times, two years' bitter fighting to overcome this territory of the Druse.

News that Arab raiders were in the area plundering travellers and villagers so terrified the few Hauran peasants with whom Louis had joined forces on the road, that they refused to go further. The next day, however, they met a troop of Turkish cavalry who had routed the Arab raiders during the night, killing several of them, whose heads bundled in a sack they were carrying back hurriedly to Soleiman of Damascus in the hope of good reward.

Some of the Druses whom Louis encountered were hostile and suspicious of his inscription copying among the many ancient sites, but others were friendly, helpful, and interesting. He much enjoyed exploring the fine ancient site of Shohba, and there copied undisturbed numerous Greek inscriptions upon capital and architrave until the sun set and he could see no more. All these he hoped would serve to throw some light on this "almost forgotten corner", with its countless remnants of antiquity.

In Biblical days the pastures and flocks of this land were celebrated, and the Israelites who here defeated Og, King of Bashan, were greatly impressed by the oak plantations. Two Druses did accompany Louis into the dark and sombre labyrinth of the inner Leja, which with its grim lava ridges and dark ruptured hills was depressing. At night it was often too cold to sleep, dogs barked incessantly and their hosts lived in constant terror of robbers. The cleft and fissured lava was difficult to traverse, the hillsides so shattered that they seemed to be in the very act of tumbling down. In his travels here Louis encountered and grew to like immensely the second chief Druse of the Hauran, one of the most amiable men he had met with in the East. Extraordinarily eager to acquire knowledge of European manners and institutions, he begged Louis to write down for him the Greek, English and German alphabets with the corresponding sound in Arabic beneath each letter, and on the following day with some pride showed the copy he had made of these. Louis found this man's kindness all the more remarkable since he could not expect the smallest return for it. He refused even to accept the gift of one of Louis's two pencils which he had admired.

In December Louis returned safely to Damascus from this strange country. When his feet healed—he had walked barefoot for a few days—he made his way back to Aleppo by way of the desert ports: Homs, and Hama of the vast creaking water-wheels and that first-found Hittite inscription. He arrived back on New Year's Day of 1811, having been away since July.

He had already, before leaving for Palmyra, written to ask Sir Joseph for a further period of study here beyond the two years prearranged, in order to acquire that *fluency* in Arabic which was absolutely essential. A six months' extension was then granted readily.

But now, on his return, he faced the unpleasant duty of inform-ing the Committee that, despite every economy, he had spent his last farthing.[23] He pointed out that he had lived on £170 in the nineteen months since leaving Malta, and all his travels had been performed in "the garb of a pauper". (Indeed so disreputable was his appearance that once on returning to Aleppo he was taken for a robber and shot at by a friend, whose aim fortunately had been bad in the dusk.) For instance: the Hauran tour of twenty-six days had cost only £4 sterling. It appears that there had been no remittances from London for some time; he regretted this mainly in that, had it been otherwise, he could have bought manuscripts and antiquities, now instead he had this uncomfortable message to convey, and was meanwhile obliged to accept Mr Barker's kind offers of a loan.

During the year 1811 he continued to work with renewed zeal at his Arabic. Having read the Koran through twice, he now learned by heart several of its chapters and many passages and, with the help of a learned Turk, he took a thorough course in the precepts of the Muslim religion, and Turkish religious law. In addition, not only was he beginning to learn the Turkish lan-guage, but he had found time to complete and send off early in May to London, via Malta, his full English journals of the tour in the Hauran, and of the earlier one over the mountains of Liban, as well as a treatise on Bedouin customs and manners, a classi-fication of the principal Arab tribes near the Syrian borders, and some geographical notes on the desert. And, as soon as he received his remittance, he sent back a large chest of Arabic manuscripts,[24] including a copy of Antar's work, "a noble Bedouin romance" which he admired profoundly, and which he hoped might be translated.

Altogether, the rare Arabic MSS which he eventually left to the University Library, Cambridge, amounted to an impressive collection of 300 volumes. One, a work on letter writing, exquisitely illuminated, its colours still bright, dates from A.D. 1418. Among some of the most important works are: histories of Mecca by Muhammad ibn Ahmad, al-Makki and by al-Azraqi; and histories of Egypt by al-Jabarti and al-Magrizi.

Letters from London continued to give warm encouragement. But those from home, however, arrived only very sparsely; there was one long gap of two years. He heard of the birth of Rosine's first baby, after a difficult labour, on the very day that Mrs Barker gave birth to a son—the child to whom Louis had promised to become godfather. As a Levantine, Mrs Barker's delivery had been easy, and Louis was all the more distressed to hear in contrast of poor Rosine's suffering.

He was now living in the Barker household and as he wrote that day it resounded with cheerful voices: "no end of yelling, music, compliments" and present-giving as a boy had been born. Had it been a girl all the relatives would have come to condole with the mother and the whole house would have been as though in mourning.

Louis now felt that he would like to give a party for the Barkers to celebrate the birth of this son to whom he was to be godfather. So, as he owed hospitality to several other people, he invited the entire European community of Aleppo—even the jealous French consul whom he could not like—to an evening of festivity and dancing. He hired an attractive hall which he decorated himself with garlands of flowers; his guests paid him pleasing compliments on the evening, praising his party as unique in the history of Aleppo, and dancing continued until one o'clock in the morning.

Unfortunately, he could not find much to say in favour of Aleppo's "fair sex" and remarked that, except for some five or perhaps six families, all the Europeans felt miserable in the lack of

1. Louis Rosine and Georg Burckhardt, 1795 (unsigned)

2a. General view of old Basle and the Rhine, by Derois

2b. Rudolf Burckhardt's house, the "kirschgarten", in Basle

3. Jean Louis Burckhardt in London, aged about twenty-four
(unsigned)

4a. Etching made by
Angelica clarke in Cam-
bridge from a London
portrait of J.L.B. by Slater

4b. Patron of exploration,
Sir Joseph Banks, Bart,
from a painting by Sir
Thomas Lawrence, P.R.A.

5. A nineteenth-century Turkish street, by W.H Bartlett

6. Mount Climax and the Bey Dag from the Antalya coast, by Katharine Sim

7a. North Syrian "beehive" houses, by Katharine Sim

7b. Krak des Chevaliers, by Katharine Sim

8. The Triumphal Arch, Palmyra, by Katharine Sim

educated and amiably feminine companionship. In this one does not get the impression that he himself was much concerned personally, the attitude applied, one feels, more to the regular European community of the place—the consuls and the merchants of the Levant Company—who spent many years working here. He had found it laughable at first to see ladies dance the waltz or minuet in long heavy skirts and "fur coats", but although he had soon become used to their dress he was forced to admit that he could not stand much of their stupid chatter.

But he was fully occupied, working hard; happy and in excellent health, but for an attack of the infamous Aleppo boil, or *habb*, which affects once almost everyone who stays for any length of time in the town; his had lasted for a year but was now healed.

There was only one European pleasure lacking, one for which he longed unassuagedly every now and then: that was "to listen for a few hours to good music". He found the sad wailing songs of the Turks, especially when they sang of love, not without merit. But the fault of their compositions is that they consist of melody only and do not "contain any of the harmonies which are the real strength of music".

Summer in Aleppo was the time for weddings; they generally took place in illuminated courtyards, coloured lights sparkling on the women's dress and jewelled ornaments, glittering on water falling in marble fountains, and whenever there was a lull in the music, the song of nightingales in cages hung in the surrounding trees made magic of the night. Sometimes there was sword dancing; sweetmeats and sugar-plums, sherberts and syrups of rose, of violets, of cherries were served—for visitors from the cold north these charming ceremonies under the warm night sky had an idyllic air.

The only wedding Louis mentions was a village one, at which, after the bridal supper, the whole party of a hundred people or so took themselves off to a field where an enormous fire was lit. While the bride and her girl attendants watched from a discreet distance, three musicians began to play and everyone, taking his neighbour by the hand, danced with increasing gaiety in a wide

circle around the players. Louis liked the melody of this dance, the
*debka*, and he sent the notes of it to Rosine in the hope that she
"might charm from it a pretty arietta", and ask one of the poets of
Zurich to write the words—since her marriage Rosine was living
in Zurich.

In his home-loving way, especially when the gaps between
those letters from Switzerland grew lengthy, Louis had worked
out that "Erndthalden" was 1,500 hours' journey distant, and in
one letter he sighed: "Oh when shall I see again the flowering
meadows and the glaciers of my beloved homeland?" It was not
often that he wrote home in this nostalgic vein; it was always
affectionately but with no trace of self-pity. Exile he might be, but
he was well content and there was satisfaction in this life of study
and adventure.

He had long planned an excursion to the Euphrates but since
the spring of that year it had been impossible, as tribes of the
Aneza had swarmed into the neighbourhood of Aleppo, attacking
the townsfolk and their allies, people of the Mawali tribe. Over a
period of several months they had ransacked forty villages, and
consumed the harvest of outlying fields, so that travel was
dangerous for all but the largest of caravans. Not to be outdone,
and despite his last experience of the Aneza, Louis contrived to
persuade some of them to act as guides. But since this would
entail employing about twenty men—one from each clan—
the price was too high and he was forced to wait until their
marauding bands should retreat.

He longed to taste the joy of the desert again; it is a strangely
gripping joy that fires all who have known it to impassioned
expressions of delight. In fact the stimulus of desert travel is quite
unbelievable to those who have never experienced it—its ardours,
its dangers and, transcendingly, the wonder of the ever-changing
sky, the play of light and shade on vast expanses, tremendous
horizons. Man is very small in the desert but he responds to the
challenge in a way that acts as a tonic to the spirit, since as the
Arabs say "voyaging is victory", and to cross the desert is to
voyage triumphantly.

Louis told his parents how well, lively and cheerful he always felt travelling in the desert under brilliant starlit nights and radiant desert dawns.*

Behold the traveller! [*he wrote eulogistically*] . . . long before dawn he leaves the tent dwellers, blesses them for their friendly shelter during the night and plentiful supper; the camels silently begin their laborious journey . . . in the darkness of the desert. . . . Then the sun rises in indescribable majesty over the sand-sea . . . and whose heart could be so without feeling that he would not praise his creator. . . . The Arabs usually greet the rising sun with merry shrieks.

But silence falls as its blazing fire approaches the zenith, and by noon thoughts begin to turn to the hoped-for cool spring of the night's encampment. Generally, at the hottest hour of the day a halt was called, the camels couched in a circle around their owners and the baggage, and each man wrapped cocoon-like in his aba tried to snatch some sleep in the shade of his beast. These were the moments when Louis would "confide secretly", beneath his robe, a few remarks to his diary. He told Turner that this vital task of recording accurate detail was *the* greatest difficulty that beset the traveller in disguise.

Sometimes, at the evening halting place, friendly Arabs were met encamped around the spring, then rugs would be spread, coffee brewed, perhaps a lamb or a kid killed in honour of the newly arrived travellers, camels' milk galore was served and the evening was spent in smoking and listening to stories.

Sometimes one hears all around the singing of the young Arab girls. The magnificent starry night led me often to leave the circle; walking round the camp I gave myself to my thoughts . . .

They were often of home: he would look as is the age-old habit of all exiles to the western—or it may be the eastern skies—for

* It is said, prosaically enough, that it is the high ozone content of the desert air which accounts for the feeling of exhilaration in desert travel!

stars under which his own country lay. But he found deep contentment in the desert's silence, and he was quite unafraid to be
among half-savage people. In fact, it seemed that nothing—the
diet, the blistering sun, the cold, the unreliable company—
nothing really had any power to worry him, except the vermin
which did distress him considerably.

In trying to explain to his parents the delight he experienced
on his journeys he contrasts the European mode of travel with
that of his own in disguise. There were several Englishmen
travelling at that time in Syria, among them W. J. Bankes, a
scholarly and adventurous man, the wildly extravagant young
Marquis of Sligo,* whom Louis had met at Cambridge; also John
Fiott, later known as John Lee of Hartwell, Buckinghamshire, and
Frederick North,† a former Governor of Ceylon, who had tried
to buy safe escort to Palmyra but failed. These gentleman
travelled with armed escorts, camped each evening in safety, even
luxury, and were everywhere overwhelmed with courtesy as
soon as they presented the Pasha's recommendation.

> My method [*Louis wrote*] . . . is just the opposite. I stop at the
> dirtiest caravanserai, use the floor as my mattress and my coat
> as a blanket, eat with camel drivers, and brush my horse myself,
> but I see and hear things which remain unknown to him who
> travels in comfort.

While on the march, except for a light breakfast the Bedouin
fasted for most of the day, not only in the month of Ramadan, so
Louis was glad of his rigorous training. At first he experienced
difficulty in keeping pace with the Arabs at the sunset meal when
a large dish of meat, rice, or whatever it might be, was set before
the men. Since they ate so heartily and the boiled stew was
invariably so piping hot, it required some practice to avoid
burning one's fingers and yet not to lag behind "the voracious
company", and he rarely retired from a meal quite satisfied until
he had acquired similar speed and dexterity.

* It was Sligo's enthusiasm for the Turkish Empire that drew Lady Hester
Stanhope to the Levant.
† The future Earl of Guildford.

When, in August, the Aneza began to retire into the interior of the desert to meet the autumn rains, and the Aleppo district became peaceful once more, Louis prepared to set out with a small caravan of people from Sokhne. These were settled Arabs who came to Aleppo annually to sell ostrich feathers and desert alkali; their isolated village was twelve hours' march north-east of Palmyra, on the route which Queen Zenobia herself had taken on her flight to the Euphrates. From Sokhne, Louis hoped to visit Deir-es-Zor and some other ruined sites of Rome's farthest outposts on the great river's banks, of which only a few stretches were known to explorers.

From the village he rode out to Rahabat, which he describes as an old castle on the bank of the Euphrates; he then followed the river to Deir-es-Zor, the ancient *Thapsacus*, which as far as he knew had not been visited by any European traveller. Perhaps not even since Justinian's greatest general, Belisarius, had struggled there to hold Rome's eastern limits. It was here that Alexander had forded the river, here Crassus had turned back, and from this point Trajan had battered his way through to Ctesiphon, beyond Bagdad.

A man feels dwarfed as he camps beside the grey Euphrates where it swirls through the vast barren land; and at sunset when the wind drops a great hush falls, even the reeds are silent then, only unseen water-birds cry out, their voices echoing across the river in the gathering dusk.

Louis wrote later, to his friend in Cambridge, that the sight of the majestic river had been worth all the weariness and the hardship; he was sure that many discoveries of antiquity would be made here, but he himself was completely frustrated in any hope of further exploration. At the very time of his arrival at the river the local people were embroiled in some sort of civil war; these "rascals of Deir" set upon Louis, stripped him to the skin, killed his camel, and made any further investigation of the ancient towns out of the question.

Louis' own description of this journey unfortunately never reached London. But, although stripped virtually to the skin, he did not lose his notebook—it is possible that the robbers considerately left him his turban, voluminous enough to conceal the long narrow book which he used. As he offered no resistance he was not harmed: this, he wrote to his parents cheerfully, was really a most excellent trait of the Arabs: "they never maltreat the traveller who agrees to be robbed".

In Aleppo he told Mr Barker that the men of Deir had at least left him in possession of his underpants: Barker was not clear whether out of delicacy or compassion. From a note elsewhere on Bedouin dress, however, Louis records that it was thought shameful for a male Bedouin to wear drawers, which are considered fit only for women. Perhaps this accounts for an incident that occurred during the long, scorifying march back to Sokhne when Louis had a hard tussle with an Arab woman who had unfortunately taken a fancy to his only remaining garment.[25]

He arrived at the village, his body blistered by the fierce rays of the sun, but unhurt; days later he reached Aleppo the "richer by many experiences", as he wrote to his people on 25 November, his twenty-seventh birthday. To them he did not recount all the hardship—for two days he had walked in that scorching heat, nearly naked, barefoot, without food or drink, but he was extremely well and cheerful. It was then the sixth year away from home: three years before he had spent his birthday in his Cambridge study, two years earlier it had been the night when taken for a robber he was shot at near Aleppo, the previous birthday he had spent in a downpour in the Hauran when his guide had lost the way; tonight he was invited to a ball:

A true image of life: crying today, dancing tomorrow . . . As an Arabian poet says: "Hold tightly, the wheel of life turns, and swings you from the bottom to the top" . . .

So another chapter of his life ended; the years of study done, he was now confident and ready to leave Aleppo for the long journey south to Egypt.

# Part III

# The Way South

# CHAPTER FIVE

## *Two Syrian Journeys*

Come with me from Lebanon my spouse, with me from
Lebanon: look from the top of Amana, from the top of
Shenir and Hermon, from the lions' dens, and from the
mountains of the leopards.

*Song of Solomon*

INCESSANT RAINS EARLY in 1812 delayed Louis' departure from
Aleppo until 14 February. He had decided not to travel by the
shortest way to Egypt since much of Syria and Palestine was still
unknown and unmapped: a country so difficult of access and of
such immense interest—not only to geography but to literature
—that it cried out to him as a challenge.

He thought himself "in some measure" now qualified to
explore it, and explaining his decision to do so he wrote to Sir
Joseph that he planned to tackle the territory as a general would,
taking "possession of any stronghold on his way, even without
express commands to that purpose".

European travellers unversed in the language and the customs
could not attempt such exploration without great expense. But
here was he, on the spot, ready and prepared and, while taking it
upon himself to travel in this way, he sincerely hoped that the
Committee would not be displeased. These journeys, he wrote—
in characteristic understatement—were, he thought, "sufficiently
laborious and hazardous not to be mistaken for tours of pleasure",
and in performing them he should complete his "preliminary
exercises and at the same time obtain some information upon
the geography of an unknown region".[1]

Among the subsequent important results culled for London,
and indeed the cognisant world, were the extent, form, and

detailed geography of the Hauran; the hitherto unknown site of ancient Apamea on the Orontes, one of the most important cities of Syria under the Macedonian Greeks; that mysterious inscription at Hama, and on the final journey south, last but certainly not least, the dramatic discovery of the long-lost capital of *Arabia Petraea*.[2]

He could not leave Syria without once more stressing the great kindness of the British consul, to whom, he told Sir Joseph, he would be "under everlasting obligations. . . . A most worthy man and of very superior talents."

It was a profound, sincere attachment that Louis felt towards this friendly Englishman, and he knew pangs of real regret at leaving Aleppo. The traveller, he thought, should try to cultivate a heart of stone to avoid becoming fond of anyone. But he was always an affectionate man, sadly destined to remain on the whole a lonely figure to the end.

Both Barker and Van Masseyk set him on the road in farewell, riding a part of the way with him beyond the city. John Fiott, the Englishman who had been staying in Aleppo for the last two months, accompanied him on the first part of this expedition.

Fiott was a Cambridge man, and he and Louis had come to know each other well by now. Turner had recorded something of an earlier ride that they made together when Louis was already passing for a true oriental. Most Europeans in disguise, Turner wrote, were at once detected by Turks and Arabs; every action seemed to betray the European—the putting on of his clothes, the manner of taking his pipe, even his coffee.

"Sheik Ibrahim" was riding with Mr Fiott (who was also dressed *à l'Arabe*) from Damascus to Aleppo. The Turks and Arabs who passed the former saluted him, but on passing Fiott exclaimed—"Frankche" (European) and laughed; this put Fiott in a passion: "Do these fellows see it written in my face", said he, "that I am a Frank, Sheik Ibrahim?" . . .[3]

Louis' reply is not recorded though one may guess that it was helpful and that he concealed his amusement at Fiott's anger. The anecdote illustrates not only his remarkable ability to act this role of "Sheik Ibrahim" but the meticulously careful study that must have gone into the creating of the part which, like any talented actor, he really lived on the so challenging stage where it was performed.

The part of the country into which the riders now headed was open to frequent attack by robber bands of Awali, then a wild predatory people—who even today retain many of their pagan beliefs; the settled half-caste Bedouin of the area suffered considerably at their hands. Probably on Barker's advice, Louis and Fiott had a two-man armed escort for the ride over the mountain into the valley of the Orontes. Once across the divide, fertile slopes led through fields of asphodel down to the river valley below, narrow here and marshy but rich with meadows, bounded on the western side by the sheer and barren Alawi Mountains, and on the north-east by the Jebel Riha.

As, next morning, they rode along the now widening, beautiful valley they soon came upon an ancient causeway and some ruined columns. This, Louis realised, must be the great road of ancient Apamea, the Seleucid city that once had a population of 120,000, and whose proud colonnaded street had been nearly a mile long. Named by Seleucus Nicator after his Persian wife, Apame, the city became the war treasury of the empire, and boasted a national stud of 30,000 mares and 300 stallions.

Riding through luxuriant pasture lands where undoubtedly the splendid stud had grazed, Louis thought of the Seleucids' herd of elephants; it was probably here that they too had fed. Marshy in winter, the land hardens in spring and grows lush pasturage. The elephants to which he refers are the notable 500 sent to Seleucus Nicator on the ceding of Macedonian-held territory in Afghanistan, by King Chandragupta in 302 B.C. Even the idea of such a gift is astounding; and the thought of that stupendous herd of great beasts marching from the far Ganges valley, through the passes of Baluchistan, across the dusty wastes of Persia and Mesopotamia, is enough to make Hannibal's feats appear relatively simple.

Apamea was not only a military centre but the seat of an

oracle, the home of a Neo-Platonist school of scholars and philosophers, and one of the last strongholds of paganism. Now little is left to show of all the glory for it was destroyed by Chosroes, "the blessed" Sassanid, in the sixth century, who sold its people down the river into slavery; it never regained its ancient importance and four centuries later it was finally shattered by an earthquake.

Where as he surmised the stud herds had pastured 2,000 years ago, Louis saw that Arabs and peasants of all the neighbouring districts had sent their horses and mules to graze. Regularly every spring the animals were left in the care of herdsmen who pitched their tents here until increasing summer heat withered the grass. Today, the best horses of Syria are still bred in this area.

From Apamea they rode through to Hama: it was during this visit that Louis made his discovery of the unknown hieroglyphics that proved to be the first found of all Hittite inscriptions.

Hama, firm city of the Faith, is famous for its gigantic wooden water-wheels, the *noria*, with their incessant creaking—a kind of droning lament that goes on day and night as it has for centuries. The *noria*, impressive in their huge ponderous way, loom darkly behind the silvery glint of water falling from their endlessly rotating buckets. Each wheel has a name; the biggest of them, "*Noria el Mohamedye*", Louis reckoned was at least seventy feet in diameter. About half the water seems to be spilled before it reaches the conduits above to be conveyed to the orchards and market gardens of the town.

The Arabs call the Orontes "the Rebel", *al-Asi*, because in contrast with all the other rivers in Syria it flows from south to north.

> If the river itself be a rebel in Hamah why hold it transgression
> That I follow its lead and I drink of the wine strong and clear?

So asked the poet, Nur al-Din, tongue-in-cheek pleading a somewhat far-fetched excuse to break the Prophet's law.

Louis climbed up above the town to look down on this rebellious river. From the heights he had a splendid view of all

Hama with the Orontes looping sleekly through its four bridges, the light-coloured buildings clustered around the tell of *Hammath* —Biblical site of antiquity; beyond lay green fields and gardens, the dark reds of Syrian soil, while further still the mountains climbed blue and cloud-chased to a bright spring sky.

It was with difficulty that Louis and Fiott extricated themselves from the friendly Hama household in which they stayed, where every evening a large company of Turks and Arabs had gathered to talk of all manner of things. Farewells must have been protracted before they could ride on towards Tripoli on the coast, and make a diversion to the castle of Masiaf, seat of the Assassins, a place rarely visited by any travellers.

Fortunately for the Crusaders, ancestors of these people had more or less sided with the invader. The Franks had, in friendly fashion, called their chief and indeed all his successors indiscriminately "the Old Man of the Mountain". These once wild, heretical members of the Ismaili sect, the original *hashish* eaters, "now turned industrious peasants" planting their lanes with pomegranate hedges,⁴ were in Louis' day still veiled in mystery, spun about by dark stories of orgiastic ritual, said to be devoted to promiscuous debauchery and to the adoration of the *pudenda muliebris*. Inter-racial feuds and secret murders too were commonplace—between Assassin and Alawi. One handsome bearded young man spoke to Louis of murderous retaliation. "Do you suppose," he said, his eyes flashing with anger, "that these whiskers shall turn grey before I shall have taken my revenge for a slaughtered wife and two infant children?"

John Fiott and Louis soon pressed on towards the coast, coming down through mulberry plantations and mountain-terraced vineyards to Kal'at al Hosn—better known as Krak des Chevaliers, the splendid castle that commands the pass leading from the coast to the desert ports of Homs and Hama. He rightly praises it as the finest building of crusader times that he had ever seen.

Tripoli in spring: hedges a blue sheen of morning glory, balconied houses laden with swags of bougainvillaea like curtains of Tyrrhenian purple over crumbling cream-washed walls, sunlit courtyards sweet with early roses, arcaded footways, old khans,

covered *souks*, low three-centred doorways. He found it a beautiful romantic place, the most lovely of all Lebanese towns, and the
only one with remnants of the country's mediaeval past.

Having knowledge of the silk business, Louis was especially
interested in the great silk trade of Tripoli. He remarked, with
fellow feeling, that since "the ruin of the French trade", France's
link with Tripoli's silk merchants had ceased. It was said that in
the Middle Ages no less than 4,000 silk weaving looms were busy
in the town.

While he was in Syria, Louis had little chance of consulting
or re-reading any classical books, and he had felt justifiably
somewhat aggrieved with M. Rousuan, Aleppo's French consul
who, although he had no Latin or Greek, owned the only classical
library in the town. Dabbling in writing himself, he was so
jealous of the precious means "to advance the literary labours of
others" that he never let his good books stir out of their place.
He was a Persian scholar, and he knew Arabic and Turkish too,
but Louis had no patience with his kind since he was:

a most clumsy genius, and ungentlemanly . . .; mean jealousy
of my pursuits made him prevent the best Arabic scholar of
Aleppo from giving me lessons.[5]

With a touch of devilment, Louis took revenge by doing his
best to encourage this Frenchman to go on with his writing well
knowing that he would make a fool of himself. On the other
hand, M. Guys, the French consul at Tripoli, was liberal-minded,
gentlemanly, and very well versed in Syrian antiquities, and it was
in his classical library that Louis was able to take his notes on the
Decapolis.

The travellers parted in Tripoli; Fiott going north to Antioch,
while Louis set out with a guide towards Damascus, intending to
pay his respects on the way to "the chief of the mountain"—the
Emir Bechir of Beit el Din.

Lebanon, the White One, rising emphatic from the sea, is the
Mediterranean's most easterly barrier, the dramatic mountain
chain which, with all its concurrent seasons, its fruits and fertility,

its snows, its cedars and its flowers, seems eternally bidding little
Europe farewell. It stands as a magnificent drop-curtain suspended
before the deserts and the immense lands of Asia that lie beyond.

Louis continued partly along the high mountain, partly down
by the sea. There is something about this golden, lotus-eating
coast that is vastly relaxing. Alpine-born, he preferred the invigo-
ration of the hills and took to them whenever possible. But the
going was difficult for his horse, the tracks abominable—indeed
the inhabitants kept them so to make invasion more difficult. He
admired the way these mountaineers cultivated the steep, narrow
terraces of their Mountain, growing vines, mulberry trees and a
few acres of corn wherever there was soil enough.

Behind Beirut he cut inland, and rode steeply up to the little
mountain town of Deir el Kamar, Monastery of the Moon, on the
side of a gorge; it was once the Druse capital, where the Emir had
a serai. Louis did not stop but rode on through a beautiful high
country of clear-flowing rivulets and little cascades where vines
and peaches grew, and so around the head of the gorge towards
the palace of Beit el Din.

During the 400 years of Ottoman Turkish rule the people of the
Mountain had maintained a semi-independence; so long as
Maronite and Druse remained on fairly amicable terms the Turks
could not break the Emirs' power. Two of these rulers especially
were outstanding, and they became national heroes; one was the
Emir Bechir. The Druses, as we know, a warlike people, were
prone to revolt against their overlords. But the Maronites remained neutral. In that they are monophysites their belief is
unorthodox; their name is eponymic, deriving, it is thought, from
that of their founder Maro, a fifth-century monk of the Mountain;
they were acknowledged by the church of Rome in the eighteenth
century.

The Emir, a Druse, received Louis very politely. A most impressive man, he was then about forty-five although he looked
older on account of his large spade-shaped beard. His dark
piercing eyes told of an immense vitality of both mind and body.
He was quite unscrupulous—he treated even his own family
badly—but it is said that although he dominated the Lebanon he

"gave as much in prosperity as he took in taxes".[6] Although head, since 1789, of the Mountain Druses he confided to Louis that he and his entire family had secretly become Christians primarily to cull favour with the Maronites—a kind of Mountain power balance between Druse and Maronite. It was a spurious belief, Louis thought, and the Emir affected publicly to observe the Ramadan and other rites. He neglected his family and he was said to be avaricious, but Louis found him an "amiable man" and if any Levantine could then be called the friend of any European nation, he was certainly the friend of the English. He was right about this for the Druses remained on good terms with the British consulates. They are a remarkable people who maintained their peculiar and somewhat mysterious religious rites and their racial independence over a period of 800 years or more. The Emir may have been amiable and a good conversationalist but his cruelties were terrible when a few years later, in 1824, the Druse Sheik rose in rebellion.

The building of his Arabian Nights palace, Beit el Din, was still not finished. Louis says that the Emir's chief expenditure was on its lavish and, it must be admitted, sometimes tasteless embell-ishments. Bechir owned a stable of about fifty horses and, apart from the creation of the sumptuous building, his only other amusement was sport with the hawk and the pointer.

It is an extremely lovely site for a summer palace: open on one side to the steep mountain, the Monastery of the Moon below, the slopes bright with the yellow and green of peach orchards and vines, its patios and pavilions glowing pale against a background of cypress command a view of the steeply terraced gorge dropping down to the blue sea some 3,000 feet below. Louis spent two days in these luxurious surroundings, in divanned rooms where clear water ran cool over costly inlaid panels and mountain breezes stirred the rich draperies of Kashmir-hung walls. Indeed he had great difficulty in getting away, for the Emir evidently took real pleasure in conversing with him and, since they spoke in Arabic, the talk was very much freer than it would of course have been through an interpreter. In fact, the Emir enjoyed Louis' company so well that he tried to persuade 'Sheik Ibrahim' to stay a few days longer for a hunting trip. But Louis was anxious to reach Damascus now, fearing that bad weather on the Mountain might make the way impossible.

Erupting as it does so steeply from the sea the Mountain knows all weathers: it was then March, late spring reigned below but winter held the summits still.

He was right about the weather on the heights; the way was throttled with snow and a thick fog lay over the crest. Had it not been for the footsteps of a man who had passed a few hours ahead of them they would have been unable to go on. Many times they sank up to their waists in the snow and, on reaching the top, they lost the guiding footprints. His man was in despair and wanted to return, but over the watershed Louis found a small rivulet beneath the snow; following it they pushed on slowly and after many headlong falls reached the high plain of the Beka'a.

Being with one of the Emir's people he was treated like a great man in the sheik's house where he alighted on the final evening out from Damascus. He mentions this as being the only instance of his receiving such honours during all his Syrian travels— except of course at Beit el Din.

On reaching Damascus, he heard that there had been further political trouble in that ever turbulent city: now it was Soleiman Pasha's turn to fall from power. The forthcoming installation of a new ruler might well be expected to set the whole Pashalik on fire: therefore Louis was obliged to bide his time until the temper of the countryside should make itself known.

Damascus grew to Arab glory under the Ummayyads who with all their riches of palaces, poetry, and desert democracy were the ancestors of today's Hashemites; their pure Arab blood was vividly appreciated then in Syria. The mixed blood of townsfolk such as the Damascenes can be accounted for in many ways; one undoubtedly was the extravagance of the slave markets of Ummayyad time—one prince might own as many as a thousand slaves. But sons born to his odalisques would be free men, so that Arab blood became diluted with Anatolian, Circassian, or Aegean Greek. It is little wonder then that the desert Arab, particularly the true Bedouin, felt and still does a superiority over the townsman in the purity of blood sustained for 2,000 years. Nor is it, in the light of these facts, surprising that for centuries the sons of Arab princes have been fostered in Bedouin tents in the hard tradition, until old enough to ride a mare.

But perhaps, generally speaking, most Arabs have one thing in common, the glib gift of exaggeration—as Louis soon learned and one day put to the test.

The Pasha was entering Damascus in state, Louis in Arab dress stood with the crowd watching at the city gates. Out of curiosity he counted the number of the retinue; it amounted to exactly 250 horsemen. Casually, he turned to an Arab standing near him and asked how many riders did he think there were in the procession.

"Eh! *Wellah—bellah!*—a *great* many!"

"Well, but just how many do you think?" Louis pressed. After a little thought the man replied: "*Ay Wellah!*—between two and three thousand!"[7]

In Damascus Louis heard that the Wahabi—now contained in Arabia by forces sent by Mohammed Ali, Pasha of Egypt—had for the time being ceased their plundering expeditions into Syria. But there was still little hope of re-establishing the pilgrim caravans to Mecca; only the most fanatic Turks—who by its cessation prophesied the fall of the Ottoman Empire—continued to hope for this. Oddly enough, it was now not only the fighting in Arabia that prevented the Syrian caravan from assembling but also another element—the lackadaisical attitude of the coffee merchants. About half the pilgrims had always been merchants of coffee and Indian goods: but, since the English coffee trade had opened during the last year between Malta and the Levant, American coffee was selling all over Syria, therefore the merchants no longer wished so devotedly to perform the pilgrimage —as they had been doing merely to buy up Mocha coffee at Mecca to sell with great profit in Damascus, Aleppo, and Constantinople.[8]

As soon as he was certain that the countryside was not going to rebel against the new Pasha, Louis set out again on 21 April eager to complete his exploration of the Hauran. He took with him a tough Damascene who had been no less than seventeen times to Mecca, and who was therefore not only used to great fatigue but also knew the Bedouin well.

In Druse territory again, skirting the Leja, this time Louis encountered a new deterrent wherever he went: a rumour circulated that having previously found treasure here, there and everywhere, he was now returning to carry away what he had left behind. He met the worst antipathy at Um-es-Zeitun, a village of thirty or forty houses near extensive ruins, where he copied many Greek inscriptions. Here he escaped ill-treatment at the hands of the villagers only by assuming a rigidly autocratic air and threatening, by dint of many lurid oaths, that if he lost a single hair of his beard the Pasha would levy an *avania* of countless purses on the village. He drew an out-of-date passport of the Soleiman Pasha era from his gown and flourished it brazenly before the menacing Druses, meanwhile hurling at them a further spate of forceful Arab oaths. The effect must have been dramatic; the courageous bluff worked, and he was able at last to ride away late in the afternoon towards the mountain of Hauran.

After sunset his Damascene persuaded him to pose as a soldier to some mountain Arabs whom they encountered, in order to get a good supper, which they sorely needed, having had only a handful of biscuit on the previous night. The scheme was effective. They supped on a dish of rice cooked in *leben*, and "were much amused by the sports and songs of the young girls of the tribe", an entertainment that continued in the moonlight until midnight —white teeth, dark eyes flashing like sudden bright pools after rain, sweet and heady singing under the sparkling clarity of the Syrian sky. But violence was never far off, as one young man that evening bore witness, showing the marks of recent fetters, and recounting his treatment at the hands of the powerful Aneza who each spring threatened the mountain and the Leja Arabs with predatory assault.

On the way to Bosra, which Louis had not risked exploring on his previous visit, he went through several villages: in one he was surprised to see a Cairene prostitute who seemed to be kept at the

expense of the whole village. It was strange since he had found the
ways of the Hauran to be almost as strict as those of the Bedouin;
there were normally no prostitutes, and adultery was punished
by death—that is of the woman, while the man was ruined by
heavy fines exacted in penalty. He recounts that only recently a
married Turkish woman caught in the arms of a young Christian
had been dragged to the market place by her three brothers who,
in the presence of the whole community, had "cut her in pieces
with their swords, loading her at the same time with the most
horrible imprecations". Her lover, however, was let off with a
fine of ten purses—that is about £250 sterling, an immense sum
for that time, and place.

At Aere, south of the Jebel, Louis met again the friendly Druse
sheik whom he had before so much liked for his kindness and
generosity. Louis had written from Aleppo and contrived to send
him a gift since he had refused to accept anything previously; now
the sheik was delighted to greet him again. His reputation for
fairness and kindness was so widespread that peasants from all over
the Hauran settled in his village. In his house, as symbol of his
hospitality the coffee pot was always boiling in the "strangers'
room".

Bosra, formerly the capital of *Arabia Provincia*, the ancient *Nova
Trajana Bostra*, once a centre of the Arabian caravan trade, quite
captivated Louis with its beautiful ruins, and its ancient streets just
wide enough to allow a laden camel to pass, where the boy
Mohammed used to travel with his uncle's caravans trading
northwards. Louis visited the House of Bahira, the monk who is
said to have predicted the Prophet's vocation. But no one would
come now "with dyed garments from Bosra", Jeremiah's
predicted desolation had come true, and of the vineyards for
which the place was celebrated even in the days of Moses not a
vestige remained, scarcely a tree grew but some wild roses, lavish
still among the ruins, were just beginning to open their buds.
The charm of Bosra was almost spoilt for him by the overwhelming curiosity of numerous Aneza who continually passed through
the ruins, and pestered him with their fly-like and most un-
welcome attentions.

He returned to say goodbye to his friend, the worthy Druse, who had engaged for him an Egyptian Bedouin to act as guide for the western Hauran—an ex-cavalry man and a murderer, who had "had the misfortune to kill one of his comrades" while in the Pasha's service. He had subsequently fled to the Aneza to whom a murder or two was nothing, and indeed neither Louis nor the kindly Druse either seemed in the least disconcerted.

One curious entourage Louis now fell in with was a rabble of thieves encamped with all their tents and donkeys, and the handsome mare of their vagabond sheik. The sheik invited Louis to drink a cup of coffee with him and it was with some reluctance, one feels, that Louis declined this offer on the advice of his companions. The talk would surely have been racy and ribald among such a band of men—they were Damascene beggars who made an annual excursion into the mountains to collect alms from the peasants.

In the plain of western Hauran he came to the Great Haj route, and spoke to some young north Africans, Mahgribins, guarding the castle that marked the first halting place on the road, at the point where the Emir of the Haj would pause to allow stragglers to collect, and also that he might restock his own stores.

He does not specifically refer to the fact but Louis' interest in the pilgrimage must constantly have been growing. It is not hard to guess that the idea of performing it himself had already taken root in his mind, through the realisation that no man in his position—that is planning to travel westward eventually across Africa with returning pilgrims—could hope to play the part fully *unless* he himself had been on the Haj.

As yet Louis betrays no inkling of this thought but it must have come to him: perhaps now, or perhaps even earlier in Aleppo as he studied the doctrines of Islam. Or in Damascus, vibrant gathering point of the Great Syrian caravan, while listening to descriptions of the Haj through long nights of Ramadan when the smoke of pipes thickened above white-turbaned heads, the fragrance of spicy foods cooking mingling with the scent of jasmine, the drone of story-tellers' voices rose and fell, and the coffee cups were filled and emptied and filled again.

Although the Haj had not reached Mecca now for six years because of the battling Wahabis, and though he had never seen it gathering, Louis knew much about it: the appalling conditions of travel for all but the wealthy and the armed, the high cost to pilgrims, the thieving and the violent robbery that was a part of the vast cavalcade. Even the Pasha's troops were known to kill stragglers during the night for the sake of their small belongings: the Pasha, it was true, often punished such crimes, and scarcely a day passed "without someone being impaled alive"; the caravan moved on leaving the tortured malefactor behind under the relentless sun to be eaten by the white-winged neophron or other birds of prey.

Louis could not have known then if he himself would ever reach Mecca; the fighting in Arabia was not then going well for Mohammed Ali's forces, nor had the idea been a part of the original plan made in London, but no one could have studied Islam as fully as he did without realising the burning need to make the pilgrimage. It would so obviously be the crowning act, completing his role as "the perfect Arab"—as he was later described by some of his contemporaries.

From the castle they continued alone along the Haj route, in danger not only from the wild Aneza but also from fanatics who lived close to the holy pilgrim road.

In spring the hills of Gilead are beautiful: a shimmer of anchusa flowers lay blue under wild pistachio trees, little oaks and stunted firs; the wadis below, brimming from bank to bank with blossom, were flushed red with oleanders—a balmy, honey- and almond-scented countryside in complete contrast with the plutonic basalt land to the north. Louis was anxious to see Jerash, which lies in the hills of Gilead, the ancient *Gerasa*, the now famed town of the *Decapolis*, which had then been discovered only very recently by Dr Seetzen.

Mounting over the steep crest of the hill, suddenly Louis looked down on the plain of Jerash and saw the ruins far below, drifting in static elegance along the valley between the green and brown hills. Sublime, apricot-coloured—fine Ionic pillars and triumphal arch, the long colonnaded street stretching north from the perfection of the elliptical forum, the sight on that May day must have made him catch his breath, so delicately and satisfyingly beautiful is Jerash.

He had to explore the ancient town unaccompanied for his companions hid themselves in terror of the Bedouin who might lead their herds to pasture or to water at the little river among the poplars, or who might be out on a raid. As his seventeen-times-to-Mecca man and the murderer-guide crept off to hide themselves, Louis faced the hot, silent ruins quite alone, and made a four-hour survey. Luckily no dark-robed figures emerged from theatre, temple, church or archway to molest him. In silence he traversed the long Roman street, lizards basking in the brilliant sunshine were the only sign of life, and his own footsteps on the hot chariot-rutted stones the only sounds he heard.

To the very end of its life Jerash was an outpost of western civilisation; early in the Roman period of its history, under Pompey it joined the league of free cities known as the *Decapolis*. It flourished and was peaceful until the middle of the first century, it had then a lively trade with the Nabataeans whose influence is evident in some typical Nabataean "crowstep" patterns of stone carving. There is too an almost illegible bilingual inscription, probably the very one that puzzled Louis, in Nabataean and Greek, and some others which refer to a temple of the Holy God, Pakidas, and the Arabian god, presumed to be Dushares, the Nabataean deity.[9]

The unseen but menacing presence of the dreaded Beni-Sakhr Bedouin made further progress impossible; Louis' men now refused to go on, and it would have been madness to do so alone among hostile tribes. So, abandoning the idea of exploring the ruins of *Ammon* (Amman), Louis turned westward again towards Tiberias.

After a march of five or six days he reached the Sea of Galilee. The water of the lake was extremely deep and very clear: thinking of the disciples fishing here, Louis swam far out, hoping to see some fish in its depths. He was a strong swimmer, and he delighted now in the pleasure of this protracted bathe after long, hot days on the road. But the night that followed was made wretched by the countless mosquitoes of the lake's low-lying shores and the "other vermin" which always attacked him mercilessly for his new-tasting northern blood. Indeed our old friend Baedeker tells us that in the last century Tiberias was notorious throughout all Syria for its fleas.

Through nomad country Louis returned towards Damascus, passing many Bedouin encampments with their long black tents of hair clustered starkly on lonely hillsides. It had been a hard journey; so much so that the difficulties of the way and the poor fodder had killed his favourite Aleppo mare.

That May he wrote from Damascus to his parents, outlining his plans, and rejoicing to have at last received a letter from them; dated eight months earlier it had been forwarded by Mr Barker from Aleppo. He told them that he hoped one day to return and build a "Negro castle" near "Erndthalden", and to live there peacefully after all the hardships he would have endured, but he confessed he was *not* yet "building any castles in the air". It was a peaceful and a not unpleasant life that he led now, and he gave really very little thought to the future. In his opinion, hope deceived and happiness seldom satisfied, so he had no wish to spoil the present by deluding himself about the future and, he wrote: "My acquaintance with the Arabs has taught me to value moderation higher than anything else." It is the philosophy of the traveller who must live from day to day: perhaps he was catching something of the Arab's fatalism too.

He continued to receive, he says, a number of letters from England but cousin Christoph (although he had had two of Louis') answered never a word: "He is a real man of the world and only thinks of his stomach and his purse. He proved that while I was in England. But I have a few good English friends on whom I can really rely."

Again the accent is on the renowned reliability of the Englishman in that golden age of the nation's story—it is no wonder that Louis was deeply hurt by the only one who deceived him.

John Barker of Aleppo was of course one of the sincere friends,

Clarke of Cambridge another, W. G. Browne of London, Renouard now in Smyrna, John Fiott too, and certainly there were others later in Egypt. All those who came to know Louis were staunch in their liking and admiration for him both as a man, a cheerful companion and friend, and as a great traveller unique in his methods and approach to the job.

# CHAPTER SIX

## *The Road to Petra*

Where lay our loosened harness?
Where turned our naked feet? . . .
Oh fountain in the desert!
Oh cistern in the waste!
Oh bread we ate in secret!
Oh cup we spilled in haste!

*Kipling*

THE SUN BEGAN to set over the mountains of the Anti-Lebanon.

God is Great!
There is no God but God . . . !

From every minaret of mosque and *madrasa* the muezzins' stirring calls rang out, bass and falsetto gathering strength, to splinter, fall and fade away along the first hint of darkness as veils of dusk crept up from the desert.

Louis left Damascus then, for the last time. He rode out alone from the city and as the sad, tenuous notes died away in a final evocative echo the clop of his horse's hooves sounded suddenly loud and lonely on the darkening road.

Since the recent Hauran journey he had remained in Damascus long enough to collect some introductions vital for the militant area of Kerak, and also to write and dispatch his travel journals. He had told his correspondents not to expect any letters until he should reach Cairo in two or three months' time. The journey would be protracted since he was going by way of the mountains east of the Jordan, the almost unknown district bordering the Dead Sea, and thence by the wilderness that the Romans had called *Arabia Petraea.*

Again he hoped to gather much new information, but the route would be dangerous and the journey hot, to say the least, since the summer heat was now rising to its scorching crescendo.

He had dressed in the most common Bedouin attire, and had chosen for his mount a very ordinary mare not likely to arouse Arab greed. Now he was riding away from the city that evening to pick up his guide at an outlying village, where he would sleep the first night.

The third week in June, the time of the corn harvest: the next day he and his man rode through sundrenched fields filled with peasants, whose dark clothes with touches of crimson about them made a pleasing contrast with the gold of grain, the light ochre stubble, and the sombre reds of Syrian soil. Young cotton plants had newly sprouted in a sheen of fresh green, and men worked among them on irrigation channels so there was a glitter of water scintillating in bright sunshine, a cheerful sound of voices calling across the fields as people laboured, harvesting one crop and preparing for another. There was laughter too from the children, to whom a harvest is always a family event, as they rode gaily on wooden sledges around the pale-gold winnowing floors.

After about three days they came down to the Sea of Galilee, passing through the ruins of Capernaum in the middle of gloomy basalt dwellings, and Mary Magdalen's birthplace, the miserable village of Magdala, on the north end of the lake. So along the western shore which Louis had not yet explored, and to Tiberias again, the town founded in the days of Jesus' childhood by Herod Antipas.

As there was no khan here Louis went to the Catholic priest to ask for the keys of the church where he thought he might sleep. But since it was swarming with the notorious "vermin" of Tiberias, he soon moved outside and settled down for the night in the churchyard, which became his headquarters for the time. This was the church of St Peter, said to have been founded on the spot where Peter cast his net.

The lake is several hundred feet below sea-level, and stiflingly hot, but Louis found much to interest him during his stay. One of the things that impressed him was the unusual freedom of the

Christians; on equal footing with the Turks they gave curse for curse roundly in religious controversy, and he even saw them striking Turks in the public bazaar, something quite unheard of in any strictly Muslim town—but the present Pasha of Acre, in whose Pashalik Tiberias lay, was tolerant.

In the large Jewish quarter he met Jews from Poland, Spain, Barbary and elsewhere, whose black-hatted rabbinical community provided him with at least one entertaining evening. He describes a singular custom which they practised while praying which struck him as being so hilarious that he had great difficulty in keeping a straight face during the procedure. While the Rabbin recited the Psalms of David the congregation joined in by imitating with voice and gesture the meaning of certain passages. For instance: at "Praise the Lord with the sound of the trumpet," they all held imaginary trumpets to their lips and tootled gaily. Whenever a "horrible tempest" occurred they huffed and puffed stormily, while at "the cries of the righteous" they started screaming loudly. It not infrequently happened, wrote Louis, that while some were still blowing a boisterous storm, others had already begun the cries of the righteous, "thus forming a concert which is difficult for any but a zealous Hebrew to hear with gravity".

That of course was vicarious amusement but another occasion was frankly gay. Among the Polish Jews Louis met a man from Bohemia, "an honest German" who was so delighted at hearing his own language spoken again that he escorted him on a merry tour of the quarter, introducing him to all his friends. In every house Louis was offered brandy, and he remarked—perhaps the brandy helped—that the women "appeared to be much less shy than they are in other parts of Syria".

While waiting to find a guide for the dangerous Jordan valley he climbed up to the mountain fortress of the Son of Ma'an—in Herod's day a robbers' nest in the rock face. When Louis saw it, it was peaceful, murmurous with pigeons' voices and the silken rustle of countless wings. On Mount Tabor's summit he was startled to find a lonely Greek family camping out to avoid the *miri*—a practical method of tax-evasion.

He returned from this little excursion to find his "old lodgings"

—the churchyard—full of strangers. One of these, an Englishman, was Michael Bruce—Cambridge friend of Byron, and of Sligo, dilettante traveller and, at that time, the lover of Lady Hester Stanhope, Chatham's proud granddaughter. Bruce had just arrived from Nazareth with a party of European priests who intended to celebrate mass in the church that night since it was St Peter's day.

> . . . Mr Bruce was thunderstruck at hearing himself addressed in good English by a bare-legged Syrian peasant with a long beard who proved to be the celebrated traveller, Burckhardt. He posed as Shaykh Ibrahim and was dressed in the coarse cotton shirt and woollen abba of the country.[10]

Louis introduced himself, mentioning St Johns, and Dr Clarke of Cambridge. Michael Bruce of course already knew of "Sheik Ibrahim" through his friend Sligo—the charming, irresponsible young Irishman so recently at Aleppo—and also no doubt through Lady Hester's correspondence with Mr Barker and with Sir Joseph Banks. It is not hard to imagine the fascination that Louis' appearance and indeed his story had for the younger man. From the moment of their meeting in the churchyard Bruce fell, at least for the time, completely under Louis' spell.

Bruce was young, wealthy, gentle, rather effeminate-looking, still wrapped up in his love affair with "the most superior creature in all the world". But from the moment when, startled by the travel-stained peasant who spoke perfect English, he had turned to see grey-green eyes in a deeply tanned, bearded face where hardship had already drawn its lines, at first interest and soon a growing admiration were aroused.

Here was a *man*, one who really travelled, who saw life through Arab eyes and yet was cultured; who spoke the language "like a native", who disregarded heat, dirt, even the fleas of Tiberias—indeed slept in a graveyard to avoid them—who went unencumbered by tents and retinues, had braved the Palmyrene Bedouin, had reached the Euphrates, and who still remained modest, even humble! The gentle Bruce was enchanted: this was magnificent—Sheik Ibrahim must meet Lady Hester, he must come with him to Nazareth!

The next morning Bruce persuaded Louis to accompany him; indeed Louis was pleased to do so especially since no one in Tiberias seemed inclined to tackle the Jordan valley except in an armed caravan. It would be one stage further on, and at Nazareth he might be lucky enough to find a willing guide.

Passing through Cana of the wedding feast, they rested at noon under an immense fig tree large enough to afford shade to all their company, a dozen men and their horses—and for Michael Bruce the conversation was absorbing.

At the Spanish monastery in Nazareth, Bruce proudly introduced Sheik Ibrahim to Lady Hester. That aristocratic Philistine took a prompt dislike to Louis, although he expressed nothing but admiration for her—at this time. She was even then preparing to make her famous, extremely costly, indeed regal, journey to Palmyra with a train of forty camels, where she was eventually crowned "Queen of the Desert" by the local Bedouin whose palms had been well greased.

Frederick North's failure to reach Palmyra had spurred her passion for this *ne plus ultra*. The fact is that until he had failed to buy his way into the Palmyrene desert she had not heard of Zenobia's fabled capital. She enjoyed braving and bribing the wild Bedouin, but she refused to visit Aleppo for fear of *le mal d'Alep*, the boil. Intrepid she certainly was but her interest could hardly be called objective, and her conversation was usually protracted— it was said that one traveller fainted away at the length of her discourse!

She . . . remained despite her travels, on the whole an ignorant woman but a gullible one. She lapped up flattery as a cat laps up cream . . . was unsparing of her tongue, inconsiderate of her friends, contemptuous towards her dependants, amiable only to her flatterers.[11]

So writes a modern commentator.

In his journal account of the meeting Louis wrote:

The manly spirit and enlightened curiosity of this lady ought
to make many modern travellers ashamed of the indolent
indifference with which they hurry over foreign countries.

But he obviously misunderstood her motives, for he continues:
"She sees a great deal, and carefully examines what she sees . . ."
This was surely over-generous but perhaps, sensing a serious rival,
she put up a superior façade of knowledge during his stay in
Nazareth. Even her young lover had been shocked at her disregard of the ancient sites of Greece, and in the Lebanon she could
not bother to glance at Tyre. Michael Bruce was the only member
of the party who troubled to look at the ruins of the Phoenician
capital, since his mistress had no interest in what she called merely
"a heap of old stones".[12]

Her comment on Tyre strikes one ironically in the cruel light
of a remark made some years later by a Frenchman describing her
as "the most interesting ruin of the Lebanon". Both Lamartine
and Kinglake, who made the pilgrimage to visit her in her
eccentric old age, saw her through more kindly eyes. To them,
especially Kinglake, who knew of her exploits from the days of
his Somerset childhood, she was still Queen of the Desert, a
pallid but practical prophetess whose large commanding features,
crowned by an immense turban, bore still all the stamp of
grandeur and "sublime pretension".[13]

But, Louis went on in gentle warning—and perhaps this faint
criticism if such it can be called reached her ears from London to
add fuel to her dislike of him—

But it is to be hoped that the polite and distinguished manner
in which she is everywhere received by the governors of the
country, will not impress her with too favourable an opinion
of the Turks in general, and of their disposition towards the
nations of Europe.

The truth was that although she was undeniably brave she
*bought* her way, not only with piastres and gorgeous gifts but with
her feminine power to astonish the sheiks. Dressed as a man, tall,

white-complexioned, a masterly rider, she delighted, mystified and startled Arabs and Turks. Her dislike of Louis, and her later rude scorn of him sprang no doubt from jealousy. So long as he was in Nazareth, and he stayed four days, he quite stole her glory; she resented him for this, and for the quiet, unassuming but effective way in which he set about his travels. He was the expert, she very much the wealthy amateur with no ambition but to impress. Her lover waxed enthusiastic over Sheik Ibrahim's exploits; even poor old Dr Meryon, her personal physician and one might almost say her slave, now paid her little attention. He too was fascinated by the celebrated Burckhardt, and followed him about asking pertinent geological questions as to the composition of the local soils—to her all distinctly boring.

She could not bear anyone to steal her limelight. When she had met him in Greece she had been jealous of Byron, and unable even to praise his beauty, let alone his poetry. Byron, Sligo and Bruce were all of an age and she, some fourteen years their senior, had been sharp with the young poet, who for his part had been sorry to see his old friend Bruce in the thrall of so overwhelming a female.[14]

> Sheick Ibrahim the traveller after leaving me at Nazareth went God knows where into the desert, and has discovered a second Palmyra.[15]

—so she wrote home, managing casually to convey relief, disenchantment and self-importance all at once.

Unable as she was to dominate the scene with Louis there she made subsequent repercussions that were trying for him. But as we have seen he was far more generous in expressions of admiration *at the time* than others were to be later and, at her especial request, he sent her from Cairo a full, knowledgeable and indeed unique note on Arab horses, for which she did not seem to be particularly grateful. Louis had studied and even dealt a little in horses while in Aleppo, and he wrote with authority on the best breed Arabians within the so-called *El Khamsa*, the Five. His letter was addressed to:

Michael Bruce Esr. In Syria *Vel ubicumque*

In it he conveyed also his polite congratulations to Lady Hester upon her expedition to Palmyra, a visit which he felt should be "recorded there by an English inscription in honour of women's minds and spirits". Before leaving Nazareth he had promised Bruce that he would write of his arrival in Egypt, and that he was as good as his word he points out:

> I hope to convince you that my word is not yet quite so bad as the clothes I wore and the nation I represented when I had the pleasure of seeing you at Nazareth.[16]

The Spanish monastery where the entourage stayed at Nazareth was in a sorry state; following the French invasion of the homeland all financial support from Spain had ceased and yet there was still tribute money of about £1,200 a year to be paid to Damascus. In Cairo later, Louis learned from the Spanish consul that when the news of the capture of Madrid, in August 1812, eventually reached Jerusalem the Spanish priests celebrated with a public *Te Deum.*

During the French invasion of the Levant Bonaparte had dined in Nazareth, the most northerly point that he reached in Syria.

Louis seldom missed an opportunity to express sincere admiration of the English, especially in juxtaposition with the hated French. Now in his journal he recounts the story of Sydney Smith, hero of Acre, of how he saved the Christians from massacre at the hands of the notorious Djezzar Pasha after the French retreat from the city.

Sir Sydney had not hesitated to reproach the Pasha for his cruelty, and threatened that if a single Christian head fell he would bombard Acre and see it burn. Djezzar had to give in, and now, thirteen years after the event, Smith's name was still remembered with gratitude by all Christians, who looked upon him as their deliverer. Louis often heard both Turks and Christians exclaim: "*His* word was like God's word, it never failed."

The same could not be said of Bonaparte, whose promise,

sworn upon his honour with many oaths, to return and relieve the Christians of their Ottoman oppressors, was never kept.

Luckily, while Louis was in Nazareth two traders had arrived from Es Salt to collect merchandise; he arranged to join their little caravan, and so left Nazareth at midnight on 1 July.

In the Jordan valley there were many nomad encampments, but as the men from Es Salt were on friendly terms with the people they travelled through in safety. Crossing the Wadi Zerka—the Biblical Jabbok where Jacob wrestled with the angel—they came to Es Salt in the Belka district. Louis was longing to reach El Kerak of the mountain, the isolated castle town on the deserted highland beyond the Dead Sea, but no guide was obtainable, and it seemed that no one was anxious to venture into that dangerous territory.

To occupy the time of waiting, Louis visited the ruins of *Ammon—Philadelphia*, modern Amman. What is now the busy little capital of Jordan was then, only so relatively short a while ago, no more than a castle and a few ravaged Hellenistic ruins by a stream whose banks were haunted by hostile Bedouin horsemen.

He started to make a plan of the antiquities, but the sight of fresh horse dung in the wadi so alarmed his guides that they rode off, leaving him alone in the theatre. Dissatisfied with his curtailed survey, he soon had to gallop off in their tracks, and when he rejoined them at half an hour's ride away he reproached them for their cowardice. A true Bedouin, however, Louis wrote, would not have abandoned his companion in this manner.

He managed, at a high price, to find a guide to take him to El Kerak, and from Es Salt he set out again on 13 July. They had not gone far when they saw ahead two men in a copse. It was the custom among Bedouin on meeting an unknown inferior force to rein in their horses on drawing near and to level their lances in challenge. Louis' guide saw the strangers from a long way off, and called to him to have his gun ready as they galloped towards the trees. The men, who were stark naked, turned and cried out: "We are under your protection!"

They had been snatched from work in their fields by men of

the dreaded Beni Sakhr tribe, stripped and beaten; they had somehow managed to escape, cut and bruised as they were. This part of the high plain flanking the Dead Sea was much fought over because of its relatively good pasturage. It is still today the land of the herdsmen.

The next morning they crossed the southern Zerka. The wadi here was so thickly grown with red flowering oleanders, all reflected in the river, that it had "the appearance of a bed of roses", the carmine of the flowers making sharp contrast with the silvery calcareous rocks erupting steeply above the scented stream.

It took them six hours to reach the stupendous banks of the Wadi Mojib beyond Diban—the Brook Arnon of the Scriptures, which divides the Belka district from that of Kerak just as it once divided the small kingdoms of the Moabites and the Amorites. Why the Bible calls it a brook is hardly understandable; it is a barren, impressive gorge, 2,000 feet deep, slicing through high tablelands.

They dismounted as the way was so broken, and it took thirty-five minutes to reach the bottom. Louis noticed part of the old paved Roman road and the broken columns of the millaria. The heat in the depths was oven-like, and the place was charged with fear. He and his guide paused at the ford, like the lost daughters of Moab, to fill their waterskins. He knew his Bible well and the Biblical connections of this place must have crossed his mind, but there was no time to linger. It was a favourite haunt of robbers who hid in wait for travellers—numerous heaps of stones were piled up along the track by every Arab passing through this dangerous wadi to provide missiles in case of attack.

The way zigzagged painfully to the flat, naturally buttressed tableland above, torrid now against a cloudless burnished blue sky. It took them nearly two hours to reach this high plateau from the ford.* Here, so his guide told him, Dr Seetzen had been partly stripped by some Arabs, but luckily they met no living soul in the crossing.

* This ancient way is now a motor road eleven miles long although the gorge tops are only two miles apart.

On the top they were following the old paved way when, towards sunset, they met some shepherds, with a flock of sheep, who led them to their family encampment concealed in that gazelle-brown land, behind a hill near the road: a camp fire glowed welcomingly among the long dark tents.

We were much fatigued but the kindness of our hosts soon made us forget our laborious day's march. We alighted under the tent of the Sheikh who was dying of a wound he had received a few days before from the thrust of a lance; but such is the hospitality of these people, and their attention to the comforts of the traveller, that we did not learn of the Sheikh's misfortune until the following day. He was in the women's apartment, and we did not hear him utter any complaints. They supposed, with reason, that if we were informed of his situation it would prevent us from enjoying our supper. A lamb was killed, and a friend of the family did the honours of the table: we should have enjoyed our repast better had there not been an absolute want of water, but there was none nearer than the Mojib [*Arnon*] and the daily supply which, according to the custom . . . had been brought in before sunrise was, as it not infrequently happens, exhausted before night; our own water-skins . . . had been emptied by the shepherds before we reached the encampment.

The next day, another six-hour ride brought them to precipitous Kerak. El Kerak—a rough-hewn, stubborn place, an eyrie that breeds tough and rugged men—towers dramatically piled on the summit of an almost isolated hill occupied from the earliest times, and now topped by a shattered but imposing Crusader castle. It was a place roundly cursed by Isaiah:

We have heard of the pride of Moab; he is very proud . . . for the foundations of Kir-hareseth shall ye mourn, surely are they stricken . . . laid waste and brought to silence . . . as a wandering bird cast out of the nest so the daughters of Moab shall be at the fords of Arnon.

The Crusaders called it *Crac des Moabites*, or *Les Pierres du Désert*. In Louis' time there was not a single boy in Kerak who did not know how to use a gun by the time he was ten years old. Even today the children of this stony town are robust and cheeky in the extreme; the Sheik of their great-great-grandfathers commanded some 1,200 matchlocks which were the terror of neighbouring Arab tribes, who no longer surged up to attack the natural fortress. Now the big, dark-skinned soldiers of Kerak in their long white robes and gleaming bandoliers maintain this fierce reputation: tradition dies hard and Kerak is still a wild, strong place despite the prophecies of Isaiah.

No sooner had Louis entered by the north gate of the town—the Christian quarter—than he was surrounded by people who seized hold of his horse's bridle. Each insisted on giving him hospitality, laughing, shouting and, as was the custom, vying with each other they practically fought over their guest. He followed the most persistent of them, and soon the entire neighbourhood gathered to join in the feast cooked in honour of his arrival. Surprisingly, however, not a soul had yet asked who he was or where he was going.

Having talked with the Greek priest in this, the Christian quarter, he felt duty-bound to pay a ceremonial call on the Sheik. He was courteously received, but he had nearly three weeks in which to repent this call. The Sheik, who was a man of immense vitality and determination, would not hear of his travelling south alone. All such suggestions were brushed aside; he was about to visit the southern districts himself and he begged Sheik Ibrahim to wait "a few days" so that they might travel together.

Haggling over the last guide's payment, and over the "present" which the Sheik now demanded, was prolonged. Daily the Sheik postponed his journey, so that Louis could not risk going down to the Dead Sea for fear of missing the escort south, and was virtually imprisoned in mountainous Kerak for twenty days while constantly changing his lodgings in order to comply with the pressing invitations of the so hospitable inhabitants. Every evening the town overflowed with visitors and their horses, since the Bedouin knew they could get good free meals here, and fodder too for their mounts. They came noisily with ringing voices, a clatter of hooves and a jingle of harness up the steep hillside. Eyes flashing, bronzed cheeks flushed above the swathed folds of the *keffieh*, they moved blithely from house to house, eating their fill.

At this time the Jerusalem clergy believed El Kerak to be the ancient Petra as the diocese was called *Petras* but, in Louis' opinion, it was probably Pliny's *Charax Omanorum*. Seetzen had already searched in vain for Petra. Now, drawing closer to the vast stony wilderness that the Romans called *Arabia Petraea*, Louis' interest was quickened afresh, and his hope stimulated, for he did not at all agree with the priests of Jerusalem that Kerak was Petra.

It was in Kerak that Louis heard of the desert "honey" which he correctly supposed was manna, miraculous food of the wandering Israelites. A juice exuding from the leaves and twigs of a tree called *gharab* (*Tamarix mannifera*), it was collected by the Arabs who made cakes of it which they ate with butter.

At last, on 4 August the powerful Sheik of Kerak decided to leave for the south—accompanied by forty horsemen all excellently mounted. The Sheik himself possessed the finest horse Louis had yet seen in all Syria—"a grey Saklawi famous all over the desert".

As they went Louis looked back from a mountain ridge and saw the southern end of the Dead Sea set jewel-blue and mysterious in its own salt-encrusted shoals, palely glimmering among rose-gold, heat-hazed rocks far below. It was a tantalising sight but Louis found consolation in knowing that Seetzen had, in 1806, already made a complete circuit of that weird sea.

There were delays, for the Sheik, being in no hurry, made countless pretexts for halting. They fared lavishly on gifts of roast mutton, the best fruits and plenty of tobacco, and at each village the party increased in size until it had doubled its strength by camp-followers bent on obtaining free meals.

At one village, where the Sheik had a house, and a wife whom he dared not move to Kerak—perhaps she was one above the legal four—they stopped for an entire day. In the evening the Sheik held a court of justice to decide disputes among the peasants.

The following afternoon they were all alarmed by a tremendous hullabaloo from the opposite mountain: men's voices rang out confused by fantastic echoes reverberating off the rocks above. Instantly, to a man, the entire party mounted and galloped away in the direction of the din. Louis was quick to follow suit. On the mountainside they found three shepherds from the village stripped naked; Arabs from the mountains of Hebron had attacked them, and each robber had made off with a fat sheep slung across his saddle.

The gang was already out of sight in the savage landscape and the men, frustrated at not being able to overtake them and give battle, began to amuse themselves with a sham fight. They displayed remarkable strength and skill in handling the lance, "and great boldness in riding at speed over rugged and rocky ground". Dust flew from beneath their horses' hooves, brown faces were flushed, excited Arab voices raised in spine-thrilling, vociferous falsetto shrieks. In the dexterous lance-play and swift manœuvre, although he was a man of sixty, the Kerakian Sheik excelled above all the younger men. "Indeed he seemed to be an accomplished Bedouin Sheik; although he proved to be a treacherous friend."

That evening, to Louis' astonishment, he took him aside and demanded a further sum of protection money. Louis reduced this from 20 to 15 piastres, and tried to bind him by the most solemn of all Bedouin oaths: the Sheik, laying his hand upon the head of his own son and upon the feet of his beautiful mare, swore that he would, for the agreed sum, conduct Sheik Ibrahim to the Huweitat Arabs in the south. But even this powerful oath was soon disregarded: the crafty Sheik laid plans for relieving Louis of some of his few possessions. Louis' saddle was a high, town one, worth 40 piastres, the Sheik's only 10, but the exchange was cunningly contrived. Louis could not, in front of the company, remind the Sheik of his secret oath since it would have revealed the sum already extorted: the Kerakian Sheik would have been reprimanded by his Bedouin followers and Louis thus exposed to his personal revenge. So Louis kept silent, and was forced to listen to the bystanders' shocked remarks.

"Is he not your brother?" they said piously. "Are not the best morsels of his dish always for you? Does he not continually fill your pipe with his own tobacco?—Fie upon your stinginess!"

They did not know that Louis had calculated on paying for part of the hire of a Huweitat guide to Egypt with the saddle's price, nor that he had already paid handsomely for the privilege of his "brotherhood".

The saddles exchanged, even then the Sheik was not satisfied. Next it was an argument over the stirrups that ensued. The Sheik's son wanted Louis' against a pair of his own which were almost unfit for use and which, Louis knew, would wound his ankles since he did not wear boots. But after two days he had to yield and, in consequence, his feet were soon cut.

He records this incident deliberately as an illustration of Arab cupidity: to the Bedouin any object was covetable, if one persisted in refusing they would not take the thing by force but they made it virtually impossible to resist without giving way to their eternal supplications and compliments. Louis had learned by experience that it was of no use to talk solemnly to Bedouin:

on the contrary I aspired to be a merry fellow; I joked with them whenever I could, and found that by a little attention to their ways and reasoning they are easily put in good humour.

They left the village of the Sheik's secret fifth wife late in the evening when the air was cooler. It was a dark night, and this was, without exception, the most dangerous route Louis had yet travelled in his life. The descent was steep, the rocks smooth, there was no regular track, the foot slipped at every step. They missed their way; then, after many of them had suffered severe falls, they all dismounted—all that is except their indefatigable Sheik, the only man not to alight from his mare whose step, he declared, was as secure as his own.

Tafileh came as a pleasant contrast with the semi-barren uplands and the parched wadis—it was a little place of many rivulets, grown with cypress and olive trees, and orchards of apple, apricot, fig, pomegranate and peach.

There was matrimonial trouble here: a man of Tafileh, having eloped with someone else's wife, had taken refuge at Kerak, and as the Sheik now intended to settle this business they delayed here for three days.

> Tumultuous assemblies were held daily upon the subject, and the meanest Arab might give his opinion, though in direct opposition to that of his Sheik. . . . Our Sheik, however, in his eloquence and address, at last got the better of them all. . . . The affair was settled by the offender's father placing his four infant daughters, the youngest of whom was not yet weaned, at the disposal of the husband and his father-in-law, who might betroth them to whomsoever they chose and receive themselves the money which is usually paid for girls. The four daughters were estimated at about 3,000 piastres and both parties seemed content . . . a white flag was suspended at the top of the tent in which we sat, a sheep was killed and we passed the whole night in feasting and conversation.

Tafileh has perhaps a special reputation as a musical community, even today the traveller is entertained there with *rebaba* music and song over innumerable cups of coffee and mint tea. Louis records that every night there was a musical party of Bedouin famous for their performances on the *rebaba*, the guitar of the desert, and all knew the latest Bedouin poetry by heart.

South of the village as they moved on the party came across a small encampment of Huweitat Arabs, and from them the Sheik recommended a guide. The charge, plus a camel for Louis and his baggage to Cairo, was fixed at 80 piastres—about £6 sterling. This was the last friendly service the Sheik performed for Louis, but the gloss rubbed off even this act when Louis discovered that he had received 15 piastres commission from the guide. Then, no sooner had the Sheik departed than the Huweitat announced that his camels were a day's march further on, he had with him one only which was needed to transport his tent; to settle with him Louis was obliged to sell his mare for four goats and 35 piastres' worth of corn. The man took the goats in payment for his services, and Louis agreed to give him another 20 piastres on their reaching Cairo. He still had about 80 piastres in gold kept carefully concealed in case of some great emergency: he knew that if he were to show as much as a single sequin of this the Arabs would suppose that he had hundreds, and would either have robbed him, or prevented him from going on by the most exorbitant demands.

It was a humble little procession in which Louis set out again. The guide and his family—wife, two children, and a servant girl: they went on foot, driving some sheep and the goats before them, and leading the one camel laden with the family tent, pots and pans, and probably a new-born lamb or two.

They went straight up over the mountain until, above Dhana, there opened out a colossal vista. The narrow cleft of Wadi Dhana led steeply down to the great Wadi Araba far below, seemingly limitless, expanding in majesic heat-hazed perspective towards a flushed and dusky western sky. He stared in wonder: this was the northern part of the gigantic Rift that stretches for 3,000 miles from Galilee, or perhaps even from the Beka'a, deep into east Africa.

A little beyond this wonderful viewpoint, they looked down into another, a smaller off-shoot valley, and saw some horsemen encamped by a distant spring. These men spotted their caravan and immediately mounted their horses to give chase.

Several travellers had joined Louis' little contingent on the road, but there was only one armed man besides Louis among them. Since it seemed that the distant horsemen were Beni Sakhr—inveterate enemies of the Huweitat—there was no time to lose. Hastily they drove the cattle back and hid them with the women and baggage behind some rocks near the road—hostile Arabs never harm women—and then the men took to their heels, bounding down towards the little village of Dhana. It was a breathless forty-five minute race in the exhausting August heat of early afternoon.

In order to run more nimbly over the rocks, I took off my heavy Arab shoes, and thus I was the first to reach the village, but the sharp flints of the mountain wounded my feet so much that after reposing a little I could hardly stand. . . . This was the first time I had ever felt fear during my travels in the desert; for I knew that if I fell in with the Beni Sakhr without anybody to protect me they would certainly kill me, as they did all persons whom they supposed to belong to their inveterate enemy, the Pasha of Damascus . . .

And his build, full curling beard and general appearance were far more those of the Damascene than of the desert Arab.

His short account of this headlong flight pictures the panicked figures flying down that steep hillside, ant-like above the vast sun-hazed Rift where it shimmers south through Syria towards the great heart of Africa.

However, after all their pursuers proved to be Huweitat who stripped only a few friends of the Beni Sakhr in the company. Returning exhausted up the mountain to the women and the baggage, they rested there among the rocks for the night and continued next day through the mountains of Seir, the Biblical territory of the Edomites. Progress was slow since the camel had gone lame, so Louis went hurrying on ahead with the guide's young son. When they reached the family encampment it was empty of all but the women who were having a great wash-day, their men having gone to Gaza to trade. Left to themselves these women felt quite free to indulge their curiosity unashamedly; they were extremely surprised to see a townsman, and still more a Damascene (for so Louis was called), in their tents. They crowded around him, a flock of lean, swarthy, tattooed, blue-gowned starlings, unrelenting with their questions and laughter. What was his business? What goods had he to sell, and *what* were the ladies of Damascus wearing that year?

The only information they gave him came as an unpleasant shock; his guide, they said, owned no camels other than the one now with him—and that was lame.

The wretched man arrived, and various delaying tactics were put into operation. Louis curbed his annoyance, believing that the man was not a true Huweitat, and having no wish to argue the matter out except in the presence of the tribesmen.

*Aug. 15th.*—We remained this day at the women's tents, and I amused myself with visiting almost every tent in the encampment, these women being accustomed to receive strangers in the absence of their husbands.

The following day they continued, still on foot, through many wadis of winter torrents, until they reached a large circle of Huweitat tents. No one moved his tent to allow theirs into the circle as would have been the custom for a fellow tribesman. Here, tired of subterfuges, Louis had the matter out with his guide; resolving to travel with him no longer, he insisted that the man should return the goats or hire him another guide instead. A sharp dispute followed, then Louis stood up, took his gun and swore never to re-enter the fellow's tent, accompanying "the oath with a malediction upon him" and those who might receive him.

As he strode out of the tent in this effective fiery mood of resolute and justified anger, the other Bedouin, who had of course heard every word of the verbal battle, surrounded him now that he was free of his so-called host and swore that they could never permit a stranger to depart thus: he should put himself under their chief's protection.

This was exactly the result that Louis had anticipated. He received back the four goats, gave the Sheik his gun in exchange for his good offices, and was directed to an honest man in a near-by encampment, who owned a strong camel and who would act as guide to Cairo.

So, driving his little flock, Louis left in the morning, with a boy to guide him to the honest man's tents. His sense of humour rarely left him, and he must have smiled inwardly at this archaically pastoral march towards Egypt, going humbly on foot, herding his goats before him.

He was welcomed as the Sheik's "brother", and soon formed a good opinion of Hamid, the Arab who was to take him to Cairo —for the four much-bartered goats, plus 20 piastres to be paid on arrival. It was a remarkably small sum for a journey of nearly 400 miles but a Bedouin put little value on time, fatigue or labour. However, had it been known that he was a European the cost would have been at *least* 1,000 piastres—£50 instead of £1.[17]

West of the road the dark pile of the Crusader castle of Shobak came suddenly into view, vastly impressive on its isolated hilltop rising from a deep ravine. As he needed some provisions Louis went to the castle. Having no cash in silver he was obliged to pay for his shopping with his only spare shirt, his red cap, and half his turban cloth, for which collection he received some flour, butter, dried *leben*—and a lean goat. This goat was to play an important part in Louis' story; it was indeed to be the excuse for, and focal point of, one of his most interesting and famous discoveries.

All along this road, at each castle or encampment he had heard, so it seems, the country people speaking with great admiration of the strange buildings and the so-called monasteries hidden away in Wadi Musa. Louis recollected that there was passage in Eusebius in which it was said that the tomb of Aaron was near Petra.[18]

But Wadi Musa branches off the desert road to Akaba, the way Hamid wished to take on the grounds that the other route through the Wadi and in a straight line to Cairo was too dangerous. So Louis had begun to seek an excuse that might enable him to enter the secret mountain fortress which he suspected did lie here. The goat was to be the pretext; he would sacrifice it to Aaron on Mount Hor. This was the stratagem by which Louis hoped to see the hidden valley on his way to the prophet's tomb: Hamid could not protest for fear of incurring the wrath of Aaron, and was therefore "completely silenced".

Six years earlier, Seetzen had been unsuccessful in his search for Petra, having taken the road leading from Hebron to Mount Sinai. Also, he had no suspicion of the long valley which Louis had seen that day above Dhana, which is called el Ghor in the north, and el Araba in the south, and which as we now know is a part of the Great Rift.[19]

Louis wrote to Sir Joseph:

the existence of this valley appears to have been unknown to ancient as well as to modern geographers, although it is a very remarkable feature in the geography of Syria and Arabia Petraea. . . . In this valley the manna is still found . . .

And the quails also upon which the Israelites lived.

As regards ancient trade routes Louis thought that a caravan laden at Akaba "with the treasures of Ophir, might, after a march of six or seven days, deposit its loads in the warehouses of Solomon —this was a valley, he urged, that deserved to be thoroughly known.

Until that day, 22 August, when he arrived at Ain Musa, Petra had been lost to the western world for over six centuries: from the time of the Crusades, in about 1200, until this summer of 1812, when Louis came south in the blazing heat with his lean goat from Shobak, and his honest Bedouin, to the copious spring of Moses rising crystal fresh among fig trees at the head of the hidden wadi.

From near the spring there is a distant view of the white dome of Aaron's tomb on the mountain top. Hamid pressed him to slaughter the goat here, and have done with it, in view of the tomb as was often the custom. But Louis pretended to have vowed to sacrifice it at the tomb itself.

Beyond, in the little fly-blown village of Elji, he hired a guide at the cost of pair of old horse-shoes, which he must have had in his scanty baggage, to escort him into the barrier of rocky cliffs to the tomb.

The guide carried the goat, and handed Louis a water skin to shoulder since he knew that the secret wadi below was dry. They followed the rivulet down westwards to where the valley narrows and the way appears to vanish completely in a sudden tumbled mass of pale sandstone rocks and cliffs, the stern bastions concealing Wadi Musa's fastness.

And it is here that the antiquities . . . begin. Of these I regret that I am not able to give a very complete account: but I know well the character of the people around me; I was without protection in the midst of a desert where no traveller had ever before been seen; and a close examination of the works of the infidels, as they are called, would have excited suspicions that I was a magician in search of treasures.

Had he lingered he would have been detained, prevented from reaching Egypt, probably stripped of what little money he possessed and of what was infinitely more valuable to him—his notebook. To future travellers under protection, he foretold, in his usual reserved manner, the antiquities of Wadi Musa would "be found to rank among the most curious remains of ancient art".

Long after Louis had given the world news of his discovery this so elusive site remained difficult of access. To see it is a unique, a much-desired experience; yet it has been only since about 1925 that any but the most intrepid and wealthy explorers were able to visit Petra, as the inhabitants, writes Lankester Harding, maintained their unfriendly attitude for a long time. They even massacred the members of the first Arab Legion police post established at Elji to protect visitors.[20]

Petra is the ancient *Sela* in the wilderness: the Greek name, a rock or stone, corresponds with the Hebrew *sela* which in Arabic means a cleft rock. Jeremiah, prophet of doom, foresaw disaster for the dwellers in the clefts of the rocks who held the heights: ". . . Edom shall be a desolation: and everyone that goeth thereby shall be astonished . . ."[21]

The Edomites, an Arab people who had snatched the fastness from the Horites, were in time driven out by the Nabataeans—a fascinating people, originally a nomadic Arab tribe who made Petra their hideout and grew rich on the proceeds of raiding spice and incense caravans from the Hadramaut. Later, they settled down under good kings of their own, levied taxes on passing caravans, and traded far afield, at one time having influence in Damascus. According to Diodorus Siculus they appear to have occupied Petra from about the third century B.C., and they remained there for at least five centuries. Recent excavations have revealed traces of very much earlier inhabitants, of the Upper Palaeolithic period—probably 10,000 B.C.

A Greek campaign to suppress the Nabataeans in about 300 B.C. failed to oust them, but Antigonus' men did manage to occupy the "Rock" briefly, but only because all the young men happened to be away at a fair. The Greeks killed many defenceless people and made off hurriedly with booty of frankincense and myrrh. The Nabataeans soon returned from their jaunt, rushed off after the Greeks to attack and massacre nearly their entire camp of 4,000 men. The Nabataeans were never caught like this again and subsequent Greek attacks failed. When their last King, Rabel II, died in A.D. 106, the Romans took over and re-designed the city with main street, theatre, and free-standing temple. Then under Trajan, the country became a Roman province—*Arabia Petraea*, one of the three famous Arabias, the others being *Arabia Deserta* and *Arabia Felix*.

Descending into the narrow chasm called *el Siq*, Louis heard the lonely voice of the wind sighing through cleft and fissure. Then, as the cliff walls narrowed, there was the sound of their own footsteps on the dry torrent bed echoing under the rocky over-hang, and again the eternally sighing moan of that wind. This is the wind that for thousands of years has chiselled strange shapes in Petra's soft sandstone, in the labyrinth of cave and carving where sometimes man's work has become confused with that of nature through the wear and rub of sand blown by this so insidious wind.

As the massive walls of the *Siq* close in, dwarfing small human figures in their depths, a traveller is enveloped, silenced by the awesome wonder of the place.

Louis had constantly to live as it were on two planes at once; now a further element was added—that of time. Now more than ever he must strive to appear the illiterate, disinterested peasant, curbing his natural amazement at the breath-taking wonders he saw, while recalling their ancient history, going back in time while living in the present as two people. This August day was a milestone in his career, and one of the greatest challenges to his powers. The strain told on him in excessive tiredness later, and little wonder: to be the first literate man to enter a place as astounding as this after a lapse of over 600 years might well be an exhilarating experience, to put it mildly. But it was his duty not only to hide his feelings and to continue to act his peasant role, but also to concentrate, to observe and commit to memory every possible detail of this extraordinary, ravishing place—while all the time his uneasy guide, nervous as a cat, hurried him on.

They had gone about fifty yards into the *Siq* when Louis saw a bridge span high above their heads, a triumphal arch across the chasm. It has now fallen, but it was in position for about eighty years after Louis' discovery. He wanted to climb up to it, but his guide assured him that no one had ever succeeded in doing so, and therefore it had unanimously been decided that it must be the work of *djinn*.

The *Siq* is one-and-a-quarter miles long, but perhaps because of its narrowness and strangeness it seems interminable. Louis took twenty-five minutes to traverse it. Then, as the rock walls twisted and parted revealing the first hint of rosy beauty, a carved façade ahead, he paused in stunned amazement: *el Kazneh* glowed in the towering sunlit cliff above a sea of red oleanders, so close it seemed that he could not see it all, unbelievably lovely as it was.

He emerged from the *Siq* and stood gazing up at the wonderful spectacle. No one can look at this work unmoved:

> the situation and beauty of which are calculated to make an extraordinary impression upon the traveller, after having transversed . . . such a gloomy and almost subterranean passage . . . it is one of the most elegant remains of antiquity existing in Syria.*

Louis was convinced that it was a tomb and not a dwelling, but the experts still argue around this point. His man told him that it was "Pharaoh's Castle", perhaps deliberately concealing the Bedouin's real name for it, "Pharaoh's Treasury", being convinced, as they all were, that its solid stone urn contained a hidden store of gold.

Whatever it may be, *el Kazneh*, unlike the rest of Petra *is* "rose-red" and hewn from the sheer rock its beauty seems to smile forth like an exquisite face whsipering from a dark frame.

As they continued into Petra, past the theatre hacked by Romans from among ancient cliff tombs, and on to where the valley opens out in the sunbaked core of the stone city, Louis was further tantalised by the sight of the magnificent façades of the

* Now Jordan.

great tombs on the eastern cliff face. They were too far off the track for him to explore without annoying his guide but he did, much to the man's surprise, enter some of the many smaller tombs and dwellings that lie within the valley. All these are bare, the interiors unadorned but many-coloured, since by carving into the living rock Nabataean tools revealed the extraordinary range of its natural colours. Veins and waves of swirling patterns gleam like watered silk in smoothly chiselled ceilings—cobalt, tan, terracotta, rose.

The guide expressed little more than surprise at Louis' diversions until they reached the Roman temple; then, as Louis turned off the path towards it, his suspicions were thoroughly aroused. He exclaimed heatedly: "I see now that you are an infidel, who has some particular business amongst the ruins of the city of your forefathers; but depend upon it we shall not suffer you to take out a single part of the treasures hidden therein. . .!"

Louis replied that it was merely curiosity that had prompted him, and that his sole intention was to make his sacrifice to Aaron. But the man remained darkly suspicious so that Louis dared not explore further in case it should lead, on their return, to a search of his person for "treasure", and the possible loss of his journal, which would certainly be taken from him as a book of "magic" were it seen.

For European explorers it was unfortunate that the idea of treasure being hidden in ancient edifices was so strongly rooted in the minds of Arabs and Turks—though perhaps it was hardly surprising when one considers that stories of Egyptian tomb robbers must have long been current in Syria. "He has indications of treasure with him" was a phrase that Louis became sick and tired of hearing.

Steeling himself to patience he marched on up the southern valley that skirts below *Umm el Biyara*—the Mother of Cisterns—from which sheer height captive Edomites were thrown to their death by the King of Judah, and so on towards Mount Hor and the little white-domed still distant tomb of Aaron. Pale vultures, the neophron or "Pharaoh's chickens", circled high above the savage peaks, soaring effortlessly in the hot afternoon sky. Surrounded on all sides by its barren cliffs the silent, awesome place shimmered, blistering with incandescent heat. But when at last they arrived on the Terrace of Aaron, at the foot of the steep mount where the tomb stands, the sun had set and it was too late to ascend.

> . . . I was excessively fatigued, I therefore hastened to kill the goat in sight of the tomb, at a spot where I found a number of heaps of stones; . . . in token of as many sacrifices in honour of the saint. While I was in the act of slaying the animal, my guide exclaimed aloud, "O Harun, protect us and forgive us! O Harun, be content with our good intentions, for it is but a lean goat! O Harun, smooth our paths; and praise be to the Lord of all creatures!"

It was dusk: the resonant Arabic chant echoed off the rock, the two lonely figures stood, the goat at their feet dying slowly Islamic fashion in a pool of its own blood. Darkness fell rapidly as the curtains of twilight descended over the empty, yet haunted valley, silent and heavy with time's imprint, charged by countless ages of man's passing.

The guide repeated his prayer several times, bowing towards the height, touching his right hand to eyes, lips and heart in reverent salutation to *Nabi* Harun. The ritual over, they hurriedly dressed the best part of the meat for their supper as well as they could, for the guide was afraid that if fire were seen it might attract robbers.

They slept there for a little while on the rocks in the cool of the night, but his guide insisted on being back early on 23 August as he was due to go with a caravan to Ma'an that day. So there was no further chance for observation; they retraced their steps in the dark along the great valleys and through the inky black, echoing passage of the *Siq*. Louis was sorry not to have been up to the tomb, whence he would have seen a great monument of which he had heard—no doubt the huge hidden el Deir, carved on an opposite mountain top.

Reluctantly he left Petra's wind- and sand-worn majesty—locked as it had been for centuries in the fastness of its rock, and locked also in the jealous minds of the local people, but no longer lost to the world. Briefly rediscovered, the triumph was his, the mapping and the surveying would have to be left to others, but once again it was he who had led the way.

It had been physically and emotionally a tremendous twenty-four hours; however, he stopped only for a brief rest at Elji and was soon travelling on again with Hamid in the direction of Akaba.

Wearied as he was in mind and body, such a splendid discovery would inevitably have lightened any hardship and, as he rode his camel south behind the Huweitat guide, he relived in thought over and over again those momentous stolen hours in unknown Petra.

"Whether or not I have discovered the remains of the capital of *Arabia Petraea* I leave to the decision of the Greek scholars," he wrote modestly in his report. But he must at heart have been convinced of the truth since, from all the information he had, there was "no other ruin of importance between the Dead Sea and the Red Sea that would answer to that city".

It was a timeless experience, an unforgettably great achievement.

# Part IV

# Into Africa

CHAPTER SEVEN

# *"The Gift of the River"*

I arrived at length at Cairo, mother of cities . . . mistress of . . .
fruitful lands, boundless in multitude of buildings, peerless in
beauty and splendour, the meeting place of comer and goer,
the halting place of feeble and mighty, whose throngs surge
as the waves of the sea . . . *Ibn Battuta. 1325–1354.*

El Misr—"Mother of the World". *Cairene saying*

AT THE IMMENSE "Brow of Syria"—*Masharif es-Shem*—Louis
turned his back finally on the north. Below the huge scarp of the
Jebel Sherra lies Arabia proper: to the west the grim desert of
Tyh, far beyond it the ancient narrow lands of the Nile—Egypt,
in Herodotus' unforgettable phrase, "the gift of the river".

As Louis and Hamid rode away on their second morning out,
the tremendous precipice barricading Petra was visible, falling
sheer almost a mile in height to the westward continuation of
Wadi Araba below.

It was now 24 August. The two men paused to breakfast that
day at an encampment of Arabs who were so poor there was no
coffee, and whose pathetic tents were no more than four feet
high; all that could be produced for the travellers was a somewhat
unappetising, though nevertheless welcome, meal of dry barley
cakes dipped in melted goat fat. But the news gleaned in these
poverty-stricken tents was "extremely agreeable": a small
caravan from a neighbouring encampment was about to cross the
desert direct to Cairo.

This was indeed a lucky chance since Louis had expected some
trouble from the soldiers of Akaba, the garrison set there by
Mohammed Ali Pasha of Egypt to keep a watchful eye not only
on the rebellious Wahabi of Arabia but also on any strangers of

doubtful origin, especially Syrians. The last was a category into which Louis most certainly fell, since he had nothing at all with him to prove what he might be doing in these remote districts, nor even—if pushed to his last resort—any proof of his European origin. It was therefore with a sense of real relief that he now altered course to find this handful of Arabs who were so fortunately intending to take a few camels to the Cairo market.

On arrival at the encampment they learned that the caravan was preparing to set out the day after next. Louis was grateful for the chance of a short rest. He was now reduced to that state which alone ensured peace for the traveller in the desert, or so he thought for he had absolutely nothing left with him that could possibly excite Arab greed.

> . . . my clothes and linen were torn to rags; a dirty keffye . . . covered my head; my leathern girdle and shoes had long been exchanged against similar articles of an inferior kind.

Even the tube of his pipe was shorn to a span for he had been obliged to cut enough from it to make two pipes for men at Kerak, and the final article of his baggage, a single pocket handkerchief "had fallen to the lot of the Sheik of Elji".

In this unprepossessing state he expected, not without reason, to be free of all further demands but he had forgotten one thing— the rags with which he had bound his ankles when cut by those wretched stirrups of that inferior Kerakian saddle. Torn from his linen garment, the rags had once been white and were of good material: the Arab women, quick to notice this, thought that they would make excellent face veils. Therefore, whenever he stepped out of his tent he was immediately surrounded by half a dozen women clamouring for the torn linen with every wile they knew, and coy beseeching gestures of thin brown hands across bold, unveiled faces. It was quite useless to say that he really did need the rags to protect his wounded ankles; unfeeling retorts came pat: "You'll soon be in Cairo where you can get as much linen as you like!"

Through incessant teasing they won their way but Louis,

annoyed at being forced to expose his wounds, ultimately foiled the girls by presenting the rags to an ugly old woman—much to the chagrin of the young ones. It could hardly have been a relaxing day.

On 26 August the caravan set out for Cairo. There were nine men and about twenty camels. They carried no provisions but flour and salt; Louis had besides this a little dried *leben* and some butter. During the journey, which was made in ten days of forced marches, they breakfasted in the morning on bread baked in the ashes after the previous night's meal, and never supped until after sunset. Louis was greatly impressed with the frugality of these Bedouin who, to save their camels, walked for at least five hours of each day on no more nourishment than about one-and-a-half pounds of dry bread. Louis tried as far as possible to imitate their abstemiousness, "being already convinced from experience that it is the best preservative against the fatigues of such a journey".

These were typical Bedouin—gaunt expressive faces, famished eyes and wide shapely mouths. They were a good-humoured bunch of men and not a single quarrel occurred during the trying journey. Although his guide, Hamid, was an honest and pleasant-tempered fellow, Louis did have some cause to be annoyed with him since he had brought only one water skin to serve them both for drinking and for cooking, and as there were several three-day waterless intervals they were on very short allowance. But Louis could not bring himself to blame Hamid, since these men, thinking nothing themselves of hardship and privation, took it for granted that other people were equally well attuned to thirst and fatigue.

It took the caravan one-and-a-half hours to traverse the great Wadi Araba, which here appeared to be one vast expanse of shifting sands, but although deep the sand was firm and the camels crossed without sinking. The heat was suffocating and intensified by a fiery south-easterly wind, his first taste of the hated *samun*; there was no trace of a road, no sign of humanity. Before this Louis had often spoken of parts of Syria, such as the highlands near Dhana, as desert, which in fact are not true desert because some sort of pasturage, however scant, does grow there; this, however, was the real thing, terrible, desolate, awe-inspiring. At sunset they reached the top of some hills and looked back: the horizon was so astonishingly translucent in the miraculous westering light that the mountains of Kerak and Dhana were clearly visible, burnished with the apricot colours of a dying sun in the huge and cloudless sky. But ahead there lay "an immense expanse of dreary country entirely covered with black flints".

Whenever Louis wanted to take bearings in the desert he did so under his aba, never letting the Arabs catch sight of his compass, since to them it would have been an instrument of magic. On horseback he had always been able to do this easily since a mare can be taught to stand quite still, but it was not possible while riding a camel, which can never be halted while its companions move on. So Louis had to leap down every time he wanted to take a bearing and squat "in the oriental manner as if answering a call of nature". The Arabs were delighted with a traveller who could jump off his animal and remount without stopping it, since the couching and rising again is tiring for a loaded camel, and the delay can be dangerous, as rest of the caravan forges ahead.

Almost incredibly, in the middle of these appalling wastes, they met a Bedouin woman who asked for water. She said she was going to her family tents at Akaba but had no provisions at all and, remarkably enough, "she seemed as unconcerned as if she were merely taking a walk for pleasure". One wonders if she got through or died of thirst in those shifting sands.

In the desert of El Tyh there were few springs or wells; some too were brackish, and as the people they met encamped at these water-holes were reluctant to feed such a miserable-looking lot of travellers they fared very badly. At one such inhospitable camp they would have come to blows over the subject of food had Louis not mounted his camel and ridden away, the others following his example.

Then there was news that a hostile tribe was in the vicinity, old enemies of the Huweitat, so they changed their tactics, travelling yet more quickly and now by night. But Bedouin do not care for night travel, since in the darkness a man may not tell the face of his enemy from that of his friend.

Among Arabs, especially in those former days when the idea of illicit dalliance was tabu, the subject of women was a constant one, and freely discussed, with little or nothing left to the imagination, the men often boasting of the good physical points of their wives in love-making. During that first night march, perhaps to keep up their spirits, Louis came in for much teasing; many jokes were made against him about the female ghouls of the desert. Possibly because of his habit of lingering behind to take bearings, possibly because they knew him to be a bachelor, a townsman and not a desert-dweller, they spoke with relish of the invisible female demons who carried off stragglers from caravans "to enjoy their embraces".

"*Wellah!*—you townsmen," they laughed, "you would be exquisite morsels for these ladies who are accustomed only to the tough food of the desert!"

They were on one of the Haj routes now, that of the Mahgribin; at every few yards lay heaps of bones, of camels, horses and donkeys, and presently they saw also numerous rough graves of pilgrims who had died of exhaustion. One in particular was pointed out to Louis, that of a woman who had died here in labour—her baby had been carried on safely the whole way to Mecca and back to Cairo in good health.

On 1 September they had their initial wonderful view of the distant sea and, perhaps even more welcome, they came to good wells where Bedouin shepherds watering a large herd of camels obligingly made way for them to water also.

From these wells they turned off in the direction of Suez; again there was no trace of a road for a caravan's tracks were immediately filled up by the moving sands which extended all around, and were piled in immense wind-fluted dunes.

Two days later they sighted the Nile, sapphire-smooth between beautiful green shores darkly fertile amid the arid wastes.

After a ride of thirteen hours the Bedouin left Louis and Hamid on the lower slopes of Jebel Mokattam and, when they had ridden away with their loose-limbed camelry, he discharged his guide, paying him with the gold sequins which he took from the skirts of his gown, much to Hamid's astonishment. It was too

late in the evening to enter the city, so he went to some Bedouin
tents which he had seen from far off, and in one of them he tasted
for the first time the sweet water of the Nile. He stayed here with
these Bedouin for a few hours, and was away long before first light.

As he mounted to the edge of the Mokattam plateau the longed-
for moment arrived. Yet it is almost without warning that the
traveller looks down on Egypt—kindly it seems and in astonish-
ing contrast with that dreadful wilderness of Tyh, the "most
barren and horrid tract of country" Louis had ever beheld. Now
below Mokattam's scarp all was covered with water glinting in
the first light as morning mists began to rise from inundated
fields and isolated villages mirrored in the flood.

Dawn had not yet broken when Louis plunged into the
crowded city, its narrow lanes already beginning to fill with
peasants and soldiers, agile donkeys, strings of laden camels.
Almost penniless, ragged and grimy as he now was from the long
journey, Louis walked quite unremarked among the gathering
throng.

Cocks began crowing, first one or two echoing each other, then
all joining the dawn chorus. From many littered courtyards
tethered donkeys too began their prolonged and anguished
braying, their own peculiarly individual morning prayer. In
opposition a muezzin's call, as ecstatic as a seraph's cry, came floating out over squalid streets and suddenly the sun leapt up from
the eastern desert over the Nile. Although he could not see it the
blind muezzin standing on the minaret's balcony at once felt its
great warmth upon his exalted face. At once too the city became
painted with gold, its drab square-topped houses sprang to
life, sharp-drawn with vivid cobalt-blue shadows, every eastern
facet bright. The burning sun climbed in brilliance, sweeping away
before it the still visible violet shades of night lingering over the
huge expanse of western desert—whose terrifying wastes cover
nearly three-and-a-half million square miles of the globe.

It was 4 September. Louis walked into Cairo, safe and sound
"by the blessing of God". It had been a tremendous journey on a
route never before taken by any European, and, what is more, he
had traversed it in the blistering heat of high summer.

Egypt, it has been said, is a farm, and so it stands in striking contrast with the eternal pastoral landscape of Syria. To Louis now after those parched uplands, the scorifying wilderness of *Arabia Petraea* and the barren Tyh, the contrast was more especially marked since the inundation was at its height. The Nile waters islanded palm-clustered villages and monuments; minarets, trees and domes stood reflected, the whole of Egypt seemed water-borne, even the mountains of rubbish which then surrounded Cairo on almost every side were lapped by these welcome "tears of Isis". This precious flood: the annual inundation which for untold millennia has watered her fields, endowed them with richly fertile silt, and brought to her miraculous narrow lands, all hemmed in by desert, the lotus flower, fruits, corn and cotton, rice, maize, tamarisk and mimosa, paddy birds, pelicans, "cranes, kites and wild water-fowl".[1]

Only a few days before Louis' arrival the dam of the canal at Old Cairo had been cut so that the waters, having rushed through the great parched ditch that bisected the city, had flooded even the dust-bowl of the Ezbekiya Square, making it now a muddy lake.

Colonel Edward Missett, then British Consul General in Egypt, lived at Alexandria but he was expecting Sheik Ibrahim to arrive in Cairo, since Mr Barker had written from Aleppo to inform him of Louis' journey, and no doubt Sir Joseph Banks had also been in correspondence with him. Louis was hoping to receive letters, and monetary bills of exchange from the African Association, upon his arrival in Cairo, especially since he had only about two piastres on him after paying off the guide. He made his way first to the house of the English agent, a man named Aziz, to whom Colonel Missett would no doubt have forwarded instructions and letters.

Louis left no record of how he arrived at Aziz' house. But an English Member of Parliament, travelling in a light-hearted casual fashion, heard of the famous Burckhardt's arrival in the city and described the incident with interest. This account forms part of what is otherwise a somewhat garbled tale but since it is akin to the meeting with Bruce at Nazareth it has a sufficient ring of truth to be quotable, and it does paint a very likely picture of Louis in his dirty rags trying to gain admittance to officialdom on that early morning in Cairo.

> He presented himself in the guise of an Arab shepherd at the residence of the English agent at Cairo. He remained in the outer courtyard for some time, and it was with some difficulty he obtained an interview with M. Aziz, whose astonishment may easily be imagined when he heard a person of such appearance address him in French.[2]

The story goes no further, and Louis did not meet Colonel Missett at this time, but they were to become good friends. Missett was a man of cultivated mind and elegant manners, much esteemed by his fellow countrymen and other Europeans, and respected also by the Turks for his firm handling of any incident affecting British prestige. Tragically handicapped, since by the time he was forty he had become completely paralysed in every limb, he was before long debarred from every pleasurable pursuit, except the conversation and attentions of the friendly circle that gathered around him. He left Egypt for Italy towards the end of 1815 and died in Florence some five years later. The friendship that Louis came to have for him, at first through letters and later in person, was both warm and reciprocal; it is therefore a great loss that not a single letter has so far come to light of what was apparently a full and lively correspondence between the two men.

It so happened that at the moment of Louis' arrival, exhausted from the strenuous journey, a small caravan of Tuat men was on the point of returning from Cairo to their home, a central Saharan between Fezzan and Timbuctu, by precisely that route in which it was intended for him to start his travels towards the Niger.[3] Tempting though this chance must have been, it was clearly inadvisable for him to contemplate joining this caravan. He had no funds with which to buy equipment—nothing had yet arrived from the African Association—he would scarcely have had time to prepare himself, new as he was to this arena—the ways of the

Egyptian and African world were very different from those of the Syrian—and above all else it would have been more than rash to hurry off on so important an undertaking before he had fully recovered physically from the last journey. Indeed the over-hastiness of his predecessors was a constant warning. But, he wrote to the Committee, there would now be no opportunity of pro-ceeding by the road to Fezzan before the next year. Therefore he planned to use the time profitably to the cause of African geo-graphy by travelling further than any explorer had yet ventured up the Nile, into Nubia and Dongola, as soon as the canals dried up and land travel again became possible. Robert Bruce before him had made the desert crossing in his amazing search for the Nile's source, and W. G. Browne had penetrated Dongola, but further to the west. Some light-hearted adventurers soon took the less dangerous but very costly way of going up-river by boat above the First Cataract. No traveller had yet followed the great bend of the Nile, and it was these river banks and the as yet unknown antiquities that they undoubtedly concealed which Louis wanted to examine.

In the meantime, Colonel Missett arranged to lend him as much money as he needed until he should receive his salary from the Committee, and Louis rented a small house set pleasantly in a big garden; a rarity this, and to him an especial delight after the rigours of parched sands. He hired "a faithful servant from Upper Egypt", by name Shaharti, from Assiout, who remained with him until the end.

Although he distinctly preferred Syria, life was probably not unpleasant as Louis began to acclimatise himself to Cairo. Its flood waters, its complicated political scene, and its fascinating hotch-potch of peoples—from fiery Pasha, and lordly officials, to humble *fellahin* toiling in the fields as Egyptian peasants have since the days of the Pharaohs. But there is a distinct note of nostalgia in one of Louis' letters home at this time referring to a little journey his parents made to Geneva.

I would have loved to have accompanied you even if I had to run on foot behind the coach.

So he wrote, and went on to lament the contrast between the free and brave Swiss peasant and the deceitful and oppressed Egyptian *fellahin*.

My future joy will be not so much to leave the deserts and uncultivated lands and to see again the blossoming fields of Europe as to move again among people who do not despise honesty as stupid.

Bustling Cairo has long had a reputation among cities as a hotbed of all the vices—"that sink of iniquity" one good lady (Belzoni's brave English wife) called it at the time. Its narrow sandy lanes were milling with pedestrians, Arabs of all sorts, veiled women on painted and bedizened donkeys, half-naked, grubby fleet-footed urchins, swaggering Ottoman soldiery who barged through the throng with boastful indiscipline and sometimes with swords unsheathed. Most people who could afford it rode on donkeys, with a servant to help clear a passage—the lanes were so narrow, ten feet or even only four feet wide, and yet men rode by often at full gallop. One had to be constantly alert, not only to avoid the donkeys and the thrusting soldiery but also the swaying burdens of passing camels.

The lanes were deeply shaded by the houses whose jutting corbelled balconies almost touched overhead; here and there dusty sunbeams struggled through to fall in pools of light. Behind the delicately turned woodwork of latticed windows like birdcages there sat voluptuous ladies nibbling sweetmeats and sipping endless sherberts, increasing that pneumatic bliss so desirable in Egyptian harems. They bulged open at the bosom, filling the whole room with themselves and their smoke—for they loved their pipes as much as their sherberts of mulberry and liquorice, their jujubes, their cardamom-flavoured coffee, often fumed with ambergris or mastic. It must be admitted that many of these women were more enticing when veiled, for then only their eyes, their finest features, were revealed. Dark, bewitching kohl-lined eyes, so evocative of those of their ancient forebears, so wonderfully drawn around with antimony wetted by rose-

9. Ba'albek, by David Roberts

10 Approaching Nazareth, by David Roberts

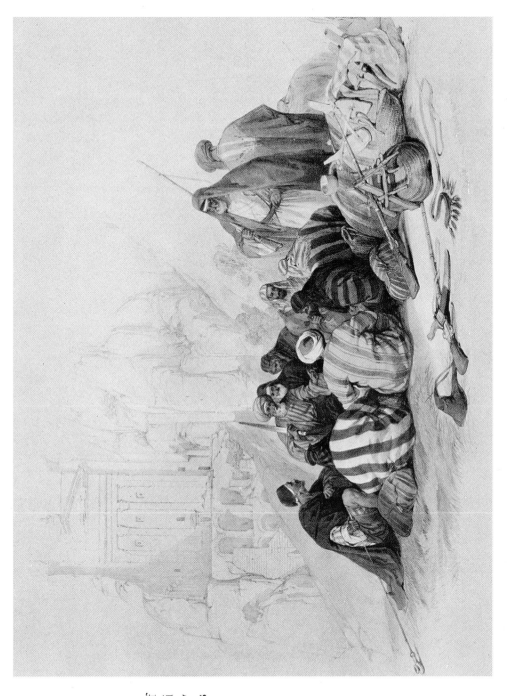

14. Group of
Arabs in Wadi
Musa, Petra, by
David Roberts

13. Approaching Petra, by W.H.Bartlett

12a. Wadi Diban, the Biblical "Brook Arnon", by Katharine Sim

12b. A part of Wadi Araba (the Rift) from above Dhana, by Katharine Sim

11. Jerash, by Katharine Sim

15. Rock-cut Nabataean houses, Petra, by Katharine Sim

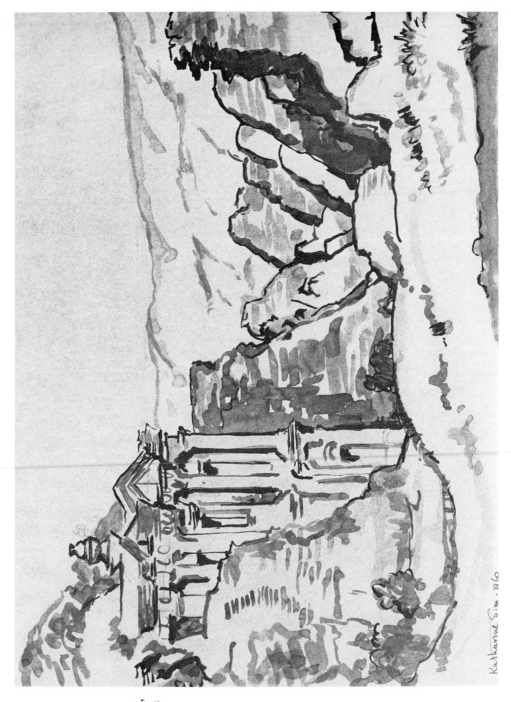

16. El Deir, Petra,
by Katharine Sim

water and sometimes mixed with ground sugar-candy or even with powdered pearls—no doubt to put a man in mind of the houris promised by the Koran, whose large dark eyes are "like pearls hidden in their shells". The veil was as flirtatious a weapon as the fan and would sometimes be lifted and moved aside as if by accident to allow a stranger to see a charming profile—if a girl was sufficiently sure of her own beauty.

Dancing and singing girls of course went unveiled; all in Louis' opinion were "strumpets". The *almeh* or singing girls were the slightly more respectable: of them one traveller wrote with distaste that nothing could possibly exceed the hoarse screaming of their voices, a mere repetition of amorous expressions without wit or feeling.[4] The so-called "belly-dancers", the *ghawazi*, danced in the streets in the costume of the harem open to reveal shapely breasts, their hennaed hands weaving lascivious gestures, and with that wonderfully sinuous movement that has been so aptly called libidinous motion of the loins—"heaven in the eye and in every gesture not dignity but love".[5] Sometimes they performed privately indoors for male parties when, amply primed with brandy, their abandonment culminated in raffish scenes of Petronian debauchery.

They are an extremely handsome people, said to belong to a tribe of their own. Their menfolk were employed by them in an inferior position as musicians and servants and, somewhat furtively, as husbands. They are perhaps descended from those very dancers who (as we know from the frescoes) in a state of complete nudity amused the earliest Pharaohs.[6]

There were also the *khawals*, some of whom can also be seen today in such places as "Sahara City", dark, effeminate young men in long skirts who perform the same kind of dances as the *ghawazi* with rather fallacious glee.

One of his Arab proverbs: "A decent public woman, rather than an indecent honest woman", leads Louis to write an interesting note on the *ghawazi* whom he describes as a nomadic tribe of prostitutes brought up to the trade, and goes on rather cynically to remark that they were not very numerous in Cairo because—"in a city where among women of every rank chastity is so scarce as at Cairo, it could not be expected that prostitution should thrive". A comment very clearly illuminating the social conditions of the time!

There was much to see: there was the river life, and that of the countryside and, of course, in the place where history began, the antiquities. The battered visage of the Sphinx by moonlight; the astounding view from the top of the Great Pyramid at dawn: mist dissolving over the flood waters, and the green demarkation line of the Nile's fertility lying in sharp juxtaposition with the very easternmost edge of those solemn Sahara sands—too huge almost to contemplate—for Louis an inspiration, a stimulating challenge belonging to the future. And, constant all the while, the swift waters of the great river coming from whence no one yet quite knew, pouring endlessly down through the deserts to the sea from the heart of Africa, from the semi-mythical Mountains of the Moon, 4,000 miles away.

In the evenings, after the sun had set in extravagantly flaming colours over the great desert, there was moonlight's metallic sheen silvering the palm fronds, and the sound of plaintive voices—Arabs singing to their tambourines. At night in the city the bazaars were lighted, especially at festival times, with innumerable little oil lamps; the small open shops were filled then with gaily dressed people sitting theatrically as if in illuminated boxes while coffee, sherbert and pipes were passed around

Other only too familiar sights in Cairo's narrow lanes were the bands of slaves, often young women in the bloom of life,

> . . . driven like cattle through the streets with merely a rag tied round their waists, the rest of the body being naked and exposed . . . while the boys in the street are pulling at, and calling to them as they pass, with impunity.[7]

So wrote one contemporary traveller; another wrote of the appalling odour of the slave market in Old Cairo and of the

> excessive state of filthiness in which these miserable wretches were compelled to exist. They were crowded together in

enclosures like the sheep-pens of Smithfield's market, and the abominable stench and uncleanliness which were the consequence of such confinement may be more readily imagined than described.[8]

Of the conditions of these poor creatures at the end of their long journey Louis does not bring himself to write, he must have known that many people had already done so. He was to witness at close quarters more than enough of their hardships and of the cruelty of their Arab slave masters, the traders, as he penetrated deeper into the south.

The slave trade was, of course, one of the oldest branches of all traffic in these lands. In the Sudan and southward from it, slave hunts were conducted periodically, and the pitiful captives marched northwards in large caravans. In fact, these Arab raiders continued their plundering up to very nearly the turn of the century. One Copt writer, whose job it had been to keep a register of slaves brought north to Cairo during a period of thirty years, affirmed that their number in general did not then exceed 4,000 over each single year.[9]

Always in search of books and rare manuscripts, Louis soon acquainted himself with the Mosque of El Azhar—"the most blooming". Created a university in the tenth century, it was considered the most important seat of learning in all Islam, and it was famous for the relief of poor travellers. Here Louis found men from Upper Egypt, and from countries as far apart as Morocco and India; Persians, Kurds, Anatolians, Afghans, Abyssinians, Syrians, Yemenis. Each people had its own separate establishment, called the *rouak*, over which one of the principal ulemas of Cairo presided, and these, Louis says, "with the ulema of El Azhar formed a body powerful enough to make Pashas tremble".[10]

Among the people whom Louis came to know in the city was a sheik in whose commonplace book he found a loose sheaf of papers—a collection of Arab proverbs made early in the eighteenth century by Sheref ed-din Ibn Asad. These formed the nucleus of the collection which in his spare time Louis set about editing and explaining. Unfortunately, he felt bound to omit from the book that resulted a considerable number so "grossly indelicate" that he could not venture to lay them before the public, "although it must be acknowledged that they excelled in wit". He also added to the collection many hundreds which he jotted down as he heard them in house or bazaar in the course of general conversation. In this work, which occupied some years in intervals between his journeys and his other writing, he was helped by many intelligent Arabs of Cairo; the book was finished early in 1817.

> To the good luck of the wedding festivities the night was short, and the female singers became penitents.

As Louis wrote these words—an ironical saying indicating a wedding that was far from successful—it so happened that the whole quarter of the city in which he then lived was webbed and caught in long filaments of light—hundreds of tiny oil lamps lit for the night before the consummation of a local marriage. Men dressed up in odd clothes were dancing and fooling in front of the groom's house; great gusts of laughter followed their clowning for they were taking off, as is a custom in Muslim countries, the unintentionally comic ways men of other nations have in speaking Arabic—there were mock French, mock Turks, and so on.

Louis had seen many nuptial processions of peasants and of people in high office at the Pasha's court, and had come to know not only the details of the public processions but also those of the more intimate ceremonies performed on these occasions. Lane writes that knowledge of such customs was easier to come by than one might think:

> for a person who has become familiar with male Muslim society in Cairo, without marrying, it is not so difficult to obtain, directly and indirectly, correct and ample information respecting the condition and habits of the women. Many husbands of the middle classes, and some of the higher orders, talk freely of the the affairs of the harem with one who professes to agree

with them in their general moral sentiments, if they do not have to converse through the medium of an interpreter.[11]

It is interesting to compare Louis' accounts with Lane's: Lane refers several times to Burckhardt's, and is also inclined to skate over some of the practices which Louis could scarcely bring himself to describe. In Lane's day an interesting if crude relic of the past was dying out of nuptial processions: one gathers that he did not witness this spectacle of so "singular" and "disgusting" a nature, but he does discreetly refer his reader to Louis' account of it, for Louis had often seen this startling masked figure parading somewhat obscenely in the forefront of peasant wedding processions:

> . . . a young man whose head, arms, legs and entire body are patched over with white cotton so that no part of the skin can be perceived . . . as if completely powdered over. He exhibits in the natural position that object which constituted the distinguishing attribute of the ancient Roman god of the gardens; this is of enormous proportion, two feet in length covered in cotton; and he displays it with indecent gesticulation in all the bazaars before the staring multitude, and during the whole procession. How this custom which is not known in other places began among the Egyptians, I am unable to ascertain; but it seems not improbably some remnant of the worship paid by their forefathers to that God whose temple at Karnak is the most considerable now existing in Egypt.[12]

One is often prompted to wish that Louis could have lived in Egypt after the deciphering of the hieroglyphics. The great majesty of that ubiquitous fertility god, Min, which Louis had seen as a priapic deity on the columns of Karnak, is vastly impressive despite its careless indecency. Louis was quick to recognise his crude descendants here in the streets of Cairo, his connecting the phallic Min with these common wedding processions welds another human link in time. It is one of those small but illuminating exercises of the mind that, by uniting us so humanly with the remote past, seem to lengthen out our own existence.

One feels that Louis would have been glad to know how right he was about this sociological and historical detail.

After the Night of the Henna there followed the Night of the Entrance, when at last the bride unveiled and her groom had to convince himself of her virginity. Lane again refers us on this subject to Louis, although he says that his account might have been more complete. However, the mode in which this ceremony was performed Louis found "sometimes so repugnant to manly feelings" that in his official journal he could bring himself to write of it only in Arabic. In those days the cutting away and sewing up of Arab women's private parts was new and horrifying knowledge to the West. In his rough notes, Louis writes in a graphically shaken hand of "agonisingly joined up flesh . . . opened at the time of matrimony in proportion to the husband's . . ."[13]

Freud said that it is impossible for us to understand the past with certainty because we cannot divine men's motives, nor the essence of their minds, in order to interpret their actions. And so it is with Louis' own private life—one often has cause to wonder since he reveals nothing of it; few letters to friends remain; one does hint with some exuberance at a passing affair. There are Lady Hester's written aspersions about his sex-life in Cairo, but then she was a jealous old woman in every way, and not particularly well-informed either. She was probably quite unaware that it was impossible for a man to live *as a Muslim* at that time in a private house in Cairo unless he was married, or unless he owned a female slave. Lane makes this very clear.[14]

It is quite obvious that while he was exploring, while he was actually on the road, any kind of private life that Louis had virtually ceased to exist, he was far too busy keeping alive among numerous besetting dangers. But, in all honesty, one has to wonder as to those long stretches of boredom spent waiting for caravans between strenuous journeys. These times must have been especially taxing for so virile a man, possessed as Louis was of inexhaustible energies both mental and physical. There was of course the usual *conventional* morality of the age; however, it seems clear that whatever affairs he may perhaps have indulged in were of a fleeting nature only. He was certainly no prude: although sensitive in matters of sex; the orgies which he was forced to witness later frankly sickened him as they would any decent human being.

As regards chaste women he was idealistic and hard to please— he sought beauty, refinement, learning and the social charms, and said later that it might well be better to remain a bachelor than to make an unhappy marriage. He believed that "a happy marriage is the most beautiful flower that a man can gather for his own pleasure",[15] and said that for himself he had no greater desire than to be a happy family man one day. There remained before him always the thought of his return, the hope of marriage, of children of his own to be brought up among those smiling ancestral orchards. But he had to admit that among all the hundreds of girls and women whom he had met in various countries there were, when he thought it over rationally, only very few with whom he might have expected to lead a happy life, and he was later to admit that he was becoming doubtful if he would ever try his luck in that "lottery which contains so few good numbers". He began even to conclude that the oriental mode of arranged marriage made sense; since it was impossible to meet a young girl of good family in Cairo one could not choose for oneself; it would seem that there was some truth in the saying that marriages made without love often endured better in the long run than those based on the attraction of physical beauty.

His mission once accomplished, he might very likely have married on his return to Europe, when his travel journals would be bringing him some wealth, and his achievements that fame which he did not want until he himself could count it well earned. This could have happened, but again one wonders whether it would have been possible for him after the experiences of such journeys to settle anywhere for any length of time. He had a strong natural love of pleasure—which, as we know, he fought against. In him too the balancing love of action was indeed powerful, in manhood well disciplined by ability and foresight, but it could have made him restless.

Of the people Louis met in Cairo a few names repeatedly occur. There was Bosari, Mohammed Ali's personal physician, whom

Louis came to know well, an Armenian who spoke Italian and Arabic; and Boghoz Bey, Mohammed Ali's favourite minister. Boghoz, a liberal-minded and agreeable man, an Armenian too, had not always found favour in the Pasha's eyes, and the story of his narrow escape from the capricious despot's wrath was widely known. Not long before he had been put in a sack by Mohammed Ali's order and was about to be flung into the Nile when some influential Turkish friend appeared and managed to delay the procedure until he had spoken to the Pasha. He interceded successfully and saved Boghoz' life.[16]

Boghoz kept a well-furnished house, a good cuisine, and all the comforts of the Levant. Louis quite frequently went to supper with him. For some reason Lady Hester had a very high opinion of Boghoz. But she denied that he was an Armenian: "although he says he is—his mother was, and so was his ostensible father, a rich merchant;—but I have found out his real father." Typically she forgot the name of this man but declared him to be a Turkish Aga who had paid clandestine calls upon the lady in question, and that Boghoz was one of the fruits of these visits.[17]

At about this time, perhaps in Boghoz' or Aziz' house, Louis now encountered two Englishmen, self-styled idle and curious, a couple of adventurous if brash tourists who seemed to have slipped so far off the beaten track more by luck than design. They were Smelt and Legh. Thomas Legh, M.P., prefaces his "Narrative" with a revealing explanation of how he and his friend came to be in such outlandish parts.

At a period when political circumstances had closed the ordinary route of continental travelling, and when the restless characteristic propensity of the English could only be gratified by exploring the distant countries of the East, an entirely new direction was given to the pursuits of the idle and the curious. A visit to Athens or to Constantinople supplied the place of a gay and dissipated Winter passed in Paris, Vienna, or Petersburgh; and the Traveller was left to imagine, and perhaps to regret, the pleasures of the modern cities of civilised Europe, amidst the monuments of the ruined capitals of antiquity.[18]

Such was the remarkably casual approach of such people to Egypt, who were vastly tickled to find themselves where:

> the *Camel*, the *Firman*, and the *Tartar* were substituted for the ordinary facilities of the *Poste*, the *Passports*, and the *Couriers* of the beaten roads of Italy or France.

Arrived at Alexandria they were armed by Colonel Missett with letters of introduction to various people in Cairo, among them Sheik Ibrahim—"a very intelligent traveller" who later gave them great assistance and much valuable information. What is interesting is that they had no idea of his real identity, and it was not until after they had returned home to England that they discovered who it was they had met.[19]

Of the important men of whom Louis would constantly have heard at this time, although some of them were absent from Egypt were Mohammed Ali's sons, Ibrahim and Tousun. Ibrahim, Pasha of Three Tails, known as "Lion of the Brave", whom he did meet, had recently been sent to chase the Mamluks from Nubia. He had clear blue eyes and a fair beard, was stalwart and powerfully built, possessed so abundant an energy that he was able to resist the fatigues of pleasure and of war alike; he was successful, young, and had that rare combination of courage and prudence—a man after Louis' own heart, one would think—but he was definitely cruel. Tousun, although he had shown great courage in the Mamluk war, was not so successful, but then he had been only eighteen when sent by his father on the first expedition to Arabia against the Wahabis. With him also had gone Ahmed Aga, Mohammed Ali's treasurer, or *Kheznedar*, a good councillor and a brave man. Of him Louis writes:

> His butcherly achievements in the wars against the Mamluks and the Arabs in Egypt had exalted him in the eyes of his master; his utter disregard of human life, his contempt for all moral principles and his idle boasting had procured for him the surname of *Bonaparte*, which afforded him much delight, and by which he was universally designated in Egypt.

His depravity, however, eventually cost him his reason.[20]

These are a few of the names which occur in the political background to Louis' story of those Cairo years, a scene that was of course dominated by Mohammed Ali. It is curious that the first seeds of Egyptian nationalism should have begun with the rise to power of this fiery foreigner, the Albanian who was to be the maker of modern Egypt.

In the Middle Ages the Arabs had been the masters. The collapse of their civilisation occurred some five centuries after its zenith with the Turkish capture of Cairo in 1517. Today some seventy million people speak Arabic, and the Muslim world numbers 350 million.

Despite early Arab mastery it was men of that unique race, the Mamluks, who reigned in Cairo from the middle of the thirteenth century until Osman Sultan Selim I of Constantinople took the city by storm, and Egypt became a Turkish Pashalik. Even then Osmanli authority soon waned and the Mamluks insinuated themselves once more into power, a power that was not broken until the first hint of nationalism appeared in reaction to the French occupation of 1798.

When the French capitulated to the British in 1801, Mohammed Ali began his ascent to power. But it was not until he ousted the Mamluks finally by his dramatic and bloody coup enacted on the heights of the Citadel on 1 March 1811 that those first early seeds of nationalism began to grow and were fostered, to develop a general Arab consciousness that was to culminate in the Arab League of this century.

Mohammed Ali was no Arab, and yet it was under him that Arab feeling intensified and coalesced throughout the whole Middle East. Indeed the aim of an Arab empire was his conception and that of his son, Ibrahim Pasha. In fact Ali's sons were more "Arab" than their father—Ibrahim especially tried to identify himself with them.[21]

Ali really climbed into power in Egypt after the unfortunate British campaign of 1807 made on the advice of Missett who, at that time, mistakenly backed the Mamluks. Mohammed Ali used these "miserable Egyptians chiefs", as he called them, as his tools, first one way and then another until he finally got rid of them. In 1810, when he was still only precariously in power, their presence in Cairo was an embarrassment to him. The Sublime Porte had repeatedly called upon him to lead an expedition against the Wahabis in the Hijaz but with the Mamluk Beys presenting a threat to his growing power in Egypt he could ill afford to leave. This was the dilemma which he ultimately solved by the massacre at the Citadel after which the remnants of the Mamluks fled into Nubia to make themselves, though only briefly, masters of the fortress of Ibrim.

Louis saw Mohammed Ali as "a man of great spirit and energy" and thought that if he were to succeed in Arabia against the Wahabis he might well prove to be a second Napoleon, and he would have in his favour that advantage which Bonaparte had not enjoyed—the backing of all "the church", that is Islam. Louis considered Ali was much more intelligent and better than most Pashas, but thought that he had "not the faintest idea of how to administer a country in a healthy way". It does not seem in the least unreasonable that the situation provoked Louis to say: "If Egypt were governed by Europeans one could make a real paradise of it"—a view common to most nineteenth-century Europeans, and applied of course to many other countries besides Egypt.

One English traveller described Ali as having "a vulgar low-born face, but a commanding intelligent eye".[22] Ali, illiterate son of an Albanian peasant, was well aware of his own short-comings. Having risen abruptly from banditry and tobacco dealing in his own Kavalla to the position of modern Pharaoh, and to what Dodwell[23] neatly calls "that life of high crime which in the East stood for politics", he strove hard to modernise Egypt. He was a great believer in the European innovations of the day: he certainly did galvanise the country into new life, and justified for himself the name "maker of modern Egypt".[24] He was extremely proud of the fact that he was of the same age as Bonaparte; there is no doubt that he liked to see himself in much the same light, and although quite unscrupulous he was a great man.

In the Middle Ages it was said that whoever was lord of Cairo might call himself lord and master of Christendom. In Saladin's day perhaps, but in these later times that was not Mohammed Ali's dream—his wish was to overcome the Ottoman Empire. He had long coveted the three Pashaliks of Syria which, under their corrupt governments, were ripe to fall.

In Cairo deadly feuds had been waged between Turkish and Arnaut (Albanian) troops; constant, almost daily street battles, violence and bloodshed were the rule. With his rise to power Ali had soon put an end to these internecine problems among the soldiery by uniting them against the Mamluks, the hated slave-race who had lorded it in Egypt for centuries and bullied the *fellahin* unmercifully.

It was in the disastrous Sixth Crusade that the Mamluk body-guard first showed their true paces, murdered their Aiyubid leader and were raised to the Sultanate throne. Cruel and oppressive at home, triumphant abroad, the Mamluks were indeed an extra-ordinary people—white slaves metamorphosed into sultans. It has often been said that they did not propagate readily in a foreign country, and that this was the reason or, as Lane puts it, *partly* the reason why this curious dynasty of slave-kings continued to import an endless succession of young white slaves to keep up their stock. It seems strange that a lusty and turbulent people should not be able to produce sturdy offspring wherever they lived, but conditions were not easy for white infants of pure stock. At any rate, the dynasty was not hereditary: they continued to buy and train other slaves so that every man in this complex pattern of a militant society knew the common experience of slavery, and any freed trooper of one year might be Emir of the next. So the Mamluks struggled among themselves throughout the centuries, fighting their way to power. Consequently violent deaths and bloody street battles were commonplace events.*

So it grew: a ruthless, soulless military structure dominating the state and the life of a hapless people—a regime toppled at last by Mohammed Ali's massacre. Adjudged brutal as the slaughter

---

* It is interesting that Alan Moorehead compares the Mamluks with that privileged priesthood, the *Arioi* of Tahiti, who practised infanticide to keep their stock rare and pure.

was, it did free Egypt from the stranglehold of her strange oppressors.

The coup was contrived by a ruse: the Pasha summoned a great number of the Mamluk cavalry to the Citadel that March day to witness the investiture of his son, who was about to lead a force against the Wahabis. From an eye-witness account the story runs that after coffee and pipes had been brought, two sets of gates at the Citadel were closed upon the horsemen so that they were caught in the narrow defile like mice in a trap. Then, as they mounted to leave, not realising they were trapped, Ali's men opened fire from every quarter. It was a scene of terrible confusion, dismay and horror, and wildly rearing horses—victims dropped by the hundreds, the narrow way ran with blood. Only one Bey escaped the carnage by leaping his horse from the ramparts over the precipice; the horse was killed but the rider escaped by hiding in the tent of an Albanian soldier in an encampment nearby. Several hundred cavalry were massacred.[25]

It was said that the great Pasha always knew when to cajole, when to threaten, when to strike, and that his caresses had something of the terrifying velvet of the tiger's paws;[26] his blows were certainly lethal. But Missett, at about this time, said that the Pasha had by his methods of severity at least made personal safety possible for people in the streets of Cairo, and this alone was a remarkable achievement in a milling city of a thousand narrow streets, where at night each separate quarter had to be locked and guarded.

As Pasha of Egypt Mohammed Ali had taken over a derelict government; Dodwell writes:

> It would be difficult to exaggerate the wretched conditions of the Turkish provinces at the beginning of the nineteenth century. An honest governor, as Burckhardt said with perfect truth, could not long hope to hold office.

Louis had already grasped this fact in Syria—from what he had seen of the machinations of the local rulers—and he knew that the problem confronting every Pasha was either to fulfil the demands of the Sublime Porte and resign himself to being a despot, or to declare himself a rebel. Somehow, Mohammed Ali contrived, as he put it himself, to have "a foot in either stirrup".[27]

He was a despot; indeed it was expected of him (his own rebellion against the Porte was to come later): he lived among people who expected and who even desired nothing more than a despot as ruler. He himself said that Egypt was barbarous: "really barbarous, utterly barbarous and barbarous it remains to this day". And yet he had hopes that his efforts were helping to render conditions somewhat better.

All who met him seemed to have formed much the same opinion that, without possessing even the rudiments of education, his natural talents were indeed great.

He was a politician of the school of Machiavel, complete master of dissimulation . . . cool and designing he found himself in a country presenting a fair field for his ambition which he determined to push to the utmost.[28]

The Englishman who wrote those words had the acute eye of an artist and he left a description of a scene in the diwan of the Citadel when the Kahya Bey, or Prime Minister, was examining some black slaves; a word-picture typical of the day. The grouping and composition of the whole were admirably theatrical, like a colourful tapestry, sumptuous with rich and varied dresses, war-like attendants standing in mute and deferential attention; the proud superiority of the Bey was impressive—around him lesser officials seemed to crouch in abject submission as glittering but minor stars encircling a brilliant planet. Fascinating, but barbaric too, since these were people who lived only by the breath of the Bey who, in his turn must observe just the same kind of abject submission to the will of the Pasha; so, likewise, the four million inhabitants of Egypt felt the influence of a single despot.

This then was the situation existing in Egypt at the time of Louis' arrival there in 1812. The Pasha's son, Ibrahim, had already hounded the last of the Mamluks from their barren retreat of Qasr Ibrim—the Roman *Primis* beyond the First Cataract, and chased them deep into Dongola. Dongola: that unmapped and dangerous territory into which Louis proposed to venture next— far up the Nile, by land, and alone.

# CHAPTER EIGHT

## South through Nubia

Come to the cataracts my love and you shall be clothed in
Cashmere, Nubia is the land of roses.

*Ancient Nubian Song*

IN LOUIS' DAY most of the celebrated Egyptian temples of the
Nile valley remained choked in sand and the refuse of ages. A
sordid jumble of Arab mud hovels sprawled over their roof-tops,
while donkeys, goats, pariah dogs and scavenging hens cluttered
all accessible parts of their courtyards. Sombre sanctuaries reeked,
immense grandiose hypostyle halls were filthy—often blackened
by the making of gunpowder from urine-saturated muck.

At Edfu, for instance, rubbish mounds reached to the tops of
the walls of the perfect Ptolemaic temple to Horus, and much of
the massive roofs was covered with houses and stables. It was the
same story at Hathor's exquisite temple of love at Denderah, and
at Kom Ombus too, where the beautiful crocodile shrine of warm
burnt-ochreous stone now towers monumentally free from the
pale sands that once enveloped it. The clearing of the temple at
Luxor was not begun until as late as 1883: before then its courts
and chambers were almost completely submerged under the
congestion of centuries of mud and garbage upon which an entire
Arab village had been built. Today, the old mosque which served
this vanished village has been left twenty feet up perched upon
the great pillars of Ammun. It is still in use, and curiously enough
keeps alive an ancient Egyptian boat festival, the midsummer
festival of Opet in Muslim guise.[29]

The Egyptian winter—a delicious time of golden skies and
moderate temperatures, and when the floods subsided in January
Louis and Shaharti set out, riding their donkeys south to Aswan.

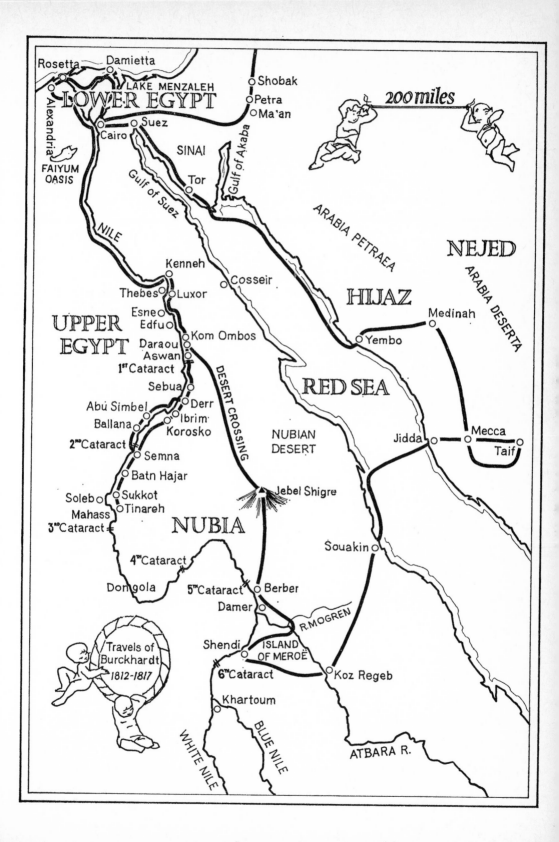

Nubia, Louis heard, was then in a fairly tranquil state and had it not been for the uneasy presence of the fiercely treacherous Mamluks somewhere in Dongola Louis might have penetrated still further. However, he was aware that these stop-gap journeys would help him to know something of the character of the Negro peoples and of the men who trafficked in slaves, and so facilitate his later travels to the interior of the continent. He intended the two Nubian journeys to take about five months, with a possible lateral excursion to the east on the old trade route towards the Red Sea. He expected to be back in Cairo to join the caravan for Fezzan in the June of 1813, but no caravan came, and none was to come through—until late in 1817.

The two men rode on in the sunshine along the fertile stretches of the Egyptian Nile closely flanked by desert—those constant golden-arid sands that hemmed in the narrow verdant strips. It was a peaceful scene: the jade of winter wheat, the glaucous green of clustered date-palms; here and there a small white mosque gleaming in the sunlight, a grave or two beside; reddish fruit showed dark on Sudan palm, the white sail of a *dahabeyah*, brilliant as an egret's wing stood out against the river's vivid blue. *Fellahin* worked in the fields harvesting the sugar-cane, or laboriously hoisting water to spring crops by the angular weighted contraption of their ancestral *shaduf*. Sometimes the only sound would be the hoarse yet soothing murmur of the Persian wheels or *saqiya*, the wistful cry of a kite overhead, and in places the only movement a heron fishing, a string of people on small donkeys silhouetted as a living frieze, or a single-file procession of black-veiled women going down to the river, statuesque with their Keneh water-jars poised high on their heads. Occasionally a few white-robed men on camels rode up the side of a pale bluff into the parched eastward hills, and there was always, at times close, at others a little distant according to the curving of the road, the vivid lapis-lazuli of the Nile's smooth, life-giving flow.

In Upper Egypt, at Esne, Louis halted for a week, to sell his two donkeys and buy a couple of fine dromedaries—light riding camels —which proved themselves splendid beasts, and here he collected a good deal of useful information concerning the present state of

Nubia. It seemed easy enough to obtain guides but no man was willing to risk his own animal on so hazardous a journey. In addition to the firmans he already held from the Pasha and his son, Ibrahim, Louis now acquired a letter of recommendation from the Turkish governor of Esne, a Cypriot, Hassan Bey, addressed to the farouche brother Kashifs, who were then lords of Nubia and to whom Louis would have to present himself in order to traverse their somewhat wildly governed territory.

It was an easy four days' journey from Esne to the First Cataract. At Aswan Louis left his servant and baggage, divested himself of his good Turkish-style clothes, and hired an old Nubian guide who agreed to take him the 140 miles to Derr, for the price of one Spanish dollar. At Derr Louis would have to rely on the Nubian Kashif to obtain him a new guide.

He must have known a great sense of exhilaration when he left romantically pretty little Aswan—from time immemorial the Gateway to the South—and began the ride into barren Nubia. The whole feeling of this Nubian journey is one of exhilaration: it was relatively brief, concentrated and dangerous. In thirty-five days of hard riding he took only a single half-day of so-called rest, and he covered on both banks of the Nile about 900 miles, all south of Derr completely unexplored territory.

Nubia: the very word has a splendid ring about it (it is said to be derived from *nub*, the gold of the ancients)—a country of golden sand, black hills, white painted houses, a land of unlikely roses. Just as cashmere indicates bridal dress, so the roses, occurring in the songs, signify affection and romance in Nubian hearts, for roses could not grow here, but there is—or was before the huge new lake Nasser covered so much of it—great wonder and austere beauty in Nubia.

About 5,000 years ago, in the archaic period, some brave Egyptians under King Djer penetrated south of the First Cataract, that natural frontier, into the Land of Ghosts,[30] ancient Kush, a part of Nubia. Remote, desolate but beautiful, it was a frightening place, the end of the world, a land of the dead. But gradually, as the centuries wore on and the Egyptians began pressing further in from the north and later the Kushites likewise, probably from the

west, frontiers receded; fortresses and temples were built. Later
still, with the decline of Egypt, that is at about the same time as the
fall of Troy, the great fortresses and shrines began to be neglected
and soon the sands crept in. Nubia then became once again the
Land of the Ghosts beyond the Gateway to the south, while
through it all the mighty Nile, flowed on eternally, impervious,
changeless, miraculous-seeming, from its far-distant mysterious
source.

After the Roman period in Egypt, when Coptic cenobites and
anchorites, those "athletes of God", spread into Nubia, much of
the land became Christian and remained so for nearly a thousand
years until the Muslim invasions destroyed the churches. There
was also during the Christian period an enigmatic civilisation, that
of the recently discovered "X—people".

Until that year, 1813, very few travellers had penetrated at all
into Nubia: Norden, the Dane, had been forced to stop at Derr in
1737. Pococke, Denon, and Hamilton had gone no further than
Philae. So now, some 500 years after the Muslims, it was once
again Louis who led the way[31] into this historical twilight—a
lonely traveller, destined to return with news of many wonders
then laying hidden or forgotten in this vast open-air "museum".

When he later dispatched his account of this journey to the
African Association he apologised in a covering letter to Sir
Joseph[32] for the rough manner in which it was written, graphically
explaining the reason. The original notes had been jotted down
when and where possible—in some wretched courtyard, against
the side of his camel, in the searing dust-laden misery of a hot
khamsin, always in secret, and sometimes while suffering acutely
the anguish of ophthalmia. Nevertheless, the journal that emerged
from these notes is a vivid part of the full Nubian account which
was to evoke high praise in London and Edinburgh, and was
hailed in glowing terms. The remarkable achievements of "this
extraordinary man", wrote one reviewer, his endurance and his
courage showed him to be a traveller of no common description.
"His simple and unstudied narrative", though never briskly
personal as that of Burton, nor couched in sculptured prose as
Doughty's, did recall to all who knew him that:

easy, cheerful and unruffled mind, that evenness of temper which he displayed in social life, and which neither fatigues nor the privations nor the insults to which he was so frequently exposed in his long and arduous journies could for a moment unsettle or disturb. . . . When the object was the acquirement of knowledge and a duty to his employers nothing was too dreadful for his endurance.[33]

On this journey Louis carried only his gun, sabre, pistols and provision bag, and had with him only the Arab clothes in which he now stood up—the common coarse *jalabiyyah*, a red *melaye*, or plaid, and a Mahgribin woollen *thabout* that was to serve both as carpet and covering.

There was no way for their camels by the river on the eastern bank near Philae, so he and his guide rode up over the mountain— about where the new Dam is now. How amazed he would have been to see this quiet, stony mountainside 150 years on, when it was the scene of ceaseless activity, a Dantesque inferno on a gigantic scale—men toiling like ants among roaring machines, blasted rock, shuddering stone in a turmoil of dust—and with a death toll rising to hundreds. But in that prescient silence of the nineteenth century the two men went quietly on their lonely way, riding south to the Tropic of Cancer into the unsullied gold and black and ochreous landscape that had slept for centuries under its immense, cloudless blue sky.

Only where the great Nile glided endlessly northwards was there a thin ribbon of life in this wilderness, a restricted thread of green. In these narrow cultivations strung out along the river's banks, the Nubians built their little houses castellated like small forts, but whitewashed and brightly painted with odd symbolic designs of ancient origin. These peasants have always loved their country, barren though it was, but so that Egypt may live they have lost for ever their ancestral painted homes now drowned with their fields under Nasser's huge lake.

The changes that have come to this land are so drastic and so recent that Louis' dangerous ride, seen in perspective, appears as if it were considerably more than a mere century and a half ago.

Curiously enough, it seems nearer in time and character to the days of those Greek and Carian mercenaries who stared in wonder at long deserted temples and carved their names upon the stones.

That first evening, as the flaming ball of the sun dropped behind the hills of the western desert, the air cooled rapidly, a gentle breeze caressed the skin. Suddenly the eastern hills flared in the afterglow, while the opposite side loomed sharp-drawn against a sky fading swiftly through dove-rose to violet. The Nile, changed briefly to a glassy lemon-yellow, ran powerfully on, oily between arid hills, and in the darkening sky a bone-white moon slowly grew luminous.

They spent that night in a small village where Louis first tasted that "dish of the country" which was to become his staple diet: thin, unleavened and slightly baked cakes of durra served with sweet or sour milk. Since the durra (or millet) was badly ground the fare was coarse, and nothing, Louis says, but absolute hunger would have induced him to eat it.[34]

They rode on towards Derr at speed: passing above the dark shining rocks of Bab el Kalabsha—the wild gateway of the river —and sleeping at night close to the foaming water.

Nubian nights are brilliant, scintillating with stars in a limitless sky. The early mornings are golden; the sun leaping up above swarthy eastern hills brightens with its swift fire each sweeping curve of flushed red sand. In the calm unruffled light of day the speeding water, innocently cerulean blue reflecting the bright sky, is shot through with gold and mirrors too the desert's tawny colours. Here and there on a sunlit scarp straggling lines of black goats stand out like drops of jet. A few women, dark caryatids, walk down to the river's brink, while far away on untouched distant sands some camels, dwarfed in the vast landscape, move slowly towards a huge horizon.

The Nubians, in their fertile strips, greeted the travellers' approach with an explosive but harmless curiosity. Louis found them delightful people, who certainly lived up to their reputation for honesty—he slept almost every night in the open outside their houses and never once was robbed—but their curiosity was quite insatiable. He thought their women slender and charming with "sweet countenances and very pleasing manners"; they were also extremely moral, which struck him as surprising since they lived so relatively close to Egypt, where "licentiousness knew no bounds".

He was amused to notice that the size and girth of the average peasant farmer varied exactly in accordance with the width of his stretch of fertile land; were it broad he was tall and strong, were it narrow he was sometimes little better than a walking skeleton. Along the wider strips the painted houses were clean and pleasant, graced with mimosa, palm and senna trees. In little bunded fields ox-drawn water-wheels creaked incessantly, while beyond—in the contrasting sunbaked hills—tawny gazelles roamed freely, brown as the sand itself, bounding from rock to rock, beautiful with all the charm of their own peculiarly delicate agility.

With an appealing simplicity Louis records the birds he saw, and some that he ate:

> . . . a small species of partridge with red legs that sometimes afforded me a welcome supper; wild geese of the largest kind, a few storks, the eagle Rakham, crows in vast numbers, the bird katta,\* but in small flights, and clouds of sparrows, which are the terror of the Nubians as they devour at least one-third of the harvest.

He also liked what he took to be a species of lapwing, and when he saw it displaying its crest he thought that he recognised it from the hieroglyphs. This was probably the elegant, lovable hoopoe: a small bird that struts and bows enchantingly in the gardens of Upper Egypt or on the sandy forecourt of some great Nubian temple, flaunting its lovely cinnamon-coloured crest which, according to legend, was given it by Solomon in place of a gift rewarding some service—a tiny golden crown which soon burdened the little hoopoe.[35]

The myriads of beetles toiling over the sands also fascinated Louis—scarabaei of all shapes and sizes. Unlike the ancient Egyptians, who venerated them as the essence of life itself, the

\* Another type of partridge which he had seen often in Syria.

Nubians loathed them, believing they poisoned all they touched. W. Hamilton, secretary of the African Association, had an interesting theory concerning the scarab and the Cancer sign in connection with the famous Denderah zodiac. He suggests that the zodiacal sign is not the crab at all, but the scarab beetle, inadvertently switched by the Greeks.[36]

Louis soon realised that he had nothing to fear from the inquisitive peasants but there were many other dangers, among which perhaps the ruthless brother Kashifs were the worst. The first of them whom Louis met was Daoud, a large dignified man, not as truculent as other members of his family, whose cussedness and bombast seemed to increase the further south one travelled. These men, all tall, handsome and fairer than most Nubians, were said to be descended from the Bosnian soldiers sent by Sultan Selim to garrison Qasr Ibrim some 300 years earlier when Egypt became a Turkish Pashalik.

Near Derr, later, Louis witnessed an incident typical of their cruel acts of despotism, and was thoroughly sickened by the cold and jealous man who perpetrated it—Hassan Kashif. He watched the Kashif, accompanied by thirty or so slaves and attendants, stride over a large field planted with ripening barley. The wrong crop, Hassan told its owner roughly—water-melons would have been better; and taking a handful of melon seed from his pocket, he commanded the peasant to uproot the barley and plant these instead. The man begged to be excused since the crop was almost ripe. Hassan merely laughed: he would sow it himself then! At once his men began to tear out the barley and to prepare the field for the melon seed. Hassan's boat was loaded with barley, and a family reduced to misery in order that the Kashif might feed his horses and camels for three days on the stalks . . .

Below the Tropic of Cancer Louis was riding in the wake of battle and the wholesale destruction that had followed the Mamluk's defeat. In all this pillaged land—where evidence of recent death and famine lay everywhere—he might have expected to meet hardly a soul, except the dreaded brother Kashifs, and the few Nubian peasant survivors of the recent holocaust of war and starvation. But, surprisingly enough, there was a nervous

Greek who was supposed to be prospecting for gold in the Alaqui Mountains with an armed guard from Esne. There was the constant threat of sporadic robbers—the murderous Alaqui—as well as the ever-haunting existence of desperate Mamluks, those shadowy but ferocious figures who were liable to cut off his head, like as not, at any chance encounter. Once there was the distant sight of a slave caravan from Mahass passing along the western bank, and there was also the surprising appearance of a young girl who sought protection for a later brief part of the journey. There were chocolate-brown women carrying plates on their heads walking to funeral feasts, glass bracelets glinting in the sun, copper anklets gleaming on slim dark legs, white teeth flashing smiles of pleasure. These funeral feasts with proffered roast meats were very tempting to hungry, hard-riding men, and so also were the many pressing invitations to breakfast.

But resisting all these, and ignoring too the Greek gold-seeker's frantic warnings of Mamluk riders, Louis hurried on, travelling boldly along the rocky shore under brilliant skies. One day he met again those two casual holiday-makers, surely the very first of Nubia's tourists, Legh and his friend Smelt, travelling up the Nile in comparative safety by boat with an American captain. They had been able to visit Qasr Ibrim in the Derr district, had then turned back for fear of the Mamluks, and were coming downstream again when they saw two Arabs mounted on camels, two seedy-looking men who hailed them in Arabic.[37]

Legh, that puzzled politician, wrote:

The fear of the Mamluks still operating upon the minds of our crew, we rowed to the other side of the Nile, and were again hailed in Arabic. On this occasion we replied, and demanded what they wanted. To our great astonishment we were answered in English and immediately recognised the voice of our friend Sheik Ibrahim, whom we had left at Siout, in Upper Egypt, extremely well dressed after the Turkish fashion, and in good health and condition. He now had all the exterior of a common Arab, was very thin, and upon the whole his appearance was miserable enough. He told us he had been living for many days with the sheiks of the villages through which he had passed on lentils, bread, salt and water, and when he came on board, could not contain his joy at the prospect of being regaled with animal food. The day before we had bought a lean and miserable sheep, for which the natives had demanded (an exorbitant price in that country) a dollar. . . . We smoked our pipes, congratulating one another on our good fortune in having met, and communicated our different plans and adventures.

They discussed the possible danger of Mamluks being in the area as bruited from several sources, and thought it likely that they had retired deep into the desert. Louis writes only in passing of this meeting, mentioning that Legh and Smelt had (rather unexpectedly, one might think) become the first Europeans to visit the Castle of Ibrim. After the good meal, and the short but welcome respite, Louis rode on south, leaving the Englishmen still quite unaware of his identity. Legh's story of this encounter on the Nile, as it appeared later in his book, probably vexed Louis when he read it in 1815, since above all he disliked exaggerated accounts of his achievements and enterprise. Lionising praise was anathema. Much of what Legh writes *is* correct but he does gush on about Louis' "various attainments in almost every living language", which was palpably absurd and must have been particularly annoying to anyone as straightforward as Louis. In his kindly way he had given these two men much useful advice, assistance and information. But he invariably kept all important details of his travels strictly for his employers only, and was discomforted when people such as Legh published what he called "exaggerated fairy-tales" about him. By then—in 1815 —he had really tasted fame but, as he wrote to his mother at the time: "fame once it has been acquired is an empty feeling".[38]

The day following the meeting he looked across the river and saw the temple of Sebua. Since most of the temples and great forts were on the western bank, he was eager to make the crossing somehow for the return journey, and the fact that a slave caravan had for the first time in memory used that bank—usually too dangerous—was a further spur to his ambition.

It was late in the evening when he reached Derr—then a place of beauty, of luxuriant vegetation, sycamore trees, palm groves, vivid green foliage—but his initial encounter there with Hassan Kashif had alarming aspects. It must have been with grave misgivings that he heard as he dismounted at the Kashif's house of the recent arrival of two Mamluk Beys. As Hassan had already retired to his harem, Louis settled down for the night in the open hall of the big house and, no doubt, feigned sleep promptly—the only refuge from the flood of questions that assailed him both from Hassan's men and the Mamluks' servants.

In the morning he awoke with something of a shock to find the tall figure of the Kashif looming over him. The inevitable suspicious questions followed. Louis answered that he was merely on a tour of pleasure, and presented his letters of recommendation. Such candour was of little use and in fact it was at once taken for deception. No one would believe that he was an ordinary traveller, like Legh or Smelt; he appeared to be a poor Arab, he spoke perfect Syrian Arabic—for once his disguise weighed against him. He must be a Turk, they said, sent to spy on the brother Kashifs by the Governor of Esne, and in this view the two Mamluk Beys supported Hassan.

It could not have been a pleasant situation but Louis writes it off as half a day of tedious negotiation, which in fact formed the "rest" to which he referred in his subsequent account! It was essential to hire a new guide here. For this service and for the Kashif's permission to proceed Louis proffered some gifts, worth about 60 piastres (between two and three pounds sterling), that would have been perfectly acceptable had not Legh and Smelt in their unthinking, wealthy way made the present seem paltry in comparison with their own, which had been worth eighteen times as much.

"And *they* wished to go only to Ibrim," complained the offended Hassan acidly. "While *you* give me a few trifles and expect to go beyond—even to the Second Cataract!"

Louis said politely that although he knew his gifts were hardly suitable, he did hold warm letters from the Bey of Esne, and in the end he got his way, partly by a stroke of luck and partly by the use of a little cunning worthy of a true oriental. He had come to adopt, with the clothes he wore and the parts he played, suitable wiles; if anything threatened to curtail his exploration he did not hesitate to counter distrust with sharp devices, and from now on he was constantly to outwit such men as these on their own grounds and at their own game.

The luck arrived in the shape of a big caravan from Mahass, bound for Esne and carrying a large amount of merchandise belonging to Hassan which he was intending to sell in Assiut and in Cairo. Louis saw his chance, and spoke to the Kashif privately, asking what would be the Governor of Esne's reaction to the disregard of his letter. If Sheik Ibrahim were not permitted to pass beyond the Second Cataract despite the letter, tribute would no doubt be levied on this very caravan—it might even be stopped from proceeding towards Assiut!

There was a prolonged and heavy silence, then Hassan said: "Whoever you may be, I shall not send you back unsatisfied. You may proceed, but *not* further than Sukkot; the road is unsafe from there you will return!"*

Louis was delighted—the implied threat had worked! He waited only to request a letter for the Kashif of Sukkot, which was immediately supplied, and a Bedouin guide was promptly found, despite the machinations of the Mamluk Beys who did all they could to prevent the journey.

The new guide was an old man named Mohammed Abu Saad, an honest fellow with much character and a good sense of humour. His tribe, the Keraish, was poor but proud—proud of the purity of its blood and also, justly, of the beauty of its girls. A kindly, hospitable people, they acted as guides and guards, pastured their cattle on the islands and sometimes made dangerous journeys into the western desert to distant nitre pits.

Louis was glad to ride away from Derr and up over the high plain. He slept that night on an island in Abu Saad's own tent. The people here were black but extremely comely and not at all negroid.[39] It was a land of butter, and those who could afford it

---

* Sukkot: the district beginning about half-way between the Second and Third Cataracts. The districts of Mahass and Dongola lie still further south.

greased themselves for the dual purpose of cooling the skin and keeping off "vermin". Naturally when the butter turned rancid the smell became overpowering; however, in common with later travellers, Louis much admired these oily young Nubian shepherdesses.

The dark hoary pile of Ibrim, with its magnificent lines seeming to grow from the rock itself, has a tragic monumental appearance, an antique appeal like the havoc of a once handsome face ravaged by time. A sad and fascinating place poised high above the river— one later traveller called it "a picturesque illusion of hovels"—it has recently afforded rich yields to the excavators. From this point Louis rode away into unknown territory; from about here the Nile begins its great westward curve.

There were graves and abandoned houses everywhere. Strange hills stood in the red-gold sand, so like replicas of Zoser's pyramid that they might well have been artefacts. On a maze of sandbanks and islands crocodiles lay basking in the sun. Eastward the land stretched away to curved, swarthy hills with sand drifts lying golden in their arms like honey in a bowl, each shadow a clear brush stroke of luminous cobalt. At sunset the hills began to glow in the westering light, their sharp escarpments accented with that same jewel-like quality of blue, and from the darkly ruddy pyramid rocks long cool fingers of shadow crept across pristine sands.

Old Abu Saad always refused to speculate on time or distances; probably through superstitious fear he carefully evaded discussion of the future, and habitually brushed aside any queries as to possible halting places, or mileages, with an unctuous saying: "May God smooth our path!" If pressed he countered with: "God is great, he can prolong distances and shorten them." All of which was rather annoying, but before they parted Louis eventually gained the day on this topic.

Another of Saad's tricks Louis managed to trump quite soon. They were riding across the top of a lonely wilderness, known as the Rock of the Girls, when Saad unexpectedly alighted, and asked for baksheesh. In certain dangerous spots, so he told Louis, tradition demanded that small gifts should be made to the guide who, were such requests refused, would make a miniature grave with sand and stones—a symbolic tomb for the traveller—as a gentle hint that from henceforth he could expect no further security.

This original method of extortion tickled Louis' fancy and since he liked the old man, he obliged with a small tip. However, the next day in another high lonely place when Sa'ad again asked for baksheesh, Louis refused, foreseeing endless demands, whereupon the old man dismounted and began to build the symbolic tomb. Not to be outdone Louis alighted also and started to model a similar grave.

"It's for you, Abu Saad," he said. "As we are brothers it is only just that we should be buried together!"

The old guide threw back his head and laughed, acknowledging defeat, and they mutually destroyed each other's handiwork. But no sooner had they remounted than Saad, quoting from the Koran, exclaimed lugubriously: "No man knows the spot upon earth where his grave shall be digged . . ."

A sentence which must have struck cold; this macabre play with toy sepulchres was rather too close to reality to be altogether amusing as this was Alaqui country, notorious for sudden and violent death.

Louis' watch had stopped, it was full of sand; they rode on all day, telling the time by the sun, often not touching a thing to eat but a handful of dates when they paused during the morning to let their camels browse on some tamarisk. Once he examined a rock-hewn temple painted over with Christian frescoes, and saw there the names of ancient Greek travellers carved on its walls.

They passed above the northern end of Batn el Hajar, the Belly or—as he calls it—the Womb of Stone, a turbulent magnificent maze of greywacke and granite in thunderous white water, the Crag of Abusir towering above—the most desolate part of Nubia, the area of the Second Cataract which spread its rapids over a distance of more than ninety miles. Beyond Mershid, the river narrowed so much, where the ancient fortifications of Semna guarded the rocky barrier, that Louis found he could easily throw a stone across.

Terrified of robbers, Saad urged the camels forward as hard as he could. After ten hours' riding they stopped with some Keraish who were so poor they had nothing but milk for supper— they had not tasted bread for months. Louis distributed a measure of durra from his own small stock on the condition that the women also ate it, for he knew that women rarely enjoyed such a luxury, bread being almost invariably reserved for the men. The women set to cheerfully to grind the flour between granite stones, and a sociable evening followed.

Plenty of bread was made and the girls sat up, eating and singing the whole of the night and being separated from us only by a partition of tamarisk branches they often joined in the conversation.

On 10 March Louis went to call on the Kashif of the Sukkot district; to do so he had to cross the river on a frail raft, an unwieldy bundle of date palm trunks. The elderly Kashif was far from welcoming, but he grudgingly gave Louis a written introduction to his son who governed southern Sukkot.

Although Louis had already reached the most southerly limit imposed by the irascible Hassan of Derr, he was determined to go on to Tinareh where, so he understood, there was a boat large enough to transport him and his camels to the western bank which he was so eager to explore.

Arrived at a hamlet opposite the island on which the old Kashif's son lived, Abu Saad announced that they could go no further since it was his duty to obey Hassan's command. In his extreme anxiety to cross from Tinareh Louis persuaded Saad with an offer of 2 piastres and a promise of the red woollen *melaye* he was wearing, and which he knew Saad coveted. With a knowing grin the old man acquiesced—should Hassan be angry with him he would say that Sheik Ibrahim had ridden on despite all pleas, and of course it would not have been *honourable* to have left him alone. . . .

There was a tremendous hullabaloo on the island, and they were unable to get by without visiting the young Kashif, who summoned them to the noisy funeral feast that was then in full swing. Women were dancing and singing glees, and the din was ear-splitting. The young man cast covetous glances at Louis' camels, and it was only the father's letter that saved them.

When they could escape from the funeral celebrations they rode on at a regular fast trot, and slept the night at the house of one of Hussein Kashif's women. These Nubian governors kept their women posted over their dominions so that they might enjoy "every home comfort", as Louis politely puts it, wherever they stopped on the ceaseless round of tax-collecting. Hussein Kashif, father of the truculent brothers, had about twenty wives, each with her own separate dwelling.

The pressure of strenuous days continued: one night, two of Saad's tribesmen rewarded Louis for a gift of durra by a skilful massage, kneading and rubbing away the numbness in saddle-weary muscles.

The next two days proved to be the worst that Louis had yet experienced in his four years of travel. He was now in the forbidden area of Mahass. While drawing near to his objective of Tinareh he passed many deserted villages; the tyrannous Kashifs had set their horses and camels to feed among the peasants' barley, and for fuel they had stripped the little houses of every possession.

At last he reached Mohammed Kashif's camp at Tinareh, as far south as even he dared venture. It was a very grave risk, but the only large boat was here, and he was staking a great deal on crossing the Nile at this point. He warned Saad as they approached to be careful in replying to questions, he must say that he knew nothing of Sheik Ibrahim's business—which was in fact quite true since Louis had so contrived it that his note-taking had never once been observed.

Mohammed and Hussein, the two brother Kashifs of Mahass, had come now to besiege the castle of Tinareh, recently taken over by a rebel. It was hardly a propitious moment. Both brothers were absent from the camp, busily engaged in taking uproarious possession of the castle. On arrival Louis and Saad were immediately surrounded by a rabble of excited men.

Presently Mohammed crossed from the western bank, and Louis went at once to pay his respects. He has this to say of Mohammed:

Born of a Darfour slave, his features resembled those of the inhabitants of the Soudan, but without anything of the mildness which generally characterises the Negro countenance.

On the contrary his expression revealed a very unpleasant disposition. He rolled his eyes at Louis like a mad man:

. . . having drunk copiously of palm-wine at the castle, he was so intoxicated that he could hardly keep on his legs.

The vanquished rebels, as well as his own men, crowded in and milled around his open hut. Two bloated skins of thick sweet palm-wine were brought, and soon everyone was drinking from little cups made of calabashes.

Only a few spoke Arabic, but it was not long before Louis discovered that he was the subject of the tumultuous discussion. The Kashif, who was "almost in a state of insensibility", had asked the stranger no questions as yet. In half an hour the entire camp was rip-roaring drunk; men staggered in with loaded muskets, a *feu de joie* with ball was fired inside the hut where everyone lolled around. Louis expected to be hit at any moment by some random shot, and frankly regretted having entered this raving camp.

Each time he attempted to rise, the Kashif prevented him, insisting that Sheik Ibrahim must stay and become companionably drunk. But, says Louis, as he had never in his life stood more in need of his senses he took care to drink very sparingly.

Before noon every camp member had fallen into drunken slumber, they lay sprawled out around him: their welcome snores afforded him time in which to think out his own next move.

A few hours later, having slept off the drink, the Kashif was sober enough to talk. Louis explained that he had travelled into Nubia to see the castles of Ibrim and of Say—the remains of Sultan Selim's empire—and that he had continued south merely to greet the brother Kashifs here, since it would have been un-civil not to pay his respects while so close. Unfortunately, as Hassan had retained in Derr the essential letters from Esne, Louis' story was met with blank disbelief.

"You are an agent of Mohammed Ali!" shouted the Kashif's interpreter, "but at Mahass we spit at Mohammed Ali's beard, *and* cut off the heads of those who are enemies of the Mamluks!"

Quietly, Louis assured them that he was no enemy of the Mamluks, he had called on the two Beys at Derr, who had treated him very politely, and—adept at understatement—Louis merely recounts that the evening passed "uncomfortably" in "sharp inquiries . . . and evasive answers".

Mohammed Kashif sat up with his confidants late into the night trying to decide what to do with Sheik Ibrahim, and whether he should live or die.

Meanwhile, his fate hanging in the balance, Louis discreetly stationed himself with his camels under cover, couched behind the Kashif's hut. While he was thus keeping out of sight huddled beside his beasts, a messenger was sent across the Nile to ascertain brother Hussein's views on the question, and whether he thought that the stranger should be allowed to keep his head.

On 14 March early in the morning, Hussein arrived with an escort personally to look over Sheik Ibrahim. The same questions were put, but Hussein's attitude was rather more gentle than Mohammed's. Mohammed repeatedly threatened to send Louis' severed head to the chief of the Mamluks, while Hussein argued that he should be allowed to return north at once, but in exchange for his life he demanded Louis' camels and his gun. He had not seen the pistols as they were hidden under Louis' *thabout*.

It was a highly charged dilemma. But Louis felt he could deal with it; he was not going to be scared into parting with his gun nor, even more vital, the camels—his only swift means of escape. So he now laid a trump card on the table, and told the brothers flatly that if anything should happen to him their mercantile dealings with Esne would most certainly suffer. They had only to send to Derr to learn the truth of his tale. And, even if he were—as they imagined—the Pasha's agent, Mohammed Ali was not a

man to allow any person employed by *him* to "perish treacher-
ously without revenging his death". Then Louis added that, since
he was merely a traveller, they really had no reason to insult him.
(No one had the slightest idea that he was a European, and he was
reserving this fact to disclose only if forced to do so as a last
resource.)

His bold arguments did appear to be making some impression
on the brothers. But Louis admits that he was extremely doubtful
as to what his fate might have been, had two nephews of the
Sukkot Kashif not arrived at the crucial moment. They confirmed
all that he had said.

The brothers then began to change their tone, but he was still
regarded with deep distrust. However, Hussein did promise to
send the boat across to ferry him and his camels over to the
western bank. But he never did so, and shortly afterwards Louis
saw her setting off downstream. It was a bitter disappointment:
his whole object in risking the dangers of Tinareh had been to
get himself and his mounts across the Nile.

Quite obviously it would be madness to go further; he was
unpleasantly close to Dongola already and, what is more, the two
Mamluk Beys from Derr were heading south rapidly, so he heard,
and it was unlikely that they would be quite so polite here, far
up-river and near their own territory.

There was nothing for it but to turn back immediately. But
when he visited Mohammed to take his leave, he was abruptly
commanded to wait until the following day when he might travel
north accompanied by the Kashif and his soldiers. This was the
last thing that Louis wanted, so he said he had to hurry back to
Derr, and that if he were not free to do so he would have to
consider himself as a prisoner in the Kashifs' camp. This final
daring remark enraged Mohammed, and completely outwitted
him. "Go then—you rascal!" he spluttered. Louis, thankful to
obey the rough command, turned on his heel, mounted promptly
and galloped off with Saad towards the north.

Within a few minutes they were out of sight. They put four
hours' hard riding between them and the camp before stopping
to sleep in a deserted hut.

Having so narrowly escaped with his life, all that now concerned Louis was the problem of how to cross the Nile—to explore those unmapped banks and examine the great temples he expected to find there. Determination being one of his strongest qualities, he undoubtedly assured himself, before he fell into the sleep of exhaustion, that he would by some means or other achieve that vital river-crossing, come what may.

# CHAPTER NINE

## *Ozymandias*

"My name is Ozymandias, king of kings:
Look on my works, ye Mighty, and despair!"
*Shelley*

UNTIL NOW, OLD Saad had been a faithful guide and companion. But at sunrise the next morning Louis found him still asleep or—as he soon had cause to think—more likely feigning sleep.

He guessed that those arak-swilling brothers had given Saad secret instructions to retard Louis' progress in every possible way, for no sooner had they mounted than Saad pretended his camel had gone lame. Then Louis was quite certain that the old fellow's intention was to allow the Kashifs' troops to catch up with them. Therefore he ordered him to dismount and to walk back to Tinareh—he himself would make his own way to Derr with the two camels. However, Saad would not leave, he rode doggedly on, but always as slowly as he could so that by lagging behind persistently all day he put often as much as a mile between them. So they progressed, two isolated figures on their camels, dwarfed in that stony wilderness, alone on the edge of dangerous robber country, far apart and vulnerable.

This time they did not cross the high plain but followed the river bank to the village of Soleb, whence Louis had a tantalising distant view of the magnificent temple opposite which he would have examined had he been able to cross at Tinareh. He thought that it appeared to be about equal in size to some of the largest in Egypt; he longed to gratify his curiosity—no wonder! And had he done so he would have been the first European to examine it at least since the decline of Rome in Egypt, more than a thousand years earlier.

So anxious was he to get across that he offered all the remaining

durra he possessed to some peasants to ferry him over and back
again—which he reckoned to be the equivalent of proffering a
guinea to a London waterman to make a twopenny ride across the
Thames. But it was no use since there was no raft to be had, nor
even a single inflated goatskin, such as the Nubians sometimes
used to help them over the Nile, and—strong swimmer though
he was—he did not think it wise to risk crossing so powerful a
river trusting in his own strength alone.

A decade later George Waddington,[40] Fellow of Trinity,
Cambridge, writing of his own experiences at Soleb, said:

> Thus far we followed in the steps of Burckhardt with his book
> in our hands: it is impossible to take leave of him without
> expressing our admiration for his character, and our gratitude
> for the instruction he has afforded us. His acquired qualifications
> were, I believe, never equalled by those of any other traveller;
> his natural ones appear to be even more extraordinary. Courage
> to seek danger, and calmness to confront it, are not uncommon
> qualities; but it is difficult to court poverty, and to endure insult.

Sadly frustrated Louis went on, but not without making an
especial note of this temple to draw the attention of some other
"more fortunate traveller".

However disappointing, it was perhaps lucky that he had not
crossed at Tinareh since the two Mamluk Beys were speeding
south on the western bank, having, no doubt with Hassan's
assistance, swum their horses across at Derr.

At the island of Say, Louis went to look at the Amara temple
and—although he does not mention it—we know that here he
carved his name, "Sheik Ibrahim". It must have been the first time
he had done this, he was not a man who readily carved graffiti.
What sudden urge had made him do so now? Was it perhaps
prompted in some way by the disappointment of Soleb? Also, a
little further north, once more and for almost the last time, he
again inscribed his name. D'Athanasi, a later traveller, in the company of several Englishmen, was to come across both these inscriptions; the most northerly one first in a small temple "called
Semnis". These later travellers were all at the time in great fear

of their lives and it cheered them to see in this remote spot the
familiar name of the man they had warmly liked and admired:

> . . . on it we found written the name of John Burckhardt,
> which we had not found upon any other edifice either in Egypt,
> or Nubia beyond the second cataract. At the sight of this name,
> we gained courage a little, on reflecting that that individual,
> despite being quite alone [*that is with a hired guide only and
> no European companion*], had dared without meeting any disaster,
> to plunge himself into these difficult localities.[41]

But at that time Louis *was* suspect, perhaps more than he
realised; a tiny slip had almost certainly revealed him to one
person at least. At Amara, D'Athanasi and his companions later
were to come across a man who recalled talking to Sheik Ibrahim,
and who had given him a bit of bread and a little milk. Had Louis
for once been dreaming? He knew the custom: perhaps it was the
thought of that great temple at Soleb more vexing than any
miraged city, as well as the strain of the recent events at Tinareh,
which put him in an absent-minded mood. For the man at
Amara told D'Athanasi that the Sheik could not have been a true
believer, because not only did he omit to give thanks to God after
he had eaten but also he put a small piece of bread left over from
his meal into his pocket, contrary to the practice of the true
Muslim who never uses on the next day anything left over from
the preceding one. Poor Louis, always so hungry and now perhaps
inadvertently slipping that scrap of bread away for the morning!

Now for two days Louis and Saad rode hard from sunrise till
sunset, until they came to the island of Kolbe where Louis hoped
to achieve the crossing. It was too late in the evening when they
arrived to attempt this major operation, so he sent Saad over to
the Kashif of Sukkot with his greetings, and with a polite request
for supper, and for the assistance of two men to help transport him
and the camels across the Nile in the morning. Saad returned
quickly with the promise of help and of food; but it was not until
late at night that a slave arrived with some barley soup, and the
good news that the two Mamluk Beys had already passed by to
the west on their way south.

The crossing proved extremely difficult. They piled their clothes, provision sacks and the camels' saddles on a small raft which one of the slaves paddled. The other slave clung to the raft with one hand and to the camels' halters with the other; an inflated goatskin was attached to the neck of each camel. When they had at last persuaded the frightened beasts to enter the water, Louis and Saad, each grasping a tail, swam with their legs only, while urging the camels across by means of a stick held in the free hand. This difficult task achieved, Louis was able to enjoy a peaceful breakfast with the slaves on the western bank, since the Kashif had set off early in search of tribute.

For several days they hurried on, finding more ruins, ancient temples, forts, and Christian churches with their wonderfully preserved frescoes of saints and angels painted in brilliant colours. They rode through wadis where the sands descended to the river in torrents, and a north wind whipped stinging granules in their faces. They slept, or tried to sleep, beside enchantingly clear pools set among rocks and tamarisks, reflecting in the dazzling dry Nubian night segments of the brilliant starry sky above. But these beautiful pools were mosquito-ridden so, when the moon rose to flood the hills with radiance, they would ride on, to sleep later on the high plains. There he could hear still the sound of the great boisterous river rushing over the wild rocks below: it was another world, a far cry indeed from the gentler voices of his Swiss rivers laden with melting snow waters in spring, hurrying through the smiling, flowery meadows that he loved.

Above the foaming granite narrows he went into the ancient fortress of Semna West, and examined the temple there,* and remarked again on the Egyptian Priapus, as he called the god, Min. To his eyes the hieroglyphics here looked somewhat roughly carved, and he wondered if they might perhaps have been the "work of young persons only learning their art..."

So much has happened in the field of Egyptology since his explorations in Nubia, when the interest even in Egypt was rather that of the antiquarian, and archaeology as such was not yet conceived, that it is necessary to recall again that the meaning of

* Built by Tutmosis III, and Queen Hateshepsut.

the hieroglyphics was still not known—and was lost since the wane of classical times. . . .

From the great strength of the fortifications at Semna Louis deduced that the enemy had been a powerful one. Nearly all was speculation for him, but he was often astoundingly near the mark; he wondered now if the "forefathers of the Blemmyes (wild Bedouin from the eastern desert) disturbed the hierarchy of Egypt as their descendants afterwards did the Roman praetors".

Their provisions were almost finished, and the sun was nearly setting as they continued at a sharp trot over the hills until they came down to the river again at a Keraish encampment. They had ridden for twelve hours, and it was late when they dismounted at the tents. Tired, but very thankful to have returned to northern Nubia, Louis celebrated by purchasing with three measures of grain a lamb which Saad's tribesmen roasted for supper.

It was one of those rare evenings when Louis could relax and lie back, listening to the Arabs' voices, savouring the wonderful scent of meat roasting out of doors, looking up at stars seen through feathery fronds of tamarisk, while firelight flickered on those beautiful dark faces of the smiling Keraish girls. At the rim of light his camels fed contentedly, and the voice of the river was loud among the rocks and islets beyond. There was another long ride the next day, and for the night another island encampment in the moonlight.

The Father of the Ear of Corn, known as Abshek in antiquity, was a rocky promontory isolated in desert wastes above the river. Once the site of a considerable city, the headland was now completely deserted. The place slept in the moonlight, bathed in white brilliance. Awaiting what?—rediscovery, or obliteration by the ever rising tide of sand? Awaiting too that strange, unpredicted, unpredictable fate which the twentieth century was to bring to its shrines—a new life as astounding as its creation over 3,000 years ago.

Calmly one great benign face, one only, smiled forth now across the molten silver of the Nile regarding the east eternally, awaiting another dawn. Ozymandias, gazing from his funerary shrine for ever towards the rising sun, with serene eyes nobly fashioned from the living rock, watching for that eternal symbol of life and resurrection by whose light his soul journeyed on through hours of darkness in its solar boat.

Stars, still bright in the dark blue sky, shone above the forbidding cliff guarding the hidden temples. The great moon began to drop towards the hill, and grew slowly pale over the western desert as details of carved rock and a sloping sandstone façade gradually became visible in the first light. A curlew called plaintively, and there was a faint twittering of unseen swifts as they began to waken in rock crevices at the brightening of the sky. Then the fiery sun mounted out of the eastern desert, the warmth sudden with it, a lisp of dawn wind stirred the tamarisks and at once the quiet place became alive with bird voices.

It was the morning of 22 March 1813: Louis awoke in a mood of intense excitement, he was filled with a growing, tingling anticipation. This was the day on which he hoped to see the great "Ebsambel"—of which he had heard so much from Sa'ad and other Arabs.

It was through rather dull flat country that they rode that morning, where scrub—*sant*-trees and tamarisks—struggled for life among blown sand. Louis had already noticed here, on both sides of the river, scattered groups of what he thought might probably prove to be tumuli. Indeed he was riding among tombs of the Ballana "X-Group" kings buried with their pole-axed camels, their favourite horses in cruel silver bits, their drugged or poisoned grooms and other servants. A strange, barbaric people of whom nothing was known until the excavations of the 1930s, they lived here in Nubia from about the third century of the Christian era until the sixth.[42]

There was nothing that Louis could possibly hope to do about such tumuli—an immense task for later excavators requiring much labour. His mind was set now on the temples that he hoped to find, and he kept looking ahead to the promontory of "Ebsambel". Approaching it as they were from above, he could, of course, see nothing of the cliff below facing the river.

He was glad to leave Saad to guard the camels on the mountain top, and to descend alone. It was an almost perpendicular cleft throttled with fine sand, down which he plunged towards the river, sinking deep into the drift at every step. When he reached the bottom he saw, to his left, the sloping rock-cut façade of Queen Nefertari's temple facing slightly to the north.

Unhampered by old Saad, who was now probably dozing on the mountain top against the flank of his couched camel, Louis was free for once to write all the notes he wished.

In about 1260 B.C. Rameses made this lovely shrine "as his monument for the Great King's wife, beloved of Mut, a house hewn in the pure mountains of Nubia, of fine, white and enduring sandstone, as an eternal work".[43]

The temple has a distinction and a delicate beauty that is quite unforgettable and entirely its own. Louis entered the pronaos through the small dark opening cut in the rock between the colossii of the façade. The six slender figures have a very youthful charm (rather quaintly Louis describes them as "juvenile persons"); they represent Rameses II and Nefertari, his most beloved of wives, with their children symbolically small at their knees. Louis took all the measurements he could, carefully pacing out the interior. He had no light with him, certainly no mirror with which to illuminate the inner sanctuary by reflected rays in the Egyptian fashion, since he does not remark particularly on the exquisite beauty of the life-size reliefs of Nefertari standing with the goddesses Hathor and Isis. Possibly the smoke of fugitives' fires (the local people retreated to this temple with their cattle whenever Bedouin from the western deserts raided their hamlets), as well as the lack of illumination made it difficult for Louis to discern the full beauty of these reliefs; though he recognised Isis and saw at once from the style of sculpture that the shrine was of great antiquity.

The marauders from the desert, he writes, came annually, moving from district to district in raiding parties of some 300 horsemen and camel-riders, plundering as they went every village on the western bank. Since no one dared withstand them—the Nubian Kashifs even visited them when they appeared opposite Derr and gave them gifts—their regular and unopposed incursions had become one of the main reasons for the Nile's western bank being almost deserted.

The temple was beautiful, but perhaps not quite as impressive as he had expected from all accounts; however, thinking that he had seen the antiquities of "Ebsambel", he began to ascend the sand drift by the same way he had come down, that precipitous gulley where the sand torrent lay thick below the brooding crest of the mountain. The warm sand streamed heavily, dragging at his feet with each laborious step. High above him the hot, deep dark blue of the sky was flecked with wind-torn nimbus; in silence all the half-buried mountain seemed waiting. There was no sound but the whisper of wind in the tamarisks by the river, the chirping of birds that nest in temple and rock crevice, the distant piping of a hoopoe flaunting his kingly crest, bowing and nodding down by the water's edge.

Something made Louis pause in his struggle up the soft drift; something made him turn slightly more to the south where a shoulder of the mountain came down beside the steep gulley. Had the Nefertari not perhaps fulfilled his expectations—did he sense there was more?

He says that he had luckily turned to the southward when it happened. And so it was that he found the Great Temple of Abu Simbel.

I fell in with what is yet visible of four immense colossal statues cut out of the rock . . . they stand in a deep recess excavated in the mountain; but it is greatly to be regretted that they are almost entirely buried beneath the sands, which are blown down here in torrents. The entire head, and part of the breast and arms of one of the statues, are yet above the surface [*this was the most southerly one*], of the next one to it scarcely any part is visible, the head being broken off, and the body covered with sand to above the shoulders; of the other two only the bonnets [*the double crowns of Upper and Lower Egypt*] appear. . . . The head which is above the surface has a most expressive youthful countenance, approaching nearer to the Grecian model of beauty, than that of any Egyptian figure I have seen . . .

Louis was right; these superb, calm faces gazing across the Nile differ from any other Egyptian statues not only in their grandeur and timeless wonder, but in an exquisite perfection of expression. To some the sublime nobility of these beautiful heads may recall the seraphically smiling ones of the Bayon deep in the Cambodian jungle of Angkor—perhaps the comparison seems strange but it is irresistible.

Tense with excitement, Louis traversed the soft sands smothering the submerged façade to come close to that one great head. The measurements he then took, alone there in the stillness, steadying his excited fingers against those features as his feet slipped into the loose sand, were later proved to be remarkably accurate. He was unable to ascertain whether the figures were seated or standing, seated he thought, and from the length of the ear—one yard four inches—he guessed their height to within a foot or two.

Gazing on these splendid features as he stood so close to them high above the river, Louis was unaware that he was staring into the face of Rameses the Great—"Ozymandias, king of kings"—as a young man at the height of his power and beauty. The same man whose aged, mummified face one can look into today in the Cairo museum; all that was yet to come. But Louis knew the work belonged to the very finest period of Egyptian sculpture, second to none in all Egypt.

It was then only seven months since Louis had revealed Petra to the civilised world; now unflagging determination had rewarded him with yet another memorable discovery. The temple of Rameses at Abu Simbel had remained unseen by European eyes certainly since the Graeco-Roman period, even possibly since the reign of Psammetichus under whom Greek mercenaries marched south into Ethiopia in the sixth century B.C. By 1000 B.C. Lower Nubia had begun to fade from the pages of history, and the sands of the western desert then started to invade the Great Temple.[44] Some 400 years after that, the Greek mercenaries marched past and two of them scrambled up the drifts to inscribe their names, and other facts useful to historian and archaeologist, upon a thigh of Rameses. Then soon the sands engulfed the façade.

Louis must have longed to be able to see into the temple that lay hidden below his feet. He shared little of the joy of such excavations, for his was always the task of the forerunner. He would never know how the first rays of sunlight pierce miraculously to that innermost sanctuary, 180 feet deep in the living rock. He would have been even more startled to see, just a century and a half after his discovery, both temples cut up into a jigsaw of 950 immense pieces,[45] numbered and ready to be reassembled on the mountain top where his old Arab and his camels awaited him then on that quiet March morning in 1813.

After his discovery no one came to Abu Simbel for another four years. It was not until 1817, inspired by his account, that Henry Salt, then British Consul General in Egypt, sent Giovanni Belzoni, a gigantic Italian whom Louis knew and had recommended, to struggle with the stupendous task of reopening the temple. He did make an entry, but the sand soon drifted back, and it was not effectively held at bay until 1892.

There was nothing more that Louis could now do. Although deeply moved and elated by the superb discovery, he had to hurry on, and so with a last lingering look at those near divine features he presently climbed up to rejoin old Saad. They mounted their camels and rode away quickly, down to the long barren shore beyond the promontory—Louis' thoughts dwelling on this new wonder that he had found.

A couple of days later they arrived back opposite Derr: Louis was duty bound to go over to pay his respects to the Kashif. As he waited for the passenger ferry to come across he saw that Hassan himself was in the boat. His greeting was very cold; news had travelled quickly.

"You had no business in Mahass," he said. "Why did you not return after reaching Sukkot?" Suspicion fell darkly like a shadow on his face. "What presents did you give my brothers?"

Louis answered truthfully—none, as he had had none to give.

"I wonder then," Hassan retorted, "how they let you pass, for you had no letters to them."

Louis replied mildly that they had treated him well, and then, embroidering a little, he added that they had even killed a lamb for him. This was not true at all, but he felt that the small fabrication was justified by way of a rebuke to Hassan who had offered him no meat during either of his visits to Derr!

This time he stayed for a few hours only, and the leave-taking was not smooth. By way of a parting gift Louis offered Hassan his pistols, since the Kashif, however hateful he was to his peasants, had not really behaved unreasonably towards him. But Hassan was in a vile humour; such pistols were unfit for a Kashif, he said, what he needed were fine long ones in swaggering holsters like those sported by the Mamluks. Louis promised to send him just such a pair, and he did not forget to order them later from Cairo, realising that Hassan would undoubtedly be most surprised to receive them. He knew well that it was unusual in the East to remember the services of anyone whose good offices are no longer wanted. But Louis was careful not to neglect such niceties —they would invariably assist any future travellers.

In contrast, the parting with Abu Saad was a friendly one. The old guide had long hankered after that red woollen *melaye*, and he was now expecting to receive it as promised. But to tease him in his own style—he who had always countered every query with his "May God smooth our path!"—Louis now gently parried the request saying "May God smooth *your* path!"—a polite phrase for ridding oneself of a beggar. The old man knew Louis well enough by now, and answered with a twinkle: "No, for once I will beg *you* to smooth it!"

Louis of course gave him the *melaye*, as he had always intended to, plus a small present of cash, and he felt confident that Abu Saad would not forget him. For Louis this is a strong statement, and it probably covers what was an emotional leave-taking, for a Bedouin such as Saad would know a good man when he saw him, and also he would not be afraid to show his feelings.

Louis then left with his new guide, recrossed the river and began to ride swiftly northwards. This part of the journey was more leisurely and he allowed himself time to enjoy the temples he saw, especially Kalabsha.* His account of the bas-reliefs there makes fascinating reading and, in the light of recent finds, shows brilliant conjecture from the historical viewpoint.

* There are coloured casts of these Beit el Wali reliefs in the British Museum.

On 30 March he came down to the river at a place where there was a small ferry boat, since he wanted to cross over to the eastern bank, as not only was there no riverside track fit for camels but he had promised himself the pleasure of seeing the Isle of Philae.

But the crossing was again extremely difficult; the boat leaked, there were no goatskins for the animals, the young rowers were slow and feeble, the camels had to be towed, and on arrival one was half-drowned. When it had recovered they rode over the mountain again and came down towards the village of Birbe, whose people kept a boat to take sight-seers across to Philae. Quite unrestricted by any Kashifs they asked vast sums for their services, and they had also a nasty habit of leaving travellers stranded on the island in order to extort more money. As he approached he was at once surrounded by half a dozen of these men, all of whom claimed to be owners of the boat and lords of the island. They demanded 6 piastres for the visit and the boat-hire.

A trifling sum really, Louis says, to be allowed to see one of the most precious remains of antiquity in Egypt. But after all his dangerous adventures in the barbaric up-river atmosphere a spirit of revolt against such minor tyranny entered into him, and he determined for once not to let himself be imposed upon by such petty extortioners. He offered them 1 piastre—one para (half a farthing) was the usual ferry boat fare in Egypt then. When they refused the piastre, he undressed, handed his clothes to his guide, put his notebook inside his turban, and swam over to the Island of Isis, secretly enjoying the small victory, an amusing climax to a swift fantastic journey. He had barely landed when the boatmen came after him in hot pursuit, and later they were glad enough to accept the one piastre for the return trip.

He spent a long, peaceful afternoon revelling in the island's beauty. There was a superb sunset over the western desert, and it was late when he arrived at Aswan, where he found that Shaharti, his faithful servant, had begun quite to despair of his ever returning from the Land of the Ghosts.

# CHAPTER TEN

## *The Desert Crossing*

God endures for ever.
The life of man is short.
The Pleiades are overhead.
The moon's among the stars.
*Bedouin chant*

FROM THE STIFLING heat of mid-summer in Upper Egypt, Louis wrote to his old friend, Dr Clarke, far away in leafy Cambridge.

> I am sitting in a half-open courtyard upon a straw mat supporting this page with my left hand, while my two dromedaries, my jackass, my servant and a swarm of mosquitoes leave me not a moment's rest. And I still find time to tell you that I am among the living, while you, lazy creature, comfortably seated in a cool room behind your bureau in an arm chair have become so stingy with your leisure time, as to make it impossible for you to throw away five minutes in order to let me know how things are with you.[46]

After the speed and exhilarating dangers of the last Nubian journey he was more than usually restless and for once desperately bored by a prolonged stay in Esne. Having heard in letters from Cairo that there was no likelihood of a caravan to the west this summer—primarily because of the disturbances caused by the Hijaz wars—he had decided to stay on in Upper Egypt; whence he would make the desert crossing, visit the banks of the Atbara, that great tributary of the Nile which joins it south of Berber, and

lastly perform his previously proposed lateral journey to the Red
Sea, travelling back along the Arabian shore to Cairo. This time
he expected to be away about ten months.

As we have guessed, he must have realised already that he could
never hope to pass as a haji with other returning pilgrims of the
great western caravans had he himself not been, at least, to Arabia.
Now, during this grinding delay in Esne it was increasingly borne
in upon him that, ideally, he should make the pilgrimage to
Mecca—to the holy city itself. It was a daring plan, a great and
dangerous challenge. But Louis was a perfectionist, and he knew
very well that for his purpose only by making himself a haji
could he establish himself unquestionably a Muslim, a true
follower of Islam in its most important tenet: if he were to travel
safely to the interior with returning pilgrims he had to be convincingly one of them.

It was a perfectly logical deduction. He later frankly admits
that this "had indeed been his principal object"[47] during all the
time that he was in Upper Egypt, and was one of the motives
which had determined him to make the second journey into
Nubia. Since the entire plan of the ultimate dangerous venture
depended on his travelling with returning pilgrims, the idea of
going on the Haj seems entirely practical, and it was accepted as
such by his employers.

In Esne he suffered two serious attacks of ophthalmia, during
the worst of which he sat indoors for seven days completely
blind.[48] He must then have gone through some pitiless self-
questioning, alone, blinded in heat and darkness between the
mud walls of his stifling little room.

He fervently desired to go to Mecca—to perfect his role as a
Muslim; while on the other hand he knew that it was his duty
*not* to jeopardise his life before the great journey to the west. He
was concerned too that any further divergence now might earn the
disapproval of the African Association. To them he did not
mention Mecca as yet, that might have seemed flying too high,
although as we have seen he told them later quite openly that the
idea had been already in his mind. Of the Red Sea journey he
wrote now from Esne:

I cannot help feeling some apprehensions lest this project should not meet with the entire approbation of the committee: as it will defer again for a twelvemonth my grand journey. As for myself, as long as I have any vigour of mind and body left, I shall look upon time as a very secondary consideration, and subservient only to the objects of science.[49]

He was regardless of how long he would be absent from Europe if he were serving that cause; but he *was* "extremely anxious" to know the African Association's opinion of his conduct in proposing to visit these unknown parts of the eastern Sudan, and in venturing across to Arabia.

He had a long, anxious time to wait before the comfort of their reassurance reached him, since he was to be many months, even years without news. He certainly was gambling on this new project; he had made no logical mistake, but he was to pay a tragic price in health. He did perfectly fit himself for the task, and yet it was in a sense this very perfection that so sadly "destroyed the best founded hopes of success, in exploring the unknown of African which the Association had ever formed".[50]

However, although these Nubian and Arabian divergencies took up no less than two-and-a-half years of his time, not a moment was wasted, since *"no opportunity of forwarding the main object of penetrating into the interior of Africa in the intended direction was lost by delay, as no caravan departed from Egypt to the westward during the whole period of his absence from Cairo."*[51]

Of this difficult time in Esne Louis wrote later:

I was then, as I am still fully convinced that the title of Haji would afford me the most powerful recommendation and protection in any future journey through the interior countries of Africa.... I knew that if I should not reach Mecca without being present at the ceremonies of the Haj, I could not hope to pass afterwards as a true Haji without exposing myself to daily detection.[52]

What more practical argument could be presented? It was accepted unanimously by the committee of the African Association,

and no one who has lived for any length of time in a Muslim
country would query the common sense of this reasoning.

The aim was to make the utmost success of the Nigerian tour:
if he were to be suspect, thwarted, or murdered, as was quite
likely, at the very outset of it, the long years of preparation and
study—apart from any other less material considerations—would
have been for nothing.

But of course to some extent, superficially, the step does
appear as a gamble: he would be away for longer than he had
intended had he followed his original plan, and he might
therefore have missed a caravan to the interior. The chances of
this had to be weighed against the manifest advantages of becoming a haji, of having seen with his own eyes the holy city at
the time of the pilgrimage. Particularly so as the Maghribins with
whom he would travel were known for being especially devout
Muslims. He knew that the Wahabi wars were still disrupting the
arrival and departure in Cairo of caravans to and from Arabia and
back to the west, so that his decision was as acceptable in his own
view as it proved to be to the gentlemen of the African Association
in distant London. His employers trusted him as a man of courage
and integrity, they knew the wisdom of allowing him to take his
own time, they were only too well aware of the dangers of un-
preparedness or overhaste. They had already, as we know, lost
two of their explorers in the west and they had no wish to lose
this most promising man of all. Not only did they approve of his
action, but moreover they were delighted with the information
that he brought out of Arabia, which proved to be the most
accurate ever received in Europe.[53] And what is more, when he
did ultimately return to Cairo (where the plague had raged for
two winters) it was to find as we know, that no caravan had
arrived or gone back to the west during his absence.

It was a triumph: he had missed no chance of the great
journey to the interior and he had, by this audacious lateral
trek, added enormously to western civilisation's knowledge
of the most secret and most holy place in the entire Islamic
world.

Nevertheless, the solitary decisions he had to make in that

suffocatingly hot long summer and protracted winter in Esne were troublesome ones, and he had far too much time in which to ponder them alone.

Having decided on the journey—the first leg of which was the terrible desert crossing that Bruce had made on his return from Abyssinia just over forty years earlier—he had to join a caravan. At Daraou, a place near Kom Ombos and about sixty miles south of Esne, some traders, "a worthless set of vagabonds", were preparing to set out for Sennar to barter for slaves. But their departure was delayed for months—first by the activities of a Mograt robber chieftain named Naim, and then by a famine in the area of their destination.

Naim was a Mamluk sympathiser who, having declared war on Egyptian slave traders, occupied himself very profitably in harassing their caravans on that formidable desert crossing. The traders were obliged to wait until their caravan gathered sufficient strength of numbers to be capable of fighting its way through should the robbers attack.

Naim, who enjoyed bragging of the pleasures of his harem, used much of his ill-gotten wealth to buy young slave girls. Since he wore on the road a strong coat of chain mail he had acquired a reputation for invulnerability, but he was eventually killed by Ababda Bedouin—with appropriate retribution—at one of his own numerous weddings. His head was taken to Egypt, his ears cut off and sent to Mohammed Ali in Arabia, and his bride was forced to marry one of the murderers.

This was in October 1813, and the caravan could have set out, but then came news of a disastrous famine near Sennar where locusts had devoured the entire winter crop, and people were killing each other for a mere measure of maize.

In his time of extreme loneliness in Upper Egypt, Louis had the misfortune to meet the merchant-traveller, James Silk Buckingham, who was, at least superficially, a very charming person. Louis was far from being the first, or the last either, to be deceived by the ingratiating ways of a man later dubbed "the most artful of adventurers".[54]

Buckingham arrived with a letter of introduction from Colonel

Missett—evidently also deceived by his garrulous charm; this, combined with the ennui of Esne, accounts for the real pleasure with which Louis greeted his arrival in Upper Egypt. Louis makes absolutely no mention of the event, or of subsequent meetings in his journals; possibly any such accounts, in view of later proceedings, were edited out. One cannot tell now, but Louis did "open his heart" to this man, as he told Renouard by letter.[55] He had trusted in Buckingham as an Englishman, and believed in his integrity as a traveller, a family man and an honest merchant. It was not until many months later that Louis received a long-delayed warning from Renouard, then chaplain to the Levant Company's factory at Smyrna. Renouard seems to have been the only person at the time to have seen the true nature of this sentimental gentleman, but his letter reached Louis too late, and Louis would have felt ashamed of having been taken in by this so insinuating man, whose copied written material and garbled verbal accounts were later the subject of a minor scandal in London.

However, Buckingham's description of their meeting by the Nile is good:

What interested me still more than any antiquities here . . . was my first meeting with Mr Burckhardt . . . whose reputation as an Eastern traveller preparing for a journey of discovery into the interior of Africa had caused him to be an object of general interest to all Europeans . . . hearing of the arrival of a boat with an English traveller, he hastened down to the river bank, came on board, and introduced himself, speaking excellent English. He was dressed in the commonest garments, as an Arab peasant or small trader, with a blue cotton blouse covering a coarse shirt, loose white trousers, and a common calico turban . . . he had a full dark beard, was without stockings, wearing only the slip-shod slippers of the country, and looked so completely like an Arab of the north—a Syrian having a fairer complexion and lighter eyes than the Egyptians—that few would have suspected him to be a Swiss, as he really was, but have taken him to be a native of Antioch or Aleppo . . .[56]

They spent the evening together at the Turkish governor's house where they supped, and agreed to meet on board Buckingham's boat in the morning.

As he was with us before sunrise—early rising being universal in this country—we had our simple breakfast of coffee and rice-pilau prepared, of which he partook; and we were so intensely and mutually interested in each other's conversation, that we continued together, seated in the boat in uninterrupted talk till sunset, with scarcely an interval of pause between; for our noon-day and sunset meals our conversation still continued in unabated volubility. The truth is, that the meeting of two Europeans in so remote a spot from their respective homes, makes them friends and brothers at once; and as each is sure to have a large amount of sympathy, bottled up as it were for want of reciprocal exercise, it is sure on such occasions to overflow. . . .

They met twice again as it so happened, each time it seems with mutual pleasure, but Louis was mistaken in putting his trust in this man, who was to talk too glibly and too widely of him as his "bosom friend".

The months dragged by and Louis was bored nearly to extinction, as he wrote to his parents.[57] Even when his eyes allowed he had little or nothing to read. Once there was a welcome parcel of Frankfurt newspapers sent on from Cairo—news of the war in Europe was then taking about two months to reach Lower Egypt. He had written up his travels long ago, often called on his friend the Bey of Esne, completed London and home correspondence, and seen the antiquities a hundred times. Apart from the painful eye trouble, he was extremely fit. He rode out every morning, and bathed in the Nile.

I may have been thought a good swimmer [*he wrote home*], in Neuchâtel, Leipzig and even London, but here I find that any little lad does it better; but they are amazed when they see me swim on my back.

He continued on the frugal diet in which he believed. His favourite dish was lentils with yoghurt, or cucumbers stuffed with rice and minced meat, and for a taste of home cooking he had taught his servant to cook the little meat pies which he calls *kuchi-pastetli*.

His active spirit fretted dreadfully at delay. But he kept himself busy by writing essays in Arabic, he even translated his travel diaries into the language—tasks he dared not have corrected for fear of revealing his identity. As it was, since he had no evident employment, bazaar gossip hummed—it was rumoured that he had chests full of dollars, or some access to treasure. Posing now as a poor merchant, in preparation for the journey with the traders he spent as little as possible in order not to attract attention. Fortunately the cost of living in Esne was fantastically low. Daily expenses for himself, servant, two camels, and donkey amounted to about 1s. 6d, his horse cost him about 1s. 4d. a month; he could buy a chicken for 6 para, and five eggs, for one, that is half a farthing.

Earlier in the year he had ridden alone to Assiut to sell one of his swift riding camels, which unfortunately died there; on returning he was caught in a violent *samun*. The blinding dust-laden inferno maddened his camel into a wild gallop. He lost the reins, was thrown heavily, and remained lying wrapped in his cloak until the wind abated, and he could see again. Later he found the animal a long way off standing by some bushes to shelter its great eyes from the furious lash of driven sand.

Louis does not record much of this visit to Assiut, though some of the things he heard or saw there obviously sickened him. Nowhere does he comment fully on the ethics of slavery. Highly civilised and humane though he was, he had come to accept it as being inevitable in these countries. Efforts to abolish slavery were then already under way in Europe, but in Africa and Arabia it ground on—as yet an ineluctable fact, however appalling.

A year later, in the slave-traders' market at Assiut, Henry Light, a captain in the Royal Artillery travelling for pleasure in Egypt, was offered a shapely seventeen-year-old Negress—"for the trifling sum of rather more than fifteen pounds sterling". The slave trader, like any horse-dealer, examined, pointed out and made the Englishman remark the good points of the girl in question.

> The poor wretch, thus exposed, pouted and cried during the ceremony; was checked, encouraged, and abused according to her behaviour.[58]

Captain Light describes the slave traders as surprisingly mild-looking men, tall and slender, dressed in long woollen gowns fastened toga-fashion, their thick hair hanging in matted plaits nearly to the shoulder exactly like that of the ancient Egyptians. But their appearance was deceptive.

There was a village near Assiut where a grisly "manufacture"—as Louis puts it—took place; the making of eunuchs to supply the ceaseless demands of Constantinople's great seraglio. This horrible job was done by two Coptic monks. Hardly surprisingly, Louis did not see them at work but he heard several descriptions of the task, and of these monks who were reputed "to excell all their predecessors in dexterity". Even the most disreputable factors of the local population regarded their loathsome profession with due contempt but, since they paid an annual tax, the monks were safe under government protection.

It was always the strongest and best-looking boys who were selected for the operation but on maturity, unlike the traditional fat guards of fictional harems, every grown eunuch whom Louis saw later in the Hijaz was gaunt and hollow-eyed, almost skeletal.

The operation, although brutal, rarely proved fatal: Louis knew for certain that out of sixty boys operated on at that particular time near Assiut only two had died, and he understood that number to be rather higher than average. He gives—in Latin—a nauseating description of the operation: it was performed by force upon these pitiful boys who, fainting from the pain, were held down fast on a table by strong men. Hot oil and some ointment, kept a secret by the Copts, effected the cure. Captain Light saw two boatloads of 150 such Negro boys, all totally emasculated, survivors of 160 operated on.[59] So eleven had died, which is a considerably higher death toll than Louis' two in sixty, but Louis' is most likely to be the more accurate account.

While he was in Assiut Louis was delighted to receive letters from his friends, Renouard, the chaplain, and W. G. Browne—once again on his travels, this time in the Middle East where he was eventually killed by Persian robbers. In reply to Renouard, Louis wrote of his Arabian decision:

> I think it my duty to make the best of myself and indeed my travelling desire increases with every new successful excursion . . .[60]

A few days later he wrote again on a rather troubled note, regarding the vexed question of circumcision:

> I have received a letter of Mr Fiott from Messina . . . in several of his letters he most seriously advises me to undergo a certain operation; saying that you and Mr Wherry . . . [*consul at Smyrna*] were equally of that opinion. To engage me still further he adds—in his last letter, the expression "I think it *would do you no harm*" (meaning bodily harm) . . .[61]

Whether he took this precautionary step one does not know; it seems more likely that, having not thought of the safeguard earlier, he would not at this stage have chanced revealing an utterly non-Muslim characteristic—apart from the fact of his very evident distaste. If, however, he did not undergo the operation he must have known that he would risk the chance of immediate death in Mecca should the physical fact become known there.

At long last, in March the following year, the caravan began to assemble for the journey, and Louis rode to Daraou to await its departure. He was now completely ready to travel, dressed much as Buckingham describes—in a coarse white linen shirt and trousers, his brown woollen *thabout*, a white cap on his shaven head tied around with a cheap cloth in lieu of a turban, and sandals on his bare feet—the peasant's dress in which he was to arrive, ragged and destitute months later in Arabia. He had fifty Spanish dollars in his girdle, and some gold sequins in a small leather amulet which he wore on his arm—the other amulet containing the scraps of silk embroidered with his initials in his mother's hair he carried always on his breast.[62] In a hidden pocket of his voluminous *thabout* were the precious firmans of the Pashas, two long scrolls with great seals, together with a letter from Mohammed Ali addressed to all the black kings on the Sennar route, introducing him as Sheik Ibrahim el Shamy, or the Syrian. Naturally his Daraou travelling companions knew nothing of this, but he gave them to understand that he was Aleppo-born, and that he was well befriended by the Bey of Esne, who governed the Daraou district. He carried on him also two small journal notebooks,* pencil, penknife, pocket compass, tobacco pouch with steel for striking a light and, stuck in his belt, the *dawayeh* or inkhorn with some loose sheets of paper for writing amulets for the Negroes.

On this barren crossing he needed to carry more provisions than he had on the Nile journey: flour, biscuits, dates, lentils, some onions, a little rice, and eighty pounds of durra for the donkey which he was to ride. He had also a metal cooking pan, a copper plate, a coffee roaster, an earthenware mortar, a wooden drinking bowl, an axe, ten yards of rope, needles and thread, one spare shirt, a coarse carpet, and a woollen covering, a small packet of medicines and three spare water skins.

In his present role of poor trader he was obliged to carry a certain amount of merchandise, so he took sugar, soap, nutmegs, razors, steels, two red tarbushes and several dozen wooden beads.

For weapons he had a gun, three dozen cartridges and some small shot, a pistol, and a *nabout*†—a useful stave reinforced with iron at both ends, it served to pound coffee beans or to defend him and was his constant companion.

* They measured 4 × 10 inches—one still remains in the British Museum.

† Burton describes the *nabout* as an ash stave 6 feet long and as thick as a man's wrist.

He was feeling physically very fit, strong enough to cope with the loading and unloading of the camel by himself—which is an extremely difficult task—so he intended to travel without a servant, and to manage alone. Experience had proved that on exceptionally hard and dangerous journeys it was better not to be hampered by a hired man whose courage and loyalty might easily break in the face of serious trial.

But when he arrived at Daraou he soon found that his preparations did not conform with the strict economy of his fellow traders. His baggage weighed too little, his camel was capable of carrying at least four hundredweight more, a freight worth 20 dollars. This was a factor he could not disregard without arousing suspicion. He was offered money to take on the additional freight, but, realising that the loading and unloading of such a burden would be too much single-handed, he decided to sell the camel, making an agreement, as part of the bargain, that the purchaser should retain the load already on the camel and take it across the desert. Although this agreement seemed perfectly satisfactory to both parties at the time, it was to lead to trouble later.

Then, because of the small amount of his merchandise, the Daraou men assumed he was running away from Egyptian debtors, so he let it be known that he was in search of a mythical "lost cousin" who, having left for Sennar some years ago on a mercantile venture in which he—Sheik Ibrahim—had invested all his property, made a good enough pretext for his present journey. The story was acceptable to these people, but they did seem to have some petty professional jealousy, believing that he would later have sufficient capital to return and make a really profitable venture in their own trade. This, he thought, was probably the main reason for their rough treatment of him throughout the entire journey. Also, he looked a poor man and therefore contemptible—hewing his own wood, cooking his own meals, filling his own water skins—indeed in their eyes he was hardly an equal of the servants whom these merchants hired cheaply for the desert crossing. In addition, although they had not the slightest idea that he was a European, they took him, because of his colouring and build, to be of Turkish origin, which alone was enough to incite ill-treatment since Arabs universally bore an inveterate hatred of their Ottoman overlords.

His position therefore in this savage caravan even from the outset was difficult in the extreme, and the reasons for his ostracism many. Although not so much alone as he had been on the first Nubian journey, he was in one sense more so, in the cruel way that a man is isolated in an unfeeling crowd, for these were callous, brutal men. Their trade naturally deadened what latent humanity they possessed—the great James Bruce wrote of "the desperate kind of indifference about life" engendered by this desert crossing.

Yet Louis seems not to have been in the least dismayed; it was as if the very animosity and revilements of the traders towards him acted as stimuli to his own verve and courage. Communally enclosed in the caravan's entity, its dangers and anxieties, he was also individually beset and hedged about by the constant aggravations and bullying of its members. He was stronger than they were, not only physically—later in Berber he often threw the toughest of them in wrestling bouts—but in his hidden possession, the strength of mind and character that lay like a palimpsest beneath the poor Syrian peasant exterior with which he confronted this uncouth rabble.

Before the loading a ceremony of blessing the merchandise took place at the village. Ababda Bedouin women appeared carrying earthenware vessels filled with burning coals which they placed before the loads and the couched camels. They threw salt on the embers and as the bluish flames arose the women cried: "May you be blessed in going and in coming!" So, Shaitan and the evil djinns conveniently deposed—or perhaps propitiated— the caravan set out on its 400 mile arduous journey.

It was a disorderly procession of some forty camels, thirty-five donkeys, and the villagers who went tagging along to see them a part of the way. The camels roaring and grumbling at their loads, ill-tied bundles falling off, a general sense of confusion—and as was the custom at the start of any long journey, they made little distance that evening. As if reluctant to leave the safety of the Nile they stopped in a small valley only a few hours away from Daraou to sit feasting and singing by firelight.

On the second day out, in a rocky defile so narrow that loaded camels could hardly pass, they were rounding a shoulder of the mountain when they heard angry voices—their advance Bedouin guard engaged in furious dispute with a strong party of armed and apparently hostile Arabs. The Ababda guides of the caravan swooped past and rushed in to the attack: stripped suddenly naked except for a rag of a loin cloth, both forces were armed with long two-edged swords and short lances, both sides used their shields skilfully to fend off the hail of stones with which the battle commenced.

Then there was a frightful din as they came face to face with drawn swords. Louis, thinking the opposition was a robber band, pressed forward to join in the defence. He was the only man who had firearms: he had already lifted his musket to take aim when one of their own Ababda yelled out for God's sake not to shoot. It was hoped there would be no bloodshed, since the attackers were also of the Ababda, intending only to levy passage money. The Egyptians then dropped back to defend the baggage, leaving the Bedouin to battle it out among themselves. After about twenty minutes' skirmishing the fight ended, both bands claiming victory.

Despite the ferocious clangour of the initial clash little damage had been done—three men only slightly wounded; the caravan had gained the day and was allowed to proceed.

So they continued, through barren granite rocks alive with locusts. At night they lit their camp fires with the dried dung of camels that had gone before them, since this was the beaten track of the traders, and encampments were bound to be where there was at least some scrub for the camels' evening feed.

None of the traders had tents, all slept in the open air under the scintillating canopy of desert night. There was beauty, but little peace; each evening brought quarrelling among the eighty or so men. They had divided themselves into a dozen groups or messes; there was a constant fear of thieves—not from robbers outside but from addicted pilferers within the camp—and no one settled down to sleep without carefully arranging his baggage close about him. In the darkness of the night an encampment was never really quiet, except when in breathless fear of attack; a stealthy footstep would arouse a light sleeper, and always, in fear or not, there would be the sound of camels grinding their teeth and belching as they brought up the cud—since a camel never seems to sleep.

With first light came the loading, and the usual protesting coughing chorus of the camel's roar as the beasts were made to rise, and once again the caravan moved on; every day the length of the march increased gradually so as to break in the animals by degrees to longer stints.

As the caravan prepared to leave each morning, every man ate a piece of dry biscuit with raw onion—nothing more. By noon they were intensely hungry; the sun's heat was tremendous by then—invariably the midday halt was loud with angry dispute. As soon as it was known whereabouts they would stop, the young men rushed ahead to choose the largest tree or some place shaded by overhanging rock for themselves and their mess. Furious arguments followed as to who had arrived first. Often as not Louis was driven from a pleasant spot, where the tracery of branches threw a cool net of shade across the sand, out into burning sunshine, and almost invariably he spent the midday hours in extreme discomfort. The customary dough cake had to be baked on the *sadj*—a hot iron plate—on an open fire in the sand. To crouch over flames in noon's remorseless heat would have been a trial to the toughest nomad. Louis does not enlarge upon his suffering but he does admit to "great distress" at these times.

The midday meal consisted simply of these hot baked cakes eaten with a sauce made of dried okra, or of butter, or honey. The customary supper dish was boiled lentils, or salted bread either baked on the *sadj*, or in hot ashes, eaten with onions and, for Louis, a cup of coffee. This last small luxury he shared with the Daraou people, so coaxing from them some slight degree of good humour —at least for a while.

On the sixth day out Louis became involved in a violent scene with the man who had bought his camel. This man had done nothing but complain, and having considerably overladen the animal he had tried continually to get rid of part of the load on to

Louis' donkey. Finally, even the camel's patience gave way and it broke down, whereupon the fellow demanded his money back, and furiously accused Louis of selling him a faulty animal. Swearing, cursing, loudly lamenting, dramatically smearing his face with dust—as sign of frantic grief—he finally won over to his side all the leaders of the caravan. Cheated, Louis was forced to enter into a fresh agreement, this time with one of the Bedouin, for his baggage freight.

It was a pitiless land: the barren, sandy plain they marched over the next day was ominously littered with the carcasses and bones of camels. Now that they were deep into the desert even the family of the people with whom Louis had lodged at Daraou, to whom he had made gifts and into whose charge he had been ceremoniously committed at the start, were no longer even civil to him. Seeing how poor he apparently was they realised there could be little hope of further presents so, having nothing to lose, they began to deride his protector, the Bey of Esne. In the desert, they said, they cared little for all the Beys and Pashas of the world. But seeing that this sort of talk in no way disconcerted Louis, they started to address him contemptuously as *walad*—"boy", varlet or serving-man.[63]

Each day these people multiplied their insults, but Louis swallowed his anger and never allowed himself to reach the point of retaliation they obviously wanted to provoke so that the quarrel might come to blows.

Louis was soon driven away from the group with whom he had messed each evening, although he had always cooked by himself. Now he remained entirely alone since the others had given out that he had stolen from their baggage. Their treatment of him reached such a pitch that he could honestly say "not an hour passed" without his being the butt of some insult, "even from the meanest servants of these people, who very soon imitated and surpassed their masters".

Louis tells the story so simply, and with such a wealth of understatement, that one must exert all one's imagination to grasp the intensity of his lonely endurance in the various predicaments arising daily.

He does not relate many incidents but this one is typical:

When we arrived at the well of Nakeyb and the camels and asses went to be watered, and the water skins were carried to be filled, some people of the caravan descended according to custom into the wells to fill the *delou* or leather bucket, while others drew up the water. Having no friend to go down for me, I was obliged to wait near the well the whole afternoon, until near sunset, to the great amusement of my companions, and I should have remained unsupplied had not one of the guides at last assisted in drawing up the water from above, while I descended into the well to fill the *delou*.

Another day, near the wells of el Haimar, Louis was fascinated by the marvellously preserved corpse of a distinguished Mamluk who, although so near to water, had died here of thirst. Looking in through the gaps in the low tomb wall Louis thought that this body, naturally preserved by the dryness of the air, was a more perfect mummy than any he had seen in Egypt.

There were many graves in the area, all of Mamluks who had died of thirst. It so happened that the wells of el Haimar lay slightly concealed in a small sandy plain set around with hills, and since one of the more unpleasant habits of Ababda guides was to keep people away from watering places and then to sell them water skins at exorbitant prices, this area became the graveyard of many travellers.

Impeded by scores of servants and hangers-on, the retreating Mamluk Corps had remained near these wells for several weeks, and it was here that the caravan had dismissed its camp-followers. Among whom were:

several dashing Egyptian dancing girls, the price of whose charms had increased in the mountains, in the same proportion as other commodities, and who had thus been able to acquire large sums of money in a very short time.

These unfortunates were later deliberately abandoned by their guides when only a night's journey from the Nile, and set upon by other Ababda who robbed them, stripped them naked and allowed them to proceed to Egypt. Louis does not elaborate on it but the tale evokes a dramatic picture of those so "dashing" girls pitifully denuded in the fracas—not only of their flimsy veils but of all their hard-earned cash as well.

To the Egyptian Arab even the worst possible desert journey, such as this, was preferable to a sea voyage however brief. Louis records a typical saying that robustly expresses this feeling: "Rather the flatulencies of camels than the prayers of fishes."[64]

The desert crossing was a most arduous one—extremely fatiguing, Louis calls it—but despite all he endured, he says that is sheer physical suffering he did not think it was as fearful as his predecessor, Mr Bruce, had made out. In fact, Louis thought Bruce had rather "overstated" his suffering in this particular desert but he adds with his usual fairness and liberality:

> ... while I think it my duty to make this remark, I must at the same time declare that acquainted as I am with the character of the Nubians, I cannot but sincerely admire the wonderful knowledge of men, the firmness of character, and promptitude of mind which furnished Bruce with the means of making his way through these savage inhospitable nations as a European. To travel as a native has its inconveniences and difficulties, but I take those which Bruce encountered to be of a nature much more intricate and serious, and such as a mind at once courageous, patient, and fertile in expedients could alone have surmounted.

A long stretch of wild and stony land now lay ahead, so rough that the camels had difficulty in picking their way. Beyond this they reached at last a wadi full of trees where every man in the caravan gave thanks to heaven, and threw down in salutation a handful of millet, as a kind of offering perhaps to the numen of the place.

Six hours later they reached another wadi in which luxuriant acacia trees were swarming with locusts feeding on young shoots. Below the trees there grew a tangled mass of gourd vines. The men began a battle-practice game, pelting each other violently with the hard round gourds, and fending them off neatly with their shields. Since Louis had no shield he very soon became the defenceless target of his Daraou "*friends*", who aimed so viciously and so often at his head that he was forced at last to put an end to the horse-play by asking the caravan leader to stop it. So he was saved from a bloody nose but earned the title of "cowardly boy"—a taunt that lasted for several days until exchanged for a fresh epithet unfortunately too coarse, in his view, for nineteenth-century London's perusal.

Despite this general atmosphere of persecution and bullying, and despite the fact that he always walked for at least four or five hours of each day's full march in order to save the donkey, and had all the labour of doing his own chores and tending his animal when tired out himself—despite all this, he says that he was never in better health and spirit. He does not seem to have given a jot for his persecutors. Certainly one good point about his isolation was that he was able to write his journal more easily than on many other journeys when almost every movement he made had been watched by his various guides, often with suspicion.

It was 13 March and they were nearing some wells at about half-way on the desert crossing, when quite suddenly panic seized the whole caravan: the terrible dread of thirst. During the day they had met a small party of slave traders travelling north from Berber with a string of captives. The traders announced that of two vital wells ahead one was dried up and the other, in the Shigre Mountains was dangerously low.

From the traders they bought a strong camel to carry water. Most of the night was spent in consultation; in the morning there were many disputes; loud, bombastic arguments continued as to what should be done. It was a two-day march to the Shigre well, already said to be low, and five days from there to Berber on the Nile, via the Nejeym wells said to be dry. They could not stay long where they were since these wells were small and the supply scanty.

The discussion became open: every man giving his opinion, even the much scorned "Lad". They were in the middle of the crossing, and they had little choice. There were two more routes to Berber, but one was dangerous, and the only man who knew the other could not be trusted.

Louis' own suggestion, typically European, was practical and drastic: it was to kill their thirty-five donkeys—whose daily water supply was at least fifteen skins—load the camels to capacity and strike out direct through the desert to Berber, by-passing the doubtful wells, and making the journey in five forced marches. But, says Louis, the Arab will seldom take such resolutions, he prefers to console himself fatalistically with the trust in God's bounty—*Allah kerim*. In the end the total result of all these deliberations was that they continued on the usual track.

With trepidation they made what preparations they could. Louis paid a man to take on his camel some extra water skins for the donkey in order to keep the animal on its feet, but it was not without great apprehension that he left the place of the wells. When they stopped for the night in a narrow valley he was over-come with tiredness, his eyes were once again sore and painful, sleep was difficult. Next day, an over-loaded camel fell, bursting several precious water skins, it broke its leg and had to be slaughtered. The following day another camel also had to be killed, and the vultures gathered quickly.

Like vultures too, the Ababda men, prompt in adversity, began to raise the question of extra payment; subsequent arguments delayed the caravan after its midday halt until nearly four o'clock. Then, at the very moment of departure, the man whom Louis had paid to carry water for him came with the largest of the four skins and slumped it down at his feet saying that his camel could take it no further. By the time Louis had filled two smaller skins from the big one, roped them and reloaded his donkey, the cara-van had moved on out of sight.

It was not until long after sunset that he rejoined it, and while following quite alone in its footsteps Louis knew the dire need of some companion. Slave traders showed no trace of compassion for any embarrassments of their fellow creatures—those who dropped behind were left to their fate.

The next day the terror of thirst was stressed by tantalisingly beautiful visions of azure blue lakes: illusionary waters, often seeming so close that they vanished at only 200 paces—exquisite mirages faithfully reflecting all the light and shade of the wild Shigre Mountains ahead on the far horizon. Sometimes Louis counted as many as twelve of these lakes encircling trudging beasts and men, each lake widening, telescoping and vanishing as the caravan toiled on, only to reform and close in again behind.

On the day following that of the mirages they entered the fantastic wildly tumbled mountains of Shigre, and climbed up to the spring. The water was good and cool, but not plentiful. The place, a narrow cavern cleft in the rock, haunt of innumerable pigeons, was difficult of access and naturally there was more trouble among the men. The ever-callous slave traders watered their camels at the spring before the Ababda guides had time to fill their water skins. With reason the Bedouin were furious; they had to spend the night up in the rocks until the well should refill, and some of them slept at the cavern's mouth to prevent anyone taking the water by stealth.

In the morning Louis toiled hard to fill two large water skins. He humped one back to the camp below intending to bring his donkey nearer to fetch the second one, which he had had to leave where it lay, sweating and full-bellied by the spring. It was, of course, empty when he returned, the traders having filled up from it, and no more drinkable water remained in the well.

Louis came away from the empty cavern, his heart heavy. A silken flutter of returning wings was bright against the dark rocks—pigeons could wait for their spring to fill, but men must press on, and for Louis now the outlook was black. His stock of water was, at the most sufficient for himself and the donkey for two days only—and it was still *five* days' march to Berber.

He tried to buy some water but without success: however, news of his plight came to the ears of the Ababda chief who sent for him just as they were about to leave the mountain camp. More to shame the Egyptians, with whom the Ababda were still very angry after their behaviour at the well, than to be just, the Sheik spoke severely of their cruelty to Louis, and made him a present of enough water to fill one small skin.

There followed an eleven-hour march through extravagantly contorted mountains, down to a vast sandy plain. From Daraou to this plain it had been a beaten trail, but in the moving sands only the experienced eye and skill of the Bedouin could guide the travellers.

Louis does not describe shifting sands since the phenomenon would be common knowledge to the members of the African Association to whom he was addressing himself. So again one must read between the lines. Shifting sands can be great dunes eighty or more feet high which move according to the wind almost overnight so that what track there is is obliterated and a caravan, confused and lost, can only too easily turn into the waterless plain where men die of thirst within twenty-four hours.

They had been nineteen days out; it was intensely hot as they continued now over this immense plain, drawing nearer to the springs of Nejeym—which they had been told were dry. However hope lingered and they sent men on ahead to dig out the wells.

When the caravan caught up with them the men were sitting dejectedly in attitudes of despair beside the choked springs. They had dug for hours in a pit twenty or thirty feet deep to find only damp sand.

Now even the Bedouin were frightened: there seemed to be nothing for it but to make an attempt to reach the Nile in forced marches.

They pressed on thirsty and desperate across the burning sands; sands which at last gave way to a dark expanse of small black flints, reminding Louis of a part of the desert of Tyh and of the wanderings of the Israelites. A dreary plain; water was low, they drank only twice a day now. Luckily there were north winds, but they suffered vilely from the incandescent heat, and tempers were more than usually frayed. There was another row in which Louis was accused of stealing water for his ass in the night, insulted with lurid imprecations—undoubtedly involving the genitals of female camels—and eventually pelted with stones.

After midnight on the twenty-first day of the journey they moved on. Following the intense heat of day the night was chilly and when they came to a wadi full of dried-up trees some of the men, to warm themselves, set branches on fire in passing, "and the flames spreading over the valley beautifully illuminated the travellers and their frightened beasts".

No doubt the Arab voices echoed then in the *hedou* song, hauntingly in the way that makes a man's blood run hot and cold with the long-drawn lilt and the thrill of it. Louis often mentions Arab songs and their differences, but the *hedou* with which they encouraged their animals on the march, especially at night, seemed to be common to all these nations, notably among Bedouin. He heard it in the Arabian deserts, and on the banks of the Euphrates, as well as on those of the White Nile.

The next day was again very hot on the burning plain; one after the other the donkeys began to collapse. Louis did not drink all day, but he gave his donkey a little water every now and again to keep up its spirits.

After a march of nine hours there were many stragglers, and all the animals were flagging, so the caravan leader called a halt in a wadi of *sellam* trees. Since leaving the pigeon-haunted spring in the mountains three days earlier, Louis had lived entirely on biscuits in order to save the water he would have used had he cooked. Again he "dined" off the same unpalatable fare and washed it down with a single really satisfying draught; there was then just enough water left for one more drink tomorrow.

> Everyone was in the greatest dejection, foreseeing that the asses must die the ensuing day if not properly watered, and none of the traders had more than a few draughts for himself.

There was now only one thing that could save them—the Ababda Sheik had advised it earlier: ten or twelve of the strongest camels would have to be ridden direct to the Nile. The nearest bank was only about six hours' swift riding time away, but since it was known to be inhabited by Arabs hostile to the traders the whole caravan could not venture there.

The camel riders were to choose a lonely spot at the river, and return at once with water. So, carrying the empty skins, they left at four in the afternoon.

For the silently waiting caravan the hours dragged by:

in the greatest anxiety, for if the camels should not return, we had little hopes of escape either from thirst or from the sword of our enemies, who, if they once got sight of the camels, would have followed their footsteps through the desert, and would certainly have discovered us. After sunset several stragglers arrived, but two still remained behind, of whom one joined us early in the morning, but the other was not heard of any more. He was the servant to a Daraou trader who showed not the least concern about his fate. . . . We remained the greater part of the night in sullen and silent expectation of the result of our desperate mission. At length, about 3 o'clock in the morning, we heard the distant hollowings of our watermen, and soon after refreshed ourselves with copious draughts of the delicious water of the Nile. The caravan passed suddenly from demonstrations of the deepest distress to those of unbounded joy and mirth.

The terror was gone, like a nightmare swept aside. A large supper was cooked and everyone sang and rejoiced until day-break, giving not a thought to the terrible fate of "the unhappy man who had remained behind".

Louis says that it was not often that people died of thirst on this route, and indeed if the Nejeym well held water it was almost impossible. But, during that memorable night, he heard an all too graphic account from a man who had very recently come to the ultimate verge of just such a miserable death. He told how in the last throes of thirst his eyes had grown dim, how his camel suddenly smelling water had broken into a wild gallop; he had fallen from the saddle and was lying unconscious, when a Bedouin chanced to find him.

It was now 22 March—exactly a year since Louis' discovery of Abu Simbel. After a hearty breakfast the caravan made a late start around 7 a.m., and stopped at noon to seek scanty shade in a wadi of acacia trees. But even the scorching heat was bearable that day since they knew they would soon reach the blessed Nile again.

The next day, as they drew near to the river—even at two hours' distance—they became aware of it from a definite increase of moisture in the atmosphere. The camels quickened their stride, the riders lifted their heads to snuff the air's delicious promise. And with arms raised, impassioned voices ringing, they roared out: "God be praised!—We smell again the Nile!"

# CHAPTER ELEVEN

## *Slaves, Swords and Drink*

Necessity is the plea for every infringement of human freedom. It is the argument of tyrants; it is the creed of slaves.
*William Pitt.* 1783

AT THAT HINT of water on the air, exhausted men and animals
braced themselves for the last lap of a hellish crossing, and before
evening the caravan arrived at a Nile village in the Berber district.

Nearly all the camels bore hideous wounds on their backs from
over-loading and the use of inferior saddles. Louis writes with
sharp distaste of the greed and negligence of men who, to save a
few piastres on the expense of a well-stuffed saddle, callously
subjected their animals to severe suffering.

Made of reed matting and mud, Berber's squat houses were
built squarely around squalid courtyards that became pig-mire
wallows after rain. Each house consisted of store-rooms, family
quarters, strangers' quarters and—almost without exception—
prostitutes' quarters. Camels, cows and sheep were kept in the
yards, the surrounding miserably ill-lit rooms were infested with
rats and mice. The chief sport of village boys was lance practice—
the rats as targets, and they killed dozens every day. These courtyards were the theatres of many lively if somewhat infernal
scenes—scuttering rats squealing under a hail of spears, grumbling
camels, and—in the background, like some dusky Greek chorus—
those lovely harlots, the *bouza* girls, singing over the making of
their intoxicating drinks.

The girls were freed slaves; their masters having tired of them,
they had no livelihood but prostitution and *bouza* making.

*Bouza* was a drink made from fermented durra: Browne knew
it as *merisa*, some travellers say it resembled beer. It was of various

qualities each with a distinctive name; the most evocative, bestowed by some cynic no doubt, was *Umm Bulbul*—the Mother of Nightingales—since that particular kind induced drunken song from throats probably not calculated to flatter the charming *bulbul*. Louis tried all the varieties, and rather liked this one, which he describes as having "a pleasant prickly taste something like champagne turned sour".

Four of these *bouza*-making whores lived in the house in which he lodged. On the night of the caravan's arrival, when the more respectable people had gone to bed, the girls came out of their quarters and approached the traders. It seemed that they were old acquaintances, and their appearance was greeted with boisterous shouts of welcome.

Most of the girls were Abyssinians by birth, women long famed for their beauty; and Louis remarks that many of them would have passed for beauties in any country. They wore over their gowns flowing white Egyptian cloaks dramatically lined with scarlet—the vivid blood-red and the white splendidly off-setting their statuesque figures, their handsome Grecian profiles and long dark eyes.

That first night, the girls gave the men from the desert "the welcome", as they called it. Promptly some *angaribs*, charpoy-like beds, were carried into the open courtyard. The men undressed to their loin cloths and stretched themselves out on the beds, while the women proceeded to massage their bodies with a kind of perfumed grease. This, a concoction of sheep's fat, soaps, musk, powdered sandalwood, with *senbal*, *mahleb* and other scents, was always used on amorous occasions. The massage lasted for about half an hour, but when it was over the whoring started. Men and girls remained together for the whole night without being "in the least disconcerted" by the presence of other people—such as Louis—who were also lying in the courtyard trying to sleep—with difficulty quite obviously, in view of a scene so flamingly erotic.

During the traders' two-week stay "these damsels", as Louis delicately calls them, came every evening to the strangers' quarters, and the women's rooms too were constantly filled with

*bouza* drinkers. Few traders would pass through this place without taking a mistress; and although in Berber not many men had
more than one wife, female slaves and mistresses were practically
*de rigueur*, and kept mistresses, Louis comments drily, were "more
numerous than in the politest capitals of Europe".

This fortnight was in fact one prolonged debauch. As if
attempting to find something good to say of the people of Berber,
Louis remarks that, in a sense, they were abstemious since they
often fasted for the whole day, but really it was only for the sake
of being able to revel all the more deliciously at night! *Bouza*
and swords marched together: nobody went to a *bouza* hut
without his sword. During the fortnight several carousals ended
in sword fights—the prostitutes often being the first to suffer.

Young Berber men who came to this house were constantly
heard boasting of the tricks they played on inexperienced
travellers by enticing them to women who, the next day, were
claimed as Arabs of pure, proud stock, whose people promptly
demanded vengeance money.

He had at first thought the Berberines very hospitable—
bread, milk and meat were sent in from various neighbours but
he soon discovered that they were simply consummate hypocrites,
since they regarded all foreign merchants as good "morsels" to
be fleeced at will, and he had to pay dearly for the so-called gifts
of food.

Another and perhaps rather unexpected trial was the insolence
of the slaves, who seemed to do exactly what they liked since their
masters never punished them for fear they might abscond to the
Bedouin. One slave tore Louis' only spare shirt to pieces in a fit
of pique because Louis had refused to give it away. All the
Berberines adored tobacco to such an extent that they were liable
to seize the very pipe from a man's mouth and smoke it until it
was finished before quite casually handing it back.

In addition to these minor trials from which all traders suffered
alike, Louis continued to be tricked and bullied by the Daraou
men, who were still doing their utmost to injure his feelings and
to make him contemptible in the eyes of the rest. At last, when
they came to realise that his physical strength was greater than

that of any of them—for it was now that he often wrestled with their strongest men and proved he could throw the best of them—he was left to the incessant teasing of the boys. That was annoying enough but he was forced to put up with it as best he could.

There are times when, reading Louis's simple account, one is astonished again and again by the sheer dogged stoicism and the astounding fortitude of the man in the face not only of real and visible dangers, but more so of ceaseless nagging aggravations such as these.

That the Daraou people hovered about him continually like a host of pestilential flies was one of the most miserable aspects of the time he spent in these countries, and it made his note-writing extremely difficult. He was never alone, and it was unsafe to walk away from the villages into the fields. But in living with the merchants there was some sort of security for him; he paid his share of the various bills, and with them he picked up a good deal of information about the trade. Of course in every way he would have been happier among the Bedouin; with the merchants there were many expenses and the state of his purse was alarmingly low.

Some travellers from Sennar were questioned about his missing "cousin" and, since it appeared no one knew of any Osmanli being in Sennar, Louis quickly had to invent another possibility, and suggested that this (mythical) person had gone on to Abyssinia. This development gave him a convenient chance to make inquiries about the desert route to Taka.

With his strong clean-cut features and his white skin—despite a deep tan it was of course still evident—Louis was thought by many people to belong to the Mamluks. He was none too pleased about this, but it seemed preferable to being connected with the Pasha in any way, since Mohammed Ali was hated by all merchants because of the heavy duties he imposed on imports from the south. So Louis was very careful to keep his large firmans well concealed.

During the Berber time Louis heard a story of a man "who was supposed to be Christian because he made notes of his journey in writing", with the result that he had been murdered by Bisharin Arabs on his way to the Red Sea. This tale more than ever convinced Louis that if he were once to be seen with his journal in his hand all hope of success would be blasted.

While in the desert mounted on his sturdy donkey he had been able to push ahead of the caravan and under some tree or rock, apparently only smoking his pipe or otherwise engaged in a natural call, he had been able to write unobserved. But in Berber and in Shendi note-taking was more than ever dangerous and difficult.

Apart from the "sour champagne" tasting *Umm Bulbul*, the only other pleasant aspect of Berber was the bathing. No one seemed to have any fear of crocodiles here, and he bathed frequently in the river, often swimming far out into mid-stream. He was not at all sorry to leave the stews of Berber when, on 7 April, the caravan started again for the south, heading towards the great market of Shendi, set at the cross-roads of the trade routes of eastern Sudan.

A day or two out from Berber they stopped at a village to pay transit duty to the Mek, or king of the district. There was a pond on the outskirts of the village and suddenly at this point the Daraou men turned to face him: they had decided to rid themselves of him once and for all. They ordered him off, the boys yelling insultingly that expression commonly used to drive dogs, away. "*Go damek!*" they shouted hounding him back, and beating his donkey so that it galloped off into the desert.

Then, since it seemed the only thing to do, Louis turned to the Bedouin: were they going to abandon him, or would they allow him to join their party? They immediately agreed, and after this the situation became materially much improved for him. He was delighted. Could he have known of current events in Europe he would have been even more elated, for this must have been the eve, if not the very day, of Napoleon's abdication and retreat to Elba.

The Mek was cold and unhelpful: the local people were villainously rapacious, surrounding the caravan with an outward pretence of friendliness but invading everything with deftly insinuating thieving hands.

Louis, who had good reason to believe the Mek would seize his gun, had already bribed the Bedouin sheik to say it was his own and so contrived to keep it for himself—at least for a while.

During the night the Mek sent his son for gifts; when none were forthcoming the young man asked for some "jolly fellow" from among them to keep him company at the local *bouza* shop. One of the Daraou men obliged, and had the dubious honour of being escorted by the princeling to a nearby brothel where they spent the whole night drinking and whoring.

The heat was increasing now, for they were approaching the rainbelt of the river where laxity and lassitude prevail. The next day was extremely hot: the Mek himself appeared in the morning freshly smeared with butter and naked except for a small loin cloth. He was attended by a retinue of slaves carrying his flask, his sword, his shield, so that despite his gleaming nudity "his Mekship had altogether a most proud and commanding appearance".

The caravan was obliged to take on a paid escort for the next stretch of country since it was terrorised by a band of intractable robbers. They travelled safely through, and came down to the high green banks of the Mogren river, which flows from the east into the Atbara. Here Louis enjoyed a full hour's rest— because the banks were so high and so steep many of the camels in stumbling down them threw their loads, causing what was for him a most welcome delay.

On the southern bank some water-wheels peacefully murmured their husky rhythm; the sound, the sparkle of the falling drops, even the resonant voices of the traders urging their camels, or calling loudly upon Allah, seemed not unpleasant in this charming spot. The blue pools of the river in its sandy bed reflected a bright clear sky and the soft foliage of tamarisks on the banks. All were sights and sounds to sustain Louis, briefly relaxed, drinking in as he always did the sweet cleanliness of any verdant scene. His so civilised mind and hard-pressed body alike were refreshed, profoundly grateful for that one chance hour of green peace in dappled shade.

But beyond there was a barren sandy plain to cross and, as they neared Damer, robber horsemen were sighted not far off, hovering about in a menacing way. However, some sheiks of

Damer dashed out on horseback to meet the caravan and escorted it through in safety.

They stayed in Damer for five days; the people were mostly Fokara or religious men. The Great Faki, their chief, came from a family of necromancers famous for the power of its spells. One tale related how the present Faki's father had made a lamb bleat in the stomach of the man who had stolen and eventually eaten the animal—a case perhaps of hypnotic dyspepsia.

These apparently law-abiding people were more amiable than the Berberines. Louis went once to kiss the hand of the venerable Great Faki who, sitting wrapped cocoon-like in a white cloak, seemed satisfied with the answers Louis gave to his academic questioning. The affairs of this hierarchical little state appeared to be well conducted. Even the ferocious Bisharin Bedouin went in awe of this regime—primarily because they feared the necromancers had power to control rainfall.

There was no regular market so Louis went out every day crying his beads for sale to make enough money to buy his donkey's feed. In this way he managed to enter many private houses and was surprised to find that, despite the austere regime of the Fakis, *bouza* shops and brothels were established all over the town. One day, as he could read Arabic, he was asked to a funeral feast to help with a Koran chanting, and on leaving was rewarded with some choice cuts of roast cow to take back for his supper.

When the caravan left for Shendi it was conducted by two unarmed Fakis who marched at its head affording protection from robbers, who feared and respected the holy men. But despite the presence of the necromancers the caravan kept very close together, and Louis carried his gun in his hand, aware that the sight of it was enough to scare a host of robbers. As was his custom when travelling he had not loaded it, and now a sheik of the Daraou men, knowing this, rode up and peremptorily ordered him to put in a ball. Louis refused, a sharp argument arose and the trader called him a cowardly rascal, unworthy of carrying arms. For once Louis replied scathingly: Daraou men he said with scorn, found sticks or scythes more suited to their hands than swords.

The Egyptian's pride was so offended by this that he struck

Louis a violent blow with his stave across the shoulders, almost levelling him to the ground.

Louis fended off a second blow with his gun, and was about to hit back with the butt-end when, fortunately, other men leapt between them or the fracas might have developed seriously.

Louis vented his wrath in "heavy curses", and everyone now, especially the Bedouin, held the Daraou man to blame. Louis winds up his account of the episode with a remarkably characteristic sentence:

> The bustle which this affair occasioned, together with our fears of the robbers, which did not permit me to quit the caravan, prevented me from taking my notes as fully as usual.

After a nine hours' ride they came down over sandhills to Hawaya. It had been an exceptional hot day; now the evening was beautiful and they all went to bathe in the Nile—the river here ran crystal clear inshore over a bed of little pebbles. They camped for the night in the middle of the village in an open space. Believing this a safe area, Louis wandered off to bargain his beads for bread but in a narrow lane he was violently set upon by two men. Although unarmed he fought back but they stole his wares and snatched his cap, and when they drew their swords he wisely took to his heels. Back at the camp the Bedouin laughed at his troubles but advised him to go to the village sheik who would be sure to discover the robbers. It was not until late that night that he found the sheik in a *bouza* hut in the middle of an uproariously drunken party. The stolen things were soon returned, but when Louis declined to join the drinkers he ultimately had to pay twice the value of the goods. He recorded this evening's escapade mainly to illustrate what little chance the lone traveller stood in these lands.

Herodotus said that after forty days' journey up the Nile in the land of the cataracts, one might take to a boat again and in another twelve days reach "a big city named Meroë said to be the capital of the Ethiopians".[65]

Meroë became the capital of the retreating Ethiopian (or

southern Nubian) conquerors of ancient Egypt who had fled from Napata, their more northerly capital, at the time of Psammetichos II's punitive incursions with the Greek and Carian mercenaries in 593 B.C. The town was situated on the east bank between the Fifth and Sixth Cataracts.

After the defeat of Psammetichos III by Cambyses in 525 B.C. Egypt became a Persian province and, Herodotus tells us, the Persian conqueror sent his spies to Meroë disguised as ambassadors bearing gifts. The Meroitic King was offended and sent back a challenging message, with the result that the Persian army marched into Nubia; this expedition ended in fiasco and most of its soldiers died of starvation in the desert. After that, all links with Egypt were cut, divided by that Land of the Ghosts between the First and Second Cataracts. Thus isolated the Meroitic state grew and flourished until the coming of the Romans at the death of Cleopatra. But the Meroë civilisation had gradually declined into a bastard culture,[66] the Pharonic hieroglyphics became debased and then lost, and a Meroitic script eventually replaced them. This script has now been deciphered but since its language is still unknown to us it remains unintelligible. The Empire of Meroë never recovered from its struggles with the Romans, after which a rapid decline set in. Little remains that can be dated later than the early part of the first century,[67] and the very site of once prosperous Meroë was lost until the nineteenth century.

During the next two days' marches Louis saw many tantalising things which he longed to investigate, for the caravan was now in the Meroë area. Of course he did not know where this was since it had been lost for some fourteen centuries, but from all that he now began to see, and from what he had read, he guessed quite correctly that this was indeed the site of ancient Meroë as described by Herodotus. With chagrin he writes: "had the wonders of Thebes" been at the roadside he could not have left the caravan. There were ruins, brick mounds and pyramidal tombs that he itched to examine. He managed to make a small sketch of one of the Meroitic pyramid tombs in their original state, not then truncated as they unfortunately were by an Italian doctor some twenty years later.[68]

The landscape was changing rapidly now as they began to enter the rainbelt. It was a most fertile district, and the way so much entangled with undergrowth and the overhanging branches of luxuriant acacias that the laden camels could hardly struggle through.

Ten days after leaving Berber, they reached Shendi of the famous market. It was 17 April 1814—just a week after the abdication of Napoleon; but here, deep in Africa, one was utterly cut off from any news, and Europe must have seemed as far distant as another planet.

In Shendi Louis found that drunkenness and dissipation were just as fashionable as at Berber. But since the governorship was in the hands of a strong man—the Mek known as *el Nimr*, the Tiger —the nightly robberies and drunken assaults did not go quite unpunished. While he was in Shendi there was a public festival for the circumcision of one of the Mek's sons: all the local horsemen gathered to escort the royal family through the town. There was a great deal of parading and prancing about but in Louis' view the horsemanship was indifferent and quite incomparable to that of the Mamluks, who rode their animals with consummate mastery. But his interest was aroused by one perfect horse in this parade; its beauty surpassed that of any other horse he could recall having seen anywhere, and he was an expert. It had been bought at the price of thirteen slaves.

Although his cavalry was not brilliant by Mamluk standards the Mek depended on his horsemen. His firearm strength was poor, in fact most of his guns were rusted or broken, and no one could repair them. Unfortunately, the Mek's men noticed Louis cleaning his own gun, and immediately supposed him to be skilled in the art. Serious proposals were soon made to persuade him to enter the Mek's service as royal gunsmith. By way of inducement he was offered one male and two female slaves, and as much durra as he needed for their maintenance. It was with great difficulty that Louis managed to convince the Mek's messengers that he was most emphatically not a gunsmith.

Having failed to acquire his services the Mek set his heart upon obtaining the gun. He demanded to see it and he kept it for

some days. When Louis begged for it back, the Mek responded
with a gift of four Spanish dollars and dish of meat sent from his
own table. Having eaten of the King's food Louis became tricked
into parting with the gun; he could make no further complaint
and had to accept the four dollars. He discovered later that this
trickery had been cunningly contrived by the deliberate ill-will
of the hateful Daraou men.

He soon came to realise that everyone here, with the exception
of the Mek, was simply terrified of firearms, a fact that led him
to conclude, correctly and with foresight, that a very small body
of well-trained European soldiers, if inured to a tropical climate,
could penetrate deep into eastern Africa. If, through their firearms, "250 miserable Mamluks" had been able to conquer and
keep Dongola then, in his opinion, a body of experienced men
with patience and prudence would not have much to fear from
these small principalities; also even the climatic difficulties were
not as much to be dreaded as those of western Africa. He thought
that if the sources of the White Nile were ever to be discovered a
small armed contingent should be used, not to do battle but
simply to ensure a safe passage for the benefit of scientific exploration. He went on to write:

England has, by her different voyages of discovery, and her
missions to explore distant countries, far surpassed all the
nations of Europe: and a successful expedition through the
interior of the African continent is alone wanting to render her
triumph complete.

Later he touches on the problem of slavery, and the praise-
worthy efforts then being made in Europe and above all in
England to abolish the trade. He knew this would in time be
beneficial to the Negro countries of western Africa. But at
present he saw little hope of the abolition of slavery in Africa
itself—a far bigger question than that of the Atlantic slave trade.
he felt, however, that no plan presented "a fairer prospect" for
Africa "than the education of the sons of Africa in their own
country, and by their own countrymen, previously educated by

Europeans". Then, and only then, he felt, would Negroes be able to resist and repel the rapacious inroads of the Muslim traders. These reflections of Louis' throw a very bright light on his character when one realises that such prescient hopes and ideas stemmed from a man still in his twenties, who made them at a dark time, and a full fifty years in advance of the great reformers of the Livingstone era.[69]

Louis' description of Shendi market runs to nearly fifty pages of his Nubian journal. In its way it is a masterpiece of meticulous detail, and a classical example of his acute powers of observation.

The market place was wide, dusty, suffocatingly hot. Markets were held daily with especially large gatherings on Fridays and Saturdays, attended by Arabs from all around; on those particular days slaves and camels were sold in the open. Rows of small mud shops like niches set one behind the other, as in some Persian markets, surrounded the square. The more opulent merchants crouched in these booths like spiders in a dark web's core, under the slatted shade of reed mats. Other merchants sat out in the blistering sun in the diminutive shade of small awnings. Countless things were sold here: cow and camel meat, fresh and sour milk and boiled chick peas brought in by Bedouin girls to be bartered for durra. There was tobacco from Sennar, snuff mixed with natron; salt, red peppers, cloves, cardamoms and tamarinds; on the great days 400 or 500 camels, perhaps as many cows, a hundred or so donkeys, dozens of spirited horses from Dongola all adding their own distinctive aromas and noises to the seething market place. These were sword blades from Germany, soap, sugar, linen and sheepskins, beads and paper, silver trinkets and pointed Mamluk shoes; ebony, ivory, and rhinoceros' horn for aphrodisiacs, honey and gold from Sennar, and above all there was in the heart of this crowded seething place that "trade in human flesh", the slaves—of all commerce in this great mart the most important.

Louis calculated that the number of slaves sold annually in Shendi was approximately 5,000, of whom about half went to Souakin on the Red Sea coast, about 1,500 to Egypt, and the rest to Dongola, or to the Bedouin in the lands east of Shendi. Those between the ages of eleven and fifteen were the most highly valued: a girl in this category would sell for from 20 to 25 Spanish dollars. Sold like cattle, they were driven off like cattle with the same phrase: *"song el ghanam go damek!"*—and a slave-owner held so many "head" of slaves as one would say head of cattle. Among these poor unfortunates Louis saw many pathetic children of four or five years old separated from their parents. Others of the same age in the market were with their mothers; most traders did show a slight degree of humanity in that, as a rule, they did not sell them separately—if such a thing did happen the vendor was generally rebuked by the crowd.

In the Sudan the slaves, although made nominally Muslim by the act of circumcision were, says Louis, never taught to pray, nor to read either, and ignominiously they often went by odd names such as Leathersack, or Goodmoney. Young slaves might be bought on trial, but there were certain defects in boys which made it impossible for the buyer to return the slave—among which were snoring at night, bed-wetting, teeth-grinding and so on.

Among the slave girls in Shendi were several called *mukhaeyt* (*consutae*, i.e. sewn-up). Louis was unable to say whether this ghastly operation was performed by the parents in their native lands, or by the merchants themselves; he had reason to believe that it was by the latter.

> Girls in this state are worth more than others; they are usually given to the favourite mistress or slave of the purchaser, and are often suffered to remain in this state during the whole of their life.

So far, what he had heard or seen of the Negroes had not given Louis a very good impression of their general character; he adds in all fairness that he had not yet seen them in their own countries but only after they had fallen into the hands "of these vile traders, who would spoil the mildest and most amiable dispositions".

Louis soon became conspicuous in the town for although he was of course now extremely tanned, he did remain relatively pale and his shaven head was alarmingly white. He once earned himself eight free onions by showing this startling pate to a country girl onion-seller, who would not believe he had a white head until she saw it. She shuddered at the sight, and swore that she would rather live with the ugliest Darfur slave than have a husband with a crown like that. His appearance in fact often excited shrieks of horror and surprise, especially among the country women who were "not a little terrified at seeing such an outcast of nature"—as they consider any pale-faced man to be—when he looked into their huts to ask for a little water or milk. In former times Chinese used to say that blue eyes were unpleasantly like sky seen through a skull—perhaps these people felt the same when they saw Louis' eyes bright in his tanned face.

Sometimes country folk, on seeing him in a market, would exclaim "God preserve us from the devil!" He soon came to realise that the chief feeling aroused by his appearance was one of disgust since Negroes were convinced that a pale skin was the result of disease, the sign of weakness. It was worse for him in the country places; at Shendi where most of the inhabitants were used to the lighter brown men of Arabia he was not quite so conspicuous except for his build. He was glad now of the company of the Bedouin, who were a protection, especially as throughout the stay the villainous men of Daraou continued to make themselves as unpleasant to him as ever—one man went so far as to spit in his face in full view of all the market. He never met any of these offensive people in the streets of Shendi without being hailed with some sort of insult. He was aware that had he responded he would have been taken before the Mek, probably with serious consequences. The Bedouin group were not over-friendly either, probably because he had shown no inclination to join their nightly *bouza* bouts; but he managed to keep them pacified with small gifts of tobacco, and once he invested in a sheep for the benefit of the mess.

The real triumph was that he had succeeded in keeping secret his European blood all this time—even at close quarters in this crowded town. In itself this was a *tour de force*, but he was at pains to point out that he was not claiming "the merit of extraordinary prudence" in mentioning this fact, only stressing that success hung upon it, for the ways from the Nile to the Red Sea were impossible for anyone except a native trader. He knew that the people of Daraou would one day probably "discover who the poor man was who travelled with them", but he was absolutely certain that he remained unknown now—to them all he was just a pale grey-eyed Syrian oddity, a poor worthless travelling merchant.

The behaviour of the Egyptians towards Louis had reached such a pitch that a dénouement seemed inevitable, so Louis devised a fresh plan, something in the nature of a quick double-cross. He had not told a soul that he wanted to go to the Red Sea; he was aware that the Daraou men still expected him to travel on to Sennar in search of his mythical absconding "cousin". Indeed, they had already started to spread bad reports of him among the Sennar merchants in the hope that the Sennar people would conveniently dispose of him en route, for they had begun to fear that should he ever return to Egypt he might one day be in a position to make them suffer for their vile behaviour. Like all bullies they were beginning to feel nervous for their own skins.

At this time, just as the Bedouin guides were preparing to return north, a caravan of Souakin merchants was also about to depart to their home town on the Red Sea coast. At this crucial point, Louis, playing his cards with finesse, let it be known that he had abandoned all idea of going on. He promptly bought a young slave boy and a good strong camel, and announced that he now intended returning to Egypt with the Bedouin.

It was a ruse which completely thwarted the Daraou men, and it made them switch their behaviour quite suddenly. Their chief, the man who had hit Louis on the march south, sent choice dishes for his supper, called upon him in person and with facile change of face even went so far as to express every wish that they might meet again in Egypt.

Meanwhile, Louis made secret inquiries about the Souakin caravan and, on the very eve of its departure, he told the Bedouin sheik of his real new intention, and managed with the aid of a little baksheesh to persuade this man to take him to the Souakin chief for personal friendly recommendation. Such subterfuge required endless patience both to devise and to carry out, and an acute knowledge of just how to oil those wheels within wheels on which all such affairs must revolve.

He had bought the slave and the camel with the last of his funds. He had acquired the slave boy, a bargain at 16 dollars, partly as a pretext for going towards the Red Sea where slaves, as everyone knew, could be sold at a profit, and had chosen him carefully from among thousands; he was to become greatly attached to him. The camel had cost 5 dollars less than the human, but Louis had an unerring eye for a good animal and it proved to be a splendidly sturdy beast. Now all was ready for a speedy get-away, but when his bills were paid he had merely 4 dollars left in his pocket—perhaps after all it was lucky that the gun had raised exactly that sum. As capital 4 dollars was meagre, but he did not feel unduly concerned then for he expected to sell the camel on reaching the coast for the price of his passage to Jidda. Also, he had a letter of credit from Cairo which he intended cashing on arrival at the Arabian port.

So it was that he left suddenly for the Red Sea to traverse a tract of land hitherto quite unexplored. It must have been with real satisfaction and a lift of the heart that he turned his back on the noise and heat of Shendi's market, the brothels and *bouza* parties, the mournful wail of fife and tamboura, and the daily din of kettledrums throbbing before the house of the Mek. Quitting most towns, especially one such as this, exchanging the bustle of crowds, the dirt and stench of the market for great open tracts, was at all times like wine to his traveller's spirit. But he could not cut adrift from Shendi's peculiar tragedy. It journeyed on like-wise as he went forward with the traders: he had to witness daily, and nightly, the sufferings and humiliations of the slaves at the hands of their masters.

As for Louis, he was now so emaciated, more than ever dis-guised by a gaunt and poverty-stricken appearance, that he was considered, by this new set of traders, as being indeed very little better than the slaves themselves.

*Part V*

# The Arabian Decision

# CHAPTER TWELVE

## *With the Slave-traders to the Red Sea*

And proclaim to the peoples a Pilgrimage:
Let them come on foot and on every fleet camel, arriving by
every deep defile:

*The Koran.* Sura xxii

As Louis left Shendi, even at the final moment there was
trouble with the Daraou men. But he was saved from their fury
by the Bedouin, from whom his leave-taking had ultimately
been quite affectionate.

In the market town the slaves had not been exactly ill-treated;
they were well-fed, seldom beaten and certainly not over-worked.
They had been spoken to kindly, even encouraged to call their
masters "father", and to consider themselves his children. But
Louis knew only too well that this attitude stemmed not from
humanity but simply from necessity: long experience had shown
the traders that slaves absconded to the Bedouin under bad
treatment, and pined away if shut up—since, to the newly captive,
house walls were as loathsome as dungeons.

Once in the desert the whole picture changed. Then, when
there was no longer any possibility of escape, the traders came out
in their true colours and showed their savage temper.

Slaves led the 200 or so loaded camels of this caravan; thirty
horses destined for the Yemen market were also led the entire way,
each by a single slave. The wealthiest merchants rode dromedaries.
In all there were about 150 ordinary traders, and some 300 slaves.
Even on these exhausting marches the slaves showed an almost
incredible hardiness; sometimes the young boys, rather pathetic-
ally, had the strength to play games after supper even despite
the fact that they had walked all day behind the caravan. Further

on in the wilderness there were places where countless rats ran among the camels' legs at every step, and Louis marvelled that the slaves found enough energy to hunt them continuously throughout the day.

Louis' own slave was greatly envied by the others because he ate exactly as his master did, that is he had butter or sauce with his durra at both meals; almost invariably, too, Louis let him ride for four or five hours in the early part of each day. Louis himself rode for the remaining time. As the average march was consistently of about ten hours' duration this seemed more than kind: it astonished the Souakin traders but Louis says frankly that although humanity did have some part in his motives, common sense had also. He knew that if both he and the boy were exhausted they could not have kept up with the march, nor coped with the cooking, the loading and unloading, the fetching of water, the endless durra grinding. Sometimes both of them were overtired, then both would ride—which must have seemed even more extraordinary to the merchants. Fortunately his camel was exceptionally strong—it was in fact to become famous in the caravan.

He discovered that of all the slaves' fears as to their fate the worst were that they might be eaten on arrival at their destination, or mutilated, or—strangely enough—terrorised by fleas, an insect unknown to them—with which dread Louis would have sympathised from experience.

In Egypt Louis had heard the traders bragging that the chastity of the handsomest girl slaves was always respected. An empty boast—with his own eyes he now saw it was utterly false. Once out in the open when the slave-girls were completely at their mercy, or lack of it, the traders threw all sense of decorum to the desert winds.

During the journey to Souakin the caravan often camped, as protection against attack, in one great circle within which night after night Louis had to watch scenes of "the most shameless indecency" enacted by the slave traders: scenes which convinced him that, whatever the opinion might be in Cairo, very few girl slaves who had passed their tenth year reached Egypt, or Arabia,

in a state of virginity, except of course those called *mukhaeyt*.
He wrote:

Many of the traders engage their female slaves to turn their
beauty to profit, which they afterwards share with them.
In our caravan one of my companions openly sold the favours
of his females for two measures of *dura*, of which he always
received one. This man also when a favourite little slave girl
died during our stay at Shendi, with the utmost indifference
ordered the body, after stripping it of every rag . . . to be laid
on an ass and carried to the Nile to be thrown in.

In Shendi the bodies of slaves were hardly ever buried, but
flung like rubbish into the river.

On the first day of the ninety-five-mile journey the caravan
paused early, as was the custom, and that night their halting place
lay within what Strabo called "the Island of Meroë", the fertile,
shield-shaped slice of country where the Ethiopian kingdom had
flourished until the second century. Then, as before on the way
south when he had seen the royal tombs, Louis was again tantalised by a fleeting discovery of ancient buildings which he knew
must be a part of the Meroitic Kingdom. At one place, to guard
his camel from some marauding Arabs who were harassing the
caravan, he drove it deep into a thicket and in doing so came across
the ruined walls of what appeared to have been part of a great
open city.

During the three-day march towards the Atbara Louis had
plenty of opportunities to study the habits and the character of
these Souakin traders, which showed in a distinctly unfavourable
light, under constant stress as they were, and in considerable fear
of hostile attacks from the fierce Bisharin through whose territory
their route now lay.

The only other strangers who had joined the Souakinis at
Shendi were some Negro traders from Kordofan, the Tekrouri,
beside whom, since he also was a stranger, Louis camped throughout the journey. They were moderately forthcoming with that
mutual aid of which all caravan travellers stand in daily need

when loading and so on, and since he responded they continued be on quite good terms, though scarcely on a friendly footing "for nobody, even in the Negro countries, is inclined to form an intimacy with a poor man". He remained very much on his guard, firmly resisting any attempt to wheedle or to steal from his baggage, so acquiring, he felt, "the character of a hardy, active man, very selfish, stingy and attentive to his own interests"— an attitude which, combined with his evident poverty, was probably the best protection devisable.

Three of the Negro traders had come originally from Bornu whence, years previously, they had travelled with a caravan to the Fezzan. Naturally Louis was particularly interested in these men, for their knowledge of this area where Horneman had vanished fourteen years previously—the very route, too, which he himself hoped to take eventually from Cairo.

The outstanding man among them, one who by his character became head of the party's mess, was Haji Ali Bornaway, slave-trader and hypocrite of the first water. He had travelled widely in Turkey, Syria and Arabia, and had performed the Haj three times. His travels in the holy land, his smug but impressive air of sanctity, won him great esteem and wherever he went he was well received by the Meks and the sheiks. He was continually reading, or pretending to read, the Koran, even when at rest under his mat shelter in the heat of the day, or while riding his camel on the march. But Louis felt that all this devotion to the holy book was little more than ostentation, a display of piety, for he was a dedicated voluptuary, spending the entire profits of all his journeys on concubines and a choice variety of other sensual delights. But, wrote Louis, to hear him preach and moralise one would think that he knew nothing of vice except by name, and although he spent half his life in devotions he had recently sold his own cousin openly in the slave market of Medinah. This wretched woman, having in all innocence left Bornu on the pilgrimage, had been unlucky enough to meet Ali by chance in Mecca. Possibly being short of concubines at that time, or perhaps warming to her appearance, he hailed her in a cousinly fashion, and promptly married her—which was quite in order since in Muslim countries a man might demand his cousin in marriage. But later, in Medinah, finding himself running out of cash he unashamedly sold her to some Egyptians and—as the poor woman was quite unable to prove her free origin—she was forced to submit to Egyptian slavery.

This unsavoury anecdote was well known in the caravan but that it did not in the least detract from the haji's reputation appears to have impressed Louis profoundly. His own deep-rooted ethics invariably made him marvel at mob gullibility, and it seems to have been hard for him to recognise the two-faced attitude of the *average* Muslim religioso. This is one reason that makes it possible to think that he could, and perhaps even did, accept for himself the *principles* of the Muslim religion without being guilty of apostasy at any time.

As we know, Louis was not a conventionally religious man but it is quite easy to understand that the faith—in one sense so austere and so virile—the desert-born faith of Islam, might have had a direct personal appeal to him. However, it was individuals such as Haji Ali and his following who puzzled him and who, so it seems, continued to do so. He never perhaps quite grasped as Doughty was to later that Islam's people "walk in a large way which is full of the perfume of the flesh purified; the debate betwixt carnal nature and opinion of godliness is not grievous in their hearts".[1]

Later in his account of this journey he writes of the great respect shown between hajis to one another, which tended to sustain the popular belief that a haji was inevitably a superior being in virtue and holiness. Certainly not a soul in the caravan was bold enough to point an accusing finger at this particularly heartless haji—sanctimonious old hypocrite that he was. For Louis, he typified that same state of moral affairs—the tyranny and the laxity—that he, Louis, had already observed in Syria, and was about to see in Arabia—an attitude utterly opposed to his own sense of discipline and his humanitarian views on the rights of the individual.

On the other hand, any revulsion that he experienced against such men as Haji Ali and the fulsome respect awarded them could only have confirmed his theory that by becoming a haji himself he would be securing almost certain success in his great ultimate journey to the interior. For him all this must have borne out the logic of his own careful planning, but he does not stress that point again. Perhaps, like many a brilliant man, he remained, as it were, innocent in spirit: although he was quite sufficiently aware of the world and of the possibility of being misjudged to be at pains, as we have seen, to make his reasons clear to the African Association. In his day those reasons were whole-heartedly accepted. It has been only in quite recent years that his intentions have been queried by a suggestion that he was too strongly drawn to the hub of the Arab world to be truly interested in its outskirts: a judgement, one feels, rather lightly given. Louis is a man worthy of deeper study; there were nuances, even mysteries in his character but whatever his faults insincerity was not among them —he was too great for that.

On the third day out a violent *samun* blew, enveloping the struggling caravan in the flying sands of its flaming breath. During the noon rest the Souakin merchants ran short of water and seized from Louis' mess what little water it had left. The entire caravan went to sleep thirsting that night, after a march of eleven hours.

Such travel frequently brings intoxicating contrast: brilliant flashes in arduous days. The next day brought a bliss so markedly at variance with the previous one's misery that even the stony-hearted slave-traders exclaimed with pleasure: "*Ba'ad el maut el jenna!*—After death comes paradise!"

The morning march took them over a parched sandy plain and brought them to within sight of the Atbara: a glittering band of azure vivid as a kingfisher's wing among luxuriant vegetation; mimosa, palms, tamarisks and a mass of wild plants all growing on a soil as rich and dark as that of Egypt. The slaves chattered joyfully on seeing great clusters of ripe fruit on the trees. To Louis' music-starved ears perhaps best of all was the wonderfully sweet multitudinous sound of bird-song in this idyllic-seeming spot. He writes of the great number of charming notes, many of which he had never heard before, and "the amorous cooings of the turtle doves were unceasing".

The whole caravan rushed eagerly forward to the river, panting to quench a raging thirst. Several camels, maddened to get at the water, broke free of their halters and galloped off with pounding raking strides; their loads loosened, swayed and fell crashing to the ground. Soon the melody of bird-song was drowned in an uproar of human and animal voices—angry shouts and yells, roarings of camels, and shrillings of nervous horses.

It was some time before the burst and scattered loads were secured again, and everyone was ready to ford the river. They crossed to the village of Atbara, where they intended halting for some days to trade: here the brief paradise ended abruptly for man was entirely vile, even dangerously predatory, and the beautiful girls heartless and mercenary to the last degree. Leopards, it was said, haunted the woods here, but Louis never saw anything bigger than hosts of enormous rats which the slaves killed and seemed to like eating.

For protection against the thieving Bisharin, Louis and his group retired to the shelter of a thick thorn grove in which each man hacked out for himself a small retreat guarded by the slaves. Despite these precautions everyone in the caravan lost some of his baggage, since these bold and handsome people, the armed Bisharin, were skilful pilferers. They also enjoyed their *bouza*; each night was loud with drunken dispute and the din of their bawdy parties. They were restless nights indeed—slaves crashing through the thorn bushes after their prey, squeals of dying rats, raucous voices of squabbling topers, and all the while a ceaseless musical background rhythm of pestles pounding in mortars— for slaves worked in shifts almost throughout the hours of darkness, grinding the next day's supply of durra for their masters.

The local people were not worthy of the name of Bedouin, they completely lacked any trace of traditional Bedouin hospitality. Not a drop of milk, nor an ounce of durra was yielded without payment, not to even the poorest of the Negro pilgrims, and the women were grasping enough to charge hire even on the temporary use of old earthenware milk vessels. But the girls were beautiful, slender and remarkably elegant, with dark brown skins, laughing eyes, fine white teeth, and they were apparently in no fear at all of their own menfolk's jealousy. However Louis soon discovered that the only reason for their so open flirtations with the travellers was to gain a higher price for milk and durra. It was all a kind of game since, unlike most Arabs, a Bishari seeing a stranger kiss his wife would merely laugh it off—but, Louis remarks in his matter-of-fact way, death would most certainly be the outcome were she to be caught in adultery.

At the end of May the caravan left the Atbara village and set out over an utterly desolate plain. There was not the slightest elevation to be seen, in all directions the haggard land stretched far away. But even in this apparent wilderness there was some life, for it was here that the rats ran day-long among the camels' legs providing sport for the slaves. For a day or so all went well until a large and menacing force of Bedouin came into view behind them, heading in the same direction. This dreaded sight flung the whole caravan into a state of deep-rooted fear; each night they camped so that they could see any move the Bedouin might make. They put the baggage in a circle as a rough barricade around the encampment and lit a great fire in the centre. Although Louis does not dwell on the unspeakable scenes that occurred then in the firelight, for him they were obviously only too poignant with a kind of fierce, horrifying beauty of their own lit by the flickering flames. With the nervous tension of mass fear working as drink does on lust, sexual and survival impulses once kindled ran unbridled. In vibrant shadow raven-dark Negro eyes showed a sudden flash of rolling white at the muffled shriek of a girl, a gust of obscene laughter. The patient animals seemed now less animal than the humans. Slave mothers crouched over their children. The adult male Negroes, feared by their masters, lay powerless, shackled at night in irons, eyes staring, angry, hopeless or wildly averted.

The expected attack did not come. Then two days later as they were drawing near to the village of Koz Rejab,[2] where they intended to stay long enough to sell part of their wares, Louis saw what he took to be an enormous building on a distant hilltop. He had always been a little short-sighted; now his vision was worse since the last two bad attacks of ophthalmia and, not being able to trust his eyes, he asked his companions what it was that looked like a building on the hill.

"Don't you see," they replied, "that it is a church? And no doubt the work of infidels."[3]

Louis was, of course, immediately filled with a burning desire to explore this interesting hilltop. It was not more than half an hour's distance so, no sooner had he dismounted, and put his baggage in order, than he started off hot-foot for the hills. But the traders saw him and their shouts brought him back.

"The whole country is infested by the Koz Rejab fellows," they yelled. "Allah!—You can't move a hundred paces without being attacked!"

Reluctantly he returned to the caravan to be told that the hill of the "church" itself was known to be the haunt of desperate Hadendoa robbers living there in a honeycomb of caverns. Despite this knowledge he still had hopes that he might be able to persuade some of the villagers to accompany him to the hilltop before the caravan moved on. But in this he was to be bitterly disappointed; there was no other opportunity because, during the night, a sudden new threat of danger panicked an unexpected start.

Before dark, some of the traders crossed the river to Koz Rejab to make inquiries as to the market. As he was on a late watch that night Louis was just settling down to sleep early, at about two hours after sunset, when the traders returned. They had been told secretly in the village that a large party of Bisharin was planning to attack during the night.

The news spread quickly throughout the camp; soon the chief came to Louis' group and cried: "O make haste! The caravan is in fear, if we stay here we shall be attacked. Fill your water skins and load your camels, we depart immediately!"

At such times, says Louis, every feeling gave way to the single one of preservation. Forgetting all else, he snatched up two water skins and ran down to the river, while the slave boy got the camel ready. By the time Louis had returned with the heavy skins, the adult slaves were already chained to their marching poles, and the chief had begun the march. They all followed along the river bank in a silence taut with fear.

They passed by the very foot of the hill of the "church" but the night was overcast and gloomy, and Louis could see nothing of the ruins. It was another of those cruelly tantalising moments to be endured alone as he always was, with his incommunicable thoughts while the caravan moved on wrapped in its aura of suffering and dread.

The traders—they were very frightened indeed—enforced the utmost silence; not a pipe was to be lit in case burning ash flying on the wind should reveal the direction of their march. There was no sound "but the groans of a few infirm female slaves, and the whips of their cruel masters who obliged them to follow the caravan on foot". These stifled moans, the swish of the lash, the general rustle and soft jingle of the caravan were the only noises of that night—except for a distant hollow barking: the robbers' dogs guarding those caverns high on the sombre hillside above.

Louis could not refrain from casting a last backward look at this forbidding place, and lamenting the ill luck which at the most southerly point of his travels had thwarted his longing to examine what he felt might perhaps have been the most valuable fruit of this difficult journey.

The following day their route lay over yet another vast plain impressive in its bleak immensity, to the Negroes from the humid south it must have seemed hell on earth. In the heat of the afternoon, marching on a gravelly surface, they were as if in a void under the great dome of the empty sky, with no tree, not the smallest shrub, no elevation, nor the slightest landmark to guide them. As evening drew on some tremendous flashes of lightning that had begun to illuminate the now threatening horizon, seemed to serve as rough direction for the march—perhaps indicating to travellers who knew the route some familiar storm-centre in unseen hills ahead.

They marched for eleven hours that day and camped exhausted in a wadi, having lost their way. The next morning they set off in a different direction. Then, as they reached the borders of the Taka district, another blinding sandstorm enveloped them.

Unable to see more than a few yards they again lost their way, greatly alarming, with their massive shadowy approach, some Hadendoa shepherds who, mistaking them for Bisharin, fled hurriedly driving their flocks before them.

The sun had set but the evening was not yet dark when they reached a friendly Hadendoa encampment where they settled down to rest. But almost at once another hurricane arose, quite the most temendous that Louis had yet seen. First, an indigo-coloured cloud appeared above the horizon, growing rapidly in height as it approached, and turning to leaden grey tinged ominously with yellow. Men, women and children, those who had never seen such desert phenomena, stared at this menacing racing darkness, dumbfounded by its terrifying magnificence. As it came towards them the lurid yellow intensified, while below it the horizon showed a brilliant serenely clear azure. It advanced soundlessly on the heels of the vacuum before it, and battened itself upon the camp. The noise broke only then as the storm enveloped them all in its rushing roaring brown darkness.

The violence of it swept their mat shelters clean away, and lifted even the heavy Hadendoa tents until the whole camp was levelled to the ground. The terrified camels arose, shattering their halters trying wildly to escape, lumbering among fallen tents and huddled people, adding hugely to the whirling chaos, the blind confusion. After what seemed about half an hour the rushing wind abated and as the atmosphere cleared Louis saw the great cloud, continuing its path of havoc, madly spiralling away to the north-west.

After the storm, they went on through wooded land to a large encampment of Hadendoa Bedouin that was protected by a thick enclosure of trees and bushes. This, the Taka district, was celebrated for its cattle, but the herds were preyed upon by lions and by what the local people called tigers—presumably leopards or panthers. Again Louis never saw a sign of these beasts but he heard their howlings often enough, and no one dared to stir outside the barricade at night. This thorny structure was:

sufficiently strong to be impenetrable to the wild beasts which prowl about it the whole night filling the air with their dismal howls, which are answered by the incessant barking of the dogs within.

As antidote to this precarious existence every Taka settlement rejoiced in *bouza* houses and prostitutes. All the women went unveiled; even the respectable ones thought it quite in order to receive a man in her tent and to be seen talking with him although her husband was absent. This, however, Louis says with perhaps a tinge of regret, never happened to him, since whenever he presented himself before a tent the women greeted him with shrill screams and shooed him away. As elsewhere in this part of the world the dark beauties were shocked and astonished by his relatively light brown skin, grey eyes, and full curling beard, especially since Bedouin beards never grow long or thick.

The Hadendoa were just as inhospitable and mercenary as their enemies, the Bisharin: the men were lazy, drunken, and indeed quite pitiless towards strangers.[4] Nevertheless, when the time came for the caravan to leave they all began clamouring for gifts. Well knowing the women's attitude to him personally, Louis indulged in a little harmless retaliation.

The people had plagued us during the whole of our stay, especially the women, who left no arts of coquetry untried, in order to possess themselves of the objects of their wishes. One of the cousins of the chief, who had just been married, was particularly importunate. Knowing that she looked on me with disdain and derision, I could not help admiring her subtlety and address in persuading me by signs that she had conceived a great affection for me, giving me plainly to understand that for a handful of cloves she would refuse me nothing. Her own people probably knew that the whole was a trick. . . .

It was some satisfaction to Louis that he was able to resist her lure and he gave her not even a single clove, let alone a handful.

They battled on in clouds of dust; again there were violent and persistent winds, once more they lost their way, and the sand-storms terrified the now wildly unruly camels.

It was on this part of the march that some Negro pilgrims joined the caravan. Such a journey often proved fatal to these penniless people. Some died from disease, hunger, or exhaustion, or from lack of clothing; others were murdered despite their destitute appearance, since the people of this so hard and savage country believed that every Tekrouri was a Sudanese king in disguise with plenty of gold about him.

To Louis' amazement one of these newcomers was blind; he had travelled all the way on foot from a place far west of Darfur, practically in the centre of Africa at the widest part of the great continent. Oddly enough, Louis saw the same man later at Mecca, and again at Medinah begging on the threshold of the mosque and exclaiming: "I am blind, but the light of the word of God, and the love of his prophet illuminate my soul and have been my guide from Sudan to this tomb!" A long walk indeed: Louis noticed that the alms the man received were generous and thought that he might well return home richer than when he left—if he were not murdered on the way.

At last the caravan was approaching the mountains—those burnt-up, red-dark nubile hills confining the dramatic Red Sea coast; a spur of these mountains lay ahead, sprawling out south and westwards from the coastal barrier of the Diabb. Now they saw again some life: inquisitive female ostriches, locusts which the slaves caught and ate, a few elegant gazelles, and here and there a herb grew that was akin to the tasty spinach-like leaf of Egypt, the *meloukia* (*chorchorus olitorious*). They used it to make a broth, but the endless durra remained their dull staple fare.

The night before they entered the mountains was wet; everybody, soaked to the skin, felt wretched having little or no shelter and no change of clothes. The slaves of course had none at all. But the morning dawned fine and clear, and at sunrise the birdsong was so sweet that slaves and slave traders alike expressed their pleasure.

The steep wadi which they ascended was rough, difficult going with many ups and downs, and a well where they had hoped to water was choked. This was a bad day for Louis in more ways than one. During the midday halt they had ridden their camels high into the mountains in search of a catchment area. He had been busy filling his water skin at a deep rain-water basin when his camel, breaking loose, had followed the others down the abrupt descent. So he had toiled on through all the heat of the day, first lugging the water skin back to where the slave was guarding the baggage, then looking for his camel. By the time he had found it again the precious rest period was finished, the hour had come to move on—when, as the Arabs say, "a man's shadow equals his height" and the march must begin once more.

All that was tiring, but nothing to what had happened earlier in the day when he had a narrow escape from being murdered. Unarmed, he had been walking as he so often did in advance of the caravan, to observe or to write his notes, while his slave rode. A Souakini trader, armed with a lance, had joined him and succeeded somehow in misleading him. Louis found himself cornered in a side valley with no exit. He was turning to retrace his steps when the man, blocking the way, suddenly raised his lance menacingly. Louis writes:

> Luckily for me, at the moment when I perceived his intention, I found a thick branch of a tree. He laughed when I took it up; but as I could not mistake his object in following me, I ordered him to stand off, threatening to become the assailant. . . .

Although it was a matter of stick against lance, the bold gesture worked, the man retreated before him, and Louis rejoined the caravan unharmed. Of course he does not say how he was able to intimidate an armed man, but obviously it was his superior courage, his build, and his strength of authority that won the day: when roused he could be as furious as a Bengal tiger.

He was sure that had he been murdered for the few dollars he possessed, nobody would have noticed that he was missing— except the slave boy—and no one would have bothered to make any inquiries. Such were the constant dangers of travel with these violent people.

Later that day the caravan passed many rain-water pools, and

Louis realised that all the strenuous labour of the hot noon-time might have been avoided. Those who knew the road were at an advantage regarding water problems, but they took good care not to share out their knowledge, and would always urge every-one to carry as much water as possible, saying: "We would trans-port the Nile itself if the camels could but carry it."

Louis felt that it was almost impossible to explain to Europeans the enormous amount of water needed for a caravan of that kind marching through such barren land. No one drank except when the whole caravan halted to do so; in both the Arabian and the Nubian deserts this custom held good. For slave caravans, the drinking times were at about nine in the morning, and twice during the afternoon march—around four and six o'clock. In the forenoon everyone drank at the rest halt and again after the midday meal, and the same rule was observed in the evening. To drink when others did not was considered most effeminate, a habit exposing a man to the scornful saying: "His mouth is tied to that of the water skin."

If a trader had many captives, the large wooden food bowl was filled and set on the ground and the slaves were obliged to kneel and drink from it like cattle from a trough; this was done to prevent the wastage inevitably occurring by pouring individual allowances. To drink only three or four times a day was con-sidered extremely short rations: when water was plentiful six or seven times sufficed for Arab and for Negro. But when the wind blew from the south-east no amount, it seemed to Louis, was enough to moisten the parched tongue, one longed to drink every half-hour or so.

As they climbed still higher to camp on the mountain pass, Louis looked back and saw a vast rocky wilderness spread below with the narrow fertile strip of the wadi twisting up through it like the coils of a green serpent. The pass in which they camped then was only about 300 feet below Mount Langay, the highest point of the water-divide, so, in contrast with the great heat of the day, the night was intensely cold. In the darkness of the rocky defile they huddled around their many separate fires: fear of robbers kept them awake most of the night, and scorpions were attracted to the glowing flames—their shining crustacean armour glistening in the light of the fires as if wet from the sea.

But the morning again was beautiful: its freshness reminded Louis of Mount Lebanon, and the clear, sweet air was more invigorating than any he had felt since leaving Syria.

The caravan descended from the pass marching as usual in that long single file typical of the slave trains, although the wadi now was wide. Each one of the 200 camels was still led by a slave, who felt the whip's lash at any false step the animal made.

Although they could not yet see it they were coming down towards the Red Sea, while marching parallel to the Diabb mountain chain. As they drew near the foot of these mountains they met coming towards them a party of Hadendoa Bedouin travelling with their women, their tents, their pots and pans, their dogs and babies. Such people on the march make a splendid sight, moving proudly through their own attendant dust cloud, their camels' disdainful heads held high, while the wild brown faces of their families bow and sway riding higher still. All the harnesses of the women's camels were fantastically decorated with coloured leather tassels, dangling white sea shells, and large bunches of black ostrich plumes that, fixed as they were on protruding poles, nodded at the camel's every stride. Perched aloft on their saddles, not one of these women managed to pass Louis without uttering a shriek at the sight of his strange bearded face. They themselves were provocative with dark mocking eyes and sidelong glances, and as each woman saw him her mouth first gaped in astonishment, then dissolved in laughter until a ripple growing in volume soon rose shrill and feminine all along the passing caravan above the deep melodious sound of camel bells.

The next day—24 June—as the sun began to rise above the last spurs of the eastern hills, they saw at an immense distance the molten gold of its reflection in the sea. It was a welcome sight to every person in the caravan, and Louis' heart lifted with thankfulness. The slaves thought it was the Nile for they had not heard of any other great water, nor of the sea.

Louis had to make the rest of the journey on foot. A camel belonging to one of the Kordofan traders fell that day and was killed: the Souakin merchants simply passed by quite regardless of its owner's plight. So, as this man had several times helped Louis when he had been exhausted, Louis now offered to assist with the load, and most of it was transferred to his camel, still the strongest in the Tekrouri party.

At midnight they loaded and marched on. When the sun rose next and they again saw its light upon the sea they knew that only some five hours' journey remained before them.

Coming down towards the almost tangible heat of the coast they encountered herds of white camels, shy and beautiful creatures, almost in the wild state, left to pasture unattended. There was a severe water shortage that day and again the Souakinis behaved meanly. Knowing the country well they had, entirely without the others' knowledge, engaged an Arab to bring several camel-loads of water from the mountains, but they refused to share a drop of it with the Tekrouris and their slaves.

When at last they reached the outskirts of Souakin the strangers put up their small mat shelters at el Geyf, a suburb divided from the town by a strip of water. Anyone who knows the Red Sea in summer may guess at the insufferable heat and dust of that stifling little shanty town in late June. A scorching hot *samun* blew; men and animals were nearly suffocated by clouds of dust-devils whirling about violently in all directions like frenzied dervishes.

Louis encamped near some wells with the Tekrouri people and a great many Negro pilgrims who, in this overwhelmingly oven-like place, had been long and patiently awaiting shipment to Jidda, and the holy land of the Prophet.

# CHAPTER THIRTEEN

## *Over the Sea to Jidda*

—said Saud ibn Saud when—having occupied Mecca—he
laid siege to Jidda (1803); and could not take the place: 'I give
it up then, I cannot fight against such a hot town: surely if
this people be not fiends, they are nigh neighbours to the
devil.'

*Doughty*

THE PEOPLE OF Souakin were notoriously mean. Louis heard
it said of them: "Though you give them water from the holy well
of Zemzem to drink when they are thirsty yet they will suffer
you to choke with thirst even when their own wells are full."

Waiting with the black Tekrouri in that parched suburb, el
Geyb, he derived some amusement from watching how these
stingy Souakinis, rather than pay the very small boat fare, would
strip, tie their clothes, sandals and swords on their heads and swim
across to the town. The expert manner in which they performed
this—almost as if walking upon firm ground, shoulders just clear
of the water—fascinated Louis, recalling for him as it did his
boyhood, and *das wasser stampfen* done in the Swiss lakes.

Foreign merchants arriving here were obliged to pay duty on
all imported slaves, and it was not long before the Emir of
Souakin himself arrived to collect the dues. As the Tekrouri had
with them some goods for which no regular tax was fixed, he
agreed to accept in lieu two of their party's camels. His covetous
eye at once spotted Louis' fine animal: he would take no other
and, trumping up some claim to all camels brought in by foreign
traders from the Sudan, he demanded it of Louis.

Louis refused: he had counted on selling the camel to pay
for his passage across the Red Sea and, besides this, he was pretty

certain that this claim of the Emir was illegal. Therefore, feeling that he was now in a position to use the firmans given him in Cairo, he demanded to see the Aga himself, promising to comply with *his* decree, whatever it might be, as to the question of the camel.

They were only a few hundred houses in Souakin, the bulk of them in ruins; the Aga's house too was far from imposing but being on one of the islands it had a fine view across the cerulean summer sea. Aga Yemak had once been a court buffoon and like his house he was unimpressive but he pompously affected the airs and graces of a Pasha—although he was patently frightened of the local Bedouin who, as Louis saw, were bold enough to insult him even within his own walls.

When the Emir took Louis to present him to Yemak, the Aga was busy attending to the affairs of some sailors. In rags Louis stood before him and bowed politely, Yemak however responded only very roughly and in Turkish. Louis answered in correct Arabic, at which the Aga exclaimed rudely in the same language and to the room at large:

"Look at that scoundrel! *Wellah!*—he comes from his brother Mamluks at Dongola, and yet pretends to know nothing of Turkish!"

Everyone in the caravan had known that, whatever his appearance, Sheik Ibrahim had come from Egypt to Shendi and could not possibly belong to the Mamluks. But, as there had been some fear that the Mamluks might try to retreat from Dongola to the Red Sea, and attempt to join the Wahabi in the Hijaz against their mutual enemy, Mohammed Ali (now at Taif planning to engage on the second Wahabi war), it did seem possible that although Yemak knew Sheik Ibrahim had nothing to do with the exiled slave-kings he might think to gain merit with his Ottoman superiors by arresting the Sheik as a spy or a refugee. When, so Louis reasoned, he would be able to seize his captive's property with absolute impunity.

"My reason for calling," said Louis with due politeness, "is to inquire if the Emir *is* entitled to my camel?"

"*Allah!*—Not only to thy camel!" roared Yemak, "but thy

entire baggage must be taken and searched. *Eh wellah!*—we shall render a good account of it all to the pasha! You shall not impose upon us,—you rascal! You may be thankful if we do not cut off your head!"

"I pray thee," Louis protested coolly. "I am nothing but an unfortunate merchant. I beg of thee not to add to the sufferings I have already experienced."

Yemak began cursing and swearing in Turkish now. Presently he called in some fellow whom, although obviously of his household, he addressed as if he were a police officer, commanding him to rope Sheik Ibrahim's hands, take him to gaol, then fetch his slave and baggage here. There is a familiar ring about this scene, a hint almost of the T. E. Lawrence incident at Deraa, however nothing untoward ensued, and it all ended rather more in comedy than in cruelty.

But to Louis it seemed high time to use the firmans. This he did—producing them dramatically from the secret pocket of his *thabout* and unrolling them with, surely, all the panache of the accomplished actor that he now was. They were extremely impressive, both in size and content.

One, in Turkish, written on a piece of paper two feet six inches long and a foot wide, was sealed with the great seal of Mohammed Ali himself. The other, a smaller one in Arabic bearing the seal of Ibrahim Pasha, referred to Louis as "our man Ibrahim, the Syrian—*Rajilna Ibrahim es-Shamy*".

The effect upon the Aga of these high-powered papers so suddenly unfurled was nothing short of remarkable: his mouth fell open, he was completely stupefied—and every single person in the room turned to gape at Louis in dumb amazement.

Still stunned, Yemak kissed the documents slowly in awe, and put them reverently to his forehead. Then, his manner now quite changed, he turned submissively to Louis begging a thousand pardons: all that he had done had *of course* been *only* for the public good. Not a word more was said about the camel, even the small duty on the slave was waived. When he had partly recovered from the shock, Yemak inquired as to what might be the cause of the Sheik's appearance, since Louis' clothing, which had been humble at the start of the journey from Daraou, was now literally in rags.

Promptly Louis replied that since Mohammed Ali had sent him to spy on the Mamluks, and to look into the state of the Negro countries, it had been convenient to assume the garb of a beggar.

The changed and wilting Aga, considering Sheik Ibrahim to be an important person, then began to fear him, and to tremble at what reports he might convey to Mohammed Ali regarding his —Yemak's—personal conduct and government of Souakin. Just as overcome with servility as he had been previously with greed, Yemak now lavished offers of presents—a slave-girl, new clothes from his own wardrobe, unlimited hospitality. All of which Louis firmly refused—but he did take advantage of an invitation to the regular midday dinner, after which he enjoyed the luxury of plentiful good tobacco smoked in one of the Aga's best Persian pipes.

These daily visitations were vastly amusing to the local populace, who laughed to see their puffed-up ruler humbled by the attentions that he seemed obliged to show to a ragged beggar. With evident and justifiable satisfaction Louis records that not only had he protection in the Aga's company and was conveniently regaining physical strength on the good fare of his table, but he was also saving expense—a most important factor, too, since by now he had only two dollars left in his pocket.

At these free daily meals he frequently met a Sherif who was, so he told Louis, under express orders to prevent any Franks, especially Englishmen, from entering Abyssinia. This remarkable piece of news was doubly interesting to Louis, since it proved that the Sherif had no inkling of Sheik Ibrahim's real identity. During the course of one of these midday gatherings the Kadi of Souakin secretly handed Louis—for delivery to Mohammed Ali in the Hijaz—a letter containing complaints against Yemak, and statements also against the Emir and his tribe.

The complaints against Yemak were that he made the Turkish name ridiculous, that he stood in too much fear of the Bedouin and that he disgraced his office by his unnatural propensities.

Of this particular failing Louis remarks succinctly that it appeared to be:

> The only crime in the east which has not yet penetrated into Africa, where all classes express disgust and horror at the descriptions given by returning pilgrims of the unnatural excesses of the Turks and Arabians.

A shrewd judge of character, perhaps Louis had already guessed at the Aga's secret weakness even before the Kadi had given him the letter. If so he does not mention the fact but, although he dined daily at the Aga's expense, he continued determinedly to wear his rags, and also to live with the black merchants and pilgrims outside the Geyf, regardless of constant and "pressing invitations of the Aga" to stay in his house.

Louis savoured outwitting this petty despot, just as he also enjoyed helping the Negro merchants to smuggle several of their slaves into town; a service which they repaid by ordering their own people to prepare some dried meat for his voyage across the Red Sea.

He sold the camel, and presently hearing that a *say*, a small boat or country ship, was preparing to sail for Jidda, he informed the Aga that he wished to leave. Yemak at once commanded the boat's *rais* to grant him a free passage, and also sent provisions on board expressly for him—dates and sugar, the very best from his own storeroom.

Louis embarked on the evening of 6 July. The *say* was only nine feet across the beam, not more than thirty-five feet long, dangerously overladen, and completely open to the brazen furnace of the sky. A ballast of durra, covered by layers of mats and hides, served as living space for some ninety people—Negro pilgrims, merchants, slaves, and crew alike. These were the conditions that would have to be endured for the ten days of the crossing, and Louis admits his heart sank when he saw the wretched vessel. But all boats would be much the same from then, the height of summer's heat, until November, which that year was the month of the Haj. Regardless of loss Red Sea *rais* so persistently overloaded their boats that disasters were frequent, but the Arab sailor would merely utter a resigned—"*Allah kerim! Allah akbar!*" and continue to follow the practice of his ancestors.

The crowded little vessel lay in port all through the next long fiery July day, awaiting her water supply. In remorseless heat the Negroes fought among themselves for elbow room and were punched by the enraged Souakini sailors who, quite ineffectually, tried to restore some sort of order to the brawling chaos of the scene. They did set sail when at last the fierce red ball of the sun sank into the western hills and merciful lilac-coloured shades deepened over the iridescent sea. But it was only to anchor at the mouth of Souakin Bay off a small ruined bastion.

Sunrise brought a spanking wind and they set off northwards, hugging the coast among coral reefs, the scintillating beauty of which was entirely new and amazing to Louis. In the afternoon they entered a narrow creek of difficult rocks and coral, where local Bedouin ran down to collect their "harbour dues".

So it continued day after weary day, from dazzling sunrise onwards, through the candescent heat of colourless noon to the flaming magnificence of sunset, and the blessed but all too humid night.

The Negroes were sea-sick, no one had enough room to stretch out his legs, everyone alike was irritable, tormented by cramp and by the sun's scorching rays. To do their work the sailors had to walk over the passengers, and the whole boat remained "a scene of confusion and quarrelling" throughout the voyage.

But countless dolphins played, leaping clear of the deep-blue water in shining arcs, and beyond violet-shadowed headlands lay great stretches of rust-coloured lands backed by pale desolate hills reaching in mile upon mile of white sand and cornelian-red sand to the blazing cobalt of the sky. Sometimes they had the pleasure of swimming ashore to sleep on the sands; revelling then in the delicious warm salt bathe, Louis would look down through the miraculous glass-blue depths to see a hint of flashing wonder beneath: coral fish like jewel-chips, as gay as flowers, drifting like butterflies or parrots, moving slender and elegant among the surprising shapes—the caves, trees, castles and platforms of the coral's growth.

Conditions were bad for everyone but infinitely worse for the Negro pilgrims; the Arab sailors cursed and beat them and, although they had paid their fares equally, often made them do the work while they themselves relaxed to smoke their pipes. Not being permitted to use the ship's oven to bake their durra loaves, the Negroes went hungry all day. They were not left even to read their prayers in peace without having buckets of sea-water flung over their papers by some contemptuous Souakini. Louis intervened fiercely on their behalf, and was assisted in his efforts by another fellow passenger.

This man, a friendly Greek sea-captain, afforded one of the few lighter aspects of an appalling voyage and Louis enjoyed his alleviating talk. He took Louis, as did all the other people on board, for a Syrian and conversed with him in broken Arabic. For Louis, one might think that these conversations recalled his own journey from Malta, and the questions that he had then been obliged to answer as to India—supposed country of his birth. He writes that he was:

exceedingly amused with the account of his [*the Greek's*] travels in Europe and the palpable falsehoods and absurdities which he uttered respecting what he had seen in England and the manner of its inhabitants.

A few of these Red Sea evenings Louis describes in words which, despite their sparseness, do evoke something of the red-gold rock and foreshore, vivid coral fish, the hot dark-blue of the sea, black goat's hair tents sprawling long and squat on sunbaked Nubian hillsides, and the great herds—brown, gold and tawny, and as stark as India ink among the sands. One evening, at the Bay of Tahile, Louis watched as the Bedouin's "immense herds of camels, sheep and goats came running down to drink at about a dozen springs among the trees close to the sea".

There was some fear that the Bedouin of this place would be hostile but that night saw hilarious carousals in the long black tents ashore, as several of the merchants and the sailors found former girl friends here. Although the *rais* had commanded everyone to return on board after sunset they defiantly remained ashore, and the noise of their protracted celebrations kept Louis restlessly awake through most of the night.

Not until they reached the Island of the Crossing Over Mount, (Jebel Mukawwar), was the boat made belatedly a little more sea-worthy; passengers and cargo were arranged so that the crew had some working space. Then, piously committing themselves to the protection of the Prophet and all the saints—whose help they sorely needed since their *rais* was a complete bungler—they headed for the open sea under a favourable wind.* They slept at night at sea, or tried to sleep for they were now cold as well as cramped, and the dazzling beauty of phosphorescence so astonished the Negroes that they could not stop chattering. To them it looked as if the sea were on fire, or had indeed turned to liquid diamonds, and they could get no satisfactory explanation of this wonderful sight from the incurious Souakin sailors to whom it was of course nothing new. However, Burton says that the Arabs do romantically enough call it the "jewels of the deep" made for the adornment of mermaids and mermen.

The *rais* was so poor a navigator that on reaching the eastern shore he missed Jidda by as much as fifty miles; this was serious as they were now in urgent need of water. He dashed the *say* wildly into a small bay, nearly capsizing her, and having arrived they found a beach that was completely barren, with no springs or well and not a Bedouin to be seen. Some of the Negro pilgrims, misled by the sailors as to the proximity of Jidda, rashly left the boat and began to walk along the shore. Louis discovered later that a couple of them had died of thirst on the way, and it was two-and-a-half days before the survivors reached the town.

While they were at sea again the following morning an almost total eclipse of the sun occurred. This dramatic and, to the sailors and Negroes, terrifying event—sudden darkness drawn like a

---

* Ibn Battuta gives the Litany of the Sea as: ". . . do Thou establish us and succour us, and subject to us this sea as Thou didst subject the sea unto Moses, and as Thou didst subject the fire to Abraham, and as Thou didst subject the mountains and the iron to David, and as Thou didst subject the wind and the demons and the jinn to Solomon . . ."

curtain over that usually so brilliant sea—caused a tremendous din for every Muslim repeated two *rikat*⁵ and then rattled swords, shields and spoons while the eclipse lasted.⁶

The next day was one of deadly, mirror-like calm. Not a drop of water was left on board so, since they were now within "gun-shot" of Jidda, Louis, the Greek captain and two Souakinis were set ashore with their slaves. They walked throughout the entire night along a barren salt-encrusted beach until they reached the Yemen road here skirting the coast, and at about an hour from Jidda they found a Bedouin encampment where they could at last quench their tormenting thirst.

During the morning they successfully smuggled into town the slaves who had walked with them, thereby avoiding the dollar-a-head duty; a useful economy since the cost of living in Jidda was very high. So, still in his rags, Louis entered the town on 18 July 1814, and laconically recorded that his arrival was "attended with some unfavourable circumstances".

He went first to see the man to whom his letter of credit was addressed, but as this had been made out in Cairo eighteen months ago, its date and Louis' beggarly appearance won him only a very cold reception, and the man flatly refused to pay the cash. He did, however, offer lodging, which Louis accepted, hoping to prove by further acquaintance that he was neither an adventurer nor an impostor. But, the man remaining adamant, Louis took himself off to one of the many public khans. He was beginning to feel desperate, since he was down to his last couple of dollars and the few sequins remaining in his amulet. Then something so very much worse happened to him that, as he puts it, there was little time for "melancholy reflections" on the monetary situation. He developed a violent fever and lay in a delirium for several days.

Possibly this illness was malaria but the maladies of Arabia are manifold. Personally he felt that its cause was his having indulged "too freely of the fine fruits" then in Jidda market, and he thought that he would almost certainly have died if the Greek sea-captain, who chanced to visit him in one of his lucid moments, had not procured for him a barber or country physician who bled him "copiously". It is something of a miracle that he survived this drastic treatment but then he was a man of remarkable stamina. To give the barber his due, it was only with reluctance that he performed the bleeding, in his opinion the remedy should have been a potion of ginger, nutmeg and cinnamon. However, two weeks later Louis was able to walk about again. Now his tiny stock of money was quite used up; even the amiable Greek was not disposed to help financially—there was absolutely nothing he could do now but sell the slave boy.

Louis deeply regretted having to take such a step: the boy had become fond of him, and wanted to stay with him, it seemed coldly inhuman to part in this way, he was more friend than slave—he had been faithful and helpful. The shared trials of that journey through Nubia, the sea voyage and illness in Jidda would all naturally have formed a bond between a master of Louis' mentality and his "slave", and he was never again to find one to equal him.

It was a bitter and a hateful moment when the captain took the boy away to sell him in the Jidda slave market—a moment that Louis cannot bring himself to enlarge upon.

The Greek sold the boy for forty-eight dollars, making for Louis a profit of thirty-two. Which means that the price of this one slave had paid for almost the whole cost of the four months' Nubian journey: small wonder that the African slave-traders found their human trafficking so lucrative!

Having miserably hardened his heart to take this poignant action, Louis was now able to re-equip himself and, throwing away his rags at last, he invested in what he calls "the dress of a reduced Egyptian gentleman". He also wrote to Cairo for money but, since he could not possibly hope to receive it in less than three or even four months and since he was quite determined, having got this far, to wait for the November pilgrimage, he had to find some means of living. Still very weak from his fever he did not want to resort to manual labour, but he was on the verge of doing so when he decided to try one more experiment first.

Mohammed Ali Pasha had gone to the Hijaz in the spring of 1813, and at Taif in the hills east of Mecca had set up the headquarters of the army with which he was intending to attack the Wahabi strongholds. Louis knew that Bosari, the Pasha's Armenian physician, was in attendance now at Taif, and he decided to ask him for help since he had been well acquainted with him in Cairo. So he wrote begging him to explain the unfortunate situation to the Pasha, and to ask if a bill could be accepted on his Cairo letters, and if the Pasha's Jidda treasurer would pay the amount.

Obviously it needed courage to do this, but the Pasha had previously expressed a favourable opinion of Louis' pursuits, and he knew something of Sheik Ibrahim's passion for travel. In addition, Louis had already had financial dealings with the Pasha's treasury so, knowing that Mohammed Ali approved of him, he hoped that he was not taking too rash a step in the writing of this letter by openly revealing his presence in the Holy Land and making so bold a request.

Although Taif was but five days' journey from Jidda and only about eighty miles distant as the crow flies, the country beyond Mecca was so difficult on account of the Wahabi that travellers rarely crossed the mountains then and caravans left only about every ten days. Therefore, Louis knew that he could hardly hope for an answer in much less than three weeks.

August in Jidda is insufferable and, to make matters worse, the fasting month Ramadan began on the 13th. Louis does not complain of the heat and makes no real attempt to describe it, but something of the sheer endurance of those weeks can be guessed at from one of the rare pen-pictures he sketches here of himself. Weak still after the fever, oppressed by the sodden, indeed baneful misery of a Red Sea summer, once the few early morning hours were over he could find no ease at all, except in the "cool shade of the great gateway of the khan" where he lodged. There he spent most of the day-time stretched out on a stone bench in what little eddy of a breeze there might be.

But he somehow found time and privacy to transcribe his Nubian journals from the small notebooks, and strength too to picture the town for us. Jidda—the very name according to some signifies "a plain wanting water"—was, as Louis saw it, filled with

a money-grasping, mainly foreign, floating population. It had no
gardens to relieve the glare of its white houses, its saline-encrusted
shores of stone and fossils glittered under the merciless sun.
There were no trees except a few miserable date palms at the
mosques, and the surrounding country was barren desert of infamous hills and perilous wastes. He encountered people from
many places: from the Hadramaut, and the Yemen; there were
Negro wood-cutters, poor Bedouin, Indian families, Malay
pilgrims, settlers from Egypt, Syria, Barbary, Europe, Turkey
and Anatolia, and a few Christians, mainly island Greeks trading
from Egypt. In his time Jidda was still the "port of Egypt" in the
direct India trade and he foresaw that if Suez were to absorb this
trade then Jidda would become no more than the harbour of the
Hijaz, as of course it is today.

He describes the little raised shops projecting into the streets
and shaded from the sun; he even counted the coffee shops—he
appreciated coffee himself; there were over two dozen, and he says
that people would drink as much as twenty or thirty cups a day.
He discovered that one of these places was the haunt of hashish
smokers, but the drug was not as widely used in Jidda as it then
was in Egypt. Hashish paste sold in Egypt was euphemistically
called *bast*—cheerfulness. He counted more than thirty tobacco
shops—he loved, as we know, to "drink smoke" as the Arabs put
it. There were eighteen druggists who sold among other things
innumerable rosebuds from the hills of Taif, used by women for
ablutions, or in conserves. There were money dealers, copper
sellers, barbers, tailors, turners, sellers of sweet oils or essences—
civet, aloe-wood, balsam of Mecca and rose-water from Faiyum
in Egypt. There were sandal makers, date sellers, soup and kebab
sellers, sellers of corn, of sweetmeats, of sugar-plums, and there
were of course countless beggars, for no man born in any of the
Holy Cities would act as a menial servant, and according to
Louis, no Jidda man would dream of working if he could
possibly keep himself by begging.

As in the khan where Louis lived, so in every building the only
relatively cool spot was the entrance hall, and he describes how at
the larger houses, as the sweltering afternoons dissolved in

languor, the master with all his men servants, hired servants, or slaves could be seen taking the siesta in the open hallway, his lawful wife shut in one part of the house, his Abyssinian female slaves in another.

Meanwhile, as Louis wrote up his journal or lay exhausted, his big frame sprawled like that of any other heat-sated "reduced Egyptian gentleman" in the shade of the great khan's gateway, the wheels were turning and relief was to come sooner than he had expected.

One result of his letter to Bosari was assistance from an unexpected quarter. Bosari's Jidda correspondent, through whom Louis had sent his letter to Taif, had mentioned Sheik Ibrahim to another doctor—Yahya Effendi, physician to Tousun Pasha, Mohammed Ali's son, then Governor of Jidda.

In Cairo this doctor had already heard much of Sheik Ibrahim's fame as a traveller and wished to meet him. He invited Louis repeatedly to his house; he was polite and helpful, and finally they came to an arrangement by which Louis received from him a sum of 3,000 piastres against a Cairo bill payable on sight. Considering the circumstances in which he was placed, Louis felt that such an offer was quite extraordinary in this part of the world, though it would not have been so in the commercial towns of Europe. However, Yahya Effendi had not the slightest doubt of Louis' respectability and solvency, so Louis was now saved from poverty at least until further money arrived from Egypt.

Almost immediately after this stroke of good fortune a reply came from Taif; Bosari wrote that the Pasha, having heard that Sheik Ibrahim had been seen walking about Jidda in rags, had sent a messenger with two fast-riding camels to the Collector of Customs at Jidda, with an order to supply the Sheik with a suit of clothes, 500 piastres for his travelling expenses and a request for him to go at once to Taif.

The invitation of a Pasha of the Ottoman Empire was equal to a royal command and, although Louis felt a deep aversion to receiving presents, rather than the loan he had hoped for, he was obliged to accept all, since he could not possibly afford to arouse Mohammed Ali's resentment.

As he was uncertain of the Pasha's intentions, he changed his 3,000 piastres into gold which he concealed in his girdle, for he thought that he might well need the cash as a bribe in effecting a quick escape from Taif. So immediately on that night, the eleventh night of Ramadan, after breaking fast at a grand supper with the Collector of Customs and a great many hajis from all parts of the world, he set off, not without trepidation, for the hills of Taif to face the power of Mohammed Ali, that wily old Albanian fox.

# CHAPTER FOURTEEN

## *Ordeal at Taif*

Conceal thy Tenets, thy Treasure and thy Travelling.
*Arab proverb*

. . . what pleasure to visit Tayif! the Eden of Mecca, with
sweet and cool air, and running water; where are gardens of
roses, and vineyards and orchards.

*Doughty*

MOHAMMED ALI'S MESSENGER from Taif was a friendly man;
Louis left Jidda with him, in the company of twenty camel
drivers of the Harb tribe who were carrying money to Mecca
for the Pasha's treasury.

Since people marched at night in Arabia because of the great
heat, Louis was disappointed to see little of the country, and in the
daytime, as he was still feeling the effects of the severe fever, he
was too overcome with tiredness and the longing for sleep to be
able to observe much.

During the first eight hours or so they travelled through bleak
country that offered nothing but a few wretched flyblown coffee
shacks and some wells of bad water until, at sunrise, they reached
a plain. At Hadda, about half-way to Mecca, they dismounted
at one of these numerous shabby coffee huts; it was filled
with:

a motley crew of Turks and Arabs in their way to or from
Mekka, each extended upon his small carpet. Some merchants
. . . had just brought in a load of grapes; and although I felt
myself still weak from the fever, I could not withstand this
temptation, and seized a few of them; for the baskets were no
sooner opened than the whole company fell upon them, and

soon devoured the entire load; the owner, however, was afterwards paid.

In Ramadan the traveller is exempted from keeping the fast, but everyone, whatever the season, pilgrim or not, on entering the territory must put on the *ihram*. *Al-ihram*, meaning prohibition or, as it were, the equivalent of our mortification,[7] stands for the ceremony of the ritual bathing *and* the name of the dress itself. It consists of two pieces of seamless cloth, one wrapped around the loins, the other thrown over the neck and left shoulder to leave the right arm free. This toga-like garment, more suitable for an equatorial climate than a desert one, can be dangerous for the pilgrim since it affords little protection from either blazing sun or winter cold.

In this coffee hut great disorder prevailed through the long sticky hours of afternoon and sleep was impossible. Not only was there a constant coming and going of soldiers who commandeered the entire supply of sweet water which had been laboriously brought in from some distance, but also rats swarmed all over the place; they were of a kind bolder than Louis had yet seen, and he was not without experience of verminous horrors of various species.

Louis left this unattractive spot with the camel-drivers before sunset, and rode with them until midnight. Then, dropping with sleep and weakness, he lay down on the sand and was lost to the world until daybreak. The others rode on to Mecca, only the messenger remained with him, but it was not wise to linger, since everyone travelled by night and stragglers were invariably easy prey.

The Pasha had given instructions that Sheik Ibrahim was to be taken by the northern way past the Holy City, but the man now led Louis along the Mecca road. Despite this favour he saw nothing really of the town then, as his guide unfortunately took a short cut: once again Louis had to repress burning curiosity while following behind and reciting, as calmly as he could, the pious ejaculations customarily uttered on entering the Holy City. Louis later travelled several times between Mecca and Jidda, and once did the journey in only thirteen hours, riding a donkey. He reckoned that it was probably a sixteen- or seventeen-hour walk, or about fifty-five miles.*

After a while he saw to the east the mountains of Taif in their full height, standing over 5,000 feet above sea level. As all this territory was holy ground, one was forbidden to break even the smallest twig from shrubs and acacias growing there. Towards the end of a long ride they passed an encampment of Hodeyl Bedouin, whose dogs lunged in to attack their camels so viciously that, although mounted, Louis had great difficulty in avoiding ferocious leaping jaws.

The next day they began climbing into the mountain chain. It was a desolate region of stratified red granite, with summits scorched quite black by the sun, and wild slopes littered with great blocks of loose stones swept down by winter torrents. At midday they rested in a pleasant spot on the mountainside beside a spring under an acacia tree, with a wide view down towards Mecca and a delicious breeze to fan their faces; here some Bedouin gave them milk to drink. Then, not far from the crest, where it was too steep to ride, they came to a beautiful little place—Ras el Kora. Louis was very tired and weak still, so he insisted on sleeping in this enchanting spot—quite the most beautiful he had seen in the Hijaz and the most delightful since leaving the Lebanon. After the scorching sands and plutonic rock of the lower country the keen air was delicious: figs, apricots, peaches, apples, the Egyptian sycamore, almonds, pomegranates and vines all grew here. He slept comfortably under a pile of sheepskins in a Bedouin hut which was neat and clean. They rode on:

> Just as the sun was rising when every leaf and blade of grass was covered with a balmy dew, and every tree and shrub diffused a fragrance as delicious to the smell as was the landscape to the eye.

Presently his thoughts returned to that rich green grass of his homeland as he halted briefly beside a rivulet:

* As a point of contrast, a modern pilgrim from Malaya told the writer that he did it by bus on the motorway in about one-and-a-half hours.

which although not more than two paces across nourishes upon its banks a green Alpine turf, such as the mighty Nile with all its luxuriance can never produce in Egypt.

He wondered, as he left this romantically beautiful and unforgettable Ras el Kora, why the merchants of Mecca did not build pleasure houses on those delicious heights.

They rode on over rough barren ground, and eventually saw Taif standing up ahead. The Bedouin describe it as "a corner of Syria transplanted and placed under the inclement sky of the Hijaz, and say that this marvel is due to all the powerful intercession of Abraham, the friend of Allah".[8] It is a healthy, fruitful place but when Louis saw it the impression was one of grim melancholy for it was still half-ruined after the Wahabi ravages of 1802, and he was never to see the celebrated gardens which lay at some distance from the town.

Indeed he was virtually a prisoner during his entire visit, and much of what occurred here, although he writes in a sense very fully of it, remains a little enigmatic.

It was about noon when he reached the town and because of Ramadan he could not call then upon the Pasha as it was customary for Turkish grandees to sleep away the day-time hours of the Fast. So he dismounted at the house of Bosari, the physician.

Bosari questioned him closely as to his intention in coming to the Hijaz. When Louis replied that it was simply to visit Mecca and Medinah before returning to Cairo, the Armenian seemed reluctant to believe him; he was apparently quite convinced that Sheik Ibrahim's real plan was to travel through overland to the Indies. On Louis' denying this, Bosari hinted, somewhat ominously, that if Sheik Ibrahim really intended to go back to Cairo he had better remain here with them at headquarters until the Pasha himself was ready to return. Even more strange, no mention at all was made of the money so urgently required although Louis was convinced that Bosari could not possibly have known that the money problem had been alleviated in Jidda.

In the evening Bosari went privately to visit the Pasha at his harem, where only friends or close acquaintances were received.

The doctor soon returned, and told Louis that Mohammed Ali would see him later in his public audience chamber. He added that the Kadi of Mecca, then in Taif for health reasons, was with the Pasha and, on hearing of Sheik Ibrahim's desire to visit the Holy Cities, had observed as if jokingly; "It is not the beard alone which proves a man to be a true Muslim!" Whereupon the Pasha had replied aptly enough that the Kadi was the better judge of such matters than he. The Kadi, so Bosari related, had then said that since none but a Muslim was allowed into the Holy Cities— a fact of which Sheik Ibrahim could not possibly be ignorant— he did not therefore believe that he, Louis, would declare himself to be a Muslim unless he really was.

Louis quotes the Kadi as having said this of him, but adds no personal comment. Perhaps he did not consider comment necessary; perhaps he took it for granted that those in England for whom he was writing knew him to be a Christian. And to his parents, years before, he had written that he would not "forget that death is the Christian's friend".[9] And yet, in the end, he himself knew that the Muslims would take his body. Was he perhaps rather more of a Muslim than he admits? It might conceivably be possible that Louis did not feel either an apostate or altogether an impostor in his self-imposed role.

H. F. M. Prescott, in writing of the Middle East, speaks graphically of that "strange and sinister territory of doubt or scepticism or half-hearted apostasy which lay between Christianity and Islam".[10] Possibly, Louis was in this state: fascinated, repelled; using his knowledge for his own genuine purpose of travel and exploration, and yet *perhaps* already half won over.

There are several points to be taken into consideration in thinking him neither impostor nor apostate. We know him to be a remarkably honest man, an idealist and perfectionist. As a scholar he would have known, and approved, of the fact that it was the Arabs who preserved through the dark ages of Europe classical medicine, astronomy, mathematics and philosophy. He would also have admired the tenets of Islam—although he never lost an opportunity to note and disapprove the hypocrisy of many of its followers, but the same goes for Christianity as

17. View from the Citadel-Cairo and the Nile Valley, by W.H.Bartlett

18. Camel train leaving the Citadel, Cairo, by David Roberts

19. Kalabsha, Nubia, by David Roberts

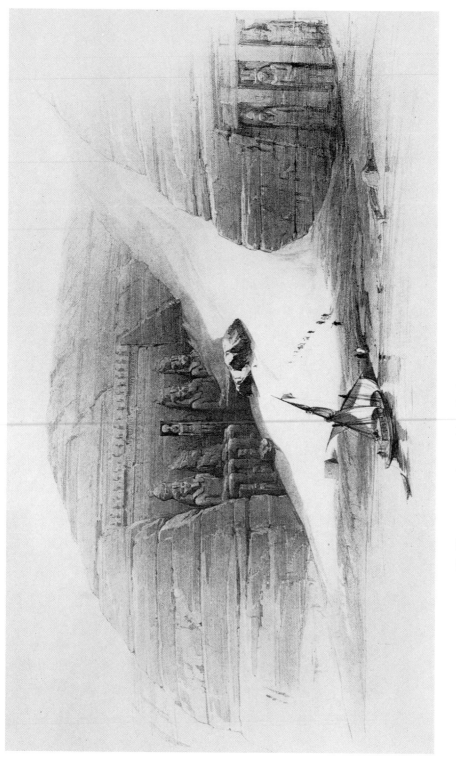

20. The two temples at Abu Simbel and felucca, by David Roberts

21. The façade of the Great Temple of Rameses at Abu Simbel, by David Roberts

22. Rameses II, one of the four colossi of Abu Simbel (photo: Georg Gerster)

23. Abyssinian
slaves in Nubia,
by David Roberts

24a. Mohammed Ali,
Pasha of Egypt
(unsigned)

24b. Jean Louis Burck-
hardt,"Sheik Ibrahim",
by Hans Hasler

well. He clearly liked Islam as a way of life—as the straight path founded upon the conviction of God's existence and His power, and as the seeking to follow in His way in daily life. But again he was undoubtedly more impressed by its precepts than he was by the majority of its adherents. In the Arab world to be born a Muslim was better than to have become one, and in the caravans and on his wild journeys we know he was taken for a Syrian. Though in circles where his European origin was known he naturally said that he was a proselyte.

We know that he had learnt austerity, and through it submission: as in Islam—a surrender to the will of God, the worship of God. A Muslim is a surrendered man, a true worshipper of the one God—as all deeply religious people are at heart. In this sense it is possible to regard Louis, who was so intensely honest, as genuine indeed; especially if God—the one God—had perhaps always meant more to him than the divinity of Christ. He was much alone with his thoughts, and so deeply involved in his role of a Muslim that he may well almost have become one—at least in as much as he was anything else—and, if neither impostor nor apostate, this was no crime.[11]

To return to that night of Ramadan in Taif: when Bosari had related the Kadi's little speech, Louis replied, safeguarding himself in a truly oriental way.

> I told Bosari that he might return alone to the Pasha; that my feelings had already been much hurt by the orders given to my guide not to carry me through Mecca; and that I certainly should not go to the Pasha's public audience if he would not receive me as a Turk.

And Turk, of course, implies Muslim. Now this was fine bluff; since the Pasha *knew* him to be a European, believed him to be English, did Ali in good faith believe that he was in truth a Muslim? Or was this belief merely assumed by the Pasha for the benefit of the Kadi? We shall never know, for Louis eventually left Taif still ignorant himself of the Pasha's real opinion. The Pasha had, he admits, treated him as a Muslim, and he says he flattered himself that his bold conduct at Taif had convinced the Pasha that he was in fact a true convert.

But on his return to Egypt the Pasha took "frequent opportunities", Louis writes:

> and indeed seemed anxious to convince Mr Salt, and Mr Lee, His Majesty's and the Levant Company's consuls, as well as several English travellers of note who passed through Cairo, that he knew perfectly well in the Hijaz, that I was no Muslim but that his friendship for the English nation made him overlook the circumstances, and permit me to impose upon the Kadhy.

It was then rather tactlessly suggested to the Pasha that Sheik Ibrahim might later boast in some of his travel accounts of how he had deceived him. Perhaps Mohammed Ali was trying to cover himself in case of doubt, for possibly *he* was uncertain either way and—as Louis neatly concludes—"to Mohammed Ali it was of more consequence not to be thought a fool than a bad Musselman"!

So we ourselves are still none the wiser, for, as Louis then remarks, despite all those later declarations of Mohammed Ali to the Englishmen in Cairo, he—Louis—did continue to live there quite unmolested and as a Muslim in the Turkish quarter. He was accepted completely as one of them by the Arabs and Turks of Cairo in that quarter since, from evidence of other travellers,[12] it was still impossible even as late as 1816—despite severe punishments imposed by the Pasha—for a *European* to be guaranteed safety from malicious assaults of Turkish soldiers, most especially in that quarter of the city.

Louis' refusal to appear before the Pasha that night alarmed Bosari, who in vain tried persuasion, saying that he himself had no option but to obey the Pasha's command and was obliged to conduct Sheik Ibrahim to an audience. However, Louis stuck boldly to his decision, so that Bosari was forced to return alone to Mohammed Ali and deliver the message. Fortunately the Kadi had now left; the Pasha merely smiled and said that Sheik Ibrahim was welcome, whether Muslim or not.

Nowhere does Louis described Mohammed Ali's physical appearance, but many other travellers have done so. One of these, William Turner, with an eye for colour and telling detail, said that when he had an audience in Cairo on the Pasha's return from the Hijaz, Ali was dressed in a dark crimson mantle, a projecting white turban, a sabre on his hip, and a dagger profusely glittering with diamonds in his sash. He had a "dark and designing countenance, and a penetrating eye. There was something savage in his look, and even his smile reminded one of Richard's power to 'smile and smile and murder while he smiled'." A comment that recalls Dodwell's description of the Pasha's caresses as having the terrifying velvet of the tiger's paw.

So this was the man whom Louis set out to meet that night: this extraordinary potentate, fifteen years his senior, resourceful soldier, brilliant capricious despot; a leader who knew the weaknesses of oriental rule and who, although striving always to maintain his own power and that of his sons, and affecting to be independent of the Porte, never ceased to be a constructive governor, a man who had, as Dodwell wrote:

a sense of the forces by which states are built up and broken down, a ceaseless struggle for improvement, a never-dulled consciousness of the defects of his administrative machinery, such as no oriental ruler had shown since the days of Akbar. His government makes a great turning point in the history not of Egypt only but of the Near East as a whole, for he led the way in adapting western political ideas to eastern conditions.[13]

Although he will always be remembered too for that bloody massacre of the Mamluks in 1811, it was not his habit to slaughter for slaughter's sake, nor was he in fact intrinsically a bloodthirsty man. He was not proud of that period of his life—the cruel struggle for power culminating in that appalling carnage at the Citadel. His own words on the subject were:

What would the world profit by the recital of this interminable tissue of combat and misery, cunning and bloodshed to which circumstances imperatively compelled me? . . . My history shall not commence till the period when, free from all restraint, I could arouse the land . . . from the sleep of ages.[14]

This then was the man whom Louis confronted in the dangerous Holy Land: a man who, although not entirely an ensanguined tyrant, had no great tenderness for human life, and who did not hesitate to take it whenever he felt justified in doing so—which was not infrequently. If Louis were nervous he does not mention it, but he must have been in very grave doubt as to his reception.

This was one of the moments that demanded much of him; he needed to draw on all his prowess and courage—perhaps this was to be the greatest test of his career. His entire future would hang on it; the success and safety of his journey to the interior of Africa, perhaps life itself. He faced it as ever, boldly and with an equanimity born of that rare combination of courage and prudence which was his.

Wearing the new robes that he had received at Jidda by the Pasha's command, he set off at about eight in the evening for the castle, which he describes as a miserable, half-ruined habitation. The Kadi had returned to the audience chamber, and the scene as it chanced to be set must have been formidable. It was a large salon: in the centre the Pasha was seated on a divan, the Kadi on one hand, and Hassan Pasha, chief of the Arnaut soldiers, on the other. Thirty or forty of the principal Arnaut officers formed a semi-circle about these three impressive figures. In the middle there squatted on the floor a number of Bedouin sheiks, whose deep eyes, like shapely pools aglitter under strong brows all turned their dark and penetrating gaze upon Louis as he made his entry, interrupting their business.

He approached the Pasha, said his "Salam Aleikum" and kissed his hand. With a sweeping gesture Ali invited him to be seated next to the Kadi, and addressed him very politely. But the subject which most interested Louis was not even broached.

After a few minutes the Pasha resumed his business with the Bedouin and when this was done, everyone was ordered to withdraw except the Kadi, Bosari, and Sheik Ibrahim.

Louis braced himself then, expecting to be put to the test. But not a word was mentioned of his personal affairs, nor did the Pasha in any subsequent conversation ever enter further into them, except to hint that he believed Sheik Ibrahim was on his way to the East Indies. He seemed to wish to talk only of politics. He was deeply interested in the fall of Paris, and in the capture of Napoleon—chiefly, so Louis thought, because he considered that Britain would now be likely to invade Egypt. Of Napoleon, the Pasha said that he had behaved like a coward: he should have sought death "rather than expose himself in a cage to the laughter of the universe".

Louis sat through two or three hours of this private conversation, speaking either Arabic through the Kadi, or Italian through Bosari, since the Pasha's Arabic was poor and Louis had virtually no Turkish. At the end of this time, when Louis took his leave the Pasha announced that Sheik Ibrahim would be expected again at the same hour on the morrow.

It was on the following evening, 29 August that the crucial test came at last.

Before sunset Louis paid a visit to the Kadi—it seems best to let him tell the tale in his own words:

[He] . . . found with him his companion and secretary, a learned man of Constantinople . . . the Kadhy Sadik Effendi was a true eastern courtier, of very engaging manners and address, possessing all that suavity of expression for which the well-bred natives of Stamboul are so distinguished. After we had interchanged a few complimentary phrases, I mentioned my astonishment on finding that the Pasha had expressed any doubt of my being a true Moslem, after I had been a proselyte to that faith for so many years. He replied that Mohammed Ali had allowed that he [the Kadi] was the best judge on such matters; and added, that he hoped we should become better acquainted with each other. He then began to question me about my Nubian travels. In the course of the conversation literary subjects were introduced: he asked me what Arabic books I had read, and what commentaries on the Koran and on the law; and he probably found me better acquainted, with the titles at least, of such works than he had expected, for we did not enter deeply into the subject. While we were thus conversing, the call to evening prayers announced the termination of the day's fast, I supped with Kadhy, and afterwards performed the evening prayers in his company, when I took great care to chant as long a chapter of the Koran as my memory furnished at the moment; after which we both went to the Pasha, who again sat up part of the night in private conversation with me, chiefly on political affairs, without introducing the subject of my private business.

At this time the state of Turkish affairs in the Hijaz was unpromising. Repeated Wahabi victories had created universal discontent, even a kind of panic among the Pasha's troops. They were terrified of the fanatical Wahabi who slaughtered all prisoners taken. The pay which sufficed in Egypt was hardly enough in the Hijaz to keep a man from starvation, and there was no loot to supplement it; since their enemies were naked savages, the best to be hoped for was a lean camel. These Turkish soldiers, at all times volunteers, found themselves now virtually prisoners of their own army and many tried to escape by sea. Louis says that he saw them himself being marched back in chains to headquarters, and he once saw on the Mecca road more than thirty of them tied together by their arms to a long rope—"an ignominy which those haughty Osmanlis could never forget".[15]

Pay was not increased and, as always in the Hijaz, there was much illness. In this sorry state of affairs it seems that Mohammed Ali was probably the only person of his court and the army who still did not despair of success. It was not for health reasons only that he had made Taif his headquarters, it was also partly to be near the Bedouin chiefs whom he hoped to win over. Some enlisted with him and he paid them generously, though he still let his own men starve. While at Taif, Louis frequently saw these Bedouin chiefs arriving; they were always presented with clothes and money. Many returned to their tents and informed the Wahabi of what they had seen at headquarters, others remained neutral.

But the Pasha, for the sake of winning the support of a few, listened to their discourse with a patience and good humour most unusual in an Osmanli of high rank.

These sons of the desert [*says Louis*] addressed him in the most blunt and unceremonious manner, calling him by his name, Mohammed Ali. One day an Ateyle Bedouin presented himself before the Pasha, kissed his beard and exclaimed—"I have abandoned the religion of the Muslims" (or True Believers as the Wahabis style themselves); "and have adopted the religion of the heretics" (so the Wahabis entitle all those Mohammedans who are not of their own creed); "I have adopted the religion of Mohammed Ali!" This unintended blunder caused a general laugh; and the Pasha answered through his interpreter . . . "I hope you will always be a staunch heretic."

In point of fact the Pasha was sceptical, and in Cairo he could not be bothered with minute and tedious religious rites which he did, however, carry out very carefully before the holy Ka'aba in Mecca. Perhaps his own scepticism was one reason for his not concerning himself unduly over Sheik Ibrahim's religion. He was much more worried about Ibrahim's intentions regarding the India trade routes, and suspicious that the English still favoured the Mamluks.

After the successful evening with the Kadi, Louis now went each night first to his house and then on to see the Pasha. They talked about many things and Louis was always politely received at the castle, but he knew that his actions were closely watched. He felt that Bosari was no better than a spy, despite his assurances of friendship, and Louis was never allowed to be alone for a moment. When Bosari asked if he kept a journal, Louis replied that the Hijaz, unlike Egypt, had no antiquities and that in its barren mountains he saw nothing worth noting.

In Muslim countries there is a strange, overhung atmosphere during the month of the Fast—a tension, an edginess—and it is not difficult to imagine that this feeling prevailed even in the court of a Pasha who was not a very strict Muslim. So that the pressures

surrounding Louis in his own personal problem must have been as
if doubled throughout long evening sessions in the restless nights
of Ramadan, at the dour half-ruined castle.

The Pasha spoke of his own fears for Egypt; now that Napoleon
was banished he felt sure the English would invade. On this topic
Louis was bold enough to say that concerning Egypt, His Highness was like a young man possessing a beautiful girl—and
although sure of her love, he was jealous of every stranger.

"You say well," the Pasha replied. "I certainly love Egypt
with all the ardour of a lover, and if I had ten thousand souls I
would willingly sacrifice them for its possession. . . ."

One senses that, although wary, these two strong and clever
men respected each other mutually. The Pasha definitely made
good use of Louis' quick wits, requiring him to give an opinion
of the Turkish translation of the peace treaty recently concluded
at Paris. After long hours spent with the Pasha's Turkish writer,
who read the document to him in Arabic, Louis was asked by the
Pasha, himself illiterate but astute, to point out and explain the
new limits of the countries involved, and other details.

So the days dragged on, and still Louis had no idea as to what
the Pasha's intentions might be. He felt that he was considered
as a spy sent by the English government, or rather by the English
Levant Company, from Cairo to inquire into the East Indian
trade.

So far as British sea-captains were concerned, even in Bruce's
day the Red Sea trade was already decaying, and they wanted to
market their Bengal goods direct in the bazaars of Cairo. But the
Porte had great fears that the Hijaz revenues would decline if the
Indian trade were to be diverted from Jidda to Suez. The coral
reefs and difficult shoals of the Red Sea did not permit ocean-going
ships from India, nor the junks of China, to land their cargoes in
the north; that was why Jidda had been for centuries the port of
Egypt. The Pasha was deeply concerned with the question of the
India trade in the Hijaz, and it was not therefore altogether unreasonable for him to suspect that Louis intended to proceed to
India. The overland route was, however, dangerous in the
extreme but from the earliest days the East India Company had,

in times of emergency, sent couriers that way, though usually via Aleppo and Bagdad, to take ship at the head of the Persian Gulf.[16]

Louis could only guess at the Pasha's opinion of him: in Cairo the Pasha had supposed him to be probably an Englishman, a man of rank, an English "milord", an impression no doubt heightened by a certain air of dignity which Louis quite rightly felt it appropriate to assume in a Turkish court "where modesty of behaviour and affability" were quite out of place.

Fear of Great Britain may have prevented the Pasha from ill-treating him, so Louis thought, but nothing at all was done to *help* him and, as far as Mohammed Ali knew, Louis had no more than the 500 piastres received in Jidda. Nothing further was said about finances, nor the money that he hoped would be given on his Cairo bill. Louis now found himself in a real dilemma: he had no desire to remain in Taif in this kind of polite imprisonment, and yet he could not ask to leave without increasing, so he felt, the Pasha's suspicions.

He therefore decided to make his presence in Bosari's house so irksome that the doctor would long to be relieved of him and would involuntarily influence the Pasha. With careful planning Louis now set himself to the role of the petulant guest, the overbearing Osmanli.

> It being Ramadan I fasted during the day, and at night demanded a supper apart; early in the morning I called for an abundant breakfast before the fast recommenced. I appropriated to myself the best room which his small house afforded; and his servants were kept in constant attendance upon me.

Eastern hospitality forbade any trace of resentment at such behaviour, and Louis points out with dry humour that he was, after all, supposed to be a great man on a visit to the Pasha. He took care in his conversations with Bosari to assure him how comfortable he was, how well the cool air of Taif suited his health, and that he had no desire to leave. The cost of maintaining him must have been high, for in the mountains provisions of all kinds were very expensive, and anywhere in the world a fussy guest is a sore trial.

The ruse worked perfectly: after some days, Bosari—for whom one almost begins to feel a shred of sympathy—asked whether Sheik Ibrahim's business with the Pasha would prevent him much longer from continuing his travels and visiting Mecca. Louis replied that there was no business, he had come to Taif only at the Pasha's request, everything was most agreeable, and what a splendid host was Bosari!

The next day the wilting Armenian again broached the subject, and remarked how very tiring it must be living entirely among soldiers, with no amusements and being unacquainted besides with the Turkish language. Louis agreed that was true but since he was ignorant of the Pasha's wishes he could make no decisions. At last then Bosari, brought to the point which Louis so desired, promised to speak to His Highness.

That very night the Pasha told Louis that as he understood he wished to pass the last days of Ramadan in Mecca (Bosari's idea this), he had better travel down with the Kadi, who was about to leave for the festival, and who would be glad of his company on the way. All exactly as Louis had hoped! The Kadi's departure was fixed for a day or two later and, most thankfully, Louis hired two donkeys in preparation for the journey to Mecca.

On taking leave of the Pasha no travel permit was forthcoming, nor the letter of introduction for which he had hoped, to the Pasha's son, Tousun, soon to be Governor of Medinah. Mohammed Ali merely said that he did not wish to interfere personally in Sheik Ibrahim's travels—the "folly and madness" of which he had already spoken.

So, neither obstructed nor facilitated in any way, Louis was at last free to go, after ten days of virtual imprisonment, and as he rode away from Taif, without waiting for the Kadi, he thanked his good stars that he was on the march again. He had found it, he writes, more difficult to avoid danger in this Turkish court than he had among all the wild Bedouin of Nubia.

# CHAPTER FIFTEEN

## *Haji Ibrahim in Mecca*

Our notions of Mecca must be drawn from the Arabians; as
no unbeliever is permitted to enter the city, our travellers are
silent.

*Gibbon*

Seventy thousand angels have the Ka'aba in their holy care,
and are ordered to transport it to Paradise when the trumpet
of the last judgment shall be sounded.

*J. L. Burckhardt*

TRAVELLING ALONE FROM Taif, Louis presently fell in with
three cheerful soldiers. As a precaution against thieves these men
had sewn up their money in bags and forgotten to leave out any
small cash for the journey; since Louis for once was solvent he
felt bound to help them. He paid their bills at the various coffee
houses on the way; they were good-humoured fellows and he
did not begrudge the extra expense at all.

His only regret, as he came down from the mountains light-
hearted to be travelling free again, was that he had not been able to
penetrate any further eastward into *Arabia Deserta*. But it was quite
out of the question since the wild country was full of hostile Wahabi.

That year, 1814, Saoud, the great Wahabi leader, had died of
fever. It was said that his last words of advice to Abdullah, his
eldest son, had been: "never engage the Turk in open plains".[17]
This related of course to the enemy's advantage of heavy cavalry
and, in Louis' opinion, had the principle been adhered to the
Wahabi would undoubtedly have recovered the Hijaz. But there
was dissension between the Wahabi of the north and those of the
south, and it was this fatal lack of agreement on strategy that
eventually led to their downfall.

Louis describes the road from Taif to Mecca and the one on
to Jidda as being literally strewn with the carcasses of dead
camels, evidence of one of the worst problems facing the Turks
in this war—the constant renewal of their baggage trains.

Nearing the Holy City, Louis had to put on the *ihram* again;
not everyone conformed, and the three soldiers did not bother.
After sunset they arrived at the coffee huts on the mountain
slopes; here they lit a large fire and boiled some rice for supper in
a big pot which they hired from the Arabs. It had rained during
the long day's march, and Louis began to shiver in the frail *ihram*.

During the night the Kadi and his party arrived. At first light
Louis went to call upon him politely, and found him smoking his
pipe and drinking coffee, taking advantage of the travellers'
dispensation from the Fast. Louis was afraid that if he were to
travel with the Kadi he might once more become virtually a
house-prisoner in Mecca, so he made some excuse now about his
donkey being tired—it might detain the Kadi, mounted as he
was on a fine mule. So Louis contrived to journey on happily with
his three companionable soldiers.

During the afternoon a violent rain and hail storm brought
them to a sudden halt. Soon water was pouring in torrents off
the mountains and when after a long time the hail stopped, rain
continued unabated for three hours. Water lay several feet deep
in the wadi, and wild streams foamed across the road. They could
neither advance nor retreat, so they sat it out on the mountainside expecting at any moment to be washed away. The Kadi—he
had caught up with them just before the storm—was in the same
plight, and his women were separated from him by torrents of
water. Thunder and lightning continued with relentless violence
and when at last the storm ended, night had come. Heavy clouds
hung around and they were in complete darkness: stumbling
along on foot they led their animals until after about four hours
they reached the coffee huts of Arafat. All were flooded but they
managed to find one in which it was possible to light a fire and
boil some water. The heart-rending wailings of the forlorn
women eventually relieved Louis of the Kadi's company—
when at last that important individual went to console his cold

and shivering females in a neighbouring hut so leaving Louis and his friends in more comfortable possession of the fire.

On the following day, 9 September, they arrived in Mecca. Louis was now completely on his own, not knowing a soul in the town, except the Kadi whom of course he wished to avoid. It is the duty of everyone, pilgrim or not, to go first to the Ka'aba and, as he was wearing the *ihram*, Louis was soon accosted by several guides. He chose one, deposited his baggage at a shop, entered the Great Mosque by the Bab es'-Salam, and started to perform the long round of ceremonial prayers required of every Muslim on reaching Mecca after a journey of more than two days' distance.

Mecca is set in a bleak and glittering plutonic landscape— *Arabia Deserta* indeed. Nothing seems to grow in the city, the encircling hills are dark and stony. Today, houses climbing up the valley sides are "crammed together like the cells of a honeycomb. Here and there an outlying building on the summit of a wind-polished rock looks as if it had been crowded out" and is waiting for a chance to squeeze into the confusion below.[18] One had only to leave the environs of the city to be in the wilderness and, says Louis, only a short way along the road one could think oneself as far from human habitations as if one were in the middle of the Nubian desert.

In this barren land, at the centre of this bleak city, is the House of God, Beitullah—the Great Mosque in the vast courtyard of which stands the Ka'aba, that monotheistic symbol at the very holiest heart of Islam. "The illustratious Ka'aba, like a bride who is displayed upon the bridal chair of majesty" proud in her mantles of beauty.[19]

Louis describes the Beitullah at length in an account which at that time was unique in accuracy and detail, the first complete pen-picture to be received in Europe, and, deriving as it did from the meticulous observation of such a man as he, it was received in London with widespread acclaim.

The mosque is so large that it is said by modern travellers to hold 100,000 people,[20] though the number Louis gives is 35,000. Writing of the Ka'aba he mentions the little lighted candles and perfuming pans of musk and aloe-wood placed below the threshold of its silver door each night, and the famous Black Stone, Adam's Seat, worn down like St Peter's toe by "the millions of touches and kisses it has received".

In his notes on the Ka'aba, culled from the works of various Muslim historians on his return to Cairo, he quotes that Adam, as the first true believer, was said to have erected the original Ka'aba on its present site. The sons of Adam repaired it; after the Flood, Abraham reconstructed it. Ishmail, his son, who had lived with his mother Hagar, that unfortunate Egyptian slave-girl, from infancy near the site of Mecca, helped father Abraham to dig down to the old foundations and eventually to rebuild it. A few centuries after Ishmail the "idols" were introduced. El Asraki, one historian quoted by Louis, says that the figure of the Virgin Mary with the child Aysa (Jesus) on her lap was sculptured as a deity on one of the six pillars near the gate. The name Ka'aba, evolved after the period of Mohammed, is said to mean ka'ab, or cube, deriving from the time that the building contained the golden vessels in the dry well it concealed. According to Diodorus it was in existence for seven centuries before the time of the Prophet.

Considering the various destructions the Ka'aba had suffered Louis could not resist commenting that he thought the 10,000 angels (these were in addition to the 70,000 to be summoned at the sound of the last trump) especially "appointed to guard the structure from accidents . . . seem from the history of the building to have been often remiss in their duty".

Seven circuits of the Ka'aba have to be done while praying, the first three at the trot in imitation of the Prophet, who contradicted a report spread by his enemies that he was at death's door by running thrice around it at full speed. The opinion among the Arabs was that the pacing round the Ka'aba was symbolically based on the motion of the planets and other heavenly bodies.*

"Most Arabic tribes were originally star-worshippers . . . at the time of Mohammed the idols around the Ka'aba amounted to 360"[21]—and every worshipper stripped stark naked, to symbolise the shedding of sin with one's garments. The Prophet of course

* As in Hinduism.

destroyed the idols in his great return to the worship of the one, the true God.

Louis performed all his *rikats*, and circuits, kissed the Black Stone, drank of the well of Zemzem, and went praying to and fro, back and forth; like poor Hagar looking for help when her baby Ishmail lay crying with thirst, and Abraham had apparently abandoned her to her fate in this parched and terrible wilderness.[22] Then the angel appeared to save her, and water hummed forth luxuriantly from the ground—from the well of Zemzem, a name which is said to mean humming.[23]

Having said the ritual prayers with his guide all the time close at his heels, Louis next went to one of the numerous barbers' shops to have part of his head shaved. The rest would be shaved after the Umra, or Little Pilgrimage; this he performed a few evenings later, walking out into the sweet desert air singing all the way. Only then was he free to discard the *ihram*.

Not knowing where to go that first day he sat for a while in a barber's shop to rest, and to inquire about possible lodgings. The town was already full of pilgrims and many places were booked for more people expected soon; however, after a prolonged search he found a ready furnished room. As he had no servant he arranged to board with the owner, who with his family retired into a small courtyard. The man was a professional guide from Medinah and although Louis lived most meagrely with him the cost was 15 piastres a day (about 6s. 3d., probably equal to at *least* £1 today!), and worse, when he came to leave the rooms he found several garments were missing from his travelling sack. But it was the guide's parting shot which was the unkindest cut of all:

On the feast day he invited me to a splendid supper, in company with half a dozen of his friends, and on the following morning presented me with a bill for the whole of the expenses of this entertainment.

On the evening before the feast day, the last night of the Fast, the mosque was brilliantly illuminated. Great crowds of pilgrims were gathered for their evening devotions, everyone carrying in his handkerchief a few dates, some bread and cheese, or some grapes. Each man set his little bundle and a jar of water before him while awaiting the poignant moment of the so stirring call to prayer that is evoked by the first sight of the new moon heralding the end of Ramadan, and the beginning of the festival.

During this period of suspense, they would politely offer their neighbours a part of their meal, and receive as much in return. . . . As soon as the Imam on top of Zemzem began his cry of "Allah ou akbar!" everyone hastened to drink from the jar of Zemzem water before him, and to eat something previous to joining in the prayer.

One can visualise Swiss-born Louis, now the "perfect Arab", sitting among a thousand other white-clad pilgrims, while golden-blue dusk quickly deepening brought alive the pale sparkle of innumerable lamps. As the Imam's resonant call rang out a united flash of pigeons' wings, turning sharply in the clear desert air, was caught as one in a sudden noose of light high above Zemzem. The Fast was over: the tiny sickle of the new moon—"the Prophet's eyebrow"—was seen floating low but bright above the western horizon.

After worship everyone returned to his lodging to supper, but again visited the mosque for the last prayers of evening.

The whole square and colonnades were lit and in addition most of the pilgrims each had his own lantern set on the ground before him. The brilliance of the spectacle and the cool breeze pervading the square caused the multitudes to linger here till midnight.

Since it was the only open space in the whole town cooling airs flowed in through all its gates—a merciful gift which the people of Mecca attributed to the fanning wings of those 70,000 angels who guard the Ka'aba. But, despite the angels, the proximity of the holy Ka'aba, *and* the guardian of the slippers, Louis remarks that he lost successively three pairs of new sandals at the House of God.

On this impressive last night of Ramadan, Louis chanced to see the utterly dedicated enthusiasm of a pilgrim from Darfur newly arrived in Mecca on that wonderful evening.

After a long journey across barren and solitary deserts, on his entering the illuminated temple, he was so much struck with its appearance and overawed by the black veiled ka'aba, that he fell prostrate close to where I sat, and remained long in that posture of adoration. He then rose, burst into a flood of tears, and in the height of his emotion, instead of reciting the usual prayers of the visitor, only exclaimed, "O God, now take my soul for this is Paradise!"

A perfect *nunc dimittis*: indeed many of the pilgrims did die in Mecca and by the end of the Great Pilgrimage the House of God bore a vastly different, even a sinister appearance. Illness and death, which often followed the exhaustion of such journeys or were caused by the frail protection of the *ihram*, unhealthy lodgings, poor food, or absolute starvation, filled the mosque with dead bodies taken there for the Imam's prayer, or with the sick carried there so that they might be cured perhaps by a sight of the Ka'aba, or at least die in the holy precincts. Louis often saw pilgrims worn down by hunger and disease "dragging their emaciated bodies along the columns" before they finally covered themselves with their rags and lay down to die.

Sometimes it was a whole day before the dead would be noticed. For a month after the Haj, almost every morning Louis found pilgrims' corpses lying in the mosque. Once, with a Greek haji who chanced to be there he:

closed the eyes of a poor Mahgribin pilgrim who had crawled into the neighbourhood of the Ka'aba to breathe his last, as the Muslims say, "in the arms of the prophet and of the guardian angels".

By signs the man indicated that he wanted Zemzem water to be sprinkled over him and, while Louis and the Greek were doing this last act for him, he died, and only half an hour later was buried. Several men were employed at the mosque to wash the places where the dead had lain, and also to bury all poor and friendless strangers who happened to die in Mecca.

Such events did not detract from the splendid impression that Louis gained of this great House of God—especially at the hours of evening prayers when at sunset a vast mass of people gathered around the Ka'aba. People of innumerable different and far-off places of the orient, of Africa, and of Muslim Europe: 6,000 to 8,000 of them, of many colours, many nationalities, all prostrating themselves at once in this superbly stylised unison of prayer— it was a spectacle, he says, which could not fail to impress even the most cool-minded onlooker with some degree of awe.

At prayer times not a sound was heard in the moque but the voice of the Imam, but at other times, during the festival es- pecially, when thousands of lamps were lit, the place was trans- formed. Always the focal point of the city, it then became a gay amphitheatre sparkling with lights, ringing with human voices, with the loud cooing too of innumerable pigeons and the beating of their wings as they wheeled in sudden startled flight above the Ka'aba. As Ibn Battuta so delicately indicates, the pigeons of the Beitullah always showed a remarkable respect for the Ka'aba.

At these times of noise and brilliance, for Louis the scene evoked more a European midnight "assemblage"—apart from the absence of women—rather than what he had expected to see in the sanc- tuary of Islam. It was then the nightly resort of foreigners, strolling or talking together often into the small hours. It was a meeting place for business men, as well as a refuge for the poor, and the diseased—so much so that it sometimes had all the appear- ance of a hospital. It was too "the scene of such indecencies and criminal acts" so abominable that he could not write of them: ". . . the grossest depravity . . . for the sake of money". Louis frequently shows this strong streak of what nowadays would probably be called prudery, but which was more likely genuine

disgust, a fastidious horror of sexual perversion, masochism, or
any brutality.

In the midst of these varied happenings, by the light of a
myriad lamps, countless devotees continued to perform ritual
circuits, accompanied by endless bawling recitations of their
guides screamed out above the loud gossiping of many idle
people and the noise of boys running, playing, laughing. But
suddenly, at about nine o'clock, it again became peaceful: "a
place of silent meditation and prayer" to the *few* visitors drawn
there by sincere motives.

At times it was the haunt also of women of that "frail sisterhood" peddling corn to the pilgrims, ostensibly, so Louis
noticed, to feed the pigeons of the Beitullah but often with the
pretext of selling not only the grain but themselves as well.
Mecca at this period was full of prostitutes whose numbers were
increased at the time of the Haj by adventuresses from abroad.
The local ones were, however, in Louis' opinion, "somewhat
more decorous" than Egyptian harlots, never appearing in the
streets unveiled. Some were Abyssinian slaves who reputedly
divided the profits of their trade with their former masters. He
records, but without comment, the interesting fact that the "frail
sisterhood" was taxed regularly by the Sherif, and additionally at
the times of the Haj. They lived in a quarter known as Shab Aamer, a
place of which Arabian poets dreamed romantically in their verses:

> Is Shab Aamer, since we left it still inhabited?
> Is it to this day the meeting place for lovers?[24]

—oddly like a familar echo of Brooke's "Grantchester" and
equally nostalgic!

It was easier to make travel arrangements in Jidda than in
Mecca, so on the third day of the festival—15 September—Louis
set out for the coast and on the way he narrowly escaped being
taken prisoner. At this time skirmishes were frequent between the
Wahabi and various tribes who had been won over to the Pasha,
while the Pasha's own forces harassed the enemy's country with
small cavalry expeditions.

Louis' caravan arrived at midnight at a watering place about half-way between the two towns to find its guard of horsemen in a state of terror, since they had just been told by some Bedouin that a small force of Wahabi was approaching. Louis' caravan therefore moved hastily off to the northern mountains hearing, even as they rode away, a sharp exchange of musketry fire in the camp behind them. It was not long before they learnt that the invading Wahabi had ransacked the camp, massacred everyone there, and carried away loot and a caravan which had halted just before their own arrival. The armed guard had put up no resistance at all but had simply galloped off *ventre à terre* to Mecca where they proceeded to spread rumour and terror. An incursion such as this was enough to stop all traffic between Mecca and the coast for a whole week, while the Wahabi, having achieved their purpose, retreated to their mountains again.

Partly because of this, Louis was forced to stay considerably longer at Jidda than he had intended; another cause of delay was the ulcerating sores which had developed on his legs. This was a common complaint on the coast, where even a gnat bite turned septic. Such ulcers are generally recognised today as one of the symptoms of malnutrition—from which it seems likely that Louis was beginning to suffer as he says that he had no appetite all the time he was in Mecca.

It must have been somewhere about now that a rather mysteriously interesting figure arrived on the scene: Donald Donald, a courageous Highlander better known as Osman. His intensely strong character comes down clearly across the years since many later travellers to Egypt wrote vividly of him. But, curiously enough, the only mention Louis makes of his name as far as can be discovered is in the account of the first Nubian journey when, passing Koshtamna, he was reminded of a lonely ride Osman had made a little while before from the Dongola Mamluks to Egypt. From this it does seem that in Cairo Louis had at least heard of Osman's strange adventures, if he had not already met him.

The boldness of such a ride naturally appealed strongly to Louis. The Highlander's story is a dramatic one. Born in Inverness, brought up firmly a Christian, Osman went to Egypt as a drummer-boy in General Fraser's forces in 1807. After the disastrous defeat at Rosetta he was taken prisoner and given the customary choice of death or of becoming a Muslim: the rite was performed on him, an enslaved and wounded boy, by force. Having then ostensibly become a Muslim, Osman joined the Mamluks and, a few years later, retreated with them to the Sudan after Mohammed Ali's famous coup at the Citadel. He subsequently made his way back alone through Nubia despite the Pasha's spies. Once in Cairo again—he was probably still only in his early twenties then—he became a slave of Mohammed Ali, married a girl of his harem, and fought under him against the Wahabi in Arabia. Most accounts say that Louis met him in slavery in Jidda; why Louis made no further mention of him remains unknown, perhaps it did not seem important but, from these other accounts, it appears that Osman must have been the rather mysterious nameless "companion" who was with Louis and his slave on the expedition to Arafat during the Haj.

Later, in Cairo, with the help of Henry Salt, Louis obtained Osman's freedom from slavery; the young Highlander eventually joined his household in the Turkish quarter and remained there until the end. The committee of the African Association obviously knew of the generous help their traveller had given to this naïve but brave and kindly Scot.

It was not until October that Louis was able to return to the Holy City. While in Jidda he acquired another slave, a Negro boy who had also travelled on that journey to the Red Sea with the traders when Louis had been in so dire a state of poverty; the boy was now quite amazed to see his changed appearance.

In a sense it looked as if Louis' luck had turned; he began to enjoy a peaceful, independent and happy time in the Holy City where—had his health only been better—he would have been perfectly content. But he felt constantly unwell, he had two bad bouts of fever, and one of dysentery. Even when he was not actually ill he felt "a great lassitude, a depression of spirits and a total want of appetite".

All these troubles he attributed to the water. It is tragic to think that, when he was barely thirty and should have been in the full flush of vigour, his remarkable strength was already being drained away by these various untreated attacks of a combination of illnesses the causes of which were still unknown.

He now rented a pleasant set of rooms in a quiet quarter of Mecca, and here in many ways he began to live more comfortably. He was neither suspect nor spied upon and his new lodging had a crowning delight—green trees grew before his windows. A rarity among these sun-blistered rocks of Mecca, and a sight that was "more exhilarating than the finest landscape could have been under different circumstances".

In the city everything naturally was of enormous interest to him—from the casual talk of the people, or their wisest proverbs, to the last detail of an ancient religious rite, the taste of the well-water, or the very stones of the desert itself. For once he felt free and at ease, since the Kadi had departed and the Pasha was still in Taif until the November arrival of the Great Haj. As he was one of the motley crowd of pilgrims from any parts of the world he was no longer the target of awkward questions. He let it be understood that he was a member of the Mamluk Corps of Egypt, living in reduced circumstances. Even had he encountered anyone who knew Egypt well enough to suspect that this was untrue there was little cause for worry since it was common enough for oriental travellers to assume a false character—especially so in the Holy City where one had to "affect poverty" in order to avoid great expenses.

So, despite his low state of health, he felt that he would always have pleasant memories of this peaceful time in Mecca. But ill-health did much to disrupt his extremely high standard of work and observation although he continued to make copious and detailed notes on the people, the pilgrimage, the mosque and the town itself.

He thought it a handsome place, its houses lofty and built of stone with numerous windows, and there were no grand buildings, no large palaces, khans or mosques to rival the islanded splendour of the Great Mosque. The streets, though not so narrow as those of Egypt and of Syria, were all unpaved; in the rainy season they were almost impassable, in dry weather sand and dust whirled about them. They were completely dark at night, being quite unlit, and one had to tread warily since all the dirt and muck of the houses was swept out into the highways.

Soon after his return from Jidda he had the bad luck to meet the Medinah guide, that avaricious and somewhat dishonest man in whose house he had first lodged. The fellow greeted him rapturously and soon began to make free of Louis' pleasant new rooms. As Louis had quickly learnt all the prayers to be said on the perambulations around the Ka'aba, he tried to dispense with the guide's services. The man countered in an awkward way; he would arrive unasked each midday to dine with Louis, and was brazen enough to bring a basket with him which he commanded the slave to fill with Louis' meats, vegetables, fruit and so on and which he later carried home with him. Every few days too he thought it time to ask for money, saying it was not the Sheik who gave it but God!

Louis could find no way of ridding himself of the pest; he told him bluntly that he really no longer needed his service. This caused deep offence, and for a short while a blessed peace reigned. But only three days passed before he returned as if absolutely nothing had happened, and asked coolly for a dollar.

"God does not move me to give you anything," Louis replied. "If He judged it right, He would soften my heart and cause me to give you my whole purse."

"Pull my beard!" exclaimed the guide, not to be outdone, "—if God does not send you ten times more hereafter than what I beg at the present!"

"*Wellah!* Pull out every hair of mine!" retorted Louis, "if I give you one para until I am convinced that God will consider it a meritorious act!"

At this the man leapt to his feet, and walked away saying in smug horror as he went: "We fly for refuge to God from the hearts of the proud, and the hands of the avaricious!"

This mixture of sanctimonious piety with brash begging was a well-known characteristic of Mecca guides, Louis says; ultimately he could not get by without one and eventually he came to some sort of gentlemanly agreement with an old Tartar who was rather more placable than the Medinah sponger.

In the longest street of Mecca, the Mesaa, Louis watched tin-smiths hammering out countless water-containers expressly for the pilgrims to carry the holy water of Zemzem back to their faraway homes. Louis found this water "heavy" to the taste but its holiness was so highly valued that, with foresight, his great Saharan journey in mind, he bought four of these tins and filled them from the well as intended presents to the Muslim kings of Africa, for them more precious gifts no doubt than offerings of frankincense and myrrh.*

In this same long street Louis found Turkish cooks of Constantinople, in the mornings selling pies and sweetmeats, at noon roast mutton and kebabs, and in the evening jellies called *mehalabie*. Here too were many crowded coffee houses, and even a couple of liquor shops where, against all the laws of Islam, strong drink was sold. The Indian fleet imported large quantities of *raki* in barrels; this highly potent spirit, akin to *pernod*, was mixed with sugar and an extract of cinnamon and sold under the guise of "cinnamon water".

The Mesaa was also the place of public punishment: while Louis was in Mecca a man was beheaded there for having robbed a Turkish pilgrim. Louis learned that many of the most cruel punishments in the history of the city had taken place in this street, and records that in 1624 two thieves were publicly flayed alive here.

On the whole, however, apart from the way the majority of them battened like parasites on the pilgrim trade, Louis rather liked the Mecca people. He found them considerably less pompous than Levantines; they had a sense of fun and they enjoyed a joke; they retained, he writes: "something of the good natured disposition of the Bedouin, from whom they derive their origin". They were most hospitable hosts; "cinnamon water" flowed at the dinners of the great merchants, after the meal rose-water was sprinkled on the guests' beards, and the room was soon filled with the scent of aloe-wood and fragrant tobacco. The wealthy all drank this so-called "cinnamon water", persuading themselves that since it was neither wine nor brandy they were not exactly

* Burton also said the water was exceedingly "heavy" to the digestion, tasted like Epsom salts and was apt to cause diarrhoea and boils.

breaking the law. "God has made us great sinners," they would
say, "but has bestowed upon us likewise the virtue of easy repentance." In defiance of the Prophet's law they played cards, drank
and were of easy virtue, merely laughing it off by saying rather
endearingly: "Oh well! The cities forbidden to infidels abound
with forbidden things!" One has to remember that all this laxity
was in the days of Turkish rule; had the strict Wahabi won in
Arabia events would have been very different. But whatever their
sins these Meccaites were a proud people and Louis liked them for
that; they were proud of their city, of being countrymen of
their Prophet, of speaking his pure language.

A narrow street off the long Mesaa called the Souega, or Little
Market, the tidiest in town, was regularly washed down and
sprinkled with water; here Indian merchants set out fine Kashmir
shawls and muslins, and perfume sellers proffered sweet oils and
balms. Here too hung strings of Red Sea coral, rosaries, sandalwood and brilliant necklaces of cut cornelians. Half-way down
this street, where it was only twelve feet wide, stone benches had
been built on either side. Here Louis often saw Abyssinian slaves
of both sexes put up for sale, most of them destined for northern
Turkey. Since, as he says, "beauty is an universal attraction" the
benches were always crowded with pilgrims young and old
who often "pretended to bargain with the dealers for the purpose
of viewing the slave-girls for a few moments in an adjoining
apartment"—a kind of nineteenth-century striptease.

The far end of the street of the Little Market was covered
over with a high vaulted roof of stone, in the cool shade of which
gentlemanly hajis lounged during the mornings and late afternoons, to smoke and talk together. It was here that Louis made
the acquaintance of a perfume seller, and habitually came to
spend an hour or two each day, sitting on the bench outside the
shop, smoking the narghile, drinking coffee, savouring the
mingled aromas of scented oils, Turkish coffee and deliciously
pungent tobacco. It was not time wasted, since this was the news
mart of the town: he would hear of the arrival of any important
people, of big commercial deals, of lawsuits brought before the
Kadi, of what was happening in the Pasha's army. Sometimes

even European events were discussed—"such as the last mis-fortunes of Bonaparte"—since pilgrims arriving from Con-stantinople and from Greece would bring with them the most recent news of Europe.

Besides this, Louis busied himself in gleaning all possible facts about the Bedouin, facts which he was later to use in his two-volume work, *Notes on the Bedouins and Wahabis*. Early each morning and again in the evening, he walked around the town and visited the coffee shops on the outskirts where he knew he would meet Bedouin. By standing innumerable cups of coffee he found that he could soon encourage them to talk about their tribes, and their deserts.

He spent the candescent hours of midday in his rooms, relaxing in the new-found freedom, sketching a little perhaps, refreshing his tired eyes with the cool look and soothing movement of those green leaves so happily framed in his window; at night he went to the great square of the House of God to enjoy the famous breeze of celestial wings. Then, like any other gentlemanly haji, shaven-headed, beturbaned, his pious tasks done, he would sit at his ease on the carpet which his slave had spread for him and, while the pilgrims were busily encircling the Ka'aba and praying, he would day-dream, indulging "in recollections of far distant regions". The green woods of beloved "Erndthalden" Alpine meadows brightening with spring flowers at the snow's dissolving edge, the mountains around Lac Léman, Cambridge leafy in high summer, the dark cedars of Lebanon, the beauty of the Nile at Elephantine with its graceful "sable nymphs". . . . He had many recollections to draw upon though he was still relatively young and, although he was first and foremost a man of action, he needed these hours of contemplation to refresh and restore body and mind, to sustain him in the curiously isolated existence which he led.

In those long Mecca nights he heard few songs except the jovial clapping *jok* of his Bedouin coffee shop acquaintances; on the whole he found the voices of Hijaz harsher than the more sonor-ous, harmonious ones of Syria. But there was one tune which appealed to him deeply, he could never hear it without a thrill of emotion. This was the song of the Mecca water carriers, sung whenever some wealthy pilgrim purchased water for distribution among the poor. He wrote the score of its melody, and this is his translation of the Arabic words: "Paradise and forgiveness be the lot of him who gave you this water." Was it the haunting sweetness alone of the music, or was it partly the words' meaning that touched Louis so profoundly—restless as he always was in his search for atonement?

He was fortunate to be present when the Ka'aba was opened, which happened only three times a year. He saw it done twice, on the 15th of Zulkade and the 10th of Moharram—for the other time, the 20th of Ramadan, he was in Taif. Ibn Battuta[25] says that it is opened by a chief of the Shaiba clan who mounts steps like those of a pulpit which are pushed towards the high entrance, evidently in much the same manner as the gangway of an airliner is today.

Louis describes the opening as taking place an hour after sunrise; "as soon as the steps touch the wall, immense crowds rush upon them and in a moment fill the whole interior of the Ka'aba" —a scene comparable in terror perhaps to the Easter madnesses in the Church of the Holy Sepulchre at the kindling of the flames. Today, it is said, only people of high rank are allowed to enter the Ka'aba.

Burton did so when it was empty of pilgrims[26] and only a few attendants were inside; even then it was so suffocatingly hot that the sweat ran off him in large drops and he "thought with horror what it must be like when filled with a mass of furiously jostling and crushing fanatics". Louis, nothing daunted, entered it with the mob—not a pleasant experience. The eunuchs were laying about them with their quarter-staves, beating the backs of men who had not paid for the privilege. In the windowless interior the heat was so intense that even Louis felt faint and was unable to endure more than five minutes of it. Many people were overcome, and had to be extricated prostrate, with much difficulty.

A certain number of prayers and *intentional* prostrations had to be done somehow and, Louis says, "it may easily be conceived how these prayers are performed and that while one is bowing down another walks over him". Prayers finished, the pilgrim was then expected to lean with arms outstretched and face pressed close to the wall while reciting "pious ejaculations".

The place was filled with sobbing and moaning voices, and Louis thought that he "perceived most heartfelt emotions and sincere repentance in many of the visitors . . . many faces were bedewed with tears".

The noise, heat, darkness and grinding press of humanity were overwhelming, so much so that even "the accurate Burckhardt", so Burton notes, made an error as to the prayers to be said, but he remained collected enough to record the moaning cries of the penitents:

> O God of the House, O God forgive me, and forgive my parents and my children! O God admit me into Paradise! O God, deliver our necks from hell-fire, O thou God of the ancient House!

The law forbade bloodshed anywhere in Mecca, not only at the mosque—and criminals often sought refuge in the Beitullah—but Louis himself once saw the Pasha's men pursue a deserter and drag him away from the very covering of the Ka'aba to which he clung for asylum. Mecca's history shows how frequently men have been killed, or even bloody battles fought, within the holy precincts—there particularly for, as Louis points out with irony, it was the most open spot the town afforded for skirmishing.[27]

He very much regretted that no Arabic histories were available here; in repeated searches for books on Mecca he noticed that it was mostly the Malays and the Persians who were similarly occupied. The Wahabi, always avid for learning, had probably taken away after their earlier conquest all there had been of historical books. He had to wait until he returned to Cairo to check many facts. He found no libraries or bookshops in the town, and he saw only one good book, a fine Arabic *kamus* which was bought by a Malay for 620 piastres.

Occasionally he attended lectures given by a sheik in the mosque, and says that he had never heard finer Arabic spoken:

". . . every word he uttered might be noted as a standard of purity." He follows this comment with a neat analysis of the Arabic dialects and pronunciations, from that of the "young Christian fops of Cairo and Aleppo"[28] to the Bedouin of Arabia, Bagdad and the Yemen—he had a most enviably accurate ear.

Again and again Louis reveals his admiration of the Bedouin. The son of a Mecca sherif was still brought up in the ancient tradition—as was Mohammed himself—that is, in the desert among the Bedouin from infancy until old enough to ride a mare. In this way a boy became used to all the perils and vicissitudes of Bedouin life, and was hardened to fatigue and privation. Of the sherifs whom Louis saw in Mecca he cannot speak highly enough; all brought up in this way, they were men of courage and good looks, spirited and handsome "with that energy, freedom of manners and boldness which characterise the inhabitants of the Desert". Some, like Sherif Rajeh, of whom Louis said he had "never beheld a handsomer man", had such a great dignity of bearing that would have singled them out among thousands. Of Sherif Ghaleb Yahya he wrote:

> . . . nor can a more spirited and intelligent face be imagined, [*and all were*] distinguished by fine manly countenances, strongly expressive of noble extraction; and they had the exterior manners of the Bedouin, free, bold, frank, warm friends; bitter enemies, seeking for popularity, and endowed with an innate pride.

That is the true "*snobisme du désert*" most perfectly expressed. Louis was acutely aware of this distinctive quality of the Bedouin so clearly reflected in the sherifs; he admired too the affection and regard in which they and their sons held the poor Bedouin who had brought them up in their tents—free in the desert, undefiled by the impurities, the greed and vices of the towns.

In the towns the true Bedouin could always be recognised by the bits of cotton he stuffed in his nostrils, or by the way he wore his *Keffieh* wound tight across his nose, or the frown of disgust on his brow.[29] Louis says that in one part of Mecca the stench of dead camels was so pestilential that, at the public's request, penniless Negro pilgrims were engaged to bring dry grass from the mountains and burn the carcases. He calculated that from the start of the war in 1811 till 1814 30,000 camels of the Pasha's army had died in the Hijaz. It was not only the dead camels that stank in Mecca, it was the sewer arrangements—or lack of them—for in those days each household emptied its privies into holes dug in the streets, and only roughly covered over.

On 21 November a man came galloping furiously into town. Louis heard the narrow streets echoing to the thunder of his horse's hooves, and to the yells of the excited mob running after him. The instant he dismounted at the Governor's house, his unfortunate horse dropped dead, ridden literally to death. This mad race announced the approach of the Great Syrian caravan and, as the first to bring news of its safe passage through the desert, this rider won the customary prize.

Early the next day the Egyptian caravan arrived, and the Pasha himself came unexpectedly from Taif to be present at the Haj. All of a sudden Mecca came alive with bustle and excitement as everyone, including Louis, began preparing for the journey to Arafat: a journey which forms so important a part of the Pilgrimage.

In his wanderings after he had been expelled from Paradise, Adam is said to have come to the plain of Arafat, and was there reunited with Eve.[30] Mohammed, shortly before he died, obeying Abraham's call to the pilgrimage, made his farewell visit to Mecca, and to Arafat where he preached standing on the side of the mountain as the sun began to go down.[31] So it is to this day, each year at the time of the Pilgrimage* every one of the many thousands of pilgrims goes out to camp at Arafat.

The Great Syrian caravan used to start from Constantinople, collecting the pilgrims of northern Asia as it passed through Anatolia and Syria. It rested at Damascus for some weeks, where it changed its Bactrian for desert-bred camels, and made preparations for the thirty-day journey into Arabia. The Egyptian

* A lunar cycle of three years.

caravan's route was extremely dangerous, along the shore of the
Red Sea through the tribal territories of wild and warlike Bedouin.
When Louis saw it that year it consisted only of soldiers, the
retinue of *Mahmal* camel, and a party of prostitutes and dancing
girls "whose tents were among the most splendid in the caravan".
He saw similar camp followers in the Syrian caravan too—evidently the "frail sisterhood"'s professional status did not preclude
their going on the Pilgrimage, indeed even dogs (unclean to the
Muslim) attended it, for Doughty says that the dogs of Aleppo
somehow managed to follow it all the way through the desert.

The Pasha's favourite wife, mother of Ibrahim and Tousun,
had travelled by sea. Her retinue, writes Louis, was:

> as splendid as the wealth of Egypt could render it. Four
> hundred camels transported her baggage from Jidda to Mecca,
> and her tent pitched at the foot of Mount Arafat equalled in
> size and magnificence anything of which we read in fairy tales
> or Arabian romances.[32]

The Mahgribin caravan, with which Louis planned to travel
to the Fezzan, used to come from Morocco via Tunis and Tripoli,
to join the Egyptian one at Cairo. It had long since ceased to be
regular;[33] the last one had passed through in 1811. The various
caravans were all falling off considerably in attendance at this
time, not only as a result of the wars, but through growing costs,
and also a general waning of religious zeal—facts which clearly
explain Louis' long wait, and more than justify his having taken
this journey into Arabia.

Despite the smaller attendance it made nevertheless a proud
showing when the Egyptians and the Syrians paraded through the
streets led by their majestic *Mahmal* camels bedizened with little
mirrors, feathers, tassels and bells, and bearing their extravantly
decorated burdens. Among the admiring crowds of Mecca Louis
stood to watch the display under latticed and jalousied balconies
that cast a complexity of shadows on tall white walls. Martial
music of the Pasha's bands reverberated among the high stone
houses. All the great men rode in ornate litters slung between tall

disdainful camels; twelve caparisoned horses heralded the Pasha of Damascus' elaborate litter, and those of his women following behind. Under the burnished canopy of desert sky Mecca throbbed with sound, and glowed with the spectrum of colour winding lavishly through the canyons of its sun-bleached streets.

On the day of the procession to Arafat, just after a violent attack of dysentery (it happens to have been his thirtieth birthday, 25 November), Louis set off on foot, with his boy and Osman mounted on camels in a vast tightly packed crowd of pilgrims. By immense good luck he was in considerably better health during the whole four days of this strenuous pilgrimage. The crowd was so dense that it was several hours before they could make their way through to the outskirts of the town, and there were many accidents.

Of the half-naked hajis all dressed in the white *ihram*, some sat reading the Koran upon their camels; some ejaculated loud prayers; whilst others cursed their drivers and quarrelled with those near them who were choking up the passage.

It was not until long after sunset that Louis eventually reached the plain where the pilgrims encamped over an area of several miles; their countless fires flickered in the darkness, and the camps of the two Pashas and the Emir of Egypt shone with high-hanging clusters of brilliant lights. Although beautiful it was a chaotic scene; people who had lost each other went wandering around among the tents calling and shouting, and it was hours before the clamour died down. Louis reckoned that there were about 80,000 people gathered on the plain.*

The night was cold and dark; men sat up praying, their loud chants rose above and rivalled the merry-making Meccaites, who were singing their jovial *jok* and clapping in unison. Sleep was impossible, Louis abandoned the idea and spent most of the night walking around the huge camp. There were about 3,000 tents but most of the pilgrims were camped under the stars. There were

---

* One hundred and fifty years later, in 1962, the crowd was numbered at one and a quarter million. (*Mecca the Blessed, Madinah, the Radiant.*)

whole streets of bazaar tents complete with provisions; the tents
of the great men were very splendid but most superb of all was
the fairy-tale seraglio of Mohammed Ali Pasha's wife.

[*It was*]—in fact an encampment consisting of a dozen tents of
different sizes, inhabited by her women; the whole enclosed
by a wall of linen cloth, 800 paces in circuit, the single entrance
to which was guarded by eunuchs in splendid dresses. Around
this enclosure were pitched the tents of the men who formed
her numerous suite.

A linen palace, beautifully embroidered, its fine work and
sumptuous colours reminded Louis of the Arabian Tales of the
Thousand and One Nights.

He had barely settled himself to sleep at last, or so it seemed,
when the guns of the two caravans were fired—as they always
were each day on the road as a signal to rise and strike camp, but
now to herald the approaching dawn of the great day, and to
summon the faithful to make ready for morning prayer.

All around the camp thousands of camels were browsing on the
dry scrub of the plain, and as soon as it was light the mettlesome
Syrian and Egyptian cavalry went dashing out to exercise. To
obtain a wider, a kind of bird's-eye view of this vast prospect,
Louis walked to the summit of Mount Arafat, where he had
hoped to take some bearings, but the crowd was too great for him
to use his compass. Surveying this amazing scene, he thought that
there could be no spot on earth where so many different languages
could be heard in so relatively small an area. In which concept,
before the days of broadcasting and great international assemblies,
he was probably quite right. He reckoned that there must be at
least forty languages spoken here, perhaps even a good deal more
than that. He was much moved by the realisation, and also by
being in what he calls "a holy temple of travellers only". It
appealed enormously to his imagination, and he admits that he
had never before at any time felt a more ardent desire to be able to
penetrate once into the remotest corners of all the countries
represented by the people whom he now saw gathered here.

Travel and the precious secrets it reveals had become a passion with him. As he wandered among the travellers' tents and bundle-enclosed pitches he reasoned that he should have no more difficulty in reaching these people's homes than that which they themselves had experienced in arriving at this plain, so he "fondly imagined", dwelling upon the idea with longing and ambition.

The thought may have been over-optimistic, but it was a challenging one typical of him—nothing now seemed too excessively difficult to contemplate in the way of travel. He had every reason to be confident then; he was one of them, an initiate, an accepted Muslim, now even a haji and a learned one at that. But in his young enthusiasm there were two factors which he seems to have overlooked—time and, sadly enough, health.

He was so deeply absorbed in his observations and in these thoughts here at Arafat that the hours rapidly dissolved. As he moved about the camp he spoke to some of the pilgrims, asking at the Syrian encampment after his Damascene and Aleppine friends and among the Syrian Bedouin for news from their deserts. Suddenly it was past midday and *lohor*—the noon prayer hour missed. Then the time of *asar* approached and the great ceremony of the Arafat plain commenced. As Mohammed before him, the preacher, riding a gorgeously caparisoned camel, took up his position on a platform on the hill and began to address the crowd, the two *Mahmal* camels standing just below him with their tall green and gold litters.

This sermon, *Khutbat el Wakfa*, which lasts until sunset, constitutes the holy ceremony of the Haj, *el Wuquf*, the standing, an essential element of the Haj without which no pilgrimage was considered valid although the pilgrim might have visited all the holy places of Mecca.[34]

The people, with their tents ready loaded, mounted their camels and crowded close to the hill to be at least within sight of the preacher, even if they could not hear him.*

The two Pashas with their whole cavalry drawn up in two squadrons behind them took their post in the rear of the deep

---

* Today there are loudspeakers at Arafat, and also in the Beitullah.

lines of camels of the hajis . . . and there they waited in solemn
and respectful silence the conclusion of the sermon.

The preacher was reading the sermon while mounted, in
Mohammed's tradition, but Louis noticed that this Turkish
gentleman was not as good a rider as the hardy Bedouin Prophet:
the camel becoming restive, he was soon obliged to dismount.

He paused in his reading every five minutes or so to stretch up
his arms:

> to implore blessings from above; while the assembled multi-
> tudes around and before him waved the skirts of their *ihrams*
> over their heads and rent the air with shouts of: "Here we are at
> thy commands, O God! *Lebeik, Allah, huma lebeik.*"

During each enthusiastic waving of the white *ihrams* the multitudinous hillside appeared to Louis suddenly to foam like a water-
fall, while the green umbrellas shielding the thousands of mounted
hajis gave the impression of a "verdant plain" below.

Looking around him Louis tried to judge from their expressions
the reactions of the people near him. Several were sobbing, a few
"stood in silent reflection and adoration with tears in their eyes".
But meanwhile, many Hijaz people and soldiers of the Turkish
army were chatting and joking and whenever the others waved
the *ihram* and called passionately upon God, they made exaggerated gestures in mimicry, ridiculing the whole ceremony. One
wonders if Louis saw any lightly veiled Meccan beauties, such as
Burton's lovely little "Flirtilla" whom he, Burton, was to chase
some forty years later at Arafat—but then unfortunately Louis
was always considerably more serious, and more reserved about
his own personal reactions to beauty than that extrovert Englishman ever was.

As the sun began to sink behind the western hills the Kadi
closed his book: the time had come for the great "Rushing
Down", the *ifada*, which must not be done before the sun has set
or the pilgrimage is nullified. When the *ifada* is signalled the
crowd, after a final blast of a "*lebeik!*", plunges headlong in the

rush with "a single surge at which the earth shakes and the hills tremble."[35]

It was an insanely tough race. Shortly before Louis' time, serious fights had occurred between the rival Syrian and Egyptian caravans, each striving to urge their *Mahmal* camel ahead of the other. On some occasions as many as 200 people had lost their lives in supporting the honour of their caravan in the mad gallop. But this year, since Mohammed Ali's power was so great, the Syrians behaved with remarkable restraint. Nevertheless, it was still a chaotic departure, there was indescribable confusion, and many people who lost their camels in the rumbustious helter-skelter went wandering about all over the plain shouting for their drivers.

Louis had told Osman and the boy to wait for him, but seeing all the others rush forward they had followed suit, or were just swept along with the massive pounding thrust of the camels, and Louis did not find them until late the next day. Meanwhile he followed on foot with the mob, and had to sleep uncovered on the sand, shivering in the *ihram*.

Night fell before the procession reached the winding valley south-west of Arafat, and soon myriads of torches were lighted; twenty-four were carried before each Pasha. Fiery sparks flew far and wide over the plain. It was a superb scene, especially as they entered the narrow defile, the crowds moving through as a river of flame, advancing like molten lava at a great pace, with an infernal din, in unutterable disorder to the thud and blast of artillery and musket fire, deafening drums of the Pashas' *nobat* bands, and swooshing roars of countless rockets. After about two hours everyone alighted and lay down to rest just where they were in the first available spot, but the Pashas' lamps blazed till dawn and the artillery never ceased firing.

At first light there was another sermon but everyone, Louis noticed, for fear of thieves in this notorious spot, was too busy brooding over his boxes to listen to a word. Then, as the first long rays of gold shot across the heaven out of the east, the Haj gathered itself together and trundled on again towards Muna for the ceremony of the stoning of Iblis—the devil: a very ancient ceremony this, associated in the Muslim view with Abraham's stoning of the devil at the time of his intended sacrifice of his son.[36]

This was another perilous moment for the pilgrim among a highly excited, tightly packed stone-throwing sea of men. Louis, fortunately, came through unscathed. Soon after the stoning there was feasting; within fifteen minutes several thousand animals were slaughtered. Louis bought his sacrificial sheep and then—this was part of the ritual—he had his head shaved, and would have changed into normal clothes, but he was still separated from his camels, men and baggage. He wandered about until at last after sunset, he found Osman and the boy encamped on the hillside. They had been worried about him, since they knew that he might easily have been knocked down and killed by a flying hoof, or even by a stone hurled at Iblis.

The Muna festival lasted for three days, but few people dared to sleep on account of the thieves. Several dozens of camels had been stolen at Arafat by the Bedouin, and someone had been relieved of 300 dollars. Two of the thieves who had been caught were beheaded at Muna by Mohammed Ali's orders, and Louis describes how their mutilated bodies lay before the Pasha's tent the entire three days with a guard to prevent their friends from removing them. Such sights did not in the least distress the Turk, hardened as he was by their frequency.

Despite the lights and the fireworks the wadi was scarcely a joyous spot by the end of the festival—with the stinking fly-ridden corpses, not only of the thieves but of countless sacrificed sheep, rapidly putrefying on the sun-baked ground. Few wealthy pilgrims could consume all they had killed; one sect—the Hanefis—were not even permitted to eat more than an eighth of a sheep. Most of the meat went to the poorer hajis, while the entrails were flung haphazard about the valley. Louis found the mosque crowded with poverty-stricken Indians encamped there busily drying meat for their travel provisions. The pavement was deep in carrion, and slices of meat were festooned on strings between the columns; it is hardly surprising that he found the sight and the stench "very disgusting". He was not the only haji to be offended by such things: obviously the poor and hungry pilgrim had every right to dry meat that would otherwise have been wasted, but hardly perhaps to use the mosque for the purpose, or so he thought. He saw many such laxities, and infinitely worse practices in these Holy Lands; however, in his strictly fair way he adds:

> our Christian holy-land is liable to some censure for practices of the same kind. The most devout and rigid Mohammedans acknowledge and deplore the existence of this evil [*in their holy places*], and prove that they are either more clear-sighted or more sincere than the Christian pilgrim Chateaubriand.*

With his unflagging love of accuracy Louis disapproved of Chateaubriand's highly coloured pictures of Palestine and its priesthood and remarks that as a traveller he could not escape blame—

> for having departed from the truth and often totally misrepresented the facts that fell under his observation.

A comment that seems worth quoting since it reflects as it were in reverse one of the clearest images of Louis himself, and his own standards of sincerity and truth. Whatever Louis' faults may have been he was a man who formed direct, clear opinions and held loyally to all that he deemed right, just as he devised bold and lonely schemes and did not hesitate to carry them out.

After the return of the Haj from Muna, the main street of Mecca became almost impassable, so dense were the crowds assembled there: merchants selling, and pilgrims buying in preparation for the long homeward journeys that would sift them out again across half the world. On the military side, too, the Pasha, preparing to open his new campaign against the Wahabi, now marshalled the entire Egyptian caravan to assist him, and used all

---

* Presumably this is a reference to Chateaubriand's *Génie du Christianisme* which Louis had probably read soon after it came out in 1802. He would have been in sympathy with later critics of Chateaubriand who agreed that although so brilliant he "dealt in false sentiment and extravagant imagery".

12,000 of the Syrian camels to transport provisions from Jidda. The animals were so weakened by this ceaseless labour that many died in the desert when finally he did allow the Syrian caravan to return north.

At about this time Louis learned that the money for which he had written to Cairo had at long last reached Jidda; so on 1 December he rode down to the coast and stayed in the town for a week. It was as crowded with returning pilgrims as Mecca had been. To him it seemed very heaven now, since people from places as far apart as Timbuctu and Samarkand, or Georgia and Borneo, constantly coming and going would, in his view, make it a most "desirable residence for an inquisitive European traveller", who might, he thought, easily attract a large number of these men to his house and by spending a small sum on provisions and assistance for them could thus collect useful information about distant and unknown parts of remotest Asia and Africa. Obviously such an idea would have great appeal for him—perhaps he saw himself as carrying it out at some later date but first he had to get on with the more practical business of the actual and the lonely exploration.

There was a Bombay ship in harbour commanded by a Scot, a Captain Bloag, from whom Louis was able to buy a good compass. This friendly man gave Louis from his own library a little volume of Milton's poems—a book which was soon to stand him in great good stead. He met two other Europeans at this time, an Englishman on his way to India, and a very unhappy Hanoverian baron—destined to die a month or so later of the plague.

The Englishman on his way to India was Buckingham—ill and in great distress after losing all his belongings at sea. Hearing of this, Osman went to visit him, treated him with every kindness and, at his request, wrote to inform Louis. When Louis arrived, Buckingham had been transferred to a cool cabin aboard Captain Bloag's ship and they could all talk freely.

> . . . the reciprocal recital of our separate adventures . . . would have made a good volume of Travellers' Tales. Poor Osman was . . . now and then in difficulty from his scruples of

conscience preventing his return to European habits and a fear of disgracing his Muslim faith. As wine was served at the cabin table with the dinner, Mr Burckhardt, though professing to be a Mohammedan, and travelling as such, nevertheless took a glass with hesitation. But Osman at first declined. Being rallied, however, by his brother Muslim, his resistance gave way, and he took a single glass also. Whether it was the motion of the ship, though at anchor, or the long disuse of wine, or both combined . . . we could not say, but in fact he became sick; and he gravely attributed this to divine wrath, as a punishment for his infringing the precepts of the Koran![37]

There is something very endearing about Osman—something half-comic half-tragic in this typical Highlander whose freckled face, light blue eyes, and sandy moustachios contrasted so oddly with his dress, manners and air, all of the real Turk.

Louis enjoyed his visits aboard the hospitable Captain Bloag's ship; and the company was interesting to say the least. The German whom he mentions was apparently a young eccentric on the run, having killed a rival lover in an affray at Vienna, who among other idiosyncrasies wore under his shirt a naked dagger hanging like a pendant from around his neck.[38] Louis, still unaware of Buckingham's unauthorised way of spending his company's funds, and of other failings, hailed him warmly as a friend and even loaned him money. Afterwards, in the New Year, answering a letter from Buckingham he wrote in his kindly way trying to give some reassurance that the pursuits of trade and commerce were no less admirable than his own work of discovery and learning. Buckingham had said that there were in commerce many practices "that an honourable mind could only consider base and degrading". Louis' warm-hearted and charitable reply came quickly: such pursuits as Buckingham's could not be called base because they were "sanctified by honour, by duty, by parental love, and connubial attachments,—the strongest ties which Nature possesses to bind a generous heart".

With his own unassuaged longing for the fulfilment of a home Louis believed in Buckingham, believed that all he was apparently doing was for the sake of wife and family. He wrote on: it was more likely *his* own pursuits that might be called degrading because they obliged him to live with what was the most "abject and wretched in human nature"—only too often among men such as the slave traders; the greedy, the brutal and the barbaric:

> Infinitely worse than all your wealth hunters. Let us both manly work through our way. . . . It is true I hope to wrest a wreath from the hands of Fame but I much doubt whether the possession of that wreath will be productive of as much heartfelt joy and satisfaction to me as will be . . . to you the endearing thanks and blessings of your family.[39]

In Mecca Louis arranged with a Bedouin of the famous and ancient Harb tribe for two camels to take him through Bedouin territory to visit the tomb of the Prophet at Medinah with other pilgrims. But these plans fell through since no caravans were able to take to the roads because the Pasha's military operations were beginning. Gathering his whole strength between Mecca and Taif, the Pasha was now ready to attack Taraba; he intended to destroy the town totally and to plant on its site an entire load of water-melon seeds. The seed was carried through Mecca with all ceremonial pomp to inspire the dispirited Osmanlis with some fresh hope.[40]

At first, remembering their old leader's dying words, the Wahabi remained in their mountains and repulsed any attacks made on them by the Pasha's approaching cavalry. The Turks soon began to despair of success; many deserters brought back exaggerated tales of various disasters and even of the Pasha's death. One day these rumours, running like wild-fire through Mecca, caused serious panic: the victorious Wahabi were on the way, every Turk in town would be slaughtered when they arrived! Hundreds of piastres were offered for any camel with which to escape to Jidda. On the very night of the rumours many people set off on foot for the coast. Others disguised themselves in nomad rags and took refuge in the castle; apparently not a soul prepared to defend the town. Louis, being convinced that flying advance troops of Wahabi would cut off all fugitives in the open desert, sensibly decided that his "safest asylum would be the great mosque, which at all times the Wahabi had respected as an inviolable sanctuary".

He and the boy therefore, taking with them his few valuables and a good supply of biscuit, went calmly to the House of God. He felt that if necessary they could live there on the biscuit and the water of Zemzem for some *weeks*.

That the whole crowd of Turks did not follow this example, may be ascribed to their judging of the Wahabi by themselves; for they could never believe that in the hour of victory a soldier would regard any place as sacred. . . .

After all, there was only one night of anxiety, for in the morning came news of the Wahabi's total defeat at Taraba. In their contempt of the Turks the Wahabi had rashly come down into the open plain, deluded by what had been a false retreat— in fact a cunning manœuvre; then, outflanked, they were compelled to fly.

Mohammed Ali fought personally at Taraba "at the moment when he ordered his cavalry to wheel about and face their pursuers"; Louis maintains that he deserved great credit for his tactics and the management of his low-spirited troops.

As soon as he saw his enemy on the run the Pasha announced that 6 dollars would be given for every Wahabi head; in a few hours some 5,000 heads were piled up before him. Only about 300 Wahabi were taken alive since few cared to beg mercy of a Turk. Whole parties of them, who had roped themselves together rather than flee, were found slaughtered in the mountains: they had fought as long as their ammunition lasted and were then hacked to pieces.

The subsequent cruelties of the now elated Turks after the victory of Taraba horrified the Hijaz. Louis recounts how the—

three hundred to whom quarter had been promised were sent by Mohammed Ali to Mecca . . . he celebrated his triumph by causing fifty of them to be impaled before the gates of Mecca; twelve to suffer a like horrible death at every one of the ten coffee houses, halting places between Mecca and Jiddah; there they were left until the dogs and vultures devoured their carcases.[41]

And anyone who has seen Arab dogs tearing at the guts of a dead donkey, or vultures feeding on the carcase of a blown cow, may have some little idea of the brutality of this picture of 170 pitiful human corpses. What happened to the remaining 130 surrendered men, Louis does not record.

# CHAPTER SIXTEEN

## *Plague*

And when his eyes shall fall upon the Trees of Al-Madinah, let him raise his voice and bless the Apostle with the choicest of blessings.

*Muslim ritual, from Burton*

At last they came to a vast plain of reddish, damp earth dotted with palm groves, wild cypresses and tamarisks.

*Emil Esin*

IT WAS NOT until the middle of January 1815, after the Taraba victory that a caravan set out for Medinah, the Radiant—and Louis was able to leave. Recently Mecca had been no longer a blessed place in which to live—it stank, filled as it was with all with all the refuse of the Great Haj. The swollen carcases of numerous camels lay rotting on the desert's edge, and in the sky vultures swooped and circled lazily, bloated on those unspeakable human remains impaled at the gates.

It was splendid to launch into the clean air of the desert; it tasted even more invigorating than usual, as fresh as the sea after the stenches of the town, a man could breathe deep again savouring that sense of well-being the desert bestows. As he has said, Louis was in the habit of walking for at least a part of the day; now after a while he strode out, away ahead of the caravan.

Towards sunset, tiring a little, he sat down under a lonely tree to await the camel train. Instantly, in the dramatic Arab way, three Bedouin sprang up behind him as if from nowhere. Their manner was threatening: they swore that he was a deserter from the Turkish army, and therefore, a lawful prize. He put up no resistance, guessing, since they made less show of force than the average determined Bedouin robber, that they were uncertain of

themselves, scared by the Pasha's recent victory. So he bluffed and
parleyed, looking impatiently meanwhile for the caravan to
come in sight. He could not imagine why it was taking so long:
it had in fact stopped for evening prayers.

The delay was difficult to endure: he sat on quietly expecting
to be stripped at any moment. Then at last the soft measured
tread of camels could be heard; simultaneously the Bedouin
vanished as suddenly as they had appeared.

Even though it was winter the heat was great. The dark,
flinty plain of el Kara (the Black) through which they rode next
day was steeped in sunlight, its shimmering heat as glittery as
mica, recalling the Nubian Desert south of Shigre.

During this day he began to make friends with his fellow
travellers; they were mostly "Malays", or more correctly Jawas
(today Indonesians), from Sumatra, Java, and the Malabar coast,
and except those from Malacca (who were no doubt true Malays)
all were British subjects.* He found them "hostile" to the English;
the opinions he gleaned from them concerning the manners
and the government of the British were interesting. Though the
worst that they could produce in evidence when pressed was that
the English—

indulged too freely in wine, and that the sexes mixed together
in social intercourse; none, however, impeached the justice of
the government which they contrasted with the oppression
of their native princes; and although they bestowed upon the
British the same opprobious epithets with which fanatic
Muslims revile Europeans they never failed to add: "but their
government is good".

He had heard similar talk among Arab sailors trading with
Bombay and Surat: the total of which was the same—the Muslims
of India hated the English, though they loved their government.
It seems a pity that "inside" knowledge such as this of Louis', no

* At this brief point in history they were so, since the various territories in
question were under British rule, except Malacca which was then under the
Dutch.

doubt of other people too, and the opinion of Burton later, who it is said predicted the Indian Mutiny,[42] was not heard or, if heard, not accepted in high places.

One brilliant night when the caravan was dawdling along, the plain shining under the cold white radiance of a full moon, Louis, drawn on by the silent beauty of the desert, again walked ahead of the camel train. After a little while, he looked over his shoulder and found that he had once more lost sight of the others. Just as he was sitting down to wait beside a cluster of tamarisks he heard an ominous thud of horses' hooves. Quickly he hid behind the trees in the inky shadow they cast under the great moon, and watched unseen as some very dubious-looking Bedouin passed by. He waited and waited for the caravan which quite unaccountably did not appear: so he retraced his steps through the scintillating night, and presently found the camels, all fifty of them in single file nose to tail, standing quietly at rest, breathing deeply in the moonlight, the jet black pools of their long shadows tracing a magnificent pattern from their feet. Every man upon them, head drooped forward, was fast asleep—and the stragglers on foot had not yet caught up.

This happened several times on the journey in the quiet of the night:

> When the camel hears no voices about it, and is not urged on by the leader, it slackens its pace and at last stands still to rest; and if the leading camel once stops, all the rest do the same.

Nothing particularly eventful happened, but Louis was amazed one day to come across an old Afghan, a man of extraordinary strength, who had walked the entire way from Kabul to Mecca, and was returning in the same manner—a distance, at a rough estimate, of about 4,600 miles.

One incident occurred which riled Louis greatly. There were several poor "Malays" who had to follow the caravan on foot, one of whom, straggling behind, was captured by the Bedouin. He had no money at all but, hoping that his fellow Jawas would pay ransom, he had promised the Bedouin 20 piastres if they would bring him to the caravan. However, the Jawas disclaimed all knowledge of their compatriot when confronted with this request, so the Bedouin said they would strip their prisoner and hold him until perhaps some other Jawas might come along and release him.

Louis was furious with the disloyal Jawas, and would have paid the money himself, but felt quite rightly that it was their duty. The caravan was about to go on and the Bedouin began to take the man away. Now the poor fellow had become quite speechless with terror: his pathetic figure roused Louis to active wrath against his callous compatriots. But they remained adamant in the face of all pleading, only swearing they did not know the man, and were therefore not prepared to incur any expense on his behalf. The camels were loaded, everyone had mounted, the leader was about to start when "the miserable object of the dispute broke out into loud lamentations"; Louis had been waiting for this moment and thanked heaven that the petrified man had at last found his voice.

Louis acted promptly then: he knew he had won the respect of the caravan and that he had the guides' goodwill; counting on this, he seized the leader's camel, made it couch, and announced forcibly that he would not let the caravan proceed until the prisoner was released. Fired with both pity and anger, no doubt he put on his fiercest expression, pitched his voice loud and commanding to make himself effectively heard above the grunting of annoyed camels, and the babel of human protest.

Having stopped the caravan and created this splendid scene, he went from load to load and, partly by "imprecating curses" and partly by "collaring" some of the Jawas, obtained from each one of them 20 paras (about 3d.), and after a long struggle made up the required 20 piastres. He took the money across to the Bedouin and, by appealing to the honour of their tribe, induced them to accept only 10 piastres. He fully realised that "according to true Turkish maxims" he should have pocketed the other ten in compensation for all his trouble; however, he presented them to the poor Jawa—"to the infinite mortification of his countrymen".

Like the Prophet, on his last ride from Mecca, they also were more than ten days on the road. They came safely through hills of moving sand and nearer to the sea until they reached the vast plain of reddish earth of Medinah the Radiant, a welcoming sight among its date groves and gardens.

Louis found some lodgings in the main street, near to the mosque—a proximity which was to prove unhappy.

While he was out shopping he heard that Yahya Effendi, Tousun Pasha's doctor, the man who had taken his Cairo bill at Jidda the previous July, was in town, and on the following day he paid him a visit. As it happened this was an unfortunate step, since on a return call the doctor noticed Louis' small treasured stock of medicines which had remained untouched on the Nubian journeys and but little used in the Hijaz, among which was a good half pound of "bark"—cinchona, or quinine. As several people at court, including Tousun Pasha himself, were ill with fever, Yahya begged Louis to give him the bark. Since he was in good health then, expected to be back in Egypt within two months, and felt naturally somewhat indebted to the doctor, Louis was glad to be able to help. Only two days later he had very serious cause to regret his generosity.

At this date Medinah was totally unknown to Europeans, and he was deeply distressed because he felt that his notes on it were quite inadequate. He offered them very apologetically to the Committee—though it was scarcely his fault that illness curtailed them. He sent a plan of the town and 147 pages of description, but this was nothing in comparison with his detailed work on Mecca.

In the great mosque that encloses the Prophet's tomb, Louis noticed some glazed tiles similar to the beautiful pottery ones covering the big stoves of Swiss and German households—for him a very unexpected reminder of those elegant tiles of his own "Kirschgarten" at home in Basle; as surprising perhaps as all those imported grandfatherly clock faces have been to later generations of foreign visitors at famous mosques.

The *Hejra*, Mohammed's tomb, stands in an enclosure with four doors, one of which was opened daily to admit only the eunuchs who swept the floors and tended the lamps. Above the tomb soars

the illustrious green dome which can be seen from far across the
desert, like a benign cloud of emerald billowing between slender
minarets. Louis writes:

> Mohammedan tradition says that when the last trump shall
> sound, Aysa (Jesus Christ) is to descend from heaven to earth,
> and announce to its inhabitants the great day of judgment;
> after which he is to die, and will be buried in this Hejra by the
> side of Mohammed; that, when the dead shall rise from their
> graves, they will both rise together, ascend to heaven, and
> Aysa, on that day, will be ordered by the Almighty to separate
> the faithful from the infidels.

Whenever Louis encountered the industrious black pilgrims
from the Sudan, the Tekrouris, he seems always to have liked
them; perhaps it was their simplicity and sincerity that moved
him, as well as their pathetic poverty. He saw they made themselves useful everywhere, as porters, wood-carriers, and so on.
They were of the Malekites, a sect that seems to carry its respect
for the Prophet further than any other, placing him very close
to the Deity in their adorations. They approached the tomb,
Louis noticed, "with a terrified conscience", and they were
utterly convinced that the prayers they said there in front of the
*Hejra*'s window would sooner or later be answered.

Once, after a brief conversation here, one of these Negro
pilgrims asked Louis if he knew what prayers might be recited to
evoke the Prophet to appear to him in dreams, as he had an
especial question to ask. When Louis admitted that he had no idea
and gently advised the pilgrim simply to pray for what he so
desired, the Negro told him with evident awe that the Prophet
had been seen here in visions by many of his countrymen.

Louis saw no sacred pigeons in the Prophet's mosque as there
were at the Beitullah, but the masses of woollen carpets spread
thickly over the entire floor space made it "the abode of millions
of other animals less harmless than pigeons" which fed on
visitors, who inadvertently transferred them to their lodgings
where they continued to feast happily and to multiply.

Possibly Islam is silent on the subject of the louse, but of its smaller neighbour it says traditionally: "Thou shalt not vilify the flea for he awaketh the faithful to prayer." It is doubtful, however, if Louis would have been much cheered by that saying had he known it.

In a delightful little garden south of the town there lived a charming saint with a large family, a man so greatly renowned for his sanctity that even Tousun Pasha himself had been to kiss his hands. As other pilgrims did, so Louis went to pay him a visit and found him to be more polite than any saint he had ever met, and not averse either to talk of worldly matters. Louis had hoped to acquire some Arabic histories from him, but the saint's learning was restricted to that of the law, the Koran and his own language. He ordered a narghile for Louis, and a dish of dates, produce of his own garden.

This so exceptionally polite saint begged Louis to repeat the visit. Louis would gladly have done so, but only a day or two later he fell seriously ill, and there followed a nightmare period that was to last for almost three appalling months.

The fever went rapidly from bad to worse, and he longed for the cinchona bark he had given away; but Yahya Effendi had already distributed it to the last dram, and had nothing left but some old gentiana powder which had lost all its goodness. Poor Louis—the fever worsened and was accompanied by terrible vomiting and profuse sweats. After a month of quotidian he had a week's respite but, lacking quinine, when the fever returned it struck with greater violence, now tertiary; the sickness too continued and was accompanied by fainting. Quite drained of strength at last he became too weak to rise from his carpet without the help of his slave-boy, "a poor fellow who by habit and nature was more fitted to take care of a camel than to nurse his drooping master".

Yahya Effendi very seldom came to call. Life looked bleak indeed, the future impossible. Louis lost all hope of returning to Egypt, and was preparing himself to die here in Medinah on his wretched louse-ridden mat. Naturally enough, desperately weakened as he was by fever's grinding rhythm and the nadir of

dredging sickness, a black depression battened upon him. It was
not so much the dying he feared: his direst apprehension was that
should news of his death arrive in England his entire Hijaz
journey might at the worst be condemned as an imprudent,
unauthorised act, or at the least an over-zealous mission.

He had one book only to help keep his mind off dismal thoughts
assailing lucid moments, that pocket edition of Milton which the
friendly Scot had given him in Jidda, "now worth a whole shelf
full of others".

Surely he more than ever regretted having been forced to part
with the original helpful boy. The present one was of little use.
While his master lay tossing, and finally quite prostrate in his
room, the boy often came home from market in tears to report
how Turkish soldiers had seized from him what food he had
bought and beaten him for protesting. Apart from the boy, the
only other company Louis had was an unseen woman, and his
guide who paid him a visit from time to time but merely, so
Louis guessed, in order to seize what he could of his baggage
when he should die. The unseen woman was an Egyptian by
birth, aged and infirm; it was she who had let him the rooms,
removing herself to a half-open upper storey from which she
could speak to him without being seen, and she would chat with
him for some little time each evening.

These were his only drab entertainments—if such they can be
called—in this fearful time. As if to crystallise the horror, he
could hear the noise of every funeral that entered the main gates
of the mosque beside which his lodgings stood cheek by jowl.
During the interminable weeks of his illness one funeral at least,
often more, passed under his window every day; he could hear
every prayer said over every corpse in the mosque and the
endlessly repetitive chantings of "La ilaha illa Ilah!"

The only possible thing to be thankful for was that in Medinah
alone it was not the custom to call in professional female mourners, whose heart-rending howls and purgatorial choruses were the
sole source of their income—they were paid by the hour for their
lamentations. To die in Medinah is considered good, so there the
normal howling practices were deemed entirely disgraceful. To

illustrate this Louis records a small drama which he heard through the thin partitions of his miserable lodging. The father of the next-door family was also desperately ill—one midnight he died. Overcome with sorrow his only son burst into loud weeping; Louis heard the mother exclaim at once: "For God's sake do not cry! What shame it is to cry! You will expose us before the whole neighbourhood!"

At last she managed to quieten her wailing boy, for which small mercy Louis was grateful, surrounded as he was with sorrow and sickness, with death and the thought of death. . . .

At the beginning of April spring began to come; its returning warmth at last brought Louis' long illness to an end, but it was two weeks before he dared to venture out, each breeze making him dread a return of the fever. The town's shocking climate, its "detestable" water, and many prevalent diseases made him anxious to leave at the earliest possible moment—as soon as he was strong enough to bear the jolting of a camel's stride again.

The streets were filled with convalescents like himself, all gaunt and pallid. It appeared that in one week eighty people had died of the fever—it seemed to have struck strangers rather more than the local people.

One interesting scene Louis witnessed from his wretched lodging exemplified the picturesque devotion of Tousun Pasha to his mother, Mohammed Ali's favourite wife. Louis appears to have been impressed by Tousun, believing him to be:

> the only member of the family whose breast harboured any noble feeling; the rest are corrupted by the numerous vices . . . but he has given in many instances proofs of elevated sentiment, and even his enemies cannot deny his valour, generosity, filial love and good nature.

But, unfortunately, he was not nearly as quick-witted as his less moral father and his cruel brother Ibrahim.[43]

Mohammed Ali's wife, says Louis, was much respected and charitable without being ostentatious about it; however, she did appear in Medinah "with all the pomp of an eastern queen' but her donations to the mosque and to the poor made the people regard her "as an angel sent from heaven". Having performed the Great Pilgrimage, she had come on to Medinah to see her son.

Sitting at his window, haggard and wretched still, Louis was glad to have something more entertaining to watch than the stream of funerals.

> Her son paid her a short visit, and left her to repose, while he himself ordered a carpet to be spread in the middle of the street, and there slept at the threshold of his mother's dwelling; offering a testimony of respect and humility which does as much honour to the son, as to the character of the mother who could inspire him with such sentiments.

Knowing well of his devotion to his own mother, one has the impression that Louis secretly felt it must indeed be satisfactory to be able to express one's sentiments in so dramatic a manner. The mental picture of himself doing so in the middle of a trim Swiss road may at least have afforded him a wry smile. But Louis had to admit that it was not only the poor who benefited from the Pasha's lady's visit, and perhaps after all it is not surprising that her son demonstrated his filial gratitude so histrionically in the highway. She had brought him gifts:

> to the value of about £25,000 sterling, among which were twelve complete suits . . . a diamond ring worth £5,000; and two beautiful Georgian slaves.

Louis had originally intended to remain only a month in Medinah, then to make his way with the Bedouin across the desert to Akaba, on the way examining the hitherto unreported inscriptions and ancient monuments of Medain Salih, of which he had heard, and to return to Cairo overland across the Sinai. He was now, as he says, panting for a change of air, but as he was far too weak to undertake such a journey, he decided it was best to go down to Yembo and on by sea to Egypt.

On 21 April he left Medinah. As he passed through the outer
gate by which he had entered on his arrival nearly three months
earlier from the desert, he thought sadly how full of health and
good spirits he had been then, of the plans he had made for an
interesting return journey to Egypt and the antiquities he had
hoped to discover during it. Now dejected and worn-out, all he
desired was a friendly and healthy spot in which he might regain
his strength.

The journey to Yembo proved hard: there were torrential
rain-storms, protracted marches, some of fifteen or even more
hours, and while the travellers tried to eat, eagles swooped down
to tear the very meat from their dishes. Louis again endured
violent bouts of vomiting; shivering fits alternated with such high
fevers that his clothes, which he could not change, were often
saturated with sweat. At last, on the seventh day, the caravan full
of sick and convalescent people crawled into Yembo.

But Yembo was far from being the haven for which he had
hoped. It was very crowded; only after a long search did he
manage to find a free room in the terrace of a khan. He left his
baggage there, and went down to the harbour to inquire about a
passage for Egypt: this appeared to be impossible. None but
soldiers, who had already taken over three of the four ships ready
to sail, were being allowed to embark. Four other ships were
preparing to transport the vast entourage of that administering
angel, the Pasha's wife, who was also returning to Cairo.

While he was sitting in a coffee shop near the harbour con-
templating these depressing facts, three funerals passed by in quick
succession, subsequently during the day he saw several more. He
did not guess the cause of so many deaths until night when he went
up to his airy room which overlooked a large part of the town.

> I then heard in every direction, innumerable voices breaking
> out in those heart rending cries which all over the Levant
> accompany the parting breath of a friend or relative.

Instantly the dread thought flashed upon him: it was the plague!
He battled with his fears, or at least tried to drown them in sleep, but

the dire threnodies kept him awake the whole night—his dread of dying in the Hijaz, of missing the next caravan to the Fezzan, added to his despondency. But he says that the acute danger in which he was at Yembo, "that abode of death" as he called it later, became more apparent in retrospect mercifully than it was at the time.

After that first sleepless night surrounded by the lamentations of, so it seemed, half the town, he went down very early into the khan where many Arabs were already taking their morning coffee, and told them of his fears. But no sooner had he mentioned the dread word—plague—than they reprimanded him angrily. Surley he could not be ignorant that the Almighty had for ever prohibited that sickness from the Holy Land of the Hijaz? To such an argument there was no reply among Muslims of that day, so he walked out to look for some Greek Christians whom he had noticed on his arrival. They promptly confirmed his fears. The plague has indeed broken out ten days earlier: it had been raging in Cairo for several months, a great number of people had died at Suez, from there ships had carried it to Jidda and so it had spread up the coast to Yembo.

It was true enough that the plague had never before been known in the Hijaz, but since the flow of traffic to and from Egypt because of the wars had never been greater it was no wonder it had developed in the Holy Land. At first the Arabs simply could not believe it was the plague. But when, a few days later, the mortality rate rose from less than twenty deaths a day to forty, or fifty—a very considerable number in a population of only 5,000 to 6,000—an absolute panic seized the people. Many of them fled into the country—the town became almost deserted —but the plague went too, and as they camped close together it spread with terrifying rapidity.

So most of them returned, excusing the shame of their flight by saying:

God in his mercy sends this disease to call us to his presence; but we are conscious of our unworthiness and feel we do not deserve His grace; therefore we think it better to decline it and fly from it.

Louis heard this careful explanation frequently.

He did not give up hope of a passage to Egypt; a little bribery might have obtained him one even then, but every ship was now crammed with diseased soldiers. There was nothing for it but to shut himself in his room and wait. If only he had felt strong he would have struck out into the open desert, but he was in a constant low fever all the time, and too weak for any exertion.

Infection was very close, always threatening. At the khan where he lived an Arab was dying in the yard. The master of the khan had already lost members of his family and he came to describe in detail, sitting on Louis' mat the while, how his son had just died in his arms. Yembo's main street was lined with the sick in their death throes begging for charity. To add to all this macabre horror, Louis' slave began going out mysteriously early each day. When Louis asked why, the boy replied that since he thought it meritorious he was assisting in the washing of the dead bodies of the poor who had died during the night. The corpses were set out each morning upon biers on the seashore.

After the first four or five days Louis began to get used to this way of living, or existing with death. He tried to cheer himself by philosophically comparing the small numbers of each day's dead with the mass of those who remained still alive and who managed to survive somehow, despite every possible contact. When he saw the numerous foreigners in the town going about apparently unconcernedly, he began to feel almost ashamed of himself for having less courage than they. This is typically unassuming of him—but he had more knowledge of contagion, and undoubtedly more imagination as to its disastrous effects than the great majority of them, and in any event few would dare to accuse him of lacking courage.

Among the poor the plague was a natural excuse for a morbid kind of protracted feasting; since every family killed a sheep on the death of any of its members and all the neighbours were entertained, the women embracing and consoling the women folk of each family. It was small wonder that the infection irrupted through the town.

Louis liked the people of Yembo (they were of Bedouin origin)

even better than those of Mecca or Medinah, and he was sorry to
see them suffer as they did at the hands of the brutal soldiery.
There were several affrays while he was there; once in the open
street a Turkish officer shot a young Arab who had refused to
comply with his homosexual advances. It was a callous murder,
committed in the full light of a hot noonday, with the greatest
composure and disregard. Having killed the boy, the officer then
took shelter from the fury of the populace clamouring for blood-
revenge in the quarters of a company commander whose soldiers
were called out in his defence.

This particular outbreak of the plague, probably because it was
new in the Hijaz, seemed to be of a most malignant kind, few
who caught it survived. The dead were buried at once: during
Louis' long days of the Yembo horror he heard of two people
being buried alive:

> the stupor into which they fell when the disorder was at a
> crisis had been mistaken for death. One of them gave signs of
> life at the moment they were depositing him in the grave, and
> was saved; the body of the other, when his tomb was re-opened
> several days after his burial to admit the corpse of a near rela-
> tion, was found with bloody hands and face, and the winding
> sheet torn by the unavailing efforts he had made to rise. On
> seeing this the people said that the devil, being unable to hurt
> his soul, had thus disfigured his body.

At long last, Louis heard that a small open boat with no
soldiers aboard was due to sail, and he arranged for a passage.
However, the sailing was postponed daily until finally he got away
from Yembo on 15 May "after eighteen days in the midst of the
plague".

Far from having escaped it though, he now found himself in
closer contact with it than ever before—the voyage that followed
was a seasick nightmare lasting twenty days. It was his duty to get
himself back to Egypt alive: life itself seemed worth little but his
sense of obligation remained firm. He paid extra for a small space
aft, but the *rais* cheated him out of this; the boat was as usual

desperately over-crowded, all he could do was to arrange his baggage around himself and the boy as some sort of protection from the fevered press of humanity.

Lying in the hold there were half a dozen extremely sick people, some in a state of raving delirium—one on the verge of death soon died; the *rais'* young brother, whose allotted place was close to Louis', had been paid to attend them. On the third day out this boy, seized with a blinding headache, began to insist on being put ashore, in order that he might somehow return to die in Yembo. After much argument he won his way.

Louis rarely mentions the trials of such things as mere heat— for instance other travellers complain of skin split and cracked by blazing sun almost to the bone, of bare feet burnt by torrid sands. But in writing about this scene Louis does get across to us the turgid oppressiveness of the incident. It occurred at noon: in an oven-like Red Sea atmosphere, summer's heat was rising again towards its crescendo; a barren red coastline above a bleak salt-encrusted shore, a very sick young Arab, the *rais* bargaining with some nomads for a camel to take his own brother back—to die of the plague in plague-stricken Yembo.

Even then, much of this Louis leaves to our imagination. He dwells on horrors only when they are protracted, and pin-pointed by small human highlights in a few weeks of dragged-out half-existence—as it was within the four walls of the room in Medinah, in the things he heard and saw there, and similarly in the fevered Yembo days punctuated by funeral lamentations. Now he says quite simply:

> Luckily the disease did not spread; we had only another death, on the fifth day, though several passengers were seized with the malady. . . . The continual sickness and vomiting of the passengers were perhaps to them a salutary operation of nature.

A very wretched voyage, and they never managed to make more than twenty-five miles a day. Where was the marvellous courage and navigational ability of those Arab sailors who some

300 years earlier had spread their faith to the Far East? He found only fear and superstition. The spirits of certain siren-like places among the coral had to be placated, and in this appallingly slow and timorous manner it took them nearly three weeks to sight Ras Abu Mohammed, the most southerly point of rugged Sinai. From that landfall boats usually struck across to Cosseir swept on northerly winds, but with the aid of a little baksheesh Louis persuaded the *rais* to put him ashore at Sherm, on Sinai, where he knew he would find friendly Bedouin to guide him overland, the nomads there having been subdued by the Pasha's Suez commander.

On the journey through the mountains there was a serious incident with a callous, trigger-happy soldier.[44] Each night Louis again suffered fever. He was so weak he could hardly drag himself over the high places where they were obliged to dismount: but on one summit he was rewarded with a splendid view down to Akaba on its blue gulf—Solomon's *Ezion Geber*—the so elusive Akaba which he was never to reach.

At Tor they saw again the Pasha's lady encamped there on her return from Medinah, she had already been waiting for a week since 400 to 500 camels were required to transport her suite and soldiers to Cairo. Hearing that the plague was still raging in Cairo, Louis decided to go into the hills to El Wadi, a village of Bedouin settlers.

He stayed very happily for a short while at El Wadi, recovering his strength in the good mountain air which he had craved so long. There were about thirty houses only in the village, each set in its own garden. He rented a small half-open building which he had covered with date palm fronds. Near it was a "shady pleasure ground, where grew palm, nebek, pomegranate and apricot trees"; in the bowery shade of all this delightful foliage was a large well of excellent sweet water. The little oasis seemed like the Garden of Eden after the horrors of the Hijaz, and he could find nothing more to wish for just then. If there was a dark skinned Bedouin Eve, there certainly was no serpent. The villagers did not suspect any strange reason for his resting here as they could see that he was scarcely able to stand on his feet, and in consequence they treated him very kindly. Indeed it was not for the last four years, not since he had left the society of his good friends John Barker and the Dutch Consul, Masseyk, and the pleasant gardens of Aleppo, that he had felt as comfortable as he did then in that mountain village among the friendly Bedouin settlers.

Even one day in this peaceful retreat "produced a visible improvement" in his health. His energy returned, no sooner was he even slightly better than he rode over to the warm bath around the corner of the mountain, and the marvellous date grove that was guarded, though to no avail, by a monk of Sinai's St Katherine's.

He spent two weeks at El Wadi and then, although not fully recovered, he decided that he *must* get back to Egypt as soon as possible. He had been without letters from Europe for eighteen months, he was impatient to reach Cairo where he knew that a great deal of mail must be awaiting him, and of course he was especially anxious to know of the committee's opinion. He was aware that the plague should be subsiding by the time that he expected to arrive since it always yielded to the influence of the hot season.

It was a long ride and a hard one; a burning stifling *samun* blew, and again his fever returned. But at Suez they were just in time to join the Pasha's Lady's caravan—now of 600 camels and under a strong guard—so with it they travelled safely through that last dangerous strip. From El Wadi he had made the whole journey to the Birket el Haj, outside Cairo, in six days, which was very quick going.

On 24 June having been away from Cairo for nearly two-and-a-half years, he entered the city again. The letters which he had sent from Medinah had not arrived; his acquaintances had given him up for dead, and supposed him buried—as he so nearly was—in the Hijaz.

The plague had nearly subsided; some of the Christians had already re-opened their houses; but a great gloom seemed to have overspread the town, from the mortality that had taken place.

His own joy at returning safely, and at the wonderful letters of praise awaiting him from the African Association, was short-lived, since among his mail he found sad news from home—his father was dead.

My joy over my return and my deliverance from many dangers lasted a few minutes only. Your letters [*he wrote to his mother*] caused me very great grief. My dear father is not alive any more. May he receive in another better world the reward of his honesty. How much I had treasured the hope of meeting him again, of assisting him in his old age, of showing him my gratitude for all the love he has given me, and of brightening the rest of his days! But fate is fickle and often destroys the hope of future happiness. Since the news of his death I feel an indescribable emptiness in my mind. Being fatherless I feel lost in a void.

You, my dear mother, are now the only support for your children. I must confess that my filial love for you has always been even more ardent than that I felt for my beloved father. It has now even increased, if this were possible, because God knows I have no one in the world but you who owns so completely my love, attachment and gratitude, and on whose existence my whole happiness depends. I am sure, dear mother, we shall see each other again. The time approaches. Together we shall devote our tears to the memory of my father. But I shall be happy then, to prove to you my undivided love and to cherish the hope that you will recognise my feelings and the thoughts I carry in my heart. . . .

## Part VI

# The Moving Finger

25a. "El Gibel Nor, or the Mountain of Light in the desert of Mecca",
probably by J.L.B.
25b. "Mozdelifa in the Desert of Arafat", probably by J.L.B.

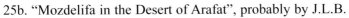

26a. "A Sacred place called Saffa", probably by J.L.B.

26b. "A View of Arafat", probably by J.L.B.

*Left:* 27a. A part of J.L.B.'s working journal

*Right:* 27b. His Arabic script in a journal

*Left*: 28a. The Mecca water-seller's song from J.L.B.'s Journal

*Right*: 28b. On a night in Ramadan, a party invitation to J.L.B. in Cairo

29. The castle at the head of the Gulf of Akaba, by David Roberts

30. Looking down on St Katherine's, Sinai, David Roberts

31. Suez, by David Roberts

32. A Muslim funeral passing the "Mamluk tombs" outside the Bab-el Nasr, Cairo, by David Roberts

# CHAPTER SEVENTEEN

## *A Month of Summer in Alexandria, the Winter in Cairo*

If a man make a pilgrimage round Alexandria in the morning, God will make for him a crown set with pearls, perfumed with musk and camphor, and shining from the East to the West.

*Ibn Dumak*

What is resumed in the word Alexandria? In a flash my eye shows me a thousand dust-tormented streets. Flies and beggars own it today. . . .

*Lawrence Durrell*

ALTHOUGH THE NEWS of his father's death—at little over sixty years of age—was a very severe blow to Louis, the warm letters which he received at the same time from Sir Joseph and from Mr Hamilton helped more than any medicine could then have been done to revive his strength and to exhilarate his depressed spirits.

Indeed the assurance which these letters contain, of my former labours having met with the approbation of my employers, has been to me the source of heartfelt joy, and the encouragement which I derived from it, has entirely banished from my mind that despondency, which my bodily sufferings had caused.[1]

But physically he remained extremely weak, and his convalescence progressed slowly. In fact there was little real improvement; the great heat of summer in Cairo could only hinder his recovery, the doctors, who were all rogues or fools, did nothing to help, and he was concerned that he could work for no more than a few hours each day. However, the peace of mind which he at last enjoyed as regards his labours and achievements so far is reflected in all his letters, especially in one to that most responsive and faithful of correspondents, the scholarly chaplain.

In his so characteristic hand—sensitive yet bold, now stronger still and more than ever well-formed—Louis sent to Renouard "a hearty salute from the verdant banks of old father Nile, and from admist the dusty bazaars of the victorious city of Misr"— to express his delight in returning safely after so long an absence and the joy he had felt on finding three letters awaiting him from this good friend.

To another correspondent he confides that Sir Joseph had written such expressions as one might expect only from a parent:

> As such I really revere him, and my gratitude towards him would alone be sufficient to induce me to pursue my task, even if so many other considerations of honour and duty did not concur in demanding from me every exertion of my faculties towards this object.[2]

But all the good intentions in the world might not then cure the long-lingering disastrously evil effects of the Arabian climate. There were several recurrences of the fever, and Louis soon realised that he could have no confidence in the set of charlatans who attended him—men whom one Englishman had already designated "the medical offal" of Europe. Of them there were many stories—of how they feared being poisoned by one another, of how they would bargain for their fees even as their patients died.

Among these impossible medicos was a Dr Mandreci, a former physician to the Pasha to whom one day as a joke the Pasha had presented the Pyramids. Mandreci immediately began devising various plans for making a profit out of such gigantic gifts: perhaps they might be railed off, fees charged for viewing them, or perhaps he could blow up Cheops in order to inspect its interior.[3] Louis himself knew that the Jewish doctor, Mapurgo, having been paid and equipped by the Palestine Society of England, had absolutely no intention of ever going to Palestine, and had in fact already profitably sold the instruments with which all in good faith he had been supplied in England.

On his return Louis had gone to stay in the pleasant house of his close friend Boghoz, the Armenian then in high favour with Pasha. Louis was happy in his company since he was a very gifted man and of an honesty Louis found rare in this part of the world,[4] but for health reasons it seemed advisable to accept Colonel Missett's repeated invitation to go to Alexandria where he might have a better chance of recuperating in the cooler air of Mediterranean breezes. Before leaving Cairo Louis began to look around for a small house that he might rent in the Turkish quarter, where he planned to spend the winter months while waiting for the caravan to Fezzan.

Early in August he wrote to his mother again of the sadness that he still felt in the loss of his father. The knowledge that Rudolf had repeatedly, even in his last days, asked after his son did much to comfort Louis, because he saw in it some proof that his father had really made his peace with him, and had forgiven him for the "sins committed" in his youth.[5] One feels that now at last Louis felt he had lived down and overcome the Leipzig experiences which had so traumatically marked his character and, equally, so served to strengthen his determination.

In this same letter, he enclosed a confirmation of the renunciation of his marriage portion, and another document by which he ceded to his mother his part of the paternal inheritance.

I have done this, dear mother, after serious consideration and it would hurt me very much if you did not comply with my wishes. Let me tell you first, that I am quite sure, I shall never need this . . . because I am certain that when I return to England from my journeys I shall make a good living there for the rest of my life.

With reason he now had every confidence that his journals of discovery and any discourses that he might write would be financially rewarding, since they were obviously already of great interest to the worlds of exploratory geography and antiquity.

At the same time he tried to prepare his mother for what he calls his "final journey", the great one towards the Niger which was to be so much longer than any previous ones. He says, gently and with some understatement so as not to alarm her, that the manifold hardships and "perhaps dangers" through which he had passed already without harm had increased his courage and his trust in a kind guiding Providence, and given him good hope for the future. He was fully expecting to be able to return to Europe within three years.

I wish it may be granted to me to embrace you again. How often I pray for it! It is my most ardent wish, and I shall be for ever unhappy if it does not come true. My hot tears will then bear witness that no absence not even the longest, can change my heart which, torn from all other bonds, lives now only for you and your happiness, dear mother—But this time is still far ahead. I shall have to surmount many difficulties before I reach it. I hope cheerfully that I shall never lack tenacity and cour- age".[6]

Just before he left for Alexandria Louis met, in Boghoz' house, a charming and talented young Englishman, William Turner, newly arrived in Cairo from diplomatic duties in Constantinople and travels in Syria. In his own book Turner recounts how much he learnt from Sheik Ibrahim, and how very good Louis was to him, especially in undertaking the laborious job of checking his travel journals.

I never talked to him without learning something. . . . After my return to Constantinople our intercourse was maintained by letter, and I confidently looked forward to his friendship as a source of pleasure in after-life.[7]

August: the time of the inundation's height; people went leisurely by boat to the Pyramids, and the great Ezbekiah square became once more a lake reflecting the lamps of festivals, and resounding with Arab song and tamboura. But Cairo was not a happy place just then: "mountains of ears" arrived, sent by Ibrahim Pasha from Arabia; and Abdullah, the youthful Wahabi leader, was brought back by the Turks in triumph *en route* for Constantinople where he was to be beheaded. An Englishwoman*\* records how the crowds went to stare at this poor young captive; exhausted, ill and weighed down by heavy chains, his expressive and attractive countenance aroused all her natural pity. The victorious Pasha, on his return to Cairo earlier that year after the Taraba victory, had failed to keep the promises made to his troops when in the Hijaz, and now as they began to show signs of revolt he shut himself up in the citadel. Louis describes how the Pasha's newly acquired reputation seemed quite to have changed his character, no longer the simple soldier, he assumed a new hauteur. He began to indulge in pomp and pageantry, and by monopolising all exports and imports for his own advantage he materially injured local workers and manufacturers alike. But perhaps most resented was the fact that he tried to introduce European discipline and drill into the ranks of his army. The Arnaut troops resisted this measure strongly—such drill performed in voluminous Turkish trousers was very funny to behold—other troops followed their example, and within a few hours soldiers had completely ransacked the shops and mercantile storehouses. The inner quarters of the town were saved from damage only by the arming of the citizens. Louis was on guard for five nights and with his companions successfully fought "a few minor battles". Although there continued to be some sporadic outbreaks, the Pasha shortly regained control of the city, and some hundred or so of the rebels paid for the revolt with their lives.

During this fight in Cairo (*Louis wrote to his brother, Gedeon*),

I couldn't help thinking of my home town where, as I saw in the papers, a garrison of 6,000 men under General Bachman is meant to defend the frontiers. . . . We got news of Lord Wellington's entry into Paris on June 5th. Europe is free now. . . .[8]

\* The wife of Belzoni.

In Boghoz' company Louis also met at this time a giant of an Italian, who called regarding some hydraulic work he was to undertake for the Pasha. This was the huge Giovanni Belzoni, strong man and one-time London show performer, a Paduan by birth, an extremely handsome man of mild appearance, with a most attractive manner and as Byron put it later, English very prettily broken. Belzoni wrote that this chance meeting with Mr Burckhardt was to prove most fortunate for him, and he would always remember it with the deepest gratitude since what he learnt from Louis was of the greatest service to him in Egypt, and he remained one of Louis' staunchest admirers. Louis felt sorry for the Italian and his English wife, short of money and out of a job as they were, and it was directly through him that Belzoni eventually obtained work—such as only a man of his strength and ability could have achieved in that non-mechanical age.

On 15 August Louis left Cairo for Alexandria to spend an extremely happy month in Colonel Missett's house, where all genuine travellers were invariably made welcome. Missett, a charming and courageous Irish gentleman, English consul and ex-officer of the Enniskillen dragoons, was a fascinating man. He kept a lavish establishment, his *chef* had trained in the cuisine of the King of Naples; he was a *bon vivant*, "as choice in his table and wines as he was in his companions . . . chivalrous to the last degree—an ardent admirer of the fair sex".[9] Even now, despite the increasing paralysis from which he suffered—he was quite unable to use arms or legs—he remained a perfect host, an amusing raconteur, a singer of after-dinner songs, and although he had to be wheeled to the table in a chair and have his food cut up for him by his valet, he still lived well.

The benevolence and overflowing high spirits of such a man were of immense appeal to Louis, especially as he and Missett had long corresponded. Louis' achievements and courage were bound to be equally attractive to this brave man, whose warmth and gaiety did not wane despite his affliction. His household consisted of Mr Thorburn, his highly intelligent secretary, and a merry Italian officer from Piedmont, Vincenzo Taberna, his *aide*, whose military and camp adventures made entertaining conversation. During Louis' visit, young Turner also arrived in Alexandria, while Lady Hester, hearing of Missett's increasing illness, sent her own faithful physician, Dr Meryon, to attend the Colonel. For some time Missett had been trying to get permission to leave his post as he hoped to take the waters at Pisa for a cure. It does not seem that Meryon was able to do anything to help the Colonel medically. The worthy doctor, however, was companionable enough and, inadvertently, afforded Louis and young Turner much amusement in the course of what seem to have been very outspoken conversations.

Louis soon began to regain his health with the sea air, the good food, and plentiful daily exercise out in the desert on the Colonel's Arab mounts. Whenever Louis was really fit and strong, and in congenial company, he seems always to have had this irrepressible sense of fun. Now it was apparently almost impossible for him and for Turner not to laugh a little at strange Dr Meryon's "profound adoration"—indeed it amounted almost to syco-phantic worship—of his exacting patroness. The subject provoked mirth and some teasing of the doctor by the two younger men, and although they remained good friends with him their hilarity was to have unpleasant if petty repercussions later from the Stan-hope fastness in the Lebanon, since Louis admits in a letter to Renouard that he had been "very free" at the time in his remarks.

The lavish expenditure which Lady Hester thought fit to make in order to gain her ends with the Bedouin he saw as a real disservice to all travellers in the Middle East. In his opinion, which it seems he may have voiced in Alexandria, she had many pre-tensions and "more foibles than a lady in man's clothes should be guilty of".[10]

Sundays in Alexandria were generally gay and colourful: the European community then paid each other visits in the mornings, and in the early evenings took their wives and daughters to stroll along the parade. However, one Sunday early that September the few French ladies who had remained in Egypt were afraid to appear, since there was a great deal of gunfire—Drovett, the French consul, having belatedly hoisted the white flag—and soldiers seemed to be everywhere. But the next day, the Roman Catholic festival of the birth of the Virgin, the French all dressed up in their best and went in the heat of afternoon to broil in the sun in a shadeless garden by way of celebrating, and in the early evening the presence of their women with lacy parasols and light dresses made the parade a charming gay place. All this and a great deal more Turner wrote up in his journal, while Louis read through and corrected for him the more serious accounts of places he had already visited in the Levant and his notes on the Arabs. When his journal was up to date Turner felt free to ride every morning with Louis.

They rose at five o'clock and rode far out into the desert: sometimes eastward, passing Caesar's camp, as far as Ramleh, where in a small garden an Arab sheik gave them coffee, and they would return exhilarated from these cool early rides to delicious late breakfasts over which Louis had many long talks with Missett and other members of the household.

Sometimes Dr Meryon, Louis and Turner, accompanied by the Colonel's dragoman, would go for a sail across the new port to look at the fort standing on the site of the Pharos. They would watch Arab divers repairing leaks in ships' hulls—men who were able to stay under water for four or even five minutes. They were told that captains were strongly advised to keep on especially good terms with these divers since, if offended or underpaid, they had been known to swim to a ship under cover of dusk and bore a hole in its bottom. Together the three men climbed to the top of the battlemented tower, which commanded a wide view of the two ports, and of the sprawling city desert-encircled, and the long lonely desolate sandhills to the west. Later, they rowed around trying to make out the ruins of the ancient Pharos said to be visible below the sea, but the waves ran high with a fresh north-westerly breeze and they were unable to get far.

Of all the places that he saw in Alexandria the so-called Baths of Cleopatra, although she had nothing to do with them, had the greatest appeal for Louis. One day, leaving the city by the Rosetta Gate, he and Turner rode on following the low coastline of jutting rocks extending along the shore from the old harbour to the mouth of the ancient canal. He thought the Baths stupendous works which alone could give some idea of what Alexandria once was.[11] They examined some of the tombs, and explored several deep caves which they expected led to the catacombs, and later they rode back gaily over the dry bed of Lake Mareotis. It was so coated with masses of glittering salt, and shone so brilliantly with numerous springs all steeped in sunlight, that they almost imagined themselves to be surrounded by sparkling sea.

One evening, Turner was much amused when Sheik Ibrahim's black slave boy came to give his master a single piastre which had been presented to him by some Turk whose baggage he had helped to carry. In the Ottoman Empire a slave's earnings belonged by right to his master, but Turner knew that most slaves did not have the honesty to comply with this unwritten rule. By the boy's natural response, the little episode seems to be another proof of Louis' goodness to those who served him.

Louis was sorry when he had to leave Colonel Missett, who would shortly be going to Pisa, but since Louis was now fully recovered it was time for him to return to Cairo. As he was by now on very friendly terms with Meryon—the doctor did not appear to have taken any exception to the light-hearted teasing—Louis agreed to sail with him to Damietta. The high northerly winds persisted for a day or two; however, not wishing to be detained any longer, Louis insisted upon embarking although it was morally certain, Turner recounts, that their boat would make no progress that night.

Did Turner perhaps have some foreboding, or was it merely that, as many others did, he sorely missed Louis' lively company? He simply says that after seeing his friend off he "passed a very gloomy evening at home". The next morning he received a note, written aboard the vessel, from Sheik Ibrahim saying that he had spent the night on a rock in the harbour. Louis persisted, however, in returning on board despite the weather and they eventually sailed at 9 a.m.

He spent two or three pleasant days in Damietta with Dr Meryon, and together they made several excursions to the ruins of ancient Egypt, and to the huge Lake Menzalah abounding with fish and fishing boats. One minuscule islet was occupied entirely by a solitary beggar who called loudly to passing boats for his daily bread. Rows of pelicans, stretching away in lines of exquisite perspective along the water's smooth surface, took to the wing at the boat's approach revealing white and rose-coloured plumage glistening in the sun.[12] It was here that an Arab poet saw the streaming locks of the reeds, as they bend in the wind's caresses, as a lover who dons a silk-tasselled turban under a mantled sky, the lightning embroidered with gold.

Their ways now separated since Dr Meryon was returning to his adored patroness in the Lebanon. He and Louis parted good friends—as regards themselves. But apparently no sooner had he reached Syria than he reported to Lady Hester "every word" Louis had said—various opinions of his, as well as gossip he had heard.[13]

Taking his time, Louis returned slowly in comfort by boat up the Nile, pausing for a few days here and there at some of the pretty country towns of the green Delta land.

He was now in full possession of his strength, "in good humour and as cheerful as ever". The hot season over, Cairo's climate would be as pleasant and mild as one could wish, with almost constantly clear skies and cool northerly breezes. Colonel Missett had lent Louis a whole box full of books from his own library and Louis was looking forward to a secluded life that winter, of reading, writing his detailed journals, and working on his Arabic with his old teacher, Mohammed. There was, of course, no news at this season of a caravan to the west, and there was not likely to be one until the next Haj, so he expected to stay the entire winter in Cairo. But if there should be another outbreak of the plague (which had happened each year for the previous three winters; during the last 40,000 had died) he would go into the desert and stay with the "faithful Bedouin" of Sinai in the cool air of their mountains rather than lock himself away indoors. He knew that fresh air and exercise were too vital to be foregone, and the Bedouin, unlike other Muslims, had a horror of the plague as much as any European, to them also it was no disgrace to flee from it.

Mr Salt, the new English consul-general, was expected to arrive that October. Louis had already met him in London, and was now looking forward to seeing him again, but there was to arise between them a hint of professional jealousy—Salt having been on Lord Velentia's exploratory expedition as secretary and draughtsman earlier in the century. This was not so much on Louis' side—he was too big for any trace of jealousy—but on Salt's. Salt was not a particularly happy man, he had been unhappy in love, and not entirely successful as an artist. However, he was sensitive and in many ways most charming; he enjoyed Louis' company, and it was not long before Louis became for him "almost the only *conversable* friend" he had at Cairo.[14]

Before the arrival of Salt, Belzoni had frequent interviews with Louis, from whom he learnt not only of the Great Temple at Abu Simbel sealed by sand, but also of the huge head of the so-called Young Memnon, the peculiarly delicate beauty of which had fascinated Louis when he had seen it where it lay at Thebes.* It is difficult for us today to understand the attitude of sincere and honest men such as Louis, Salt, Banks, Elgin and many others towards the precious antiquities of countries other than their own. Sir Joseph had indeed especially requested Salt to collect "antiquities and curiosities" for the British Museum. But it was a fact that such works were not then appreciated by the Turks, or the Arabs. According to Belzoni, Sheik Ibrahim had several times tried to persuade the Pasha to send the lovely head of the Young Memnon to the Prince Regent as a present, but the Pasha had merely laughed, considering it too trifling a gift for royalty.

At night, Mohammed Ali always sat in his garden after firing practice across the wide Nile, when earthenware pots were used as targets. As soon as dusk fell he would retire to sit in a leafy alcove, or on the rim of some cool fountain with all his attendants around him, and numerous buffoons and clowns would fool around to keep him amused, and here he received Belzoni. Flooded with the white radiance of a swelling moon this courtly

* This head, then erronously called the young Memnon, is really of Rameses II—the same Pharaoh whose sculptured features had enchanted Louis at Abu Simbel, it comes from the Ramesseum at Thebes, *circa* 1250 B.C.

scene was beautiful, under the languorous shade of the low-hanging foliage the light caught here a glint of gold, there a flowing hem of some silken robe.

Belzoni had finished his work on the hydraulic machine for the Pasha but the local people objected to its being used for fear it would create unemployment. So once again the gigantic Italian was at a loss. Louis knew that of all men he had the strength and the will to arrange for the head of Memnon to be removed from Thebes. On his part, Louis was most anxious to have this piece of sculpture sent to England without delay. He considered it one of the most beautiful in Egypt and akin in feeling to the superb heads of the Abu Simbel colossi—whose "incomparable serenity and godlike mildness" was so remarkable. In those days the idea of collecting antiquities was becoming widespread. Ambassadors were naturally in a better position than anybody else to achieve this object since it was easier for them to arrange transport and obtain permission. It never seemed to occur to anyone that such acts were in any way dishonourable, nor that the country in question was being raped of valuable property, and their successors continued as in all innocence with the practice throughout the century, from Elgin to Layard and others later still.

Louis was so keen about the idea of the Memnon for England that he mentioned it to Mr Salt very soon after his arrival in Cairo that autumn, in fact Louis always turned the conversation to the subject of Upper Egypt in the course of daily discussions which greatly excited Salt's ardour and curiosity.[15] One day Louis took Belzoni to be introduced, and spoke at length about the Italian's prowess and suitability for such work, and, assuring Mr Salt that it was most providential that such a man had arrived, he tried to persuade the Consul to employ him to remove the great head from Upper Egypt. Nothing was decided at this first interview, and it was not until Belzoni returned accompanied by his English wife who related, with tears in her eyes, all the hardships and difficulties her husband had endured in the service of the Pasha, that Mr Salt relented. Then, on Sheik Ibrahim's advice, he decided to employ Belzoni, and sent him to Thebes. After what were literally Herculean labours, Belzoni removed the great head of Memnon. It was eventually presented to the British Museum—where it stands today—by Henry Salt and Louis Burckhardt.

It looked as if for once the winter that year was going to be free of the plague. The time passed very happily for Louis in his little house above Bab el Hadud with a backroom in which he worked overlooking one of the canals. Osman, the enslaved Scottish ex-soldier, had returned from Arabia, and with Salt's help Louis now contrived to get him made a free man again through Pashalik grace. No longer a slave, Osman had no means of livelihood, so Louis gave him a place in his own household and helped him to become an excellent dragoman; in which capacity he was to be very well known in Cairo later.

Early in the new year of 1816 Louis wrote to his mother that he was living in his little rented house quite alone with two servants, presumably Shaharti and Osman (he made no mention of his slaves since naturally it would have been hard for her to understand).

My work increases more and more every day because I want to write my diaries as detailed as possible so that these at least can be sent off as a result of my journey if I do not return myself. Occasionally I go hunting to keep fit. But I have never been a very good shot, and my sight has indeed not improved since my young days. My lively and very personal correspondence with Colonel Missett of Alexandria is a recreation for me and gives me many pleasant hours. Colonel Missett is one of the noblest and strongest characters I have ever met. Furthermore he is the only man who can restrain the powerful Mohammed Ali Pasha. . . . I hope Switzerland will have a long time of peace and Basle will not have to suffer another bombardment. But I think Russia will set Europe on fire again and the general peace will not be very long. Here too everyone is in a bellicose mood. . . . The lovely meadows around Basle will now be covered in deep snow and people will be skating under the Rhine bridge, while here, now that the floods have gone, spring is coming and all the fields are green. . . .

After the ending of war in Europe there was quite an influx of English travellers now. Among them the young Mr Bankes of Dorset, to whom Lady Hester had taken a violent dislike when he had visited her in the Lebanon on his way south; she thought him a conceited and very self-opinionated young man. Not so Louis, who liked him, and made him promise to visit Rosine personally in Zurich, probably in the summer of 1817. Whatever Bankes' personal weaknesses may have been—as Lord Byron hinted later —he was a scholar and a gentleman, as Louis was quick to realise; Salt too appreciated his high intelligence and scholarly company.

If Louis' parents had in the difficult earlier years showed him perhaps rather little warmth of affection when he was away from them and often in trouble, it did not seem to be lacking now in the letters he received from his mother, every line of which, he wrote, showed him her "loving maternal heart". He was deeply touched by them and told her that they were infinitely dearer to him than anything else. He rejoiced in the fond expressions and praise which he had so long craved from her, and as regards their personal relationship he could now write:

I have now achieved all that I have been aiming at for nine years, since I took my sad leave of you, namely to prove to you that youthful exuberance could not completely eradicate the feelings of honesty and honour in me. The hope of attaining this goal—I may confess it now—was the main reason for my undertaking this journey. . . . This career of mine is wonderful, far better than my wildest hopes suggested. To return with the job half done would reduce my standing with my superiors, with the public and, I am sure, with you too. A few more years of perseverance and I shall either have achieved all that you could want for me, or I shall be defeated with honour.

In this century so long a stint without home leave in a good climate, after even a fraction of the hardships he had endured, would be virtually unheard of, but the question of it probably never entered the minds of his employers, and clearly, even if he had been tempted by it, he would not have contemplated such a thing before he had brought his task to its desired end, or to the death.

But life also had its lighter side. In a letter of this time to Dr Meryon he speaks of the fair Rosalie, whom it seems he had met and no doubt danced with in Missett's house, now newly wed to the madly jealous and somewhat drink-fuddled Mr Schutz* just returned from Rosetta. Louis clearly much admired this young woman who now that she was a bride received him only very coldly, but it appeared that he still did not lose all hope of kindling some fires in that quarter even yet.[16] Whatever such flirtations, or rebuffs, may have been they did not seem to affect him deeply— his work remained his primary and all-abiding interest.

A letter which he wrote to Renouard at about this time is perhaps phrased rather ambiguously, but one has to recall that he had learnt English only from the age of twenty-two and his meaning is sometimes a little difficult to disentangle. One can only conclude that this particular letter refers to his own discretion as regards his incognito in the Levant where, he wrote, he had not opened his heart to anyone except Barker, Missett, Fiott, and Buckingham—remembering that many English travellers who might have heard of his pursuits in London were indiscreet enough probably to talk of them in the Levant. He continues:

Luckily however I am now *nearly above* the bad effects that might else have been produced by such disclosures and I assure you that I tread upon very *firm ground*. However, I hope that prudence shall never abandon me; long experience has taught me that prudence and patience are the cardinal virtues of a traveller, more company to him than even courage, and I shall always be ready and happy to listen to any strictures my friends may apply to my conduct for real or supposed want of foresight or prudence, *sauf le droit de me justifier!*

He goes on in a more flippant vein to warn Renouard that M. Aslin† was becoming quite insatiable and indeed untrustworthy

---

* English pro-consul at Alexandria.     † The French consul-general.

in his orders for books through other people whom he did not
always pay in full, and he recounts also some little stories
which he had heard through Aslin of the indefatigable Lady
Hester. Being a Frenchman, Aslin enjoyed her letters and cherished
his remembrances of her and her admiration for the French, and
he had informed Louis that her ladyship was waiting for the
Messiah. A case surely, wrote Louis, frivolously winding up his
letter to the chaplain—"for you Reverend gentlemen to decide
how long she may still be detained in the Holy land".

In February 1816, Louis sent off the full journal of his tour
through Nubia to Souakin and Jidda. It had been ready for some
time but in the hope of a daily expected slave caravan he had
delayed sending it in order that he might clear up some doubts on
various points by further questioning of the traders. But he could
wait no longer, and now he was completing his Arabian journals
which were soon to follow.

> I am sorry to say [*he went on*] that my hopes of departing from
> Cairo are not likely to be quickly realised. No Maghribin
> caravan has arrived, although the yearly epoch of its arrival in
> Egypt has passed by. Almost out of patience myself, I am little
> able to intreat my employers not to lose theirs. . . . I am far
> from feeling myself comfortable in Egypt, and every private
> motive engages me to wish for a speedy departure. . . .

No caravan came, and then at the beginning of April the plague
broke out in the town. While the fatalistic Muslims disregarded
it, the Europeans barricaded themselves in their houses behind
double doors. The space between the doors contained large jars
of water changed every twenty-four hours, and a fumigating box
for letters. An Arab stationed outside would for a small sum
receive orders and buy provisions each day; all foodstuffs were
put into the water jars for a while, except bread which for some
odd reason was thought to be safe if eaten cool. So the Europeans
lived incarcerated for weeks, seeing in the streets below the
horrible attacks of the plague as it first laid hold upon its victims,
who—from their agonised gestures—appeared to suffer sudden

violent pains in the head, and were simultaneously seized with fearful retching and black vomiting.[17]

Small wonder then that Louis, who refused to shut himself up as other Europeans did, decided, as the plague worsened after nearly three weeks, to leave for Sinai and the Bedouin.

His plan was to push on if possible to Akaba, in order to trace the direction of the eastern gulf of the Red Sea which, as far as he knew, had never been seen by any European traveller.[18]

# CHAPTER EIGHTEEN

## *The Desert of the Exodus*

> As the naked wilderness could not maintain a people of
> hunters, they rose at once to the more secure and plentiful
> condition of the pastoral life—the same uniformly pursued by
> the roving tribes of the Desert; and in the portrait of the
> modern Bedoweens we may trace the features of their
> ancestors, who in the age of Moses or Mohamet dwelt under
> similar tents, and conducted their horses and camels and
> sheep to the same springs and pastures.
>
> *Gibbon*

SINAI—AN ANTIQUE land. The very name booms across millennia giving man his basic law, evoking echelons of mountains—
mysterious sounding-gongs of granite—flights of quail in shuddering fall, sugary manna's viscid glint. Israelites desperate on
the march, Moses and God's burning tamarisk—and the white
serpent prophetically suspended in the wilderness.

Throughout the ages a stupendous peninsula, a thrilling, a
barren but beautiful place, small and yet so important in the
history of mankind—then never before described in detail, even
now a challenge to the traveller.

Unlike the Israelites in their wanderings, for his part Louis had
not the slightest cause to yearn for the fleshpots of Egypt during
his journey into Sinai. It was a strenuous, mostly happy time,
exciting too, and once or twice even extremely dangerous. But
he was well, active, busy, in his element with the Bedouin, and
able to breathe again the "pure air of Switzerland".[19]

The chief discoveries he made there were the general structure
of the peninsula and many new facts of its geography—one of the
most important of which was the extent and form of the Gulf of

Aelana, now Akaba, which had been until then "so imperfectly known as to be either omitted from the maps, or marked with a bifurcation at the extremity, which is now found not to exist".[20]

To travel to Mount Sinai and St Katherine's it had for a long time been necessary for pilgrims and others to obtain a permit from the Greek convent of Cairo. This Louis did, but he waited in vain for a letter from the Pasha to the principal Sheik of the tribes of Tor which would have helped him on the dangerous way to the castle of Akaba. For some reason, the Pasha failed to reply to the application sent politely enough through his drago-man, and Louis was forced to leave without this important document.

Keeping a little to the south of the pilgrim route he crossed the plain from Cairo towards Suez with his guide, and Sharhati his servant. The area was still a dangerous one: many people were murdered here by the dreaded Omrah who plundered and skirmished almost at will, until Ali Pasha's firm reprisals began to have effect.

Louis found Suez to be a decaying dump, more Arabian in feeling than Egyptian. The stench of its low-lying miasmic lands and stagnant creeks had long since driven its inhabitants to the bottle, but however liberal or frequent the brandy dose it could do little to counteract either the stinks or the malignant fevers of the place. In this pestilential town Louis was able to engage a guide named Hamid, a Bedouin of the Towara (from Tor, that is), who proved himself to be a useful, brave and honest man.

They left very early in the morning, riding in a northerly direction. The tide was at high flood, so they had laboriously to circumnavigate the creek at the head of the Gulf of Suez—at what is now the southern end of the Canal. Later, they rested for a while at the famous wells of Ain Musa—Moses' spring among the date palms. The next day, after nearly eleven hours' riding, they slept in the barren Wadi Amara, their camp fire making a small bower of light, homely beneath the glittering immeasurable panoply of stars.

Ahead was an enormous rampart of mountains rising towards the climax of the great central plateau with, near its southern apex, the holy mount itself. They soon began entering hills of wildly flamboyant strata—in some places jetty black, in others lustrous with the transparency of agates. Rock bands and swathes of warmer colours, reflecting the sunlight, gleamed as if polished with flowing oil. Louis found himself thinking constantly of the Israelites in their flight from Egypt, of the direction of their march, the springs at which they must have stopped, of what Moses could possibly have used to sweeten the bitter wells of Howara. It could perhaps have been the juicy berries of a little shrub that grew in one of the wadis.

Early next day they rode across a high rocky plain; the air was gloriously fresh, the dawn—heralded by those long foxes-brush type of cloud painted in a glowing sky—was sublime. In Arabia there was nothing that Louis enjoyed more than this ever-amazing spectacle of the rising sun, and the cool breeze that always accompanies its so sudden appearance burning up over the rim of the world.

> It was an invariable custom with me, at setting out early in the morning to walk on foot for a few hours in advance of the caravan; and as enjoyments are comparative, I believe that I derived from this practice greater pleasure than any which the arts of the most luxurious capitals can afford.

Now they were in a rugged landscape torn and devastated by wild torrent courses dry since beyond the memory of man. Then the area of sandstone began: painted hills of Petra-like colours, a fabulous confusion of mountains, a silent beauty of naked rock more wonderful than any temple or cathedral made by human hands—God-inspired, a fit place for man once to have heard the voice of God. There, sandstone glows in warm hues of rose, copper and mellow russet, and laminated rocks of quartz, feldspar and mica reveal ochre-yellow or olivine green channelled with purple, crimson and black. "In the granite districts red, brown, white, rose and grey are the chief colours . . . the glaring whites and greys of cretaceous strata . . . often streaked with brilliant clays of lilac, maroon and crimson".[21]

THE DESERT OF THE EXODUS 373

They paused at noon in a wadi below a large overhanging rock which, so Louis thought, had for ages afforded shade to travellers. While his guide and servant lay asleep here and one of the Arabs had gone to a near-by well to water the camels, he walked around the huge rock and was surprised to find inscriptions—he copied some—similar to those which had already been noted by Seetzen and by Niebuhr in Wadi Mokatteb, the six miles long "Valley of the Writing" further south.

At this point an Egyptian who had joined the caravan earlier left them to ride on ahead alone, being in a hurry to reach his Bedouin bride who lived somewhere in this area. Later that same day the caravan saw him again; he was completely exhausted, his eyes already so dimmed with thirst that he could scarcely recognise the men. He had lost his way in a sandy plain, and ridden helplessly about the mountains and deathly silent cleft ravines until he had luckily chanced to meet with them. He would probably have died had they not seen him. Louis' companions laughed at this "effeminate Egyptian", as they called him, for so foolishly presuming to travel alone in an unknown district.

They struggled next up a steep ascent, a mountain of moving sands, the summit of which commanded a wide view north bounded by the far blue ranges of el Tyh's southern escarpment. Each day the ascents grew steeper and wilder, buttressed by shattered rocks of shining black porphyry. Then, from over the crest of Lion Mountain, they dropped down a little into a wide wadi covered with good pasturage. To Louis the scene recalled his Alpine valleys, and the scent that met them was delicious, "a spicy gale wooing man's approach with all the perfumed herbs of Arabia"—sweeter even than the fragrance of Hymettus' honeyed slopes.[22] Here they met some Bedouin peacefully collecting brushwood of the flowery broom to make charcoal for the Cairo market.

That night, after another very long ride, they slept at a Bedouin encampment where, since the sheik was absent, the Arabs held a long, fierce dispute among themselves as to who should have the honour of providing the travellers with supper, and with breakfast the next day. A lamb was killed—an act of great hospitality for these Bedouin were very poor. During the evening Louis joined his hosts in singing some popular songs.

Of the *mesamer* and the *kazyde* which he heard so often in the dead of night in Sinai, he has written very fully.[23] Some two or three hours after sunset a group of young people, either the girls or the men, would gather near the tents and begin to sing. It was an invitation that continued until those of the opposite sex came out to range themselves in a long line, facing but never intermingling with the other. One of the men would then begin the *kazyde*, a repetitive melody, all the men joining in the chorus clapping their hands and swaying in unison. Then one or two of the girls would advance dancing shyly towards the opposing line, each veiled girl held a blue *mellaye* spread over her outstretched arms. It was all intensely modest and romantic, in complete contrast with the sensuous dances of Cairo, and Louis preferred it "in the highest degree" to any of the dances of Egyptian or of Syrian women.

The men were not allowed to call the girls by name but would sing the homely expressions of command or encouragement by which they made their camels obey them. "Get up O camel!"—"Walk fast!"—"The poor camel is thirsty!" and so on. Some of the gayer young men spread out their turbans or *keffiehs* on the ground to represent food for the "camel", and if a girl were daring enough to snatch these away the owner would redeem his belongings when the dance was over by paying a small fee. Louis himself once retrieved a handkerchief by giving the girl who had seized it a pretty string of mother-of-pearl beads, saying it was meant as a *"halter* for the camel"; delighted she hung the baubles round her neck.

If a girl came dancing bravely close to the men's line they showed their approval by stretching out their arms as if to embrace her:

this dance, which continues frequently for five or six hours and till long after midnight, and the pathetic songs which often accompany it most powerfully works upon the imagination of the Arabs, and they never speak of the *mesamer* but with

raptures. The feelings of the lover must on this occasion be
carried to the highest pitch. The veiled form of his mistress
advances in the dark, or by moonlight like a phantom to his
embraces; her graceful, decent steps, her increasing animation,
the general applause she receives, and the words of the song . . .
which are always in praise of beauty, must create the liveliest
emotions in the bosom of her lover, who has at least the satisfaction of being able to give full scope to his feelings by voice
and gesture without exposing himself to any blame.

The songs, often extempore, always related to the beauty and
the qualities of those girls who moved apart from their companions to dance separately. Obviously he found it all refreshing
and very appealing. He wrote:

The Bedouin are perhaps the only people of the East that can
with justice be entitled true lovers. The passion of love is,
indeed, much talked of by the inhabitants of the towns; but I
doubt whether anything is meant by them more than the
grossest animal desire; at least I have never witnessed among
them any instance of preserving affection amidst misfortunes;
while, on the contrary, many persons daily evince the most
perfect indifference after enjoyment. The seclusion of women
forbids the possibility of becoming acquainted with the beloved object's character, as the first interview with her leads
invariably to possession; and where the minds cannot understand each other, it is scarcely possible that sentiments of
friendship should assume any degree of sublimity; which, I
imagine, constitutes the difference between animal and rational
love.

It would appear that those two words—"I imagine"—unless
they are used to cover himself, are enough proof that Louis had
yet to experience real sexual love as opposed to carnal desire. He
craved all his life, it seems, that spiritual companionship which
elevates love above lust.

He had little opinion of the amorous verses of the Arabic

townsman which had no reference to the qualities of mind or heart but only to ample physical charms. And when one recalls the poet who sang admiringly of his mistress whose face resembled the full moon and whose haunches were like a pair of cushions, one is inclined to agree with him.

> But the Bedouin have frequent opportunities of becoming acquainted with the daughters of their neighbours: their love is often conceived in their youthful days, and fostered during a series of years; and . . . a Bedouin girl . . . whatever may be her sentiments with respect to a lover . . . will seldom condescend to let him know them, and still less to suffer any personal liberties, however convinced of a reciprocal affection. The firm assurance of her chastity must powerfully influence his heart; and as a Bedouin's mind and imagination are always strong and sound, not pampered into sickly sensibility or depraved fancy like the townsman's, it is to be supposed that virtuous impressions being once made take a firm hold.

He had to admit, however, that the universal Islamic custom of easy divorce was not much in favour of lasting attachments. But where the Beduoin were concerned he found even for that an excuse: he would "rather ascribe it to the unruly temper of those sons of the desert, than to any want of feeling in their character".[24]

He began to learn more also of Bedouin marriage customs. A girl was not consulted on her choice. As she brought the herds back to camp one evening she would be met by her future husband wearing a green sprig in his turban to show that he was taking a virgin.* With the help of his young friends he would then carry her off by force to her father's tent. If she knew of the ambush she would defend herself fiercely with stones, often wounding the young men even if she liked her suitor for, according to custom, the more she struggled, bit, kicked and shrieked the more she was applauded ever afterwards. Then, completely covered in an aba

---

* The Malays seem to have inherited this custom, perhaps from the Arabs who brought them Islam—in the *tajok mahkota*, the groom's "crown's aigrette", which figuratively in romantic Malay verse means—"my princess, my love".

in her father's tent, she would for the first time hear the name of her husband. After that the ceremonies were much the same as those of other Muslim peoples—except that the bride was expected to keep up a convincingly violent show of protest throughout. One tribe Louis mentions in Sinai—the Mezene— had an unusual bridal custom which appealed to the strongly romantic side of his nature. After being wrapped in the aba the girl was allowed to escape from her tent at night and run away in- to near-by mountains. The bridegroom would go in search of her —sometimes it was days before he found her hiding place—while her girl friends, who were told of her whereabouts, kept her supplied with food and water.

> If the husband finds her at last (which is sooner or later, accord- ing to the impression that he has made upon the girl's heart) he is bound to consummate the marriage in the open country, and to pass the night with her in the mountains. The next morning the bride goes home to the tents, that she may have some food; but again runs away in the evening, and repeats these flights several times . . .

His love of open air and of the mountains, the romanticism of idyllic-seeming customs, the spare tawny beauty of these desert people, all conspired to captivate Louis, drawn more and more as he was towards the real Bedouin of that time, and to their simple if archaic pastoral way of life. Here in a sense he saw, or thought he saw, that kind of purity which he himself so deeply admired.

Through narrowing defiles they were now approaching the great summits of Sinai; isolated Jebel Serbal, glistening "Coat of Mail", lay ahead, and on one hand immense abrupt cliffs black- ened by the sun enclosed the mass of red granite—Mount Sinai itself, or Horeb, the Mountain of God, of Moses, of the Law.

In one pass he was shown, as Arabs have shown men through the centuries, the stone on which Moses was said to have sat as he pastured his flocks at "the backside of the desert", as the Bible has it, and Louis saw that the Bedouin kept the seat covered with fresh or with dried herbs, and that some of them kissed or touched it in passing.

After a long ride through sun-scorched granite it came as a surprise to him when, on reaching the stony plain beyond, he saw suddenly, darkly revealed in the deep shadow of the holy mountain's towering mass, a beautiful garden of cypresses and almond trees. It belonged to the Monastery of the Transfiguration—the so-called convent of St Katherine, itself rock-like among the unexpected greenery of its trees.

In the fourth century A.D. many of the early "athletes of God", Christian anchorites and hermits fleeing from persecution in Egypt, had come to live in and around the holy mountain, and in the near-by oasis of Feiran—where the wadi's slopes were honeycombed with their cells and tombs, the one in fact often becoming the other. Feiran was the site of the first bishopric and although for nude anchorites shivering in the wilderness the oasis was kinder than the bare mountains, existence was precarious in either place. In the sixth century the two communities united at the Holy Mount when the Emperor Justinian built this fortress monastery for their protection over 1,400 years ago. It was later that the place became known as St Katherine's, after the torture on the wheel and subsequent martydom of the brave and beautiful Katherine of Alexandria. Her body was said to have been miraculously transported to the fastness of Sinai—a story akin to that of the Virgin of Loretto. Two dents in the rocks of Jebel Katerina above the convent are said to have been made by the angelic posteriors of the robust pair of messengers who bore her there.[25]

Louis' little caravan crossed the plain and, reaching the shadow of the mountain, halted under the monastery window through which the *papas* communicated then with the semi-hostile Arab world outside. When Louis' Cairo letter had been drawn up and read by a monk, someone fastened a pole across the rope, and so Louis was hoisted to the window. He was made very welcome, and shown to the small neat room which the prior assigned in those days to all strangers whom he received with any mark of distinction.

There were many interesting notes pencilled on the walls of his room, the names of the most recent European travellers were there, including that of Seetzen now dead of poison in the Yemen. Some Louis recorded, and some he later sent to amuse his mother. One written by two Frenchmen in the ninth year of the Republic of France and the third after the conquest of Egypt had been neatly capped by two Englishmen who arrived eleven years later: "*7 ans après la destruction de la République Française et 11 ans après l'expulsion des Français de l'Egypte par une armée Anglaise . . .*"

Louis does not mention the amazing view from this room but a later traveller who has a flare for descriptive writing says: "It would seem as if *Arabia Petraea* had once been an ocean of lava, and that while its waves were running literally mountains high, it was commanded suddenly to stand still."[26]

Louis was surprised to find a Greek woman staying in the monastery: he whets one's appetite to know who she might have been and how she had arrived there, but he says no more.

Monks of the Greek Orthodox church today still maintain this famous monastery as they have done since the age of Byzantium. Their numbers have varied enormously; at the time of Louis' visit there were only twenty-three. With regard to their daily routine and strictly meatless diet, Louis considered the discipline severe. But the fruits of their amazing garden in the heart of the burning solitude were superb—oranges, lemons, almonds, mulberries, apricots, peaches, pears, apples and olives, melons, beans, lettuces too, and all sorts of culinary sweet herbs were grown. Apart from these delights their one real indulgence, their only solace, Louis calls it, appeared to be the brandy which they distilled from the dates they grew. As they do now the monks supplied the Bedouin twice daily with bread as part of tribute for protection. Louis thought the monastery bread excellent, but the kind that the Bedouin received from the window was a very third-rate sort; in fact, it was said to be of a quality that no decently brought up ostrich could swallow without endangering his digestion.[27] Perhaps it was no wonder then that the Bedouin sometimes demanded meat meals in addition to this diet. Louis also says that they had been known if disgruntled to beat up any monks they encountered outside on the mountain, or to destroy the gardens, and sometimes they fired off their muskets alarmingly from neighbouring heights. The monks had a fine armoury and used to fire back, always taking good care not to kill anyone.

If the monks had cause to fear the Arabs against whom they were barricaded in this wilderness, the Arabs also had some respect at least for the monks, since they were convinced that these humble *papas* had power to call down rain. Louis saw that this unwonted reputation had become a terrible nuisance for the monks—though he thought that to some extent they had brought it upon themselves in order to gain credit with the Bedouin. The Bedouin appeared to believe that the rains were under the immediate control of Moses, and that the monks' prayers and actions with the Book of Law, which they were convinced was concealed here, prevailed upon the weather. Therefore, not unreasonably, in reverse the monks were often held responsible for droughts, when the Bedouin would come *en masse* to force the *papas* to take to Jebel Musa and pray.

Once, after extremely efficacious prayers, a violent cloud-burst occurred over the peninsula. It caused so much damage to crops and drowned so many animals that the Arabs rushed back to the monastery to expostulate. It was a curse the monks had called down, rather than a blessing! One or two furious men opened fire on the monastery. They were finally quietened with gifts, but did not go away before stipulating that the rains would have to be more moderate next time.

Louis discovered that it was a favourite belief among the monks that the young Mohammed himself had once alighted beneath these walls on one of his trading journeys north, and that out of veneration for Moses' Mount he had later presented a firman to secure for the monastery the respect of all his followers. Louis thought that although it was a very pleasing story it was only a fable, and that the supposed firman in the Sinai convent of Cairo was merely a fake. That other link with Islam, the mosque inside the monastery walls, was said to have been built in the sixteenth century to save the place from destruction by Selim after his conquest of Egypt. But Louis found an account which clearly stated that in A.H. 783 (A.D. 1364) some Turkish stragglers from the Great Haj caravan had become its servants, so it was obviously very considerably older.

Another Islamic touch which interested Louis was that in the modern Arabic inscription commemorating Justinian's building of the monastery in A.D. 557, it was curious to find a passage from the Koran—probably done, so Louis guessed, by a Muslim engraver without the knowledge of the monks, who could not read Arabic.

On the whole he found these Greeks—they were mostly from the islands then—to be extremely ignorant men. Their wonderful library was always closed, but Louis contrived to examine volume after volume, and the prior made him a present of "a fine copy of the Aldine Odyssey and an equally fine one of the Anthology". The priests assured Louis that they had documents proving how long the various valleys and oases had been in their possession but either they could not, or they would not, show him their archives in any detail without permission from the prior at Cairo. "Indeed all their papers appeared to be in great confusion." This remark is interesting in view of the important find twenty-seven years later of the world famous *Codex Sinaiticus*.

Louis lamented too the fact that the monks seemed to know little or nothing of the Old Testament—such knowledge would after all have been a link with their close Muslim neighbours. Louis goes on to castigate in no uncertain terms (which makes one think that he might in another era have made an excellent literary critic of Arabic) the appalling Arabic translations of the Bible, as perpetrated by the Bible Society of England. No Muslim scholar would have been tempted to read such stuff since the "whole construction was generally contrary to the spirit of the language, so harsh, affected and full of foreign idioms". In style and phraseology it differed "from the Koran more than monkish Latin from the orations of Cicero".

On his first visit he stayed only three days in the monastery since he was anxious to explore the unknown territory eastwards. The monks did all they could to discourage him in his desire to reach Akaba as they were in constant fear of the Bedouin, but when they saw how firmly he was resolved, they realised they could not prevent his leaving.

Hamid had recently met an uncle of his, old Saleh, who swore that he knew the way to Akaba; Louis therefore thought it would be reasonable to journey on with these two men. Leaving the monastery very early one morning they plunged at once into still wilder rocky country. Great bands of porphyry, running perpendicularly from the very summits of the mountain to its base, glittered wonderfully with embedded crystals and thin bits of quartz in a universally roseate surrounding.

In this labyrinth of coloured rock it was not long before Uncle Saleh had to admit that he was hopelessly lost. Indeed, so Louis guessed, had he ever known the way he had probably not ridden over it since his boyhood. Luckily, they met some Bedouin charcoal burners who put them on the right track.

The district was more barren than anything that Louis had yet seen in his travels, except perhaps parts of the desert of el Tyh— even the Nubian valleys seemed pleasure gardens by comparison. Not the tiniest leaf was to be seen; even the thorny mimosa which remains green in Nubia with the slightest of dews was here quite withered, and so dry that it caught fire from the lighted cinders which dropped from their pipes as they rode past.

That evening they fell in with two elderly half-naked Towara Bedouin who, with their ichthyophagous dog, were going down to the sea to fish. One of these men was deaf "but so intelligent that it was easy to talk with him by signs; he had established a vocabulary of gestures with his companion . . . his fishing partner for ten years". The name of the deaf man's friend was Ayd. He showed himself to be one of the hardiest and shrewdest of all the Bedouin Louis had ever met. And, in his younger days, he had been a well known or, perhaps Louis should have said, a notorious robber. Indeed, in Egypt once he had been so severely beaten for his crimes that his back had become permanently bent; despite this and his age he remained as robust, active and high-spirited as any young man.

Sharing Louis' supper that evening in the barren mountains, the two fishermen shook their heads gravely when he told them he was bound for Akaba. The old ex-robber did not take long to discover how very little Uncle Saleh knew of the road, and reproached him for having deluded Sheik Ibrahim by false promises.

Louis felt that there was so much sense in all that Ayd said about the country that he decided to ask him to join them on the venture up the gulf, as soon as they reached the seashore.

The next day, after riding through a majestic defile of perpendicular rock, he saw the Gulf of Akaba blue and scintillating far below. An hour or so later they were down on a sandy beach, where there was a well among a grove of date palms close by the shore.

Ayd was eventually prevailed upon to accompany Louis and Hamid up the coast, while old Uncle Saleh began to show some signs of treachery. After breakfast of fish broth and bread, the deaf man was told to wait for Ayd's return, and the other four set out, skirting a small bay. The sands were patterned with crisscross marks of what Louis took to be serpents' tracks—which made him think again of the Israelites: "and the great and terrible wilderness wherein were fiery serpents and scorpions and drought and where there was no water", and of the Lord God who had brought them forth water out of the rock of flint, and fed them in the wilderness with manna.[28] Louis knew manna, *mann* as the Bedouin call it, as a kind of sticky dewy substance that exudes from the twigs of the *tarfa* tree, or tamarisk. It does not seem to have been until later that it was discovered—as even more of a disillusionment—to be the secretion of a stick larva.

Uncle Saleh was a persistent nagging nuisance; he was always ready to dismount, always wanting a meal, or grumbling at setting off, and constantly trying to persuade Hamid and Ayd to turn back  But they pressed on north through a long succession of bays, riding often like Alexander in the waves. At noon Louis saw a beautiful sight—a herd of gazelles coming gracefully down from the furnace of the hills, leaping lithe and tawny out of the tawny wilderness to bathe in the brilliant sea.

That afternoon the men halted below a steep headland where in a rocky valley there grew some acacias and a little grass. Ayd swore that there was a natural rain-water cistern in the mountain above. In the hope of persuading young Hamid to make the climb he described the place in so elaborate and confused a way, and with so much pomposity, that Louis, who felt sure he was inventing the whole thing, told him he was a babbler.

"A babbler!" the old man exclaimed indignantly. "*Allah!* Nobody in my whole life has ever called me that before! I'll show you which of us two deserves that name!" Grabbing one of the large water skins, barefooted as he was he began rushing up over the sharp, loose stones of the mountainside. Soon out of sight, he presently reappeared further on, now climbing an almost perpendicular goat-path. One-and-a-half hours later he returned by the same way, carrying on his bent back the bulging water skin which could not have weighed less than a hundred pounds. He slung it down at their feet and said:

"There!—Take it from the babbler!"

Louis was so overcome with shame at his own ill-considered words that he was at a loss as how best to apologise, but as soon as Ayd saw that Sheik Ibrahim did really feel himself in the wrong he was quite pacified, and nothing more was said about it for a while. At night though, when he saw Louis taking a deep draught of the water, and heard him saying how sweet it was in comparison with the brackish water of the coastal springs, he held up a reprimanding hand and said: "Young man, in the future never call an old Bedouin a babbler!"

They came next to high cliffs abutting the shore and were forced to make a long detour inland through the steep and winding ways of Wadi Mezeiryk. Many sweet-scented herbs grew here and the acacias were remarkably green. This, the Bedouin said, was owing to a tremendous rainfall in the north during last winter—although the south had scarcely seen a drop of rain for two years. On arriving at the shore again eight hours later, they continued between the sea and a range of black basalt cliffs until they reached the sandy flats known as Wadi Taba. Here they dug out a choked well and watered their camels, which had not drunk for some days.

Taba was the furthest point to which Ayd had promised he would go; already they had passed the limits of the Towara

Arabs and were in the territory of the infamous Huweitat and their allies—the intrepid Alowein robbers, and the murderous Omrah. They had not met a soul on the way but they had seen one set of footprints in the sands, which Ayd thought probably belonged to a Huweitat friend of his who fished in this area and who would have acted as guide ensuring safe conduct here, could they have met up with him.

To reach Akaba it was inevitable that they would have to pass through dangerous valleys of unfriendly peoples: flatly Ayd would go no further. Hamid bravely offered to go wherever Louis went, but without either Huweitat guide or the Pasha's firman there was really no alternative but to go back. Louis knew well enough that these people, the Omrah particularly, not only robbed but murdered travellers who went unescorted by one of their tribe or of allied tribes.

Early in the twentieth century there was an "incident" at Taba when Turkish forces crossed the Egyptian frontier and established themselves there.[29] The dispute was eventually settled, and a commission of British and Turkish officers was set up to determine the boundary. The line then created left Taba inside Sinai and until the recent Arab-Israeli wars this narrow angle remained the division where the sharp point of Palestine's southern limits cut down between Egypt and Jordan, thus making—after the post-World War II creation of Israel—all access impossible from Sinai to Akaba except by sea. So in Louis' day, in Lawrence's, and now, it remains a curiously difficult and dangerous little corner of the world.

Disappointed, Louis strained his eyes to see Akaba, which he could distinguish only as a black line in the distance. His more sharp-sighted companions clearly saw the date palms surrounding the castle which he had so much wanted to reach. The little garrison town and haven lay only five or six hours away at the head of this hitherto unmapped gulf, where the great Wadi Araba ends in the sea.

Dusk soon fell and they could see no more. The next day broke lowering, and so overcast by a hot sand-laden *samun* that they could not see across the gulf. Louis went swimming but was not refreshed, so heavy and sticky was the day. Once more near to Syria his thoughts went back to the journey he had made four years earlier, in 1812, from Damascus to Cairo, and of how then also it had been impossible to reach Akaba. From both the north and now the south he had come so close—it must have been devilishly frustrating.

As they retraced their steps along the shore the overpowering *samun* continued to blow, and it did not drop even with the sunset. Their fitful sleep was disturbed too by the sudden barking of Ayd's fish-eating dog. Ayd sprang up saying he felt sure that someone was near in the darkness, so they got their guns ready and sat by the fire the whole night—for however hot the season the Bedouin must have his nightly fire. It was an edgy experience; they had the feeling of being watched, and Saleh was very frightened, but morning came without an attack.

They made their way back below the dark basalt cliffs and little bays, and re-entered Wadi Mezeiryk. As they had seen no one at all and were coming into the friendly districts of Towara Arabs they no longer felt any fear—they were even laughing at Ayd who kept telling them to hurry past the valley mouths.

It happened when Saleh was ahead driving the camels: Louis was following leisurely, while Hamid and Ayd were walking about fifty yards behind him.

Louis' gun was on his camel. He had just strolled peacefully around an angle of the wadi, when he heard Ayd suddenly cry out with all his might: "Get your arms!—Here they are!"

Instantly, Louis sprinted towards the camels for his gun. But at that same crucial moment cowardly Saleh, instead of stopping to help, struck the camels violently with his own weapon so that they galloped off, charging full speed up the valley. Always fast on his feet, Louis contrived to catch up in time to seize his gun in full flight. But before he could return to the others he heard two shots followed by a war-whoop from Ayd.

"Have at him!—Are we not Towara!"

Next Louis saw Hamid come springing around the bend of the wadi: his eyes flashing rage, his shirt sprinkled with blood, gun in one hand, in the other his knife—its blade vermilion in the sunshine. His foot was bleeding, his turban lost, and his long black hair hung wildly over his shoulders.

"I have done for him!" he exclaimed as he wiped the blood from his knife. "Let's fly!"

"Not without Ayd!" retorted Louis.

"No!—*wellah!*—without him we'd all be lost!"

Together they raced back around the corner and saw Ayd running desperately to catch up. Beyond him, about forty yards away, three Arabs stood looking down at a fourth man lying inert and bloody at their feet. Louis and Hamid each seized Ayd by an arm and with him between them ran headlong up the wadi after their camels. They did not know how far the animals might have gone since Saleh had frightened them so badly. It was half an hour before they were found: one of them had burst its girths and thrown both saddle and load. Fear quickening every action, the men worked feverishly to secure and replace the gear: when Ayd was mounted they ran on behind the camels, passing safely through a rocky defile into rather more open country where an ambush was less likely.

As they regained their breath a little, Hamid told Louis of how first Ayd had seen the four Bedouin running down the hillside to attack. Evidently they had meant to stage the ambush at the wadi corner but had arrived a fraction too late. When Hamid heard Ayd's yell of warning, he had just enough time to strike a light to the matchlock of his gun, while the boldest of the four ran to within twenty paces of them. The man took aim at Hamid and fired. The ball passed through Hamid's shirt: he returned fire instantly but missed. Then, while the robber began coolly reloading, Ayd had cried out to Hamid to set upon the man before the other three could reach them. Hamid then rushed in drawing his knife; he received a javelin wound in the foot, slashed into his adversary and—as Louis described it later—"cut him to pieces".

If the man died on the spot, Ayd said, they would undoubtedly be hunted down for blood revenge. Had he only been wounded the others would stay with him.

Ayd urged them on fearing pursuit. Louis was certain that these men had intended to murder them all, contrary to the usual practice of the Bedouin, and—as Huweitat—they could not afford to let any Towara escape. Having studied the little group of travellers by the light of last night's fire when Ayd's dog had barked so furiously—

> they had no doubt resolved to kill the whole party, as the only effectual mode of avoiding all disclosures. . . . I do not believe [*Louis writes*] that such atrocities often occur in the eastern deserts . . . but these Huweitat Arabs are notorious for their bad faith and never hesitate to kill those who do not travel under the protection of their own people. . . . [*He goes on stoutly defending the Bedouin as always*]: Scarcely any other Bedouin robbers would have fired till they had summoned us to give up our baggage, and had received a shot in answer.

Louis dressed Hamid's wound as best he could; it was not serious and in four days had nearly healed. They pressed on through the night, and on 10 May they met Ayd's deaf friend again at the coast. Foiled in his hopes of Akaba, Louis now planned to explore to the South, and to return to the monastery by a westerly route. Timorous Uncle Saleh had had more than enough; he returned to St Katherine's with the deaf man, while Ayd agreed to conduct Louis and Hamid along the coast.

As they went, Ayd spoke of the strange hollow sound sometimes heard here, the mysterious noise that accounts for the "booming Sinai" story so often told by Muslim and Christian alike. It seemed to issue from the upper country, and was mostly heard in summer when the wind was strong. The Arabs said that Moses' spirit, descending then from Jebel Musa, flies across the sea calling a farewell to his beloved mountains. Some little time later Louis climbed Omm Shomar's torrid sun-blackened cliffs where he had expected to find a volcano which might have accounted for this long recorded "booming", but he found nothing—all was "utter desolation and hopeless barrenness".

By this time Louis was so expert at writing in concealment that he could now manage it with ease even on a camel. By throwing the wide aba over his head in the Arab way as if to protect himself from the sun, he could write even if another person rode close beside him: it was as essential as ever not to be thought a treasure seeker or a magician. Since the skirmish and the hasty flight from the wadi there had been no chance for him to write, either while riding or while feigning sleep, for they had travelled too fast and hard. So now on the third evening he had to resort to his other method—that of going away as if to answer a call of nature, crouching down Arab-style under his cloak. He had so many notes to record and remained so long away from the halting place that Ayd's curiosity was aroused.

> He came after me, and perceiving me immovable on the spot, approached on tip-toe, and came close behind me without my perceiving him. I do not know how long he remained there but suddenly lifting up my cloak he detected me with the book in my hand.
> "What's this?" he exclaimed. "What are you doing?"

Since they were companions, Ayd said, Ibrahim had no need to answer at once but he would have to do so when they returned to the monastery. But in rejoining Hamid at the camp fire, Louis asked Ayd to say what he had to say now.

"You write down our country," Ayd answered passionately. "Our mountains, our pasturing places, and the rain which falls from heaven . . ."

Others had done it before; *he* did not wish to help the ruining of his country—and so on. Louis tried to reassure him: he liked the Bedouin too well to hurt them—he must realise that. He *had* written down a few prayers since leaving Taba, he said, suggesting that had he not done so they might all have been killed. This startled Ayd (as well it might), and for a while he seemed almost convinced, but presently he went on with a long story about some travellers years before who had come to Sinai and written down everything: "stones, plants, animals, even serpents and spiders". Since then little rain had fallen, and game had decreased alarmingly.

It was the same story as that which Louis had found among the

Bedouin of Nubia, who believed a sorcerer, by writing down certain charms, could stop the rains and transfer them to his own country.

Louis realised that the travellers Ayd referred to were Seetzen, eight years previously, and shortly before him Agnelli, who had travelled for the Emperor of Austria inquiring into the flora and fauna of Sinai. These men may have been more open in their approach; Louis could not afford to be so, he had too much at stake for the future.

It was difficult for Louis to soothe Ayd, hot-blooded old fellow that he was. However, he simmered down and remained pacified during the rest of the journey, but on their return to the monastery he spread a report among the Arabs that Sheik Ibrahim was a writer like those others before, and Louis lost their confidence almost completely.

As in Arabia men perfumed the *keffieh,* so here the women of Sinai perfumed their hair, which they wore in a thick bang above the forehead. Louis soon found that these girls of the long tents were not at all shy—although they kept their distance—and he frequently joined in their friendly pastoral scenes.

One evening, some goat girls led the travellers to where their mothers were spinning, or gathering herbs to feed the lambs and kids that frisked gaily about them and their small children. Ayd, who knew the women personally, shook them by the hand and kissed their babies, but Hamid and Louis kept at some distance. They all supped well that night when the men returned, off a dish of fresh-caught turbot followed by roast meat, for all of which Louis paid and shared around with everyone. The whole encampment became very cheerful since, as Louis remarks, one way to the Bedouin heart is certainly through an abundance of food—and Bedouin appetites are enormous.

Another evening was spent in the company of a beautiful girl of about eighteen and her mother, whom Ayd knew. Louis and Hamid had discreetly sat down a little way off but after sunset the woman and her lovely daughter joined them. Louis thought the girl quite as graceful and as charming as any well educated European girl could be. Indeed, in comparing the Bedouin girls with Europeans—even those of the most polished cities—he saw that grace and modesty were, just as much as beauty, the gifts of nature.

There was no meat served that night, only milk, for the men were away, and these graceful women were poor. Elsewhere, Louis has recorded one particularly festive night spent in the mountains with the Bedouin, when Ayd made him laugh by fitting his actions, comically exact, to a well-known Arabic proverb.[30] "He resembles the bread on seeing only the smoke"— a saying that indicates a man so hopeful that he begins to break his bread expecting broth to follow.

They had alighted at a small encampment at evening, and had hardly been made welcome before Ayd strolled off, to return shortly carrying two large stones. When Louis asked him why, the answer was that he meant to use them to break the bones to get at the marrow of the sheep he expected would be slaughtered in their honour—although there had as yet been no sign of a feast. Everyone present began to laugh at such a show of optimism; but Ayd was proved to be quite right—very soon afterwards a gargantuan steaming dish of meat was set before them.

It was revitalising to come up again from the heat of the coast into the mountains on the way back to the monastery. Presently, following a tiny stream, they came upon a charming little grove in bright viridian contrast with the bare dazzling rocks hemming the small spot in. Besides the date palms there was an onion patch, and another, a more sinister crop—Indian hemp. Not a soul was to be seen, some camels fed on the grass beside the rivulet, and in the branches of a tree hung several baskets and a gun. Here the Bedouin had no fear of robbers, and allowed their camels to pasture untended—it did not matter if they strayed since every man knew his own camel's footprint.

There was dancing and more feasting that night at an encampment in the hills, and *mesamer* singing was protracted until the small hours. Louis had little rest that night since, when the dancing at last was over, as guest he was expected to sleep in his host's tent beside several other men whose idea it was to honour him by keeping him company. Crowded quarters, shared fleas, lack of fresh air were anathema to Louis, but one could not sleep outside—partly because of the dogs which hated all strangers, and partly because one might inadvertently see into the women's quarters.

They left the camp before dawn and were soon looking down from the summits on that fabulous monastery and its garden cradled in the rock far below. Hamid was increasingly worried about the blood fine which he would most probably have to pay for the killing near Taba—if killing it proved to have been—and now he made the others give their solemn oath not to mention the fight. However, out of some jealousy Uncle Saleh divulged the whole story on their return to St Katherine's. It eventually became known that the man had been mortally wounded, and after some months Hamid had to pay two camels—which the Towara sheiks gave for the fine plus $20, a sum which Louis felt bound to reimburse to him in Cairo later. Had Hamid not paid up, the Bedouin concerned would inevitably have "struck sideways"—that is, taken oblique blood revenge on his own people.

Louis took two days' rest at the monastery, enjoying the delightful garden, and the date brandy, examining more books, and seeing the charnel house which the monks had previously been reluctant to show him. Then, escorted by the Jebelis, he set out on a pilgrimage of the various holy places in the hills around.

The Jebelis, or mountaineers, have an interesting history. They are descended from Christian slaves sent by Justinian from the Black Sea coast to act as servants to the monks. Now Muslim, they look much like any other Bedouin but their girls are especially famed for their beauty— "a circumstance which often gives rise to unhappy attachments, and romantic love-tales, when their lovers happen to belong to other tribes".

From Jebel Musa Louis went on to spend another cool night high among the peaks, accompanied by his servant, the Jebali and a young Greek, a former Red Sea sailor, "who appeared to have turned monk chiefly for the sake of getting his fill of brandy from the convent cellar". Again there was roast lamb for supper, and when two women and a girl appeared most of the night was spent in the *mesamer* despite the fact that the mountainside was so steep one could hardly stand up firmly, let alone wheel around in the dance.

He was up and away in time next morning to watch the sunrise above the Gulf of Akaba from the summit of St Katherine's mount, and he gazed out in wonder across Sinai's great granite heart, the rocky wilderness of serrated peaks, irrupting echelon upon echelon.

This height was too good a vantage point to be missed, and from it he took many bearings. The Arabs were shocked and appalled: they had thought him one of them; now, compass and pencil revealed, their worst suspicions were aroused. He had come to the mountains to practise enchantment—he would carry away the rain!

In consequence, the return journey to Cairo was very much less happy than the outward one. It might have been extremely unpleasant had "the faithful Hamid" not been at his side, and of more service to him then "than all the firmans of the Pasha could have been".

After the episode on Jebel Katerina, the trip to Omm Shomar, the previously mentioned attempt to discover the source of the "booms", had to be made in secret with Hamid. On their return to the monastery Louis was met by furious Arabs who argued threateningly at length. Knowing their appetite for meat, he managed to pacify them by a gift of mountain goat.

The monks and Sharhati were greatly relieved to hoist him back safely into the monastery, having fully expected him to be killed by the Bedouin. That night several Greek friends of the monks who had arrived from Tor and Suez were so generously plied with date brandy in the priests' private rooms during the evening that they all retired to bed tipsy.

In an outer wall of the monastery there is a shrine to el Khidr—a first class saint among Bedouin.* The brother of a sheik who seemed still friendly towards Louis was about to give a thank-offering feast before this little chapel, and Louis was invited.

* *Kadar* or *Khidr* means power. The saint appears to be St George (of Beirut), England's patron saint. *Khidr*, or the "animating power of nature", is also associated with both Elijah and Alexander the Great.

Much against the monks' advice he lowered himself down by rope from the window, and sat for several hours with the Arabs over the sanctified meal. In the course of the evening he was invited to yet another feast, which was due to take place the following day in Wadi Saleh. But as he had offended so many people by the incident of the compass bearings, he thought it might be as well to leave for Cairo unseen in the small hours, while the feast was still in progress in the wadi.

Having then said goodbye to the monks, especially to the worthy prior, who presented him with a newly shot leopard's skin, some rock crystals and a few small pieces of Sinai cinnabar, he set out secretly long before dawn with Hamid, his brother, Shaharti and two camels. Hamid's brother, however, proved treacherous: when he realised that Louis intended to climb Mount Serbal that morning, he left them and hurried off to inform the feasting sheiks in the wadi. Whereupon a messenger was sent to waylay Louis on his return.

The climb of Jebel Serbal was completely exhausting. Louis and Hamid tackled it alone, barefooted. With difficulty he managed to reach the summit and copied some strange inscriptions there. He thought it probably a very ancient site of worship —no doubt similar to the Nabataean High Places of Petra.

When he awoke the following morning in Hamid's garden down in Wadi Feiran, he found himself surrounded by some thirty furious Arabs, all agog to pick a fresh quarrel about his pursuits on their mountain tops. Since he paid little attention to their loud chorus of protest, and merely sat where he was calmly beginning to pack up his belongings for the journey to Cairo, they changed their tune and began asking for supplies, and coffee beans. Eventually everyone was satisfied, and in return for his gifts they loaded him with milk, cucumbers, and a paste of ground lotus seed.

But a little further on yet another vociferous group barred the way.

I gave them nothing, telling them they might seize my baggage if they chose, but this they prudently declined to do. Ten years ago I should hardly have been able to extricate myself in this manner.

So, in his quiet way he expressed his readiness, his ability to handle dangerous men, his complete qualification for the great journey still to be done—when that long awaited caravan should at last arrive in Cairo.

# CHAPTER NINETEEN

## *The Caravan Moves On*

The innumerable caravan, which moves
To that mysterious realm, where each shall take
His chamber in the silent halls of death.
*William Cullen Bryant*

DESPITE THE FACT that he had never ventured across the desert beyond Suez, Hamid readily agreed to go on to Cairo, since, as Louis said, "fear seemed quite unknown to this excellent young man".

The plague was over in the city: Louis was eager to return, and willing to risk starting the journey on their own as they expected very shortly to catch up with some Towara charcoal burners, who had preceded them from Suez.

But near the Castle of Ajerud after sunset, they saw the lights of several fires in the distance and rode towards them in the darkness, thinking to meet the Towara Bedouin. It was a shock to see instead the dreaded Omrah camped around a well. Using all his ability to bluff, with a fine assumption of Turkish hauteur Louis effectively made out that he belonged to the Pasha's army—and the two young men retreated hastily with Sharhati to the castle. They found its Turkish garrison in distress, and virtually water-less, the Omrah having command of the only supply. The brave Hamid made several fruitless sorties while the blockade lasted. On the third day the castle was relieved by the arrival of a large caravan from Suez, and soon afterwards Louis re-entered Cairo.

The two months spent in Sinai—if dangerous—had been as exhilarating as an adventurous holiday. He had only once, towards the end, had any recurrence of the fever, the mountains had been a delight, and the contact with the Bedouin stimulating.

Louis was a soldier's son—had it not been for the effects of the Napoleonic era upon Basle he would very likely have been a soldier himself; it was natural that he should feel this kinship with the Bedouin and, despite the petty annoyance of their superstitious fears, he recognised their courage and proud spirit of independence. For, as Gibbon said: "the patient and active virtues of a soldier are . . . nursed in the habits and discipline of a pastoral life".

Louis' experiences had taught him, as he wrote now to Gedeon, that he had reached the age—he was thirty-one—at which a man's body is best able to endure the greatest hardship. Heat, physical discomfort, poor food had never held any terrors for him, only "unhealthy air and bad water" were the things that not even the toughest physique could stand. His hopes and assurance had never been higher. The last thing he wished for was to linger on in Cairo: his only desire was to complete his mission for the African Association.

While his job was to tackle the problem of penetration from the eastern side, news now arrived that the English government had recently equipped two large expeditions intended to explore Central Africa from the western approaches. Hearing of this he wrote to his mother a few days after his return from Sinai:

one of them is meant to travel up the River Congo by boat, the other to visit the sources of the Niger, about which the explorer Mungo Park has previously given some hints. It would be pleasant if we could meet in Central Africa, and if I could leave very soon it might be possible. But there are still delays, and I cannot fix the date when I shall be able to leave Egypt. To remain here begins to depress me.[31]

His mother replied to his letter evincing anxiety that the big English expedition might deprive him of the recognition of his work in that area; on this score he told her not to worry:

People have some sense of justice, and will be able to differentiate between an expedition by a corps of soldiers, and a single

person who travels without any escort. . . . Whatever my fate
may be in the future I hope I shall have achieved something
which will free me from envying others for their discoveries,
and which will bring honour to my name.[32]

He goes on to thank his mother for her care in not talking of
his plans and letters so as to avoid anything about him getting
into the newspapers. He warns her again that when he left Egypt,
which would be soon, he hoped, she must be prepared to be
without news of him for two or three years since there was little
chance of being able to correspond with Europe while he was
away.

But my superiors in London will see to it that they get news
about me secretly, and I promise that you will be informed from
England if anything is heard of me.[33]

In July 1816, he wrote sadly to the Committee to tell them that
the accustomed time had again gone by when a Fezzan caravan
might have arrived in Cairo. It was a situation which left him in
an almost unbearable state of suspense—suspense so acute was
hard to control. Rumour had it that the great Mahgribin caravan
was to pass through that October, after many years cessation, on
its way to Mecca for the Haj. If this were true it might be possible
for him to join it on its return some months later—should no
earlier opportunity arise—and so reach Fezzan by a circuitous
route.[34]

The prospect of so long a delay was deeply depressing: but
he was too wise and experienced to be driven into taking any ill-
advised steps, however strong his feelings might be. He wrote
that he would prefer to submit himself "to the temporary im-
putation of a neglect of duty rather than act with rashness"
against his convictions.

On his return from Sinai Mr Salt had waiting for him a pair
of pocket compasses sent by the Association, and a letter that was
more than welcome. Louis had written then in gratitude to Mr
Hamilton:

This letter was from my mother; and I can find no terms adequate to express my thanks for your kindness in informing my mother of my welfare, and of the satisfaction which my services have caused to my employers. Next to the desire of contenting the latter, that of contributing to the happiness of my mother is the most fervent I have in this world. So flattering a testimony as that which came from you, could not fail to excite in her heart very lively emotions, and has created in mine sentiments of lasting and heartfelt gratitude towards their authors.

Each year, towards the end of June, a great stillness seemed to herald the inundation. Then gradually the flood waters rose, spreading out until all Egypt was a lake mirroring a blaze of golden dawns and fierce vermilion sunsets. Every morning the water level's nightly increase, checked as from time immemorial was announced by a town crier. Every evening seemed a festival: in merry mood the people—as the ancients had before them through untold centuries—rejoiced at the annual miracle of the Nile bringing on its swelling flood promise of abundance and fertility to all their fields. At night fireworks deluged velvet-dark skies with gaily cascading lights: dancing monkeys, dancing dogs, dancing girls, all contributed to the festive feeling of the inundation's height.

Now brimming full, the canal behind Louis' little house had become a place of beauty affording him great pleasure. On moonlit evenings the water rippled silvery in the wake of innumerable gondola-like boats, laden with people, plying up and down leisurely, to mandolin music and wailing Arab song— none too melodious to Louis' ears, but nevertheless there was gaiety and enchantment for him in the visual scene.

Louis waited and waited through hot languorous moonlit nights and still days, half listening as he worked to the cool plash of water and the soft thud and thrust of small boat sounds beneath his window, all the time throttling his growing impatience as best he could with the magic of work.

There was much to be done and it helped although nothing

could compensate for the delay. He worked on Arabic literature, the details of his journals and treatises, and studied Makrizi, the fifteenth-century Arabic historian and geographer. The letters he wrote to the Committee during this period show how deeply he felt the disappointment caused by the non-arrival of any caravan from the interior.[34] They also contained much information and wise observations on current events in Egypt, as well as other travellers' tales annotated with his own shrewd comments. All this was of immense use and interest to the Association; and since the comments of the average transient traveller were only too often "replete with error" the Committee valued his letters enormously.

> The remarks of a person who unites good sense and judgment to local knowledge and experience, are of the highest value in countries where every branch of enquiry presents results so different from our preconceived notions . . . where accurate information is very difficult to acquire.[35]

There is in Leake's *Memoir* a feeling of deep sympathy, and understanding of what their traveller was going through now in those long months of uncertainty in Cairo. They had the highest possible hopes of him—their most brilliant traveller.

To the vast majority of orientalists of that day the spirit of the East was still largely a sealed book. To them the East, as far as they knew it, was colourful, interesting, fascinating, remote; indeed several Englishmen of the time wrote of it in language that was more vivid than Louis as a foreigner could command. But they saw it in a slightly patronising way, as superiors, and also superficially from the outside. Louis was within; and to him the spirit was unobscured. It seems fair to say that not until the classic works of Burton nearly half a century later, and those of Lane, not from the literary aspect comparable to Burton but having a wonderful insight, did any other European surpass him in his knowledge of that field.

Of the Bedouin in particular he had a remarkable and, it appears, the first real understanding—of their pride, nobility, and independence. Even today they are only too often, in loose political thought, lumped with other Arabs—so that the modern tragedy of Jordan, for instance, is rarely visualised in full.

The Italian, Belzoni, who so much admired Louis and may well have been quoting him said: "the Bedouin are no more like the Arabs of Egypt than a free man is like a slave"—this, of course, in the days of Mohammed Ali's despotism.

From Cairo that autumn of 1816 Louis wrote to London:

The repeated notices I have transmitted concerning the Bedouins of Arabia, will show how much I am interested in them. I believe that very little of their real state in known in Europe, either because travellers have not sufficiently distinguished Bedouins from Arabs in general, or because they have attempted to describe them without having the advantage of seeing them at leisure in their own tents, in the interior of the desert. Their nation is of the original stock from which Syria, Egypt, and Barbary derive their present population . . . they acquire a still greater interest when we consider, that amidst . . . depravity . . . and decline (in the middle-eastern world) . . . the Bedouin are the only . . . nation who have preserved unchanged their ancient customs, and the manners of their forefathers, and who still continue to be what they were twelve hundred years ago, when their emigrating tribes conquered part of Asia, Africa, and Europe.*[36]

He then goes on to apologise for sending his papers in what he called so imperfect a state. He was in excellent health, but his eyes were bothering him again; they were far from being as he would have wished. Since the serious attacks of ophthalmia in Upper Egypt his eye trouble had recurred only too often, and again just recently he had suffered severe and painful inflammation.

Now also a stupid embroilment with Lady Hester had begun which, although trifling really, was obviously provoking. It was an irritant that he sometimes surmounted by making flippant, or

* The Hyksos, first conquerors of ancient Egypt, were men of the Sinai Bedouin, according to Gibbon.

even caustic replies. Those were the days *par excellence* of letter writing, but all things considered one would think he might have been better advised to leave the matter alone, and not commit his remarks to paper. Lady Hester's huge and virulent hand, witty though its sentences may have been, was surely only too familiar to her numerous correspondents and too well known for the gossiping jealousies and slanders it conveyed to be taken over-seriously.

In a letter to his mother, Louis refers to Lady Hester as "that evil woman" in Syria:

> If one does not humbly submit to her orders, kiss her hand, and permit her to dominate one completely, one exposes one-self to her malicious tongue. She keeps writing rude letters to me, which I answer with funny and highly flattering expressions, or sometimes very rudely so that she gets quite furious. But she is too well known to find anybody who will believe her slanderous talk about me.[37]

That he wrote such retorts does not sound characteristic of him but at least he seems to have been very honest as to his reactions to Lady Hester's onslaught, perhaps inadvertently she served him once again with some light relief. At any rate no one did seem to take much, if any, notice of her reports against him.

Towards the end of the year the correspondence by which they had attacked each other mercifully ceased,[38] but she then began hatching various complaints against him in letters to England and, loving the French as she did, was now bent on assuring people at home that the famous Sheik Ibrahim's attachment to England was a mere sham, and that he had once offered his services to Bonaparte.

And since she was quite in the dark as to the reason for his long stay in Egypt she ascribed it to laziness:

> and says that the quietness of Cairo, and its prostitutes, have deprived me of all activity and strength . . . she also persecutes with her hate Mr Bankes, the traveller, to whom I gave a letter

for you last year [*he wrote to his mother*] and who . . . in Syria was not inclined to pay much attention to her insane and domineering behaviour. As he will have arrived back in England by now and moves there in high society, I suppose he will defend himself and myself also, and expose the high and mighty person to the ridicule she deserves. She wishes that I should go down on my knees and pray for her forgiveness and *de baiser la main qui frappé* to make sure of her patronage. But . . . my own superiors could tell her how unable I am to humble myself for the sake of being patronised.—Don't be worried about this quarrel . . . she cannot do me any harm except for her slander which might perhaps be believed by those who do not know me. But I care very little about it because I wish to be loved and respected only by those whom I respect and love myself.

To his faithful correspondent, Renouard, now installed at Cambridge as professor of Arabic, he mentions lightly in "a gossiping way" this "deadly warfare with her travelling Ladyship" —as a direct result of that cheerful time in Alexandria with Turner and Missett the previous summer. It had first produced "a very angry and extremely pointed letter from her Ladyship", which she had followed up "with a kind of circular letter" to all his friends in the Levant endeavouring to blacken his name. She had given "this quarrel a publicity it did not deserve," he wrote.[39] However, none of it seemed to worry Louis very much; if anything her insinuations served as a spur to even harder work and study.

He was far more concerned to learn from the belated letter of Renouard that Buckingham, to whom he had "opened his heart" in Esne and in Jidda was not to be trusted. It seems that something of Louis' real intentions in Africa had leaked back through Buckingham's letters and accounts to reach the English press. Renouard wrote to warn Louis of Buckingham's only too garrulous and "knavish tricks", but the letter had arrived at least a year late. Louis felt that he had no excuse for having "been imposed upon by this virtuous and sentimental gentleman who has since been playing so many tricks", except the loneliness and lack of good company he had experienced during the long delay in Esne, and again in the Hijaz when he had mistalenly thought he could trust Buckingham and confide in him.

Earlier, before Christmas, 1915, Buckingham had returned to Cairo, having been banished from India. Louis had greeted him amicably once more, still having not received Renouard's warning—still not yet knowing "what sort of a narrator" Buckingham really was[40] with his liability to sabotage important efforts of discovery, and a habit of plagiarizing other people's works.*

Louis felt so strongly about the Buckingham scandal that he sent a very sharply worded paper to London (now in the India Office Library) so that others might not be taken in. W. Bankes wrote later: "Sheik Ibrahim was too open and too honourable to wish others to be deceived as he had been for a time himself."[41]

Buckingham again set off for India, now in the character of a Turk. When belatedly, in Syria, Barker heard from Alexandria of this adventurer's true nature, the Consul was authorised to take his dispatches from him and to dismiss him. But as he was already on his way to Bagdad "a Tartar was sent expressly after him for his recall but died accidentally upon the road !"[42]

Throughout his life Louis' nature remained friendly, warmly sociable, and in Cairo during this final and perhaps most difficult of all delays it was the company of real friends that he missed. Osman was a kindly man but quite lacking in the education that would have made any profound companionship possible. As for the newly arrived consul-general, Henry Salt, whom Louis had been looking forward to meeting again, he was often away and at first there was little time to get to know him. It was later that Salt came to find in Louis a most excellent friend.

Louis wrote to Gedeon:

Were I in Syria, or Arabia, I should not be so impatient, as I have friends there and would find the people of greater interest. Here I have neither the one nor the other, and if I

---

* From Buckingham's own evidence (in *Arab Tribes*) Murray refused to publish his book on Palestine, and it was only after much hesitation and apparent reluctance that Longmans eventually did so in 1825.

could not pass the time studying my Arabic manuscripts, I should scarcely be able to stay quiet.

In October that year some Bedouin arrived from the mountains of Sinai bringing him a camel-load of delicious pears from their orchards, and the skin of a leopard which they had recently killed. These were, no doubt, Hamid's relatives with news of the blood fine for that killing.

Louis' little household would have been pleasant enough had it not been for the restlessness of this time. He had his faithful Egyptian servant, Shaharti, Osman whom he must have been beginning to train as a dragoman, a slave-boy for the donkeys, and a slave-girl to do the washing and cooking. He was careful to live in a simple way still, so as not to pamper himself or allow his body to soften.

News that October of the safe shipment down the Nile of the colossal head of the Memnon was cheering and pleased him greatly. A hundred and ten *fellahin* working to Belzoni's ingenious instructions had taken a whole month to move the huge bust from where it had lain at Thebes to the river bank. Now Belzoni was in Nubia working on his first attempt to clear the torrents of sand from the Great Temple at Abu Simbel, found by Louis four years previously.

The joint enterprise with Salt—Louis was extremely punctilious about the payment of his share down to the last piastre—for the removal of the great head of Memnon gave Louis immense satisfaction. He felt convinced it was a treasure which the British Museum would be glad to own, and he really hoped that the enterprise, of which he was not a little proud, would "resound in England to the honour of every Swiss".[43]

Just before Christmas, he wrote as was his custom to wish his mother a happy New Year, expressing himself even more warmly than usual. It was the last time that he would be able to write for this occasion—for some years at least.

But believe me that when in Central Africa the date comes again, I shall send my wishes for you to Heaven, and that as long as I am alive, with every new year, I shall carry you more sincerely and always gratefully in my heart as my dearest mother and best friend.

Salt had repeatedly promised to paint Louis' portrait to send to Switzerland. But as consul-general he was very busy, and often away for quite long periods in Alexandria—also there was still that nuance of *jalousie de métier* between them, or so Louis felt. As yet Salt had found time to make a pencil study only: Louis hoped to persuade him further by translating, especially for him, a rare Arabic manuscript on the history of the pyramids—which would be invaluable to Salt since he was writing an essay on the subject.

Louis was thirty-two that November but he thought he looked more like a man of forty, and he warned his mother gently that he was no longer *"le joli homme"* he once had been. His face was brown and creased by blazing sun and searing sands, but he hoped that when the time came to shave off his beard, and to shed the Turkish clothes which he habitually wore, he might be quite *"présentable"* again one day.

So the winter passed in work. In March 1817, he received an enthusiastic letter from Mr Hamilton written on behalf of the African Association as a whole. The warmth of its unanimous praise more than rewarded him for all he had been through, and proved that he had the Association's profound trust. Whatever his future fate this assurance was of immense consolation now, and it showed that Lady Hester's slanders had borne no fruit in London among those who mattered to him in his work. In addition, Mr Hamilton had promised to call upon Frau Burck-hardt and Rosine when he was next in Switzerland. Hamilton, Louis wrote to his mother, would be able to tell her more about him than any other person could since he had read all the travel journals; she was sure to like him, he was a very learned man but not in any pedantic Teutonic way.

Early in June 1817 he sent off, in the care of a captain sailing for Malta, the last package of his works: the manuscript of the Arabic Proverbs.

High summer again: the beginning of the inundation once more, a time of brimming beauty, islanded villages mirrored in the glinting saffron flood, and the delight of those loveliest of all Nilotic flowers, "the brides of the Nile"—the lotus.

Some grew profusely in one of the *birkets* near Louis' house.[44] He loved them. He knew how the children played with the hollow stems, and saw how closely the seed vessels in their small brown hands resembled those painted plants held by Theban priests of the ancient murals. He describes too the fully opened bloom, a circlet of pointed petals of hyacinthine blue that swims on the surface of the water for some days until it is engulfed.

Once, at Damietta, a boatman had told him how the plant died and decayed when the floods subsided; it was therefore, Louis thought:

a fit emblem of life in all its vigour and luxuriance while it blossoms during the inundation . . . the certain cause and forerunner of plenty in Egypt. It is an emblem of death also when quite open as the flood retires. Or it may be understood differently, (and I believe the Egyptians did understand it in both senses;) as indicating while in blossom that everything is covered with water, and nature as it were asleep; and indicating when in a state of decay that nature is restored to life, for soon after that period seeds are sown by the husbandmen—this, inundation is life in one sense, and death in another.

He was right; the ancient Egyptians had visualised the creation of the world out of moisture, symbolised in the lotus.[45] From the mud rises the jewel in the heart of the flower—the aspiring spirit of man, the mystical *omne padme hum* of the Buddhists.

Everywhere the boats were out again, the canal behind Louis' house brimming once more, gay with people and song. July came, and still no sign of a caravan from the west. He wrote to his mother that month in gratitude for a letter the tone of which had breathed contented peace in every line. This contentment of hers, arising as it did from the praise he had received, gave him further great consolation. Not that he was unhappy, he hastened to assure her, but the waiting made him all too restless, and now he was bothered by "a number of acquaintances" whom he sincerely wished he had never met. He thought that perhaps he would one day be justified in keeping apart from people who did not really interest him—though in doing so he would probably be considered odd. And in his humble way he wondered if he would ever be able to return to his own country without being labelled peculiar should he deviate slightly from strictly conventional behaviour. Not that the thought worried him greatly.

Of his writing he said:

> As soon as they hear in London that I have left this place they will start to publish my reports and I hope at least some parts of them, e.g. my two journeys through Nubia and the one through Arabia, will be translated into French or German. When I return I shall edit a German translation myself.

Egypt was now "teeming" with European travellers, though none had yet dared to venture up the Nile as far as he had.[46] All were busy collecting antiquities, even squabbling like a pack of hyenas over their finds; while Cavilglia, the Genoese captain, had just discovered buried beneath sand the beautiful temple between the paws of the Sphinx, below godlike Mykerinos.

There had been a severe famine in Syria recently and—aftermath of war—a general shortage throughout Europe. In consequence Egypt's trade flourished and her ports were full of foreign ships loading her grain. Louis told his mother that he expected they had most likely eaten Egyptian wheat at home that year. News of dearth and poverty in Switzerland had touched him deeply. His funds were low on his first hearing of it—there had been the extra expenses of the Memnon head—but on 20 August he was able to send a cash draft which he enclosed in a brief letter to his mother asking her to distribute the money realised among the needy Swiss of Zurich.

> It is so little that I cannot imagine that I have done much good, but if this small sum is used for blankets and clothes it may help a few families to face the coming winter more comfortably.

September: the inundation began to subside; as the flood waters waned and fell away so the blue lotus flowers which he loved withered and died. Egypt's soil, again exposed, lay bare, refertilised and ready for the new season's crops.

Then at last it happened: among pilgrims bound for that year's Haj a small party of Maghribin arrived in the city *en route* for Mecca. They expected to return by the same way, through Cairo and across the Fezzan, around about the middle of December. Louis was overjoyed.

Often now in the early evenings he would walk and talk with Salt—they were beginning to know and like each other better—in the pleasant garden of the British Consulate. It was a small walled garden laced with many leafy paths, where one might quench one's burning eyes in cool shade. The day's work done, they would frequently stroll up and down talking of the latest news from Belzoni at Thebes, of the long awaited caravan to the Fezzan, of Louis' coming great journey to the unknown interior. Together too they would smile over the recent "ephemeral productions" of some superficial travellers whose garbled accounts of Egypt were then winning praise in London that was palpably absurd; glib writers who, as an Indian once so nicely put it, simply—"take walk make book".

It was all very pleasant; Louis' happiness and anticipation made him more than ever companionable, Salt was growing to value his friendship and to respect him greatly as a man. At this time too news came from Nubia of Belzoni who had managed at last on the second attempt to open the Great Temple of Abu Simbel and—by the Naval officers who had helped him—he sent back descriptions of its astoundingly beautiful interior. He was now in upper Egypt to dig in the Valley of the Kings.

Salt decided to go up the Nile to see for himself something of all this new work—in about the middle of October it might be possible for him to get away. Louis, of course, would not accompany him, he would be keeping himself fit and in readiness, writing letters of farewell, making his final arrangements to join the caravan to Fezzan.

One evening in Salt's garden Louis met Lord Belmore, then on a tour of the eastern Mediterranean, and his personal physician, Dr Richardson, a pleasant man who, like so many others, found considerable enjoyment in "the enlightened and agreeable society of Burckhardt".[47]

Spare but broad-shouldered, sturdy, and as he was then at the height of his strength, Louis appeared remarkably healthy. He was a highly entertaining conversationalist, always cheerful and animated, in fact to look at him one would have thought that never was there a man more likely to live to a good old age, he seemed physically so sound and full of vitality.

But suddenly, at the beginning of October a slight attack of dysentery began. When, by the fourth of the month, the symptoms had increased he consulted Dr Richardson privately at Mr Salt's house. The doctor gave him what medicines he could: they all continued to meet frequently in the Consulate garden, and Louis retained every appearance of health.

On 10 October, Mr Salt took Lord Belmore and Dr Richardson to see the pyramids of Gizeh, Dashur and Sakkara—an expedition lasting a day or two. On the evening of their return downstream to Cairo the wind dropped before sunset; taking to their oars the boatmen sang cheerfully to the rhythm of each stroke. Painted houses on the vivid banks shone like daubs of chrome in the westering gold. The day's labour done, numerous boats ferried people from one side to the other as they have since the times of the Pharaohs. The boatmen were merry, the whole riverine scene was animated and yet deliciously peaceful, lapped in the apricot colours of dying sunlight. But for Richardson, the evening's charm was drastically destroyed when he found several notes from his "worthy and intelligent friend, Mr Burckhardt" awaiting him at the Consulate.

During the Consular party's short absence at the pyramids, Louis' health had deteriorated alarmingly. Now, to make matters worse, it was impossible to visit him in the distant Turkish area, since each separate walled quarter of the city was locked at eight o'clock every night.

Very early the next morning, Shaharti was waiting anxiously at the Consulate, and Dr Richardson was led to see Louis, for the first time in his own house. For the next few days the doctor continued to give him every professional assistance in his power. But all efforts were ineffectual to combat an illness which had taken so deep a hold on an intestinal system already weakened by previous attacks. One wonders a little if Dr Richardson realised, at the time, just how serious was this illness. There was however no remedy—even the cause of dysentery was then still uncertain. Fatally obstinate, it took rapid toll despite Louis' physical strength, and his tremendous will to live.

Osman and Shaharti, or both, were constantly at his bedside doing what little they could for him in his pain and sleeplessness. He lost so much blood; with terror they watched the visible weakening of their stalwart, lovable master. At night, as the candles burned low it seemed that before their very eyes his sun-tanned face draining of colour was becoming more pallid even than the wax itself.

14 October: ironically, "Burckhardt Day"—the day of the annual family gathering at Basle. Louis' thoughts, if he knew the date as one fears he did, must have turned painfully to his home-land then.

On the next day, only the eleventh since the first serious signs of his illness—Monday 15 October—he felt the battle was almost finished. He knew that he had not long to live. That morning he asked Dr Richardson if Mr Salt might now be sent for: he wished to speak to him.

The unaccustomed visits of Europeans at Louis' Turkish house had already drawn a crowd of neighbours, most of whom knew that their Sheik Ibrahim was dying. They had great respect for him, indeed veneration—the young, the learned, the brilliant haji—in their eyes he even had, it was said, something of the aura of a saint.*48 They did not want the Christians to take his body: they began clamouring that it must be buried in the Muslim cemetery, the City of the Dead beyond the Bab el Nasr.

When Salt received Louis' message he had been on the point of

* Until recently there was a street in Cairo called Shari al-Shaykh Barakat, said to be the name adopted by Louis or for him by his Muslim friends—*barakat* meaning blessings, a pleasant play on words.

departure by boat for Thebes and, although he set off for Louis'
house immediately, it seems there was some delay for it was not
until afternoon that he reached the Turkish quarter. The crowd
before Louis' door, while staring at the arrival of another European and so high-ranking a one at that, parted in silence to let him
through.

The scene in Louis' room as Salt then beheld it affected him
so grievously with sadness that it was to cast a shadow over the
few remaining years of his own life.[49] The tragic wastefulness,
and the pitiful yet magnificent courage of the man struck to his
heart. He wrote afterwards to London saying that he could find no
words to describe how shocked he was at that hour, to see the
terrible change which had taken place in his friend in so short a
time.

> On the Tuesday before, he had been walking in my garden with
> every appearance of health, and conversing with his usual live-
> liness and vigour; now he could scarcely articulate his words,
> often made use of one for another, was of ghastly hue, and had
> all the appearance of approaching death. Yet he retained his
> senses, and was surprisingly firm and collected. He desired that
> I should take pen and paper, and write down what he should
> dictate.[50]

The sun set, and the xanthic light of *mahgrib*'s hour began to
fill the room. There was a brief silence as Osman fetched paper
and ink, then from a neighbouring mosque a blind muezzin's call
to prayer drifted out above the rooftops, melodiously melancholy:
"*La ilaha ila Allah taala!*" When the last long-drawn note had
died away, and Salt was ready, Louis began to speak with difficulty.

"If I should die now, I wish you to draw upon Mr Hamilton for
£250—money due to me from the Association—and with the
2,000 piastres I have in Mr Boghoz' keeping make the following
dispositions—. Pay up my share of the Memnon head. . . ."

This Louis repeated again carefully, fearing that Salt should
think he had already contributed enough as Salt had once hinted,

knowing him to be far from wealthy and very generous in his commitments to others.

With increasing effort Louis struggled on: "Give 2,000 piastres★ to Osman, and 400 piastres to Shaharti, my servant. Let my male and female slaves and whatever I have in the house—which is little—go to Osman. Send 1,000 piastres to the poor at Zurich. . . . Let my whole library—except my European books—go to the University of Cambridge . . . to the care of Dr Clarke . . . also the manuscripts now held by Sir Joseph Banks. My European books—I leave to you, Mr Salt. Of my papers make a selection as you think fit, and send them to Mr Hamilton. . . . I was starting in two months' time with the caravan—going to the Fezzan,—thence to Timbuctu . . . but it is otherwise disposed. . . ."

With deep compassion Salt noticed how painfully he then bit back his emotion: the expression of his face as he spoke of the intended journey was "an evident struggle between disappointed hopes and manly resignation. Less of the weakness of human nature was perhaps never exhibited upon a death bed."

Mastering defeat, Louis mentioned next his affairs in Europe and his will held in London: according to which if he was not heard of in Central Africa before 1 January 1820 (eleven years after his departure from England), he was to be considered dead. By this will, after showing gratitude to a relative who had helped him during that difficult Leipzig period, he appointed his mother to benefit from all sums that might accrue from his work with the African Association. The Consul wrote on gravely, his heart leaden: the room was growing dark, and Shaharti came to light the candles moving the central one towards the table at which Salt was sitting. Louis spoke again, his voice now only a rasping whisper.

"Give my love to my friends . . ." and he mentioned several people whom he knew well in Cairo. ". . . write to Mr Barker . . ." Then he paused and finally with painful exertion said: "Let Mr Hamilton acquaint my mother with my death and say my last thoughts . . . have been with her . . ."

He could hardly trust himself to speak of her, and had left it strictly to the end; exhaustedly he added: "The Turks will take

★ About £100.

my body,—I know it,—perhaps you had better let them . . . it's not worth making a fuss about the place where these bones are deposited . . ."

There was a silence. Salt finished writing, and looked up from his papers at Louis. Dr Richardson and Osman stood quietly by. Louis then expressed a wish for the Consul to leave, and shook his hand as in taking a final farewell.

This tragic finality and deep sense of loss Salt bore heavily away with him—a burden that he never forgot. Richardson and Osman stayed with Louis until the end. *Isha* was sung out from the neighbouring minaret, the last call to prayer of the day. The gates of the Turkish quarter were shut. There was a murmuring of *sura* from the people waiting at the street door, the distant echo of a plaintive Arab song, the yelping of a pack of dogs, then the city fell quiet and slept, while above it a myriad stars sparkled in the wide clarity of the Egyptian sky.

At a little before midnight, only six hours after that long talk with Salt, Louis died. He went as bravely and quietly as he had lived—without any moan.

The funeral, as he had desired, was a Muslim one, conducted with all proper regard to his rank as haji, scholar and sheik. On foot the procession wound through the streets; Osman, the Scottish Muslim, Louis' old teacher, Mohammed, learned men from el Azhar, his many Turkish acquaintances, schoolboys and the blind professional mourners all followed the bier towards the Gate of Victory in the city walls. Prayers and appropriate *sura* were chanted as they went.

> Ya sin, by the wise Koran!
> Surely of the Sent Ones, Thou,
> Upon a right path!
> A revelation of the Mighty, the Merciful,

and:

> He it is who created you of clay—then declared the term of your life: and with Him is another prefixed term for the resurrection. Yet have ye doubts thereof!

Leaving the city by the Bab el Nasr they had only a little way to go for the tomb prepared for Louis' body lies near to that gate, at the edge of the great wilderness that he was so soon to have crossed.

Grievously shocked, Salt wrote many letters to England about his friend. This irreparable loss was:

a terrible blow to the African Association, which had built all its hopes and with justice upon him; he was enterprising, yet cool and prudent, had been ten years preparing himself, had become the perfect Arab, and in two months intended to set out . . . God has otherwise disposed it.[51]

The effects of Louis' death would never be erased from his mind, and bitterly convinced him "too strongly perhaps, of the futility of most of our pursuits. . . ."

The tributes from England are of a braver, wiser kind:

As a traveller he possessed talents and acquirements which were rendered doubly useful by his qualities as a man. To the forti-tude and ardour of mind, which had stimulated him to devote his life to the advancement of science, he joined a temper and prudence, well calculated to ensure his triumph over every difficulty. His liberality and high principles of honour, his administration of those generous qualities in others, his detesta-tion of injustice and fraud, his disinterestedness and keen sense of gratitude were no less remarkable than his warmth of heart and active benevolence, which he often exercised towards persons in distress, to the great prejudice of his limited means. No stronger example can easily be given of sensibility united with greatness of mind, than the feelings which he evinced on his death bed, when his mother's name, and the failure of the great object of his travels, were the only subjects upon which he could not speak without hesitation. By the African Association his loss is severely felt, nor can they easily hope to supply the place of one to whom birth, education, genius and industry conspired to render well adapted to whatever great enterprise his fortitude and honourable ambition might have prompted him to undertake. The strongest testimony of their approbation of his zealous services is due from his employers to their late regretted traveller; but it is from the public and from posterity, that his memory will receive its due reward of fame; for it cannot be doubted that his name will be held in honourable remembrance, as long as any credit is given to those who have fallen in the cause of science.[52]

From another source came:

. ._. his place will long remain unfilled, he was a traveller of no common description: his record shows what manner of man he was . . . In the deserts of Syria, Arabia, or Nubia, and in the hospitable mansion of the venerable patron of the Royal Society, was always the same cheerful and contented being . . . this extraordinary man. . . .[53]

In Constantinople, Turner, trying to complete his notes on the Arabs with which Louis had helped, was so moved by the news that he could not face his work without experiencing real distress.[54]

At the very time of Louis' death Belzoni, digging in the Valley of the Kings, had made his important find of the tomb of Seti I. A month later, Salt went to visit him in his triumph, but brought the sad news of Louis' death, which came to the Italian too as a cloud of grief and bitterness. It seems that it was from that moment at Thebes that Belzoni resolved to reach Timbuctu as if on behalf of the man he had so greatly admired for his integrity and unselfishness.*

Some years later, near this very tomb of Seti I, an English traveller found many inscriptions in Greek and Latin, signed with English, French and German names. Among them was one before which he stood a long time; written in pencil it ran: "*Ibrahim—Post Reditum suum a Limitibus Regni Dongolae*". A man felt small when he contemplated a life such as Burckhardt's—spent "in

* Belzoni died in this attempt.

patient toil, and self-denial, in study without remission and in the sad and cheerless path of lone and solitary enterprise".[55]

Solitary it certainly had been but not sad. Louis had travelled, as he once told the Pasha, because he had much pleasure in exploration, and cared very little about personal fatigue.

Osman, who subsequently became a well-known dragoman attached to the British Consulate, escorted many later travellers in Egypt, and sometimes he would take them to where, a little beyond the Victory Gate among crowded graves, Louis' small tomb lay. When the feast of Ramadan was ended this huge silent City of the Dead became suddenly a fairground. People went out to tend the graves taking palm fronds and sweet basil to lay upon them. There were chantings and prayers, lamentations and songs. Picnic meals were carried forth; the wealthy lavished food upon the poor; children's swings soared gaily. Voluptuous dancing girls swayed erotic hips, and after dark a web of furtive intrigue pulsated among tombs and tents.

One Englishman whom Osman took with him to tend Louis' grave on this festival felt that although the stone was modest the great traveller needed no written eulogy for he had died lamented by Muslim and Christian alike. "And sometimes when speaking of him to his friends you see a tear glisten in the eye, so animated are they in praising him."[56]

So his body was buried on the edge of the desert that his spirit loved: the immense wilderness stretching away from the city's walls under the clean air and the starlight, and the surging dust of fiery winds; all sun-scorched by day, at night the haunt of hyena, wild dog, and ghostly screech-owl, where in westering light Mamluks' pompous turrets and towers stood crumbling in fire and gold—regal tombs among the thousand humbler stones of which his was one.

Not that he would have cared how humble it was, nor where it lay—he had always known that "no man may tell the place in which his grave shall be dug . . ."

Less than two months after his death, the vanguard of the returning Mecca caravan approached the city riding westward from Suez—a line of camels stretching away across the desert as far as the eye could see. The main body of the pilgrims would arrive a day later but many light-hearted ones who had gone ahead, reaching their homes quickly, now sallied out of town again with flags and drums to meet their friends. Women sitting at the wayside sang in welcome of the pilgrims. And with the great caravan there rode a small contingent of tall gaunt men from the west—bound for the Fezzan and far beyond.

# Bibliography

Adearne, J. H. *Girlhood of Maria Josepha Holroyd.* 1896

Armstrong, Martin. *Lady Hester Stanhope.* 1927

Atiyah, Edward. *The Arabs.* 1958

Bankes, W. J. *Narrative of the Life and Adventures of Giovanni Finati* (2 vols). 1830

Bankes, Viola. *Dorset Heritage.* 1953

Barker, B. B. *Syria and Egypt under the last Five Sultans of Turkey. Experiences of Mr Consul General Barker* (2 vols). 1876

Bartlett, W. H. *Forty Days in the Desert.* 1849

Blanch, Lesley. *The Wilder Shores of Love.* 1954

Belzoni, Giovanni. *Narrative of the Operations and Recent Discoveries, etc., etc., in Egypt and Nubia.* 1822

Bodley, R. V. C. *The Messenger—the Life of Mohammed.* New York. 1946

Breasted, James Henry. *A History of Egypt.* 1905

Browne, W. G. *A Journey to Darfur,* etc. 1814

Bruce, Ian. *The Nun of Lebanon: The Love Affair of Hester Stanhope and Michael Bruce.* Their Newly Discovered Letters. 1951

Bruce, James. *Travels to Discover the Source of the Nile.* 1805

Buckingham, James Silk. *Autobiography of James Silk Buckingham.* 1855

— *Travels Among the Arab Tribes.* 1825

Burckhardt (Jean Louis), John Lewis (Johann Ludwig) *Travels in Nubia,* edited by W. M. Leake and with a *Memoir* by him. 1819

— *Travels in Syria and the Holy Land,* edited by W. M. Leake. 1822

— *Travels in Arabia* (2 vols), edited by Sir William Ouseley. 1829

— *Arabic Proverbs, or the Manners and Customs of the Modern Egyptians,* edited and with notes by Sir William Ouseley. 1830

— *Notes on the Bedouins and Wahabis* (2 vols). 1831

Burckhardt-Sarasin, Dr Carl. *Scheik Ibrahim* (Johann Ludwig Burckhardt) *Briefe an Eltern und Geschwister.* Basel. 1956

— *Oberst Johann Rudolf Burckhardt (1730–1813) der Ebauer des Kirschgartens.* Basler Jahrbuch. 1957

Burton, Sir Richard F. *Personal Narrative of a Pilgrimage to Al-Madinah and Meccah* (2 vols). New York. 1964

Byron, Lord. *Letters and Journals.* 1838

Bryant, Arthur. *Years of Victory. 1802–1812.* 1944

Caillaud. *Voyage à Meroë, 1819–22,* and *Plates with Descriptive Letter Press* (2 vols). Paris. 1823

Carrington, Richard. *The Tears of Isis,* the story of a new journey from the Mouth to the Source of the River Nile. 1959

Cleveland, Duchess of. *The Life and Letters of Lady Hester Stanhope* by her niece. 1914

Cochrane, R. *Gallery of Notable Men and Women.* 1879

Cotterell, Leonard. *Anatolia (Lost Worlds).* New York. 1962

Crichton, A. *Memoir of Burckhardt (Naturalist's Library Vol. 31).* 1843

Crowfoot, J. W. *The Island of Meroë.* 1911

Curzon, Lord. *Monasteries in the Levant.* 1849

D'Athanasi, Giovanni. *A Brief Account of the Researches and Discoveries made under the direction of Henry Salt Esq.* 1836

Dawson, Warren Royal. *Who was Who in Egyptology.* 1951

Denon. *Description de l'Egypte.* 1809

de Staël, Madame. *On Politics, Literature and National Character.* 1964

Dodwell, Henry. *The Founder of Modern Egypt.* A Study of Muhammad Ali. 1931

Doughty, Charles M. *Travels in Arabia Deserta* (2 vols). 1888

Edwards, Amelia. *A Thousand Miles up the Nile.* 1889

Emery, Walter B. *Egypt in Nubia.* 1963

Esin, Emel. *Mecca, the Blessed; Madinah, the Radiant.* 1963

Fisher, W. B. *The Middle East.* New York. 1957

Forster, E. M. *Alexandria, A History and A Guide.* New York. 1961

Fairburn. *Life of Thomas Coutts Esq.* 1822

Fedden, Robin. *Syria, an Historical Appreciation.* 1946

Gau, François Christian. *Antiquities de la Nubié.* 1822

Gibb, Sir Hamilton. *The Travels of Ibn Battuta A.D. 1325–1354.* Vol. I. 1958

— *Islamic Society and the Western World.* 1950

Gibbon, Edward. *The Decline and Fall of the Roman Empire.*

— *Autobiography* of (edited by Lord Sheffield).

Haik, Farjallah. *Liban.* Paris. 1958

Hallett, Robin. *Records of the African Association 1788–1831.* 1964

— *The Penetration of Africa to 1815.* 1965

Halls, J. J. *The Life and Correspondence of Henry Salt Esq. F.R.S. His Brittanic Majesty's Late Consul General in Egypt.* 1834

Hamel, Frank. *Lady Hester Stanhope.* 1913

Hamilton, W. R. *Several Parts of Turkey*, etc. 1809

Hansen, Thorkild. *Arabia Felix. The Danish Expedition of 1761–1767*, translated by James and Kathleen McFarlane. 1964

Harding, Lankester G. *The Antiquities of Jordan.* 1959

Haslip, Joan. *Lady Hester Stanhope.* 1945

Heisch, P. I. *The Memoirs of Lavater.* 1842

Henniker, Sir Frederick. Bart. *Notes During a Visit to Egypt, Nubia, the Oasis, Mount Sinai and Jerusalem.* 1823

Herodotus. *The Histories.*

Herold, J. Christopher. *Bonaparte in Egypt.* 1962

Hill, G. B. *The Memoirs and Life of Edward Gibbon.* 1900

Hill, Richard. *Biographical Dictionary of the Anglo-Egyptian Sudan.* 1951

Huxley, Sir Julian. *From an Antique Land.* 1954

Idris, Shah. *The Exploits of the Incomparable Mulla Nasrudin.* 1966

Irby, The Hon. Charles, and Mangle, James. *Travels in Egypt and Nubia, Syria and the Holy Land.* 1844

James, E. O. *From Cave to Cathedral, Temples and Shrines of Prehistoric, Classical and Early Christian Times.* 1965

Keating, Rex. *Nubian Twilight.* 1962

Kinglake, Alexander. *Eothen.* 1844

Knight, G. Wilson. *Lord Byron's Marriage: The Evidence of Asterisks.* 1957

Laborde, Leon, et Linant. *Voyage d'Arabie Petrée.* Paris. 1830

Lacarrière, Jacques. *The God-Possessed.* 1963

Lane, Edward. *The Manners and Customs of the Modern Egyptians.* The 1860 text with introduction by Mursi Saad el-din. 1963

Lawrence, T. E. *The Seven Pillars of Wisdom.* 1943

Leake, William Martin. *The Memoir* prefacing J.L.B.'s *Travels in Nubia* 1819

— *Preface* to J.L.B.'s *Travels in Syria*, etc. 1822

Legh, Thomas (M.P.). *Narrative of a Journey in Egypt and the Country Beyond the Cataracts.* 1816

Light, Henry (Capt. of the Royal Artillery). *Travels in Egypt, Nubia, Holy Land, Mount Libanon and Cyprus, in the Year 1814.* 1818

Luke, Sir Harry. *Malta, An Account and an Appreciation.* 1949

MacQuitty, William. *Abu Simbel.* 1965

Marsden, J. H. *Memoir of W. M. Leake.* 1864

Maundrell, H. *A Journey from Aleppo to Jerusalem.* 1810

Mayes, Stanley. *The Great Belzoni.* 1959

Meryon, Dr Charles. *Life and Memoirs of Lady Hester Stanhope*

Miller, William. *The Ottoman Empire. 1801–1913.* 1913

Mitchell, R. J. *The Spring Voyage.* 1964

Moorehead, Alan. *The Blue Nile.* 1962

Morris, James. *The Hashemite Kings.* 1959

Mountfort, Guy. *Portrait of a Desert.* 1965

Norton. *The Letters of Edward Gibbon* (3 vols, edited). 1956

Otter, The Rev. W. Editor of: *The Life and Remains of E. D. Clarke,* Prof. of Mineralogy Cam. (Vol. II). 1824.

Palmer. *Desert of the Exodus.* 1871

Parmelee, Alice. *All the Birds of the Bible. Their stories, Identification and meaning.* 1960

Philby, H. St John. *Forty Years in the Wilderness.* 1957

Planta, Gervais. *History of Switzerland* (abridged). 1825

Plowden, J. M. C. *Once in Sinai.* 1940

Posener, Georges. *A Dictionary of Egyptian Civilisation.* 1962

Prescott, H. F. M. *Once to Sinai. The Further Pilgrimage of Father Felix Fabri.* 1957

Prothero. *The Private Letters of Edward Gibbon.* 1896

Redding, Cyrus. *Fifty Years Recollections.* 1858

Richardson, Dr Robert. *Travels along the Mediterranean and Parts Adjacent in company with the Earl of Belmore during the years 1816–17–18* (2 vols). 1820

Roberts, David and Brockenden, R. A. *The Holy Land, Egypt and Nubia* (3 vols). 1842–9

Rodwell. Translation of *The Koran.* 1909

Salt, Henry. *Egyptian Antiquities.* 1835

Sherer, Moyle. *Scenes and Impressions in Egypt.* 1824

Shinnie, Margaret. *African Kingdoms.* 1961

Thesiger, Wilfred. *Arabian Sands.* 1959

Turner, William. *A Journal of a Tour in the Levant* (3 vols). 1820

Waddington, George (Fellow of Trinity, Cambridge). *Journal of a Visit to Some Parts of Ethiopia.* 1822

Walsh, R. *Account of the Levant Company.* 1825

*Journal of the Society for Army Historical Research.* Vol. 34

*The Calcutta Monthly Journal.* 1823
*The Quarterly Review.* 1809–1820
*The Gentleman's Magazine.* 1819
*The Journal of the National Geographic Society*, Washington. D.C. Vol. 129. 5 May 1966.

Photostat copies of the Sutro papers
W. R. Dawson's *Calendar* of Sir Joseph Banks' letters
Letters and MSS in the British Museum
Dawson's transcription of the *Westcar Diary*. MSS. B.M.
MSS in the Public Records Office
MSS in the Historical Commission
MSS in Cambridge University Library
and some privately held papers and letters belonging to the Salt family.
*Encyclopaedia of Religion and Religions.* Royston Pike. 1951
*Encyclopaedia of Islam.* 1st edition
*The Atlas of the Bible.* L. H. Grollenberg.
Baedeker's *Egypt and the Sudan.* 1929
— *Syria and Palestine.* 1893
— *Switzerland.* 1885
*Dictionary of National Biography* (D.N.B.)

# Reference Notes

## INTRODUCTION

1 *Petra* I. 132. John William Burgon. (Burgon has an odd link with Burckhardt, through Renouard, the scholarly priest by whom he—Burgon—was baptised at Smyrna in 1813. Renouard was one of Burckhardt's most trusted correspondents.)

2 *Memoir* in the Life and Travels of John Lewis Burckhardt (afterwards referred to as *Memoir*) by W. M. Leake in *Travels in Nubia* by J. L. Burckhardt. 1819.

3 *Scheik Ibrahim* (Johann Ludwig Burckhardt) *Briefe an Eltern und Geschwister* (afterwards referred to as *Briefe*). Edited by Carl Burckhardt-Sarasin and Hansrudolf Schwabe-Burckhardt. Helbing and Lichtenhahn, Basel, 1956.

4 *Dictionnaire Historique et Biographique de la Suisse*. Neuchâtel; 1924.

5 *A History of Egypt*. James Henry Breasted. 1905.

6 *The Years of Victory*. Arthur Bryant. 1944.

7 *The Encyclopaedia Britannica*.

8 *A Memoir of John Lewis Burckhardt*. Dr Andrew Crichton. Vol. 5. *The Naturalist Library*. 1843.

9 *Personal Narrative of a Pilgrimage to Al-Madinah and Meccah* (afterwards referred to as *Burton's Narrative*). Sir Richard F. Burton. Preface to Third Edition p. xx, Vol. I.

10 *Nubian Twilight*. Rex Keating. 1962.

11 *Ibid*.

12 *Travels in Arabia*. J. L. Burckhardt. Vol. I with a preface by Sir William Ouseley. 1829. (Afterwards referred to as *Travels in Arabia*.)


## PART I—THE EARLY YEARS

*Chapter One: Swiss Childhood*

1 *Letters of Gibbon*. Vol. II, pp. 332, 339.

2 *Memoirs of my Life*. Gibbon, p. 236.

3 *Ibid.*, p. 214.
4 *The Founder of Modern Egypt.* Henry Dodwell, p. 9.
5 *Briefe*, p. 168.
6 Bode, on Goethe.
7 *Ibid.*
8 Carl Burckhardt-Sarasin, p. 52. *Oberst Johann Rudolf Burckhardt* (1750–1813) *der Erbauer des Kirschgartens.*
9 *Ibid.*, p. 43.
10 Planta. Chap. XXXI, *History of Switzerland.*
11 Crichton. *Memoir* of J.L.B.
12 Planta. Chap. XXXVII.

*Chapter Two: In Malta—The Start of the Adventure*

13 This term is apparently in use today among those who deal with money both from the historical and the banking viewpoint: sources checked were a London banker and the Dept of Numismatics at the British Museum.
14 Add. MSS 27620. The B.M. letter to Renouard from J.L.B. dated 21 August 1808, from 114 Great Russell St, Bloomsbury Square.
15 *Dictionary of National Biography* (afterwards referred to as the *DNB*).
16 *The Penetration of Africa to 1815*, p. 173. Robin Hallett.
17 *Ibid.*, p. 196.
18 The Sutro Papers (photostat copies of the R.G.S.).
19 Letter written at Athens by G. Finlay Esq. in *Brief Memoir* of William Martin Leake. Hertford County Council Records Office. No. 85555.
20 Leake's *Memoir* to *Travels in Nubia.* p. v.
21 *Records of the African Association*, 1788–1831. Robin Hallett, p. 222.
22 Report of a Committee held in Sir Joseph Banks' house, March 21 1808. Photostats of the Sutro papers (the African Association records at R.G.S.).
23 Letter contained in the *Memoir*, p. vi.
24 *Penetration of Africa.* Robin Hallett, p. 379.
25 *Memoir*, p. vi.
26 *The Life and Remains of E. D. Clarke.* Vol. II, p. 617, edited by W. Otter.
27 *Ibid.*, pp. 585–6.

PART II—INTO ASIA

*Chapter Three: Eastwards—Beyond Antioch*

 1 Letter in *Memoir*, p. xi.
 2 *Ibid.*, p. xx.
 3 *Syria.* Fedden, p. 30.

*Chapter Four: The Aleppo Years of Training*

 4 *Travels of Ibn Battuta.* Vol. II, p. 97.
 5 J.L.B. *Syria*, etc., p. 146.
 6 *Anatolia.* Cotterell. *Lost Worlds*, pp. 300 and 312.
 7 Appendix to *Syria*, etc. J.L.B., no. II, p. 654
 8 *Encyclopaedia of Islam.* Vol. II, p. 572. 1st edition.
 9 J.L.B. *Syria.* Appendix II, p. 654.
10 *Travels in Egypt, and Nubia, Syria and the Holy Land.* Irby and Mangle, p. 72.
11 *Syria and Egypt under the Last Five Sultans of Turkey.* The experiences of Mr Consul General Barker, p. 28.
12 *Ibid.*, p. 153.
13 *Syria.* Fedden, p. 31.
14 *Syria*, etc. J.L.B. Appendix I, p. 634.
15 *Journal of a Tour in the Levant.* W. Turner. Vol. ii, p. 484.
16 *Bedouin and Wahabi.* J.L.B., p. 34.
17 *Memoir.* p. xxxi.
18 *Memoir*, p. xxxviii.
19 W. Turner. Vol. iii, p. 437.
20 *Syria*, etc. Baedeker, p. 193.
21 Fedden, p. 76.
22 Letters to Clarke, p. 593 (Otter).
23 *Memoir*, p. xxxviii.
24 *Ibid.*, p. xlii.
25 *Ibid.*, p. xli note.

PART III—THE WAY SOUTH

*Chapter Five: Two Syrian Journeys*

 1 *Memoir*, p. xliii.
 2 W. M. Leake, preface to *Syria*, etc., p. v.
 3 Turner. Vol. iii, p. 472.

4 Fedden, p. 157.
5 Letter to Clarke from J.L.B., p. 598 (Otter).
6 Fedden, p. 189.
7 Turner. Vol. iii, p. 478.
8 Letter in *Memoir*, p. xliii.
9 *Antiquities of Jordan*. Lankester Harding, p. 83.

*Chapter Six: The Road to Petra*
10 *Life and Letters of Lady Hester Stanhope*, the Duchess of Cleveland,
   p. 124.
11 *Malta*. Sir Harry Luke, p. 156.
12 *Lady Hester Stanhope*. Haslip, p. 116.
13 *Eothen*. Kinglake, p. 74.
14 Haslip, p. 84.
15 *Life and Letters of Lady Hester Stanhope*, p. 151.
16 *The Nun of Lebanon, the Love Affair of Hester Stanhope and Michael
   Bruce*. Ian Bruce, p. 159.
17 *Syria*, etc. J.L.B., p. 416.
18 *Memoir*, p. xlvi.
19 Leake, preface *Syria*, etc., pp. v–vi.
20 Lankester Harding, p. 117.
21 Jeremiah 49:17.


PART IV—INTO AFRICA

*Chapter Seven: "The Gift of the River"*
1 *Narrative*. Sir Richard Burton, p. 32.
2 *Narrative of a Journey in Egypt*. Thomas Legh M.P., p. 11.
3 *Memoir*, p. xivii.
4 *Several Parts of Turkey*. Hamilton, p. 342.
5 *Notes*, etc. Henniker, p. 74.
6 Lane, p. 387.
7 *Travels*, etc. Dr Richardson. Vol. i, p. 83.
8 Legh, p. 387.
9 *The Founder of Modern Egypt*. Dodwell, p. 231.
10 *Nubia*, etc. J.L.B., p. 410.
11 Lane, p. 181.
12 *Proverbs*, etc., J.L.B., p. 116.
13 B.M., MSS 30240a, p. 33.

14 Lane, p. 161.

15 *Briefe*, p. 173.

16 Turner. Vol. ii, p. 359.

17 Lady H. S. *Life and Memoirs*. Dr Meryon. Vol. iii, p. 65.

18 Preface, Legh.

19 *Ibid.*, p. 84.

20 *Bedouins and Wahabis*. J.L.B., p. 224.

21 *The Arabs*. Edward Aityah.

22 Henniker, p. 68.

23 Dodwell, p. 29.

24 *The Ottoman Empire*. Miller, p. 88.

25 *Narrative*, etc. of Finati. Bankes, p. 107–11.

26 Dodwell, p. 258.

27 *Ibid.*, p. 86.

28 *Travels*, etc. Light, p. 26.

*Chapter Eight: South through Nubia*

29 *From Cave to Cathedral*. E. O. James, p. 109.

30 *Nubian Twilight*. Rex Keating, p. 17.

31 *Travels*, etc. Irby, p. 35.

32 *Memoir*, p. li.

33 *Quarterly Review*. Vol. 22, xliv, art: viii, p. 437.

34 durra: there are two species of holcus cultivated in Egypt, alike in appearance but each bearing very different types of grain—one being maize in the north, the other a small millet-like grain in the south. Both are, or were then, called *dhura*.

35 The hoopoe appears in his charming plumage in a wall-painting done 3,700 years ago, in a rock tomb of Beni Hassan. Parmlee. *All the Birds of the Bible*, p. 121.

36 Hamilton, p. 212.

37 Legh, pp. 82, 84.

38 *Briefe*, p. 184.

39 Perhaps it was from people such as these, who spoke Arabic as well as Nouba, that Louis drew up his vocabularies. Linguistically Nubia was divided into two parts, Wadi Kenous and Wadi el Nouba. From Louis' evidence the Nouba language appears to decline the verb to love in several tenses, but the Kensy apparently in one only—or else it must be concluded that he went no further with that verb in Kensy than the first person singular of the present tense.

*Chapter Nine: Ozymandias*

40 *Journal.* Waddington, pp. 24, 25.
41 *Brief Account.* d'Athanasi, pp. 42, 46.
42 *Egypt in Nubia.* Walter Emery, p. 64.
43 Keating, p. 55.
44 *National Geographic Magazine.* Vol. 129, No. 5, May, 1966. Washington D.C., p. 725.
45 *Ibid.,* p. 748.

*Chapter Ten: The Desert Crossing.*

46 Clarke (Otter). Vol. ii, p. 604.
47 "Shendy". *Travels in Nubia.* J.L.B.
48 *Briefe,* p. 147.
49 *Memoir,* p. li letter in, Leake.
50 *Ibid.,* p. lviii.
51 *Ibid.,* p. xlix.
52 *Travels in Nubia.* J.L.B.
53 *Memoir.* Leake.
54 *Travels Among the Arab Tribes.* J. S. Buckingham, p. 639.
55 Letter from J.L.B. to Renouard, 10 July 1815. No. 29. Add. MSS 27620.
56 *Autobiography* of James Silk Buckingham. Vol. ii, pp. 179–80.
57 *Briefe,* p. 146.
58 *Travels,* etc. Light, p. 44.
59 *Ibid.,* p. 46.
60 MSS 27620, No. 21 25 June 1813.
61 *Ibid.* No. 24. 6 July 1813.
62 *Briefe,* p. 172.
63 The author has heard modern Egyptians discuss the link between this word *walad*, and the English noun—lad. But which derived from which seems uncertain, perhaps lad through the Crusaders, from the Arabic.
64 Proverbs. J.L.B. No. 381.

*Chapter Eleven: Slaves, Swords and Drink*

65 Herodotus. Book Two, p. 31.
66 *Egypt in Nubia.* Emery, p. 224.
67 *Ibid.,* p. 227.
68 Keating, p. 68.

69 *Penetration of Africa.* Hallett, p. 375.

PART V—THE ARABIAN DECISION

*Chapter Twelve: With the Slave Traders to the Red Sea*

1 Doughty. Vol. ii, p. 407.

2 Bruce wrote: that after leaving Shendi and passing through the five or six villages of the Jaheleen he alighted and here "begins a large island several miles long, full of villages, trees and corn, it is called Kurgos. Opposite to this is the mountain Gibbainy, where is the first scene of ruins I have met with since that of Axum in Abyssinia." Vol. iv. *Travels*, etc., p. 538.

There seems to have been something here, but it remains a mystery. Bruce guessed that this was a part of Meroë, whose latitude should be 16° 26″, and Kurgos to be Purgos—the tower or observatory of that city. *Travels.* Vol. iv, p. 539.

In Caillaud's Map, vol. ii, plate lv, *Voyages à Meroé* a "T" marks the spot at Koz Rejab indicating: "*lieux ou existent des temples*" and Leake in his preface to *Syria*, p. xix, says that Djebail, where Louis saw the ruins, is the same as Mount Gibbainy and that the place was afterwards "more completely" explored by M. Caillaud.

3 As in Jordan, so here also: the modern Egyptians often called their ancient temples churches, ascribing them to the work of Christians.

4 Besides being unlike true Bedouin in their extreme inhospitality, treachery also was not considered a crime or a disgrace; J.L.B. says here that a Hadendoa seldom had scruples about killing a companion on the road for his own gain and yet oddly enough the blood retaliation existed in full force. He heard too of a "horrible custom said to attend the revenge of blood among the Hallenga, a neighbouring tribe, who originated from Abyssinia; when the slayer has been seized by the relatives of the deceased, a family feast is proclaimed, at which the murderer is brought into the midst of them bound upon an *angarib* (bed), and while his throat is slowly cut with a razor, the blood is caught in a bowl, and handed round amongst the guests, everyone of whom is bound to drink of it at the moment the victim breathes his last." Louis with his characteristic attention to absolute truth, points out that he could not personally vouch for this but he had been told of it by several different people, and not a soul had been heard to contradict the truth of it. The method of killing is the Muslim way of slaughtering

an animal, so as to *avoid* the consuming of forbidden blood. In this connection the author is tempted to recount here the story of a young Muslim in modern Malaya who was reputed to have, and who boasted of having, tasted the blood of a freshly murdered middle-aged man (whose reputation as a great lover of women was wide)—so that he himself might acquire the dead man's prowess. But later this young Lothario also went too far in his own amorous escapades and was eventually hanged for murder in Kuala Lumpur gaol in 1958.

## Chapter Thirteen: Over the Sea to Jidda

5 *rikat*, Arabic—the hands on knees posture in ritual prayer.
6 This is identical with some Far Eastern customs. Not so very long ago the Chinese believed that in an eclipse the sun was being swallowed by a "celestial dog" and gongs were sometimes beaten to scare the monster away. Can such widespread archaic fear be a relic stemming from the Flood legends?

## Chapter Fourteen: Ordeal at Taif

7 *Narrative*, etc. Burton. Vol. ii, p. 138.
8 *Encyclopaedia of Islam*. Vol. iv, p. 621. 1st edition.
9 *Briefe*, p. 109.
10 *Once to Sinai*. H. F. M. Prescott, p. 133.
11 He was much criticised by the Rev. C. Francis, though upheld by Burton. *Narrative*, preface xx, Vol. i.
12 Turner, Vol. ii, pp. 386, 394, and *Narrative* etc., Belzoni, p. 6.
13 Dodwell, p. 37.
14 *Ibid.*, p. 38.
15 *Bedouins and Wahabis*. J.L.B., p. 282.
16 Dodwell, pp. 3, 4.

## Chapter Fifteen: Haji Ibrahim in Mecca

17 *Bedouins and Wahabis*. J.L.B., p. 285.
18 *The Messenger*. The Life of Mohammed. Bodley.
19 Ibn Battuta. Vol. i, p. 188.
20 The writer's Malay *munshi* in 1964. Haji K-R Ja'amat.
21 Rodwell's Koran. Note i, p. 455.
22 Genesis 21:14.
23 *Mecca the Blessed, Madinah the Radiant*. Emil Esin, p. 18—but Burton says: "the word Zemzem has a doubtful origin. Some

derive it from the Zam Zam or murmuring of its waters, others from Zam! Zam! (fill! fill! i.e. the bottle), Hagar's impatient exclamation when she saw the stream."

24 Ibn el Faredh, quoted by J.L.B. in *Travels in Arabia*, p. 234.
25 Ibn Battuta. Vol. i, p. 196.
26 *Narrative* Burton. Vol. ii, pp. 207–9.
27 *Travels in Arabia*. J.L.B. Appendix vii, Vol. ii.
28 *Ibid*. Appendix viii.
29 *Narrative*. Burton. Vol. ii, p. 179.
30 Emil Esin, p. 17, and R. V. C. Bodley, p. 319.
31 J. Esin, pp. 112–15.
32 J.L.B.'s *Bedouins and Wahabis*.
33 Turner, Vol. III, p. 470, and *Travels in Arabia*, J.L.B., Vol. ii, p. 13.
34 Ibn Battuta. Vol. i, Note 217, p. 244.
35 *Ibid.*, Vol. i, pp. 244, 245
36 *Ibid.*, Note 231, p. 246.
37 *Autobiography*. Buckingham. Vol. ii, p. 294.
38 *Ibid.*, p. 283.
39 *Ibid.*, p. 301.
40 J.L.B.'s *Bedouins and Wahabis*, p. 323.
41 *Ibid*.

*Chapter Sixteen: Plague*

42 *The Wilder Shores of Love*. Lesley Blanch, p. 23.
43 *Narrative etc*. Belzoni said that Ibrahim Pasha was the terror of the Arabs; a vile man, who actually had two Arabs roasted alive like rabbits on a spit at a slow fire, and fired a man off the front of a cannon, and so on (p. 22). Dodwell says more mildly that he had not his father's charm.
44 In justice to the Turk of today it must be pointed out that these so brutal soldiers of the Ottoman Empire were drawn not only from Turkey but very largely from Albania, the terrible Arnauts, who were the terror of the population wherever they were quartered. Burton said that he had never met a more reckless brood, wild, trigger-happy ruffians, "man-shooting appears a favourite sport with them" (vol. i. p. 133).

PART VI—THE MOVING FINGER

*Chapter Seventeen: A Month of Summer in Alexandria, the Winter in Cairo*

1 *Memoir*, p. lix. A letter from J.L.B.
2 *Ibid.*, p. lxi.
3 Turner, p. 487.
4 *Briefe*, p. 155.
5 *Ibid.*, p. 153.
6 *Ibid.*, p. 150.
7 Turner, p. 359.
8 *Briefe*, p. 158.
9 Buckingham, *Autobiography*. Vol. ii, p. 152.
10 J.L.B. Letter to Renouard. B.M. MSS 27620.
11 J.L.B. Letter to Clarke (Otter), p. 623.
12 Henniker, p. 35.
13 J.L.B. Letter to Renouard. B.M. MSS.
14 *Life*, etc. Salt, p. 131.
15 Athanasi, p. 6.
16 J.L.B. Letter to Meryon. Add. MSS 4251, University of Cambridge Library.
17 Legh, p. 135.
18 *Memoirs*, p. lxvi. Letter from J.L.B.

*Chapter Eighteen: The Desert of the Exodus*

19 *Briefe*, p. 166.
20 *Syria*, etc. Leake's Preface, p. v.
21 *Desert of the Exodus*. E. H. Palmer, p. 71.
22 Henniker, p. 15.
23 *Bedouin and Wahabis*. J.L.B.
24 *Ibid.*, Vol. i, p. 277.
25 Prescott, p. 85.
26 Henniker, p. 230.
27 Palmer.
28 Deut. viii:15.
29 Plowden, p. 151.
30 *Proverbs*, J.L.B., p. 222.

*Chapter Nineteen: The Caravan Moves On*

31 *Briefe*, p. 166.

32 *Ibid.*, p. 171.
33 *Ibid.*, p. 177.
34 *Memoir*, letter in, p. lxx.
35 *Memoir*, p. lxx. Leake.
36 *Memoir*, letter in, p. lxxi.
37 *Briefe*, p. 173.
38 *Ibid.*, p. 176.
39 Letter to Renouard, ff. 37. B.M. MSS. 27620.
40 *Ibid.*
41 *Arab Tribes*, Buckingham. Appendix, p. 618.
42 *Ibid.*, p. 607.
43 *Briefe*, p. 181.
44 *Proverbs.* J.L.B., p. 220.
45 *Dict. of Egyptian Civilisation*, p. 152.
46 *Briefe*, p. 187.
47 Richardson. Vol. i, p. 53.
48 Burton. Vol. i, p. 85.
49 Salt. Vol. ii, p. 40.
50 Salt, letter in *Memoir*.
51 Salt to Sir Francis Darwin. Vol. ii, p. 40,
52 Leake, end of *Memoir*.
53 *Quarterly Review.* No. 36, Vol. 22, p. 437.
54 Turner. Vol. iii, p. 463.
55 Sherer, p. 109.
56 *Westcar Diary*, p. 272. Dawson's transliteration. MSS. B.M.

# Glossary

aba     Arab robe of light wool

Aga     Turkish title meaning chief or master

*almeh*     singing and dancing girl in Egypt

Arnaut     Albanians

*avania*     extortionate tax

*agal*     the corded, often silken, circlet holding Arab headgear in place

Bey     Turkish title meaning "lord", junior to Pasha

*birket*     large water tank

*bouza*     drink made from fermented millet

*dahabeyah*     Nile sailing boat

*djin*     evil spirit

dragoman     from Arabic *tarjuman*, guide or interpreter for foreigners, contractor for the management of expeditions. Dragomans attached to embassies had special privileges.

Druse     A Syrian people inhabiting the Jebel Druse or Hauran, and parts of the Lebanon

Effendi     Turkish title, deriving from the Greek, meaning master

Emir     Arabic title meaning governor or prince

durra     millet

*faldetta*     Maltese women's head-dress

*fellahin*     Egyptian peasants

firman     a passport

*ghawazi*     "belly dancers"

Haj, *el*     The Mecca pilgrimage

haji     a pilgrim

*haram*     forbidden

*imam*     religious official of the mosque

*ihram, el*     the ritual bathing *and* the robe of Mecca pilgrims

*jalabiyyah*     long loose cotton gown worn in Egypt

Janissary     "new troops" of the Ottoman Empire

Kashif     governor of a district, responsible for collecting its revenues *khamsin*    hot dust-laden wind that blows in Egypt on about fifty days of the year

Kadi    Arabic judge

Kaya Bey    Prime Minister

*kawal*    effeminate male dancer of Egypt

*keffieh*    Arab muslin headkerchief

khan    caravanserai, the Arab inn

*kiblah*    the direction of Mecca

*kus-kus*    Basic north African dish of meat, grain and vegetable

*leben*    yoghourt

*madrasa*    theological college

*Mahmal*    the splendid tall camel bearing an ornate, empty litter on the pilgrimage, a mere emblem of royalty

*mahgrib*    the west

Maghribin    western Arabs, or Moroccans

Mamluk    slave-king of Egypt

Maronite    Christian Arabs of Syria, and Mount Liban; are now uniate catholics

Mek    Sudanese king

*melaye*    Egyptian stole or shawl

*mesamer*    Bedouin love dance

*miri*    general land tax

Misr, el    Cairo

*muezzin*    he who calls the faithful to prayer

*nabout*    a stave of Moroccan style

neophron    the white vulture or "Pharaoh's chickens"

Pasha    Ottoman Empire title of certain high ranking civil and military officials. A Pasha of Three Tails was the highest rank, the title derived from the number of horses' tails borne before him as standards commemorating an early Pasha who, seeing his standard cut down in battle, lopped off a horse's tail to bear instead in exhorting his troops.

Porte    see Sublime

*rais*    a captain

Ramadan    the month of fasting

*saqiya*    Persian water-wheel

*salam aleik*    polite greetings

*samun*    hot, dry, dust-laden wind moving in a straight, narrow track

*say*    a small boat

*shaduf*  pole with bucket and counterpoise, Nilotic irrigation gear

*souk*  a market

Sublime Porte  The first gate of the Old Seraglio (Eski Serai) at Constantinople, the Bab-i-Humayun, or 'Sublime Porte' gave its name to the Turkish government in its foreign relations

*sunt*  the acacia

*sura*  a chapter of the Koran

*thabout*  a large Moroccan style woollen cloak or burnous

ulema, or olema  Muslim doctors of sacred law and theology

Wahabi  the strict Puritans of Arabia whose name derived from their founder Wahab ibn Saud

*walad*  lad, boy

*wellah!*  "By God!"

# Notes on Illustrations

Frontispiece: this colour wash and line drawing was made by the author in Petra in the course of an overland journey from India in 1960.

The coat of arms on the title page is the Burckhardt Arms.

1. This charming water-colour by an unknown artist, of the Burckhardt children playing is reproduced by courtesy of the Historisches Museum, Basle.

2a. Old Basle by Dero is from a lithograph in the British Museum.

2b. From the Staatsarchiv, Basle.

3. This drawing of J.L.B. is from the print department of the British Museum, unsigned, it is perhaps from a study done for the missing portrait by Slater, made in London in 1808.

4a. This etching was made by Angelica Clarke expressly to send to Louis' mother. The original Slater portrait has so far not been traced. Photograph by courtesy of Radio Times Hulton Picture Library.

4b. From an oil painting in the board-room of the British Museum.

5. A photograph bought recently in Turkey, made apparently from a painting by W. H. Bartlett, but unacknowledged.

6, 7a, 8b. From original pen and ink (and one pencil) drawings by the author.

8. From a water-colour by the author.

9, 10. From David Robert's "View of the Holy Land", from prints in the British Museum.

11, 12a, 12b. From originals by the author. 12b was done from just above the village of Dhana where J.L.B. was chased by hostile Bedouin —looking down towards a part of the Rift known as Wadi Araba, of particular interest to J.L.B. since he was the first European to see this vast distant valley running at right angles to the small wadi, and to realise that it was a part of the Great Rift. The author made the sketch by chance for the beauty of the place—before being aware of J.L.B.'s story.

13. From the title-page vignette called "Approach to Petra" in W. H. Bartlett's book *Forty Days in the Desert on the Track of the Israelites,*

1849—that is nearly forty years after Burckhardt's discovery of Petra.

14. David Roberts, accompanied by a retinue and armed escort, made many superb studies in the Holy Land, Egypt and Nubia, thirty to forty years after Burckhardt's journeys, and published five huge volumes of prints from work done there.

15, 16. From originals by the author done in 1960.

17. From W. H. Bartlett's frontispiece to *Forty Days in the Desert on the Track of the Israelites*, 1849.

18. From Vol. 3, 1849, *Egypt and Nubia*, by Brockenden and Roberts from Roberts' print of the "Citadel of Cairo, Residence of Mehemet Ali".

19, 20, 21. From Vol. 2, Brockenden and Roberts, *Egypt and Nubia*.

22. With the permission of Dr Georg Gerster, Zurich.

23. From Vol. I, Brockenden and Roberts, *Egypt and Nubia*.

24a. From a print in the British Museum, artist unknown.

24b. From a lithograph made by Hans Hasler (1840–1903) *possibly* from a portrait done by Henry Salt in Cairo. Photograph by the kindness of Galerie berühauter Schweizer, Zurich.

25a. Gebel Nur is where Mohammed is thought to have received the light of his revelations.

26a. This is a place near the mosque where the richest foreigners stayed in Mecca at the time of the pilgrimage. It is possible that J.L.B. did this sketch from the window of his lodging.

26b. At Arafat there were the ruins of a small mosque where Mohammed was accustomed to pray, and several large reservoirs lined with stone, two or three of these are close to the foot of Arafat, or were in November 1814.

25a, 25b, 26a and 26b are from original sketches in the possession of Mr Rodney Searight, and it is considered that they are probably the work of J.L.B.

27a, 27b, 28a are from the MSS department of the British Museum. So is 28b; it was found among a collection of J.L.B.'s letters to Renouard, apparently sent to him as being an attractive example of Arabic script. It is an invitation, probably from one of the many acquaintances who were inclined to disturb Louis' peace during his last year in the Turkish quarter of Cairo, and it reads: "In the name of God, the Beneficent, the Merciful, You are invited, Shaik Ibrahim tomorrow at 3 o'clock after midnight to the [house of] poor Karran Mattar so that with Karran Mattar and Al-Arshi, Arshi may have a seance but not a musical concert" signed "The poor Karran Mattar".

29. From a print in the British Museum by David Roberts. This picture of Suez in white heat gives a true feeling of the Red Sea area.

30. Also from a print in the British Museum. Nearly forty years on, Roberts with his friends and retinue were able to reach this point which Louis had strained his eyes to see while in danger from imminent attack.

31. From a print in the British Museum.

32. From Vol. 3 of Roberts' *Egypt and Nubia*. Roberts was drawing the scene outside the Bab-el Nasr when this funeral happened to emerge from the city gate heading for the Muslim cemetery. Appropriately he included it in his study.

### NOTES ON THE SEVEN HALF-PAGE LINE DRAWINGS

1. From "Voyage de l'Arabie Pétrée" by Leon de Laborde, Paris, 1830. Man with tambour.

2. The ceremony of the New Year Greetings in the "Kirschgarten," a line drawing by the author from a half-tone illustration in Daniel Burckhardt-Werthemann's book *Hauser und Gestalten aus Basels Verganenheit*, Basel, 1925. It presumably depicts Rudolf Burckhardt seated, Gedeon presenting the greetings, with Georg and Louis marching behind, and Rosine clinging to Sarah's hand.

3. Leon de Laborde, a Scribe.

4. Ibid., a Syrian—probably Damascene Arab Sheikh.

5. Ibid., Arab with javelin.

6. Ibid., a man smoking.

7. From *Egypt Delineated* by Denon, 1925. Denon comments that these four Arab portrait heads are of men appointed to act as officials by the people of Rosetta. The first, on the left, was chosen because he was brave—having once rescued women of Rosetta who had gone out to weep over the tombs of relations and had been carried off by Arabs of the desert. The second as he was of a kind and placid disposition; the third because he was a man of information; and the fourth because he was the wealthiest and most distinguished person. Could any magistracy have been better composed? If each one, argues Denon, had possessed the qualities of all four, the harmony of the whole might not have been so perfect . . .

All illustrations from the British Museum are reproduced by permission of the Trustees of the British Museum.

# Index

# Index